Democracy in Latin America

Changing Nature of Democracy

Note to the reader

The United Nations University Press series on the *Changing Nature of Democracy* addresses the debates and challenges that have arisen as "democratic" forms of governance have blossomed globally. The march of democracy has defined the close of the twentieth century; the fulfillment of individual and collective aspirations, good governance, and the nurturing of civil society form the benchmark of political organization. However, democracy defies a universal model, and the definition of democracy continues to be elusive. Moreover, the performance of democracy often fails to live up to its promise. This series explores two areas. Firstly examined is the theoretical discourse of democracy, such as the tension between procedure and substance, the dialectic between principles and institutions, the challenge of reconciliation and peace-building in democratic transition, the balance between universal and communitarian notions of democracy, between participation and efficiency, and between capital and welfare. Secondly, the series explores how these themes and others have been demonstrated, with varying effect, in a number of regional settings.

Titles currently available:

The Changing Nature of Democracy edited by Takashi Inoguchi, Edward Newman, and John Keane
The Democratic Process and the Market: Challenges of the Transition edited by Mihály Simai
Democracy, Governance, and Economic Performance: East and Southeast Asia edited by Ian Marsh, Jean Blondel, and Takashi Inoguchi
Democracy in Latin America: (Re)Constructing Political Society edited by Manuel Antonio Garretón M. and Edward Newman

Democracy in Latin America: (Re)constructing political society

Edited by Manuel Antonio Garretón M. and
Edward Newman

**United Nations
University Press**

TOKYO · NEW YORK · PARIS

United Nations University Press
The United Nations University, 53-70, Jingumae 5-chome,
Shibuya-ku, Tokyo, 150-8925, Japan
Tel: +81-3-3499-2811   Fax: +81-3-3406-7345
E-mail: sales@hq.unu.edu
http://www.unu.edu

United Nations University Office in North America
2 United Nations Plaza, Room DC2-1462-70, New York, NY 10017, USA
Tel: +1-212-963-6387   Fax: +1-212-371-9454
E-mail: unuona@igc.apc.org

United Nations University Press is the publishing division of the United Nations University.

Cover design by Joyce C. Weston

Printed in the United States of America

UNUP-1068
ISBN 92-808-1068-5

Library of Congress Cataloging-in-Publication Data

Democracy in Latin America : (re)constructing political society / edited by
Manuel Antonio Garretón M. and Edward Newman.
      p.   cm.
Includes bibliographical references and index.
ISBN 92-808-1068-5
1. Democracy—Latin America. I. Garretón Merino, Manuel A. (Manuel
Antonio) II. Newman, Edward, 1970–
JL966 .D4544   2001
320.98—dc21   2001006274

Contents

Acronyms

AD	Acción Democrática (Venezuela)
ADN	Acción Democrática Nacional (Bolivia)
AI-5	Institutional Act No. 5 (Brazil)
APR	Acción por la República (Argentina)
APRA	American Popular Revolutionary Alliance (Peru)
ARENA	National Renovation Alliance (Brazil)
ARENA	Alianza Republicana Nacional (Salvador)
BL	Movimiento Bolivia Libre
CACIF	Comité Coordinador de Asociaciones Agrícolas, Comerciales, Industriales y Financieras (Guatemala)
Causa R	Causa Radical (Venezuela)
CODE	Confederación de Partidos por la Democracia (Chile)
CONAIE	Confederation of Indigenous Nationalities of Ecuador
Condepa	Conciencia de Patria (Bolivia)
COPEI	Comité Organizativo para Elecciones Independentientes (Venezuela)
CRIC	Consejo Regional Indígeno del Cauca (Colombia)
CORPI	Consejo Regional de Pueblos Indígenos (Central America)

ECLA	Economic Commission for Latin America and the Caribbean
EZLN	Zapatista National Liberation Army (Mexico)
FAR	Fuerzas Armadas Rebeldes (Guatemala)
FEDECAMARAS	Federación de Cámaras de Industrias, Comercios y Bancos (Venezuela)
FEI	Federation of Ecuadoran Indians
FMLN	Frente Farabundo Martí para la Liberación Nacional (Salvador)
FREPASO	Frente del País Solidario (Argentina)
FSB	Falange Social Boliviano
FSLN	Frente Sandinista de Liberación Nacional (Nicaragua)
IACHR	Inter-American Committee on Human Rights (OAS)
MBL	Movimiento Bolivia Libre
MDB	Brazilian Democratic Movement
MERCOSUR	Southern Cone Common Market
MINUGUA	U.N. Mission for the Verification of Human Rights in Guatemala
MIR	Movimiento de Izquierda Revolucionaria (Bolivia)
MNR	Movimiento Nacional Revolucionario (Bolivia)
MPs	Medidas Provisórias – Provisional Measures (Brazil)
MR-13	Movimiento Revolucionario 13 de Noviembre (Guatemala)
MST	Movement of the Rural Dispossessed (Brazil)
MVR	Movimiento Quinta República (Venezuela)
NEP	Nueva Política Económica (Bolivia)
ONUSAL	UN Observation Mission (Salvador)
PAC	Patrullas de Autodefensa Civil (Guatemala)
PAN	Partido de Avanzada Nacional (Guatemala)
PCN	Partido Conciliación Nacional (Salvador)
PDS	Social Democratic Party (Brazil)
PDT	Labour Democratic Party (Brazil)
PFL	Party of the Liberal Front (Brazil)
PMDB	Party of the Brazilian Democratic Movement
PPB	Brazilian Progressive Party
PPS	Popular Socialist Party (Brazil)
PR	proportional representation
PRD	Partido Revolucionario Dominicano
PRD	Revolutionary Democratic Party (Mexico)
PRI	Institutional Revolutionary Party (Mexico)
PSB	Brazilian Socialist Party

PSDB	Party of the Brazilian Social Democracy
PT	Workers' Party (Brazil)
PTB	Brazilian Labour Party
RN	Renovación Nacional (Chile)
SERPAJ	Servicio Paz y Justicia (Uruguay)
SINAMOS	Sistema nacional de movilización social (Peru)
UCR	Unión Cívica Radical (Argentina)
UCD	Unión del Centro Democrático (Argentina)
UCS	Unión Cívica Radical (Bolivia)
UDI	Unión Demócrata Independiente (Chile)
UNI	União de Nações Indígenas (Brazil)
UNO	Unión Nacional Opositora (Nicaragua)
UNIS	Unión de Indígenos de El Salvador
URNG	Unidad Revolucionaria Nacional Guatemalteca

Introduction

1

Introduction

Manuel Antonio Garretón M. and Edward Newman

Democracy offers great opportunities for Latin America after a turbulent and sometimes painful recent history. It also presents a host of challenges in the context of international economic and political trends that condition the dynamics of political communities from the outside. (Re)-democratization in most of the region has had to confront the legacy of civil war and repression, and also the social dilemmas inherent in the integration of the region into the global market-based economy. Moreover, the struggle for (re)democratization has had to address a destabilizing colonial legacy of social and ethnic division and power structures that preceded democratic institutions. The evolution of Latin American democracies – as countries that have recently experienced conflict and authoritarianism – and the degree of success in consolidating democracy hold great importance for the people of the region. This process also has implications for divided societies elsewhere which share similar obstacles to the attainment of true democracy.

This volume examines democratic transition and consolidation in post-authoritarian and post–civil war Latin America. A range of issues can be embraced within such a remit: justice and reconciliation; integration into global economic institutions and the transition to market economics, with the accompanying social and political impact this has brought; the manner in which external actors – such as the United Nations, international financial institutions and multinational corporations – have conditioned or facilitated democracy; the role of civil society; the problems of achiev-

3

ing a sense of citizenship in many communities in Latin America; and the gap between the procedure and the substance of democracy in some of these countries.

Themes

This is a broad range of issues, which requires a focus. Thus the premise of this volume is that the fundamental prerequisite of democracy is the existence of a healthy polity or polis – described here as a "political society." Therefore, political democratization and democracy in Latin America involves the (re)construction of the political society, which is not complete in many societies. In this sense three main transformations in the region in recent decades have tended to have contradictory effects on the erosion or enhancement of the polis.

First, political democratization has reinforced the polity but in every case this democracy is weak – if not irrelevant – as regards managing and addressing the problems and challenges that all political regimes should resolve. Second, cultural and structural transformations, and particularly the changing development model towards one in which globalization and market economics have eroded the classical role of the state, have had implications for political relations, and conditioned the political impact and voice of different actors. Arguably, these transformations have dis-articulated many socio-political actors and pervaded the public political sphere in a number of ways. Third, the relationship between the state, the party system, and civil society – in fact the very nature of politics – has been dramatically changed and in different situations new formulae for reconstructing a socio-political matrix, as an alternative to populism and authoritarian or neo-liberal models, are being sought.

This volume examines the (re)construction of democracy in post-authoritarian or post–civil war societies in Latin America in the context of these themes, from both empirical and normative perspectives. These themes will be applied not on a national case study basis but in terms of four "scenarios" of political democratization on a regionwide basis.

Dimensions

The application of these themes to the (re)construction of political society raises a number of challenges that envisage democracy as broad and mul-tifaceted process and public good. Thus, democracy is very much seen in terms of substance – its output, results, and ability to address social prob-lems and provide social goods – in addition to procedure. The framework for political (re)construction in the context of Latin America faces three main challenges.

The reconstruction of national community: Reconciliation with the past and the challenge of bridging new cleavages

As democratic forms of government replace authoritarian regimes and civil conflict, a critical issue in the success of this transition is the management of past human rights abuses and crimes against humanity. With the memory of atrocities still fresh, justice and accountability for the past are central to sustainable democracy and to installing a sense of confidence and trust in public life. Moreover, this is not just a historical issue: past "disappearances" continue to impose intolerable cruelty upon family members and human rights abuses continue to occur. Conversely, the appearance of impunity for past crimes undermines confidence in new democratic structures and casts doubt upon commitments to human rights, which are integral to successful consolidation.

Simultaneously, however, the search for the truth can be destabilizing and can prolong, even obstruct, the consolidation of democracy. Moreover, in many cases the transition from authoritarian rule depended upon the cooperation of actors and individuals directly involved in human rights abuses in the past. This has involved a delicate balance. The victims' demands for justice must be met, but the participation and support of all major actors – including the perpetrators of crimes and their supporters – in the democratic system is essential for its short-term sustainability. The lack of democratic support of some actors – sometimes including the perpetrators of crimes and their sympathizers – clearly challenges the stability and credibility of democracy. Reconciliation has thus been difficult. Amnesty – even immunity, in the case of Chile – has been a necessary component but inevitably it has been difficult to forget, much less forgive, the suffering that has occurred.

There is a paradox to be solved: justice is necessary to move forward; it is integral to the democratization process. But stability and the inclusion and support of all actors make the search for truth and justice difficult. How are countries managing this dilemma? With what degree of success? To what degree, and with what effect, does the management of the past condition democratic politics? How are the lessons learnt from earlier experiences applied to more recent cases?

The second dimension of reconciliation concerns the reconstruction of the national community so as to produce a new consensus or social pact. In many Latin American communities wide social inequality, ethnic division, the presence of organized crime, casual and organized violence, insecurity, lack of confidence in (unaccountable) police, and corruption in public institutions undermine the ethos of citizenship. In many cases the colonial legacy has left ethnic and social divisions that remain to this day. Indigenous peoples often continue to be disadvantaged, poor, and outside the political mainstream. It is notable that during times of repression, uprising, and civil war, ethnic divisions became pronounced and reflected deep socio-economic conflicts. The Zapatista uprising in Chiapas, Mexico, was only the most dramatic demonstration of a widespread feeling that certain sections or classes of society in Latin America are alienated from "democratic" institutions. Many less publicized challenges to established politics demonstrate a lack of faith in new, "elitist" democratic structures. The real challenge concerns a new national consensus or project. What will this project involve and entail, and is it possible?

The reconstruction of the political system: Towards a new socio-political matrix

The traditional or classical national-popular matrix of relations between the state, the party system, and the social actors (or "civil society") and the mediating role between the three within the institutional framework of politics is in question. This volume seeks to examine the ways in which structural transformations – especially new modes of development – affect the changing role of the state, the disarticulation and recomposition of the party system, the emergence of social actors, and new questions of citizenship. Whilst the bare procedural requirements may exist – in terms of elections – the substance can be shallow. The degree of participation, the quality of debate, the availability of real political choice are doubtful. The tendency towards presidentialism – and in particular the tendency of presidents to suspend constitutional practices to enhance their powers or extend their terms – would appear also to cast a shadow over democracy.

There have been various labels for this: "illiberal democracy," "façade democracy," and "neo-authoritarian electoral regimes," among them. According to those who use these labels, traditional power structures, ethnic divisions, and the gap between rich and poor continue. Important research questions, therefore, concern the substance of democracy. Do the processes and institutions of democracy offer real opportunity for political choice and change? What is the degree of confidence of the people in this? Has the tradition of popular sovereignty, of social revolution, ended? How has the separation of powers worked in Latin America?

Social actors – "civil society" – have played a central role in these questions. In the liberal tradition civil society forms an array of free associations in between the family and the state, involving ideas, interest groups, and political agendas. In Latin America civil society has tended to play a somewhat different role in post-authoritarian and post–civil war societies than in established liberal democracies. The region's recent history, in many countries, of repression has resulted in civil society existing as a form of opposition, especially as organized political parties were often prohibited or severely emasculated. In conflict and authoritarian situations civil society – including the Catholic Church – organized resistance and self-help, and raised consciousness, often in opposition to the state. A number of questions arise. What does civil society really mean in Latin America, and what is its relationship with politics and the state? What is the role of civil society in the search for truth and justice, and in forming political agendas? How has civil society responded to the neo-liberal predominance?

The reinsertion of society in the world: Globalization and international community

Two transnational forces condition the reinsertion of Latin American democracies into the world; its integration into the world economy and its interaction with the actors of the international community. The (re)-birth of democracy in Latin America has often been accompanied by a transition to market economics, which clearly gives rise to market-oriented models of development. In fact the two processes are inseparable, and have conditioned each other. The history of the region has presented a variety of economic models. Populist welfare-based experiments, and free-market and nationalist command economies are among them. However, there has been a swing to free-market neo-liberal policies in conformity with external economic patterns and structural adjustment programmes of international financial institutions. A socially disturbing process has thus paralleled political democratization. "Shock" economics, a movement away from traditional economic practices/lifestyles, and an emphasis upon opening up the economy and exporting have had an impact. Globalization – demonstrated in the opening up that has accompanied NAFTA – has altered the political equation. In some cases this privileges certain political actors – such as exporting business elites – over others, such as social reformists.

The emergence of "limited" democracies, conditioned by a neo-liberal agenda, also demonstrates the extent that external actors have forged the agenda of democratization in Latin America. Foreign banks and governments, international financial organizations and multinational corporations have arguably made an alternative to "limited democracy" impossible. Yet at the same time, there is growing opposition to the neo-liberal agenda of mainstream democracy which often takes the form of extra-constitutional resistance. This raises serious questions regarding the ability of democratic structures to accommodate the desires and aspirations of those who have not seen their material positions enhanced through economic development.

How has the background of socio-economic change and neo-liberalism conditioned democratic agendas and choices? Have certain actors been privileged at the expense of others? Have external actors – such as multinational corporations – been likewise privileged above domestic citizens? Are there alternatives to "limited" democracy? Can democracy that is conditioned by a neo-liberal agenda be genuinely inclusive?

In most Latin American countries democracy has been conditioned as much by external as by internal forces. External inputs have both positive and negative connotations. Democratization, traditionally, is considered in the context of the political, cultural, and socio-economic complexion of a particular political community. Indeed, according to the communitarian ethic, it is necessarily a culmination of "domestic" processes. In recent decades it has become clear that transnational processes, international organizations, and the free flow of information have inevitably had a bearing on – and in fact have promoted – the process of democratization, sometimes with dramatic effect. In a more practical sense, international organizations played a crucial role in negotiating the transition from dictatorial rule to democratic rule in some Latin American countries, especially those emerging from civil war.

To what extent is democratization conditioned by "internal" and "external" processes in Latin America, and is the balance changing? Can the UN and other external actors have a decisive and substantial (rather than just a facilitative) impact upon democratization? What values does an external agent or organization bring with it to the democratization process? Practically, how successful has external assistance been in terms of consolidating democracy in Latin America – what is the record? In post–civil war situations the democratization process involves particular sensitivities; democratization is an integral part of the peace-building process. In such a situation, the issues of justice and reconciliation, and of the legitimacy of political actors, raise particular challenges for external involvement. How have other international actors – such as multinational companies, international economic institutions, and international human rights and civil society groups – had a role in conditioning and forming the democracy agenda in Latin America?

Scenarios of democratization

Clearly, the forces that underlie the (re)construction of political society in Latin America do not affect the whole region uniformly. Latin America reflects enormous diversity in culture, history, and political processes.

The units of analysis here will not be single national cases, but four constellations of national cases, conceived as "democratic scenarios." Thus, instead of studying different single national cases, the volume will analyze the dimensions of four different democratic scenarios reflected in the process of political democratization in the region. In the first part of the volume, "Scenarios of Democracy and Transition," countries will be grouped under the following situations:

Transitions: when democracy is the result of movement away from a military or formal authoritarian regime through political mechanisms. This is the case with such Southern Cone countries as Chile, Argentina, and Brazil, and also Bolivia.

Reforms: when a democratization process is initiated by the government to extend or enlarge a restricted or semi-authoritarian democracy. This is the case with Mexico and Colombia.

Democratic foundations: when democracy is installed for the first time after civil wars or revolutions. This tends to be the case in Central America.

Regression and crisis: when a new or a consolidated democracy suffers a major crisis that threatens to regress to a non-democratic situation. This is the case with Venezuela, Peru, Ecuador, and Paraguay.

Within the framework of these democratic scenarios, Maria D'Alva Kinzo presents the democratization of Brazil as a transition case characterized by the gradual and faltering reestablishment of civilian rule after the military's peaceful return to the barracks. She begins by outlining some of the main elements of Brazil's authoritarianism, observing that it was marked by periods of repression alternating with periods of political relaxation, followed by the eruption of political crises and repression. Brazil's democratic transition was the most prolonged: a gradual and slow process of liberalization that took eleven years to re-establish civilian rule and another five to have a head of government elected by popular vote. This gradual opening up saw the military, at first the main player in determining the political dynamics of the transition, giving way to civilian actors, against a background of mounting economic crisis and the creation of new political parties. Democracy in Brazil was not preceded by a rupture with the previous order. Indeed, the reconstruction of the political system was the result of the amalgamation of new and old structures and practices.

Yet political democracy has left serious challenges as yet unmet. Social inequalities continue to obstruct the deepening of democracy. Brazil's institutional framework has several aspects that have constrained the better functioning of representative democracy and democratic government. The combination of presidentialism and federalism with a fragmented party system has produced a situation in which the process of decision-making is complicated by the presence of a multiplicity of veto powers, increasing dramatically the costs of both political negotiation and consensus building.

Marcelo Cavarozzi examines Argentina, Bolivia, Chile, and Uruguay through the same analytical lens. In the 1980s the four countries made the transition from military authoritarianism to representative democracy, and these transitions coincided with a "second transition" from the state-centered matrix to an alternative socio-political matrix defined by the predominance of markets over politics and the erosion of national sovereignty as a result of globalization. Cavarozzi demonstrates how these two processes – the consolidation of representative democracy and the change of the socio-political matrix – have contributed, in turn, to the reform of the models of government and the reshaping of the party systems in these countries, albeit through different paths. Considering democracy as a socio-political movement, Cavarozzi concludes that political change in these countries is related to deeper change in contemporary South American societies, in particular the relationships between politics and other central dimensions of society, especially the economy and culture. This is defined by two pervading challenges. Firstly, globalization has increased the level of social disintegration within national societies in South America, as elsewhere. Secondly, and connected with this, is the widespread loss of interest in citizenship, rooted in the increasing loss of relevance of the democratic political system for settling economic and social conflicts, and for influencing the day-to-day life of the majority of the population.

Turning to the "reform" scenario of democratization, Laurence Whitehead presents a "paired comparison" of Colombia and Mexico, exploring the hypothesis of a distinctive path to democratization through this scenario, with its own logic and internal structure. Whitehead first explores the hypothesis as a logical construction – considering what it would imply in its "pure" form – before attempting to apply it to Colombia and Mexico. In view of the divergences that are as apparent between these two cases as the similarities, the essay also includes a methodological discussion about the use and limitations of the method of paired comparisons. It also highlights patterns shared by the two cases not emphasized by the reform model. Whilst retaining some reservations about "reform" as a sub-type, Whitehead observes certain patterns: the unevenness of national integration; the instability and lack of definition of constitutional checks and balances (including centre-local relations); the recentness of the "level playing field" in party competition; and the persistence of ongoing conflicts over the scope and contents of citizenship rights all illustrate these constraints. In conclusion, he considers whether the concept of democracy "by stealth" may be more fitting: neither of these countries has experienced the kind of dramatic discontinuity that would provide the basis for resocializing the voters and the political class according to the norms of a properly democratic regime. It may be that the July 2000 presidential elections will turn out to have provided just such a discontinuity – but it is too early to be conclusive.

In approaching Central America through the theoretical framework of "foundations," Edelberto Torres-Rivas examines patterns amongst societies that have mostly had to embark upon a democratic project after devastating civil wars. He sets this scenario against a backdrop of economic crisis and foreign debt and the challenges of constructing the foundations of democracy. The first part of the essay introduces the disorder that characterized the recent history of Nicaragua, Guatemala, and El Salvador, examining the causes and effects of the civil wars and the peace negotiations that brought these to a conclusion. Torres-Rivas then goes on to analyse how the construction of political democracy is becoming possible by means of the reconstruction of the political system, the electoral system, and the state. The essay concludes with some observations regarding the relationship between society, citizenship, human rights, and the evolving international context. A key argument of Torres-Rivas is that the most important cause of the crises that led to war in the region was revealed in the character of the state – a weak state, infiltrated by corruption and a military dictatorship that maintained its power through the use of force. As a corollary of this, he argues that democratic consolidation is structurally related to the strengthening of the state, and the emergence of a healthy relationship between the state and civil society. This rests upon the development of a democratic political culture, respect for human rights, tolerance, and dialogue.

The final essay in the first part of the volume, by Heinz Sonntag, examines the theme of "crises and regressions" in Ecuador, Paraguay, Peru, and Venezuela. For a number of complex and different reasons – although with some parallels amongst them – these countries have experienced severe instability and significant regressions in their democratic systems. In some cases, this has represented a significant challenge to consolidation, in others a threat to the democratic system itself. Sonntag puts the tumultuous history of these cases into the context of a crisis of developmentalism: the emergence of contradictions that undid the commitment to development among the different (and often emerging) classes and sectors. Weak governability and scarce political governance, the fragility of the national project – including indigenous challenges – and the misappropriation of newfound wealth by a narrow political elite also characterized, to different extents, the instability in these countries. In Ecuador and Peru the redemocratization process itself has, he argues, essentially failed because both societies had already earlier overcome authoritarian regimes. In Paraguay, it is the democratization process itself that is at stake. And in Venezuela, the attempt of fostering democratic and state reforms not only failed to succeed but also led to a profound deterioration during a period of transition which has lasted seven years and whose definite outcomes are unclear. Sonntag presents the most important issues in each of these countries and discusses some common challenges that result from the regressions and crises for all Latin American societies.

The second part of the book builds upon these scenarios by examining a number of themes and issue-areas. Central among these, Rodolfo Stavenhagen examines how, with the (re)emergence of democratic regimes in Latin America, the "indigenous question" has presented a series of deep-rooted problems which must be addressed if the consolidation of democracy is to be a reality. He argues that large sections of the population, namely the indigenous peoples, lack effective citizenship and have been excluded from the political community for most of their history. The uprisings of indigenous people – in Ecuador and Mexico, to take two prominent examples – are an expression of a much wider phenomenon: the rights of indigenous people, denied for long, are an integral part of the process of democracy in the region. The history of "nation-building without Indians" has seen the emergence of indigenous movements as political actors with a serious political agenda. This indigenous agenda is crucial for the future democratic evolution of Latin America. Stavenhagen highlights the right to land and the recognition of indigenous territory, the right to culture and to bilingual and intercultural education, local autonomy, "functional" self-determination, and political representation.

Edward Newman's essay addresses a seemingly perennial challenge: how democracies have dealt with a history of human rights abuse and dictatorship in the context of democratic transition and consolidation. How to balance the needs of justice, truth, and reconciliation in a viable and progressive democratic project? Even when democratic transition and consolidation are no longer jeopardized or threatened by regression in the search for justice and accountability – in countries such as Chile, Argentina, Uruguay, and Brazil – this does not mean that the past does not have an impact upon the quality of public life and democratic institutions. The deficiencies of dealing with the past, of achieving truth, justice, accountability, and transparency – the elusiveness of reconciliation – may not threaten the "procedural minimum" of democracy. Yet these deficiencies continue to impose constraints upon democratic institutions, upon a sense of reconciliation, upon a unity of purpose in an inclusive progressive democratic project, as the legacy of the past continues to divide society and bring the legitimacy of democratic institutions into question. This issue is thus central to the (re)construction of political society in many Latin American societies. Newman explores the modalities of reconciliation, of dealing with past abuses of human rights, in the context of different trajectories of democratic transition and consolidation. He discusses the successes and deficiencies of dealing with the past, which have often left an ongoing struggle for truth and accountability, and he offers some comparisons of "national" attempts at reconciliation – such as in Chile, Argentina, Brazil, Uruguay – and "international" attempts at reconciliation which reflect a greater prominence of transnational norms of humanitarian conduct and governance. The essay considers whether the growing prominence of transnational forces is changing the balance of power in favour of accountability and justice, and challenging the trade-offs and impunity that earlier appeared to be the necessary price of democratic transition. Indeed, whilst conventional political science invariably argues that the modalities of dealing with a past of human rights abuse are conditioned and in most cases constrained by the terms and pace of democratic transition, this essay suggests that the international dimension is altering this equation.

Manuel Antonio Garretón's essay on "The New Socio-Political Matrix" revisits the typology of democratic scenarios in the Latin America and considers the relationship between the state, political regimes and parties, and civil society/social actors as a matrix. It is this evolving relationship, he argues, that constitutes the socio-political matrix and the space for meaningful discourse. Latin American societies have been living through profound transformations. Political-institutional models of concertation and conflict have replaced the dictatorships, civil wars, and revolutionary modalities of previous decades. The model of "inward development," of the dynamism of the public and industrial urban sector, has been replaced by formulas of adjustment and stabilization that seek new forms of insertion into the world economy, characterized by phenomena of globalization and transnationalization of market forces. Social structures have also been transformed, with an increase in inequality, poverty, marginality, and the precariousness of the education and labor systems. This has produced a recomposition of the system of social actors and a questioning of the traditional forms of collective action. Finally, Garretón argues, there is a crisis of the model of modernity associated with Western modernization and the North American mass culture predominant in Latin American society – at least among the leading elites – and a resultant emergence of indigenous and hybrid formulas of modernity. Hidden by these transformations, suggests Garretón, is deeper change that affects the wider world: a shift away from the basic referential societal type, the national-state industrial society, as a result of globalization and an expansion of the principles of identity and citizenship. This means a disarticulation of this societal type, although in different degrees according to particular situations.

Amparo Menéndez-Carrión takes up similar issues in "The Transformation of Political Culture in Latin America." She addresses the question of "politics-and-culture," acknowledging it as a concrete realm of experience, a contested field of knowledge, and a key point of entry to reflect upon the question of "transformations" within Latin American. Her focus is on three interrelated questions: How has the relationship between politics and culture in Latin America been portrayed over recent decades? What can be said about the meaning of politics as lived and experienced in today's Latin America? What implications emerge from the answers to these questions for grappling with the question of political culture, for portraying the interplay between politics and culture in the region's increasingly complex milieu, and for envisioning the (re)construction of political society?

A basic premise of this chapter is the acknowledgement of the interplay between politics and culture as a strategic and open-ended terrain, occupied by concrete actors in concrete situations and contexts. The analytical emphasis is placed throughout on shifting practices, shifting narratives, and shifting terrains of culture as they interact with and transform the realm of politics. The realm of situations and experiences, rather than the realm of individual attitudes and orientations, is stressed throughout as the locus for understanding the interplay in question.

In the final essay, "The International Dimension of Democratization and Human Rights in Latin America" Ellen L. Lutz and Kathryn Sikkink consider the impact of international norms upon the processes of democratization and the interaction between international and domestic dynamics. Lutz and Sikkink analyse cases from each democratic scenario and explore what role international and regional actors played, apart from and in conjunction with domestic actors. In addition, the essay considers how international and regional laws, norms, institutions, and policies on human rights and democracy have changed over time. The deepening of regional networks relating to human rights and democracy and increasing international scrutiny of the human rights records of Latin American societies – a "norms cascade" – combined with domestic processes of democratization, served to strengthen a sense of accountability and respect for human rights. Lutz and Sikkink illustrate these processes by describing the role of international actors and norms in the promotion of democracy and in making peace in "foundational societies," and the role of international law – including extradition procedures and international arrest warrants – in the remarkable cases of Argentina and Chile. These two cases demonstrate well the interaction between domestic and international processes, and how international and regional processes have reinvigorated national efforts towards justice and accountability. The essay also gives attention to international and regional pressures in the reform processes of Mexico and Colombia.

In all of these cases, international pressure was at work, but the outcomes depended on how these pressures interacted with domestic political processes. International pressures were effective in helping contribute to some change in at least one case from each of the four scenarios. Thus, the particular democracy scenario does not determine whether or not international pressures will have an impact, according to Lutz and Sikkink. The clearest variation in the amount of international pressure was not between countries or scenarios, but over time. The most important explanatory factors for the changes in human rights practices in this chapter appear to be the existence and strength of the norms cascade, the intensity of international and regional human rights pressures, and the level of domestic political will and pressure to conform to the norms. Where domestic pressures are strong, as in Chile or Guatemala, international pressures can provide critical leverage; where domestic opposition is weak or divided, international pressures have less influence.

An overarching issue that runs through all of the chapters concerns the cleavage between the substance and the procedures of democracy. The norm of democracy is becoming embedded in regional and national politics. Yet there is a sense that democracy is losing its meaning for the lives of citizens, for the fulfillment of their aspirations and needs. Moreover, the disarticulation of state-society relations in the context of neo-liberal economic forces and globalization contributes to this problematique: the (re)construction of political society relies upon consensus about what government is for, and what public goods the state must provide. The essays in this volume suggest that this consensus does not completely exist. Yet on the positive side, democracy has also made great strides. Post-conflict and post-authoritarian societies show no serious signs of reversal. Despite the crisis and threat of regression in some societies, the region is largely stable and democratic, albeit with the caveats made by the authors in this volume. Justice and accountability for past human rights abuses, whilst very far from complete, have progressed beyond what many people would ever have hoped for in countries such as Chile and Argentina. Taken together, the prognosis that these chapters suggest for the (re)construction of political society is neither entirely positive nor negative. What is certain is that the journey to meaningful democracy is unfinished.

Scenarios of democracy and transition

2

Transitions: Brazil

Maria D'Alva G. Kinzo

Introduction

More than 20 years have passed since the so-called "third wave of democratization"[1] reached Latin America. In some countries, civilian rule replaced military-authoritarian regimes after a peaceful transition; in others this was only possible after several years of civil war. In countries where authoritarianism had never had the form of military dictatorship – as in Mexico – the wave of democratization came with reforms that significantly expanded political competition. In still others, this wave reached the beach but retreated in the face of instability or reversion, such as in Peru and more recently in Ecuador and Venezuela. This variety of experiences within a region whose countries have shared similarities in their processes of development, suggests the importance of assessing Latin America's democratization in the light of the diversified paths it has taken.

Brazil, together with Argentina, Bolivia, Chile, and Uruguay, forms the group of transition cases: a pattern of democratization resulted from the reestablishment of civilian rule after the military's peaceful return to the barracks. The examination of Brazil as a separate case of transition is due less to any singularity arising from this country's continental size and complexities, than to the assumption that most of the achievements and limitations of Brazil's democratization concern specific features of Brazil's transition which, in turn, are related to some peculiarities of its experience of a military-authoritarian regime. Thus, an assessment of Brazil's current

19

democratic setting requires, first, a characterization of that regime as well as of the political dynamics that led to its liberalization and transition to democracy. This process will be the concern of the first two sections of this essay. In the third section, democratization will be assessed by looking at its impact upon the polity and society, attempting not only to assess Brazil's current democratic setting, with its achievements and limitations, but also to deepen our understanding of this specific pattern of transitional democratization.

Military-authoritarian rule

In relation to other military regimes established in Latin America in the 1960s and early 1970s, the Brazilian case has distinctive features that deserve consideration when we try to assess the influence of long-term factors on democratization.[2] Some of these features concern the political institutions under which military rule operated; and others, in the realm of the economy, have to do with the economic development model adopted by the military and its consequences.

In the political realm, at least two important features characterized the Brazilian case. First, it was a military regime in the sense that the armed forces as an institution controlled the government after a successful coup conducted both by the military and by civilian politicians in opposition to João Goulart's government. Two implications followed. First, since the government was conducted by the military as an institution, politicization of the military corps was intense, and the internal power struggle between factions within the army had an impact not only on the military organization itself – albeit sustained by hierarchy and discipline – but also on the political process at large. The conflict between the moderate military officers and those with a more radical orientation permeated all twenty-one years of military rule as a source of instability. Second, since the 1964 coup was a joint military and civilian action, the civilian supporters of the "revolution" had to have a place in the new order. This leads us to the second feature characterizing the Brazilian case: the regime established after the 1964 coup did not suppress all mechanisms and procedures of representative democracy. The Congress and the judiciary were not closed, even though their powers were severely limited and several of their members were purged. Alternation in the presidency of the republic continued to take place, as did periodical elections for several positions, although both were strictly controlled institutions. Party politics continued to function, although the parties of the 1945–64 democratic period were dissolved in late 1965 and an artificial two-party system was created in the following year. In sum, the political order that emerged was a mixture of military-authoritarian rule with institutional mechanisms of representative democracy. By underlining that the Brazilian case is atypical in the sense that the regime maintained some mechanisms and procedures of the previous democratic order, I am not trying to underestimate its repressive and undemocratic character. Rather, my intention is to point out that this peculiar institutional arrangement affected the dynamics of the political system and was a source of political instability. In fact, the period of military rule in Brazil cannot be characterized as a typical case of institutionalized authoritarianism. It was rather a process marked by periods of repression alternating with periods of political relaxation, and permeated by the eruption of political crises. These crises – which ended in waves of repression – were largely the result of this institutional arrangement whose ambiguous nature stimulated conflict among groups within the military establishment and between these and the democratic opposition.

A good example of these dynamics followed President Castelo Branco's decision to hold elections for state governorships in 1965, in spite of the reaction of the more radical authoritarian groups – both military and civilian – who saw an election as an unnecessary risk for a regime that was not yet consolidated. The election outcome, a victory of the opposition in two important states, led to a serious political and military crisis, resulting in the decreeing of the Institutional Act No. 2 and a new phase of repression.

The same political pattern can be seen in the events of 1968. A period of "decompression" had started when the second general-president – Costa e Silva – took office, signaling prospects of democratization. The new political climate opened the way to a wave of student demonstrations, strikes, and a more radical stand taken by some parliamentarians from the MDB (Brazilian Democratic Movement) – the legal opposition party created in 1966.[3] The political temperature soon rose, leading to a political stalemate when Congress refused to approve a petition to punish an MDB deputy for having criticized the armed forces. Once again repression was the outcome: the military decreed the Institutional Act No. 5 (AI-5) which intensified political purges, and made the president's power even more arbitrary and concentrated. This saw the beginning of the most repressive period of military rule (1968–73).

By the end of Médici's government (late 1973) the military seemed to have been able to consolidate themselves in power, but it was also at that time that signs of political decompression started to be seen again. This time, however, the signs proved to be of a different kind, as they turned out to be effective steps of a planned strategy of controlled liberalization that would be carried out by Ernesto Geisel – the fourth general-president who took office in early 1974. But the regime's same dynamics of relaxation and compression persisted: the political decompression opened the way to a mounting opposition movement – this time channeled through the election process by the opposition party. The emergence of a crisis within the system would lead to renewed political "compression": Congress was temporarily closed and a series of restrictive measures to regulate the elections and Congress representation was decreed by the president. But the political compression was less tight than in previous periods, indicating that the government's intention was to correct the course of the process of controlled liberalization that the 1974 election outcome had released.[4] In fact, the country was already going through the first phase of political transition, which at that moment was seen much more as a kind of reform of the regime than a step towards democratic transition.

In sum, the nature of the regime's dynamics and the conflicting process resulting from the power struggle among the actors involved were related to the hybrid character of the regime, which combined formal institutions of representative democracy with direct military rule. The instability that accompanied military rule in Brazil – in other words, the regime's difficulty of institutionalization that made Juan Linz characterize Brazil's authoritarianism as a situation rather than a regime[5] – was largely a consequence of the establishment of this mixed political framework. This feature would have an impact on the way transition took place in Brazil. Before examining the process of transition, another feature characterizing the Brazilian case needs to be mentioned – one that relates to the economic realm.

In contrast to the Chilean or the Argentine cases (where the military established new economic models or destroyed the old one) the Brazilian military did not innovate in economic policy. With the exception of the first three years of military rule, during which all efforts were concentrated on a stabilization program to bring down high rates of inflation, economic policy under military rule followed the same development model that had been in place since Vargas. The so-called "Brazilian miracle" of the 1967–73 period was sustained, on the one hand, by the conditions resulting from the 1964–67 stabilization policy and, on the other, by a development plan that consolidated and extended the import-substitution model now directed to exports and with a still stronger entrepreneurial role for the state. By 1974, in spite of the signs that the miracle was over – clearly manifested by the impact of the 1973 oil crisis on Brazil – the military opted for keeping on the same track. The strategy followed was what O'Donnell called "deepening of industrialization,"[6] an attempt to keep the economy growing through an ambitious policy of import substitution in capital goods and basic raw materials, sustained basically by public sector investments and foreign loans.

This strategy was successful in sustaining high rates of investment and economic growth until 1980 and in making the overall experience of military rule in Brazil be seen as a case of good economic performance. However, it also resulted in serious social and economic imbalances.[7] The problems that had been one of the main causes of the 1964 military intervention – high inflation and economic stagnation – re-emerged with greater intensity and remained in the background of the process of transition.

The long transition

If some peculiarities marked Brazil's experience of military rule, others marked its democratization process.[8] Among the cases of democratization through transition, Brazil's was the most prolonged: a gradual and slow process of liberalization that took eleven years to re-establish civilian rule and another five to have a head of government elected by popular vote. For analytical purposes we can divide this process into three phases. The first, from 1974 to 1982, was the period in which the political dynamics of the transition were determined by the military and appeared at the time to be more a reform of the regime or the establishment of a guided democracy than the initiation of democratic transition. The second period, from 1982 to 1985, was also characterized by the military's political dominance, but other players had a role in the political process. In the third phase, from 1985 to 1990, the military was no more the major player in the game (although keeping some veto power), having been replaced by civilian politicians – both ex-supporters of the former regime and those from opposition sectors – and by the organized sectors of civil society. As these phases have different components and dynamics resulting from the interplay of the main political actors, they should be examined in detail.

The first phase, 1974–1982

The inauguration of Geisel's presidential term in 1974 and the announcement of his project of "gradual and secure" political relaxation marked the start of a new period of military-authoritarian rule, a period which would also be the starting point of Brazil's democratization. The partial revocation of press censorship and signs that the 1974 legislative elections would be freer than previous contests indicated that the new president's statements were more meaningful than the frequent promises of a return to democracy made by his predecessors. The way this project of liberalization was conducted and the dynamics of the political process that eventually led to democracy were nonetheless very complex and prolonged. This phase of the transition, from the beginning to the end, was entirely conducted by the military government, which defined both its pace and scope. But several factors influenced the course of the process. The first factor was the elections. The gentle breeze of liberalization allowing freer conditions for the 1974 electoral contest led to an unexpected outcome: the remarkable electoral performance of the opposition party (the MDB) which won 16 out of 22 seats contested for the Senate, had an increase of 46 per cent in its representation in the House of Deputies, and gained a majority in six state assemblies. In fact, the 1974 elections resulted not only in a manifestation of popular dissatisfaction with the government and the regime, but also in the legitimization of the MDB – the legal opposition party whose creation in 1966 responded to the military government's decision to establish a two-party system. In other words, the outcome of the election made it clear that the regime, which was responsible for remarkable rates of economic growth in the previous six years, lacked popular support; it also made clear that the "tame" opposition party, allowed to operate so as to provide a formal competitor to the government party (the ARENA – National Renovation Alliance), had become an effective channel for the opposition, an instrument to be used not only on the electoral scene but also in the political process at large. Thus, if the liberalization policy was to be kept under government control, it needed to neutralize the impact of both the elections and the MDB.

The second factor was the military institution and its internal conflict. In fact, one of the main factors explaining the government's initiative in promoting liberalization was the military's need to withdraw from politics. As Rouquié observed, "a permanent system of military rule is almost a contradiction in terms. The army cannot govern directly and durably without ceasing to be an army."[9] But Geisel's initiative exacerbated the conflict within the military, making the reaction from the military faction most opposed to the opening up of the regime more forceful. The intensification of police repression in 1975–76 by hardliners in command of the armed forces headquarters in São Paulo State was clearly a reaction to Geisel's liberalizing moves.

Thus, two sources of pressure had to be controlled by the government to guarantee the implementation of its project of "gradual and secure" political opening. On the one hand, there were the pressures from within, that is, from the hardline military officers, against political relaxation. These required the neutralization of the hardliners to ensure that they would neither undermine President Geisel's absolute command of the political process, nor interfere in the crucial issue of the presidential succession. On the other hand, there were the pressures from the opposition sector demanding democratization. These involved the neutralization of the democratic opposition, particularly the MDB, to prevent this party from having further electoral success and becoming an obstacle to the government's controlled liberalization.

Geisel was quite successful in neutralizing those problems by playing the game in both directions at the same time. By altering the electoral rules and legislative procedures, and by purging some of the more outspoken MDB parliamentarians, Geisel appeased the hardline officers and reinforced his control over the democratic opposition. By reacting against the hardliners – for example, by dismissing the São Paulo army commander after the torture and killing of a journalist and a metalworker – Geisel showed his absolute command of the political process. He managed not only to continue his program of liberalization but also to control the presidential succession. Thus, by the end of 1978 liberalizing political reforms were carried out in accordance with the gradual and guided character of the political relaxation policy. The new president – General João Figueiredo, who was to be in charge of continuing that policy in the following six years – had been elected in strict accordance with Geisel's determination to impose his own choice.

If Geisel showed great political skill in dealing with the potential opponents to his political objectives, he was less skillful in addressing the third factor influencing the process of political liberalization: the economic problem. Signs that the Brazilian "economic miracle" was over started to be evident.[10] The economic problem was certainly a crucial element to be taken into account if the military's aim of a secure and gradual return to the barracks was to be achieved. It seems that considerations of a political nature must have influenced the way Geisel responded to the impact of the first oil shock (and consequent world economic recession). Instead of economic contraction, as happened in several similar economies dependent upon oil imports, the policy adopted was to promote economic expansion by deepening the import-substitution model to the detriment of internal and external imbalances. Thus, an ambitious program of import substitution in the sectors of basic raw materials and capital goods was put into action, involving significant state investment in energy and infrastructure and high levels of external loans. The course of this policy was not reversed during the first years of Figueiredo's administration, which means that while the expansion of the economy was maintained, both the external accounts and inflation rates kept deteriorating. The aggravation of the external problems finally forced Figueiredo's economic team to radically change the economic policy. An attempt at economic adjustment was for the first time carried out, leading to a sharp fall in the level of economic activity and a rise in unemployment. Another external shock in 1982 aggravated the conditions of an economy extremely vulnerable to changes in the external environment.[11] From then on, economic crisis – meaning inflation and deterioration of the external and internal accounts – would accompany the political transition and the democratic governments that followed it.

Thus, from the beginning to the end, the transition process had as its background a mounting economic crisis, the tackling of which would be postponed due to the military government's resistance to changing a policy that in the past had been very successful, and also because of the negative impact that an economic adjustment could provoke at a time when the regime was liberalizing. In other words, the process of political decompression ended up limiting the government's capacity to tackle the economic crisis. Factors such as the election outcome, the internal conflict within the army, and the emergence of serious problems on the economic front were therefore elements constraining the process of controlled liberalization. It was only in 1978 that President Geisel made further moves towards liberalization, the most important being the revocation of the draconian Institutional Act No. 5.

In 1979, under Figueiredo's administration, Congress passed an amnesty bill, which, although limited, allowed the return from exile of most of the politicians and left-wing activists who had been banned during the years of repression. A new party law was also implemented, putting an end to the two-party system compulsorily created in 1966. As a consequence, in addition to the two prevailing parties which were reorganized under new names (the ARENA became the PDS – Social Democratic Party – and the MDB became the PMDB – Party of the Brazilian Democratic Movement), three other parties were created in 1980: the PT (Workers Party), the PDT (Labour Democratic Party) and the PTB (Brazilian Labour Party).[12] The reform of the party system represented an important liberalizing measure, but it also reflected the government's intention to divide the opposition forces so as to keep the transition under control. Among the factors to be controlled, the most crucial were those related to the presidential succession to take place in 1985 when civilian rule was planned to be reestablished. For that, it was indispensable to ensure not only that the next president would still be chosen by an Electoral College rather than by general suffrage, but also that the government keep the majority in the Electoral College. Thus, election rules were altered to increase the government party's chance of victory, as was the composition of the Electoral College so as to reduce the opposition's chances of electing a larger number of delegates there.

The second phase, 1982–1985

In spite of all this interference, the process of liberalization entered a new phase with the 1982 elections. New political parties were created and participated in the elections; politicians who had lost their political rights in the 1960s re-entered politics; and for the first time since 1965, state governors were elected by popular vote.

The first electoral contest held under the new party system certainly resulted in important gains for the military government, as the results guaranteed its majority in the Electoral College which would choose the next president. But the opposition gains were also important, particularly for the PMDB, which kept its place as the main political force in opposition to the regime. It received 40 per cent of the overall vote, elected the governor and the senator in nine states, and obtained 200 seats in the Chamber of Deputies. In spite of the fact that the military was still the major player of the game, from 1982 on, some new players would influence the process, undermining the government's plans to retain full control over the process.

The most important episode was the presidential succession, which needs to be examined as a two-act drama. The first consisted of the PMDB's attempt, in 1984, to change the rules of the presidential election by proposing a constitutional amendment bill re-establishing elections by popular vote. Aiming at raising popular support for the bill, all the opposition parties joined together to mobilize the population for the campaign in defense of prompt re-establishment of general suffrage for the election of the next president. The so called "Diretas-Já" campaign, which counted on the crucial organizational support of the governors of the three most important states – which were all controlled by opposition parties – resulted in an impressive popular mobilization with millions of people, carrying banners and wearing T-shirts with the slogan "Diretas-Já," attending public rallies all over the country. Observing the mobilization at that time, one could have had the impression that civil society – which had showed its existence with the emergence of social movements by 1978 – had finally woken up, and that this mobilization could finally change the course of the liberalization. In fact, this was the perception of some sectors of the opposition. The movement was so impressive that some PDS parliamentarians started deserting their party, concerned with the popular impact if they sided the government and voted against the amendment. In spite of this climate the amendment bill was defeated. The number of PDS dissidents was not large enough to enable the opposition to reach the two-thirds majority required for constitutional amendment bills. Moreover, to make sure that the bill would not pass, the government not only exerted its full influence to keep the PDS in line, but also imposed a state of emergency in Brasilia, the capital, and blocked all access roads to prevent demonstrations at the Congress on the day of the vote.

The outcome of this episode showed that the military was determined to maintain full control of the presidential succession. It also indicated that, in spite of the support of popular mobilization, the opposition was numerically too weak in Congress to be able to defeat the regime if it were to keep operating under the established rules of the game. This meant that there were only two alternatives for the opposition: either to search for the support of potential dissidents in government, or to attempt to break the established rules of the game through the mobilization of society. The decision to go one way or the other would depend on the position and the relative strength of each of the different groups in the opposition, that is, the PMDB with its internal subgroups, the PT, PDT, and PTB. The PTB had voted with the government against the direct election bill in exchange for governmental offices. The PDT was also unpredictable to the point that its main leader – Governor Leonel Brizola – suggested an extension of Figueiredo's presidential term in exchange for the direct election of his successor. Thus, two players were left: in favor of the first alternative was the PMDB, more specifically its moderate group, which was the largest and controlled the party leadership; and in favor of the second, the PT – a party strongly identified with the social movements – followed by a small fraction of the PMDB which was also linked to the popular movement.

The PMDB's decision to take the first course – that is, to attempt to influence the presidential succession by playing by the rules of the game – was the second act of the presidential succession drama. It was certainly the product of the moderate posture of the party's leaders for whom a negotiated solution would prevent the risks of popular mobilization, namely, a reaction of hardline military officers against any attempt at radical change.[13] In any case, the PMDB leaders were determined to participate in the presidential election even under limited conditions. In fact, while the PMDB worked for the "Diretas-Já" campaign, the party – especially its moderate faction – was already working for an alternative strategy, should the amendment be defeated in Congress. The alternative was to present Tancredo Neves, the governor of the state of Minas Gerais, as the opposition candidate in the presidential contest at the Electoral College. With the defeat of the direct election amendment, the PMDB started working for Neves's candidacy. But this was not a simple task. As the opposition did not have the majority in the Electoral College, the PMDB's candidate could only win if he could benefit from the split within the government parliamentary camp. The opportunity was opened when a group of PDS politicians refused to support the government candidate who won the nomination at the party's convention. Negotiations between the PMDB and the regime's dissidents (who left their party to create the PFL – Party of the Liberal Front)[14] led to the creation of the Democratic Alliance whose aim was to form a united front to defeat the government candidate. In return for the PFL support for Tancredo Neves's candidacy,

Senator José Sarney – a dissident who had resigned the position of PDS national chairman – was nominated for vice-president. The strategy followed by the moderate opposition was indeed successful insofar as the military government was unable to impose its presidential candidate. But it would have two important consequences: first, it made it possible for the regime's dissidents to have an important role in the new regime – in fact they have ended up being a government partner ever since. Second, the strategy provoked criticism from the more radical sectors of the opposition, namely the PT, whose position was against participation in the indirect election of the president. On the grounds that the Electoral College was illegitimate and unrepresentative, the PT refused to take part in the election. As the number of votes the PT had in the Electoral College was not decisive it was more profitable for it to mark a position against the so-called negotiated transition, thus distinguishing itself from the moderate opposition. This strategy proved to be correct for a party that was trying to create its own identity and searching for a space on the left of the spectrum of the new political system.[15] The problem, however, was that by stressing the limitations of the "negotiated transition" the party helped to erode the basis of the legitimacy of the new order inaugurated in 1985.

The third phase, 1985–1990

With the election of Tancredo Neves and José Sarney on 15 January 1985, the second phase of the transition ended. But the inauguration of civilian rule was still to be affected by the unexpected: Tancredo Neves suddenly became ill on the eve of taking office and following his death, Vice-President José Sarney became head of the first civilian government. Thus, in addition to the fact that the return to civilian rule resulted from a compromise between the moderate sectors of the opposition and the regime's dissidents (which therefore lacked the support of an election by popular suffrage), the death of the political figure who was supposed to lead the new government made democratization still more complicated. This was all the more the case because the negotiated transition had largely been the result of Tancredo Neves's political ability in making the opposition's project acceptable by the military.

This meant that civilian rule was reestablished under very fragile circumstances, particularly for a president who had to face the challenges of a mounting economic and social crisis. Thus, Sarney inaugurated his government without clear program guidance. Moreover, he had a serious deficit in legitimacy. His former links with the military regime, as well as the facts that he had not been elected president by popular vote and was not attached to the party that was expected to lead the new government (the PMDB),[16] were all elements contributing to his political weakness. This made his administration vulnerable to all kinds of pressures, whether from the heterogeneous political forces that composed his government (each aiming at enlarging its influence), or from the opposition parties and organized sectors of civil society calling for democratization in all senses of the term.

As for the PMDB, having waited for so long for the day of its accession to the central power, it ended up having to share it with its old opponents. This placed the PMDB in an ambiguous situation in which it was the main party of the government coalition but did not constitute the government. From then on, the PMDB's capacity to influence the political process was reduced as a consequence of its difficulties in defining a party line to orient its actions. In fact, much of the PMDB's problems resulted from its peculiar origins and development. A party whose objective was to fight for democracy, it had been able to become a broad opposition front while it did not need to take clear position on potentially divisive issues. Its organizational structure established throughout Brazil was a political resource important enough not to be ignored by the party's several and heterogeneous groups. This made the party remain as a broad front even after 1985 in a democratic context. Although the PMDB continued to be an important stabilizing force in the new order and maintained its position as the major party in the country, it was entangled in a crisis of identity that deeply aggravated its problems of internal dissension. One of the main consequences of this was the party split that led to the creation of the PSDB (Party of the Brazilian Social Democracy) later in 1988.[17]

In any case, with the return to civilian rule, the Brazilian democratic transition followed its course in the new political environment. In the socio-economic realm the post-1985 period was traumatic: between 1986 and 1994 Brazil had four different currencies and no less than seven different stabilization plans. With the exception of the last plan – the Plano Real which was partially successful – all of them failed in their objectives, in spite of the variety of experiments. The succession of failures resulted not only in the aggravation of the economic crisis and social problems, but also in the erosion of the state's capacity to govern, making the problem of governability an enduring reality.[18]

In the political realm, this last phase of the transition was a period of intensification of Brazil's democratization. The most important signs were the establishment of free conditions of electoral participation and competition (with the revocation of all limitations to the right to vote and political organization) and, above all, the rebirth of Brazil's constitutional framework with the promulgation, in 1988, of a new constitution.

The drawing up of the 1988 Constitution was a good indication of the complexities of the Brazilian case of transition. From beginning to end, the process involved a heated debate amongst all sorts of groups aiming either to enlarge or to restrict the scope of the social, economic, and political framework to be established. This climate can be seen mostly as a side effect of the history of the transition. Political forces linked to the former regime tried to ensure their space in the new order, whilst the progressive sectors acquired much more prominence than could be expected from their numbers in the Constituent Assembly. In this regard, it is worth noting that the transitional nature of Brazil's democratization – that is, the fact that it was the product of a negotiated pact – had an important influence on the constitution-making process. It had the effect of making the political leaders who had conducted the transition, especially those more committed to democracy, more vulnerable to criticisms of the limitations of the new democratic order and to pressures from those political forces advocating more profound democratization. Consequently, the resulting constitutional framework was possibly much more democratic than could be expected under the conditions of a controlled process of transition.

The Constituent Assembly (which was initially criticized on account of the fact that it also functioned as the regular Congress) was the most democratic experience in Brazilian constitutional history given the procedures under which the constitutional deliberations were carried out. First, the procedures had a very decentralized structure in the sense that all Congress members were able to participate in the several phases of the constitutional work. Second, the proceedings were very open to society in the sense that all organized sectors were able to participate either directly, in subcommittee hearings, or indirectly, by applying pressure for the approval of their propositions. Third, as political forces were very fragmented and the parties weakly organized, the assembly was highly susceptible to interest group pressures. Fourth, as the assembly was not dominated by any monolithic group, majority votes were the product of endless negotiations on almost every particular issue.

The result was a constitution that, in spite of its serious imperfections, represented a clear democratic advance. All the mechanisms of representative democracy were guaranteed, and some of these involved direct democracy, such as the plebiscite, the referendum, and the people's right to initiate bills. Moreover, power became less concentrated in all senses of the term, as a consequence of the strengthening of the legislature and the judiciary as well as of the subnational elements of the federation, and the guarantee of freedom of party organization. Although the new framework would have serious consequences for the functioning of decision-making, it was indeed a clear democratic move. In the social realm, the charter marked important advances in the standards of social protection in the direction of a more egalitarian and universalist format. This was indicated in the innovations introduced, such as the widening of social security provisions. The Constitution also innovated in the protection of minorities with the introduction of rigorous penalties for discrimination against blacks and women.[19] However, given the social and political setting within which constitutional rebirth came about, the new was bound to cohabit with the old. This was the case with the secular problem of landownership concentration, which was left almost untouched, and of the military, which kept its prerogative of intervening in case of serious political crisis if requested by any of the three branches of government. The legacies of the Vargas era were also revived in the nationalistic and statist inclination of some of the charter's economic clauses and in the preservation of some features of the corporatist structure of interest representation. As Sallum remarks, "although decadent, the national-developmentalist model (certainly under more democratic clothing) was juridically consolidated through the 1988 Constitution."[20]

In fact, the Constitution reflected the impact of several contradictory forces that managed to exert influence on a process that took almost two years to be completed. Its articles and clauses are much more the embodiment of a mosaic of contradictory interests of a heterogeneous and unequally organized society than the final outcome of a pact on fundamental and consensual issues. The fact that the Constitution included in its transition acts provisions for constitutional revision five years later was symptomatic of the lack of consensus. Thus, several features of the 1988 Charter were so controversial that a constitutional revision soon became a fundamental item in the political agenda.

The election of a president by universal suffrage in 1989 was the last step of Brazil's long and complex process of democratic transition. There were 22 candidates, and in contrast to the 16 million voters who participated in the previous presidential election (in 1960), more than 72 million went to the polls in 1989.

The inauguration of the government of Fernando Collor de Mello marked symbolically the end of Brazil's long period of 16 years of democratic transition. But political developments thereafter showed that Brazil's emerging democracy had to pass several tests before it was stabilized in the present situation. Among the outstanding events that made the period a succession of economic and political crises, several stand out. First was the drastic economic stabilization measures embraced by the Collor Plan, issued the day after he took office – a heterodox economic stabilization program that attempted to promote full-scale trade liberalization. As happened with the preceding shock stabilization plans, the Collor Plan resulted in failure, quickly eroding the president's strong popular support. Then came the impeachment of President Collor in 1992, on charges of corruption, after an impressive popular mobilization and a decisive and legitimate action carried out by Congress. This was followed by the accession to the presidency of Vice-President Itamar Franco whose faltering leadership contributed to increase economic and political uncertainty. Then, the 1993 plebiscite, held under the provisions of the 1988 Constitution to establish the future system of government, reconfirmed the adoption of the current presidential republican system. Next was the constitutional revision in 1994, which was dragged down by short-term political considerations and produced no substantial change, although the need for some reform was widely accepted by almost all political parties. There followed the corruption scandal in the Congressional Budget Committee, leading to the creation of a parliamentary commission of inquiry and the disclosure of massive levels of corruption. Then, the adoption of another economic stabilization program (Plano Real) in 1993–94, created a fictitious unit of account (UVR) to break inflationary expectations and introduced a new monetary unit (the real). Not much later, the 1994 presidential election campaign turned into a plebiscite on the government's economic policy which had managed to produce a sharp decline in the inflation rate, and so led to the election of Fernando Henrique Cardoso, the government's candidate and the architect of the Plano Real. Finally, a succession of world financial crises – the Mexican in 1995, the Asian in 1997, and the Russian in 1998 – almost buried both the efforts of economic stabilization of the Real Plan and the popularity of the president who was its mentor.

Since 1994, other elections have been held, corruption scandals have daily covered the front pages of the press, and social protest has emerged everywhere. These are events that have become part of the day-to-day life of Brazil's democracy. Does this suggest that democratization has been completed, that Brazil's democracy has been consolidated? This will be the main topic of the next section.

Democracy in Brazil: Between achievements and limitations

There is no doubt that Brazil's current regime has gained clear features of a polytical democracy. If we take as a reference Dahl's two dimensions of a polyarchy, Brazil has certainly enlarged considerably the conditions of public contestation and political participation.[21] The effective recognition of the right of parties to contest an election irrespective of their ideological orientation or social basis has been confirmed in all electoral contests since 1985. The most significant evidence is the emergence of the PT as a real competitor in national as well as regional and local elections. In this respect Brazil's democratization was quite an innovation, since the reestablishment of competitive party politics brought about the creation of a new party that was marked not only by the typical features of a mass party but also by its close links, particularly during its formative phase, with social movements. As a result, its collective identity was built upon its association with both the salaried workers and the organized sectors of civil society, stressing, therefore, the principle of participatory democracy.

The significant improvement of the conditions for political participation is evident not only in the considerable increase in the electorate, but also in the increase in political uncertainty resulting from the free exercise of the voters' will. The Electoral Court has played an effective role in keeping electoral fraud under control.[22] At the same time, conditions of uncertainty are ensured by the fact that elections have taken place in a predominantly urban society, rather than in rural areas where electoral fraud and political control were common practices.

The economic growth experienced under military rule produced serious distortions that aggravated the problem of poverty and social and regional inequalities in Brazil; but it was also responsible for a rapid process of industrialization and urbanization that resulted in the emergence of a mass society with all its complexities. Several consequences followed from this. One was the enlargement in the number of dispossessed people who are not socially integrated to society but are in the electoral arena, having considerable weight in elections;[23] another was the substantial increase in the contingent of industrial and urban workers who became the basis for the emergence of social movements and progressive parties. Although apparently less prominent than during the period of democratic mobilization, urban social movements are an important element of the new democratic polity. In fact they have undergone a redefinition of their approach in response to the disarticulation of the state, or have institutionalized themselves as social organizations in response to the political opportunities opened by decentralization and participation at the local level. Referring to the positive impact that the post-authoritarian process of decentralization has had on society, Martins suggests that "the municipalization of social policies has opened ample space for the participation of civil society by delegation from the state," and that in several places social movements have made use of the new possibilities of social intervention to expand the state's capacity to respond to social demands.[24]

The economic transformations undergone in the agricultural sector in the last three decades – making it an amalgamation of rural capitalism with old forms of land property and production – has aggravated the problem of social exclusion, but they have also produced the social cement for the intensification of the agrarian reform movement which, led by the strongly organized MST (Movement of the Rural Dispossessed), has become the most important manifestation of social disobedience in

Brazil. The MST's relationship with the government has been contentious, since there is little room for negotiations between two actors defending positions so far apart: on the one hand, the government's policy of incremental land reform and, on the other, the MST's actions based on land occupation as a means – according to its leaders – to pressure the government for a rapid solution for the landless problem. In spite of its radical positions and questionable means of action – such as the recent occupation of government offices – the MST mobilization has kept the agrarian reform issue on the political agenda.

The importance of the press and the media in general should also be seen as a means of improving contestation and participation. Though it is true that the media, in Brazil as everywhere, have been very influential in electoral campaigns in favor of the establishment, it is also true that they have had an important role in denouncing all sorts of political manipulation and corruption, thereby becoming an appropriate instrument of democratic political control. Even if the media sometimes exacerbate popular sentiments against politicians and representative institutions in general by filling the news with political scandals, thus contributing to discrediting democracy, it has also contributed to the improvement of political morality and political responsiveness.

As regards the demilitarization of the political system – a crucial factor in assessing the conditions of democracy in countries that experienced a military dictatorship – several signs indicate that changes in the relationship between the armed forces, the state, and society have taken place in the last decade. First is the attitude of the armed forces in distancing themselves from the serious crisis that led to Collor de Mello's impeachment. In addition, the recent creation of the Ministry of Defense has deprived the commanders of the three services of their ministerial status and brought them under the rule of a civilian ministry. Finally the recognition by the state of its responsibility for the victims of political repression during the military regime has led to the creation of the Committee of Missing Persons as a result of a law enacted for the benefit of the families of people who disappeared under the military regime.[25] These developments, together with the fact that in spite of several crisis situations the armed forces have remained quiet in their barracks, are evidence of a significant change. This does not mean, however, that they are guarantees that Brazil's democracy is immune to military intervention of any kind.

To affirm that the conditions for the consolidation of a polyarchy have considerably improved does not imply that Brazil's democracy is fully consolidated. In fact, there are certain limitations to democratization which have to do not only with the "quality" of public contestation and participation of the citizenry but also with the effective operation of a democratic and representative government.

The first is certainly the social question. There is no doubt that extreme social inequalities are a crucial factor limiting the chances of deepening democracy. Moreover, Brazil is known for its deep and unsolved inequalities, a legacy of the past that the present experiment of democratic government has not made less acute. Figures for 1998 indicate that 33 per cent of the Brazilian population lived in households whose family income was below the poverty line. Using data for the 1977–98 period, Paes de Barros et al. observe that, in spite of some fluctuations resulting from a period of economic instability, the intensity of poverty has shown a very stable pattern.[26] The level of poverty reached its height during the recession of 1983–84, when the proportion of poor people surpassed 50 per cent. It was at its lowest in the period of implementation of the two economic stabilization programs: in 1986, the year of the Cruzado Plan, the percentage of poor dropped to 28 per cent, going up again to above 40 per cent in the following years; and following the Real Plan (1995 onwards) the proportion of poor declined to 33–34 per cent. This declining tendency registered since 1995 indicates an improvement in the pattern of poverty, but the improvement remains insignificant given that 33 per cent represents no less than 50 million people. Moreover, the reduction of the magnitude of poverty has not affected Brazil's extremely unequal pattern of income distribution. Examining the same period (1977–1998), Paes de Barros et al. observe that during those two decades the Gini coefficient was remarkably stable, and referring particularly to the post–Real Plan period, "there is no evidence that it has produced any substantial impact on the reduction of the level of inequality despite the fact that the level of poverty has undergone a significant reduction."[27] They also produce evidence to demonstrate that although economic growth is an important means to tackle poverty, it requires a long period to produce a significant effect. This makes it essential that economic growth be accompanied by the adoption of specific policies to reduce the extreme concentration of income.

The long period of acute economic crisis, the accumulation of unsuccessful attempts to tackle uncontrollable rates of inflation, and the side effects of the current policy of economic adjustment have eroded the traditional role of the state. As the introduction to this volume observes, Latin American democratization has been accompanied by the erosion of the socio-political model in which the state was in the center of collective actions. The fact that Brazil was a latecomer in the process of economic restructuring means that it has also taken longer to restructure the state. This became clear in the limited scope of government interventions in the social area in this fifteen-year experience of democratic government. The current government led by President Cardoso, despite having prioritized its actions in the economic stabilization front, has attempted to tackle the social problem by concentrating efforts in the area of education, agrarian reform, and the so called Solidarity Community Program.[28] The results, however, are still limited, or may be visible only in the long run – as is the case with education policy.

Notwithstanding large disagreements regarding the role of the state in this changing context, the restructuring of the state involves not only the redefinition of the basis of its relationship with society – for which there is still a long way to go before definite contours of a new relationship become visible – but also the creation of mechanisms to respond more effectively to the imperatives of social inequality, economic stabilization, and economic development. In this respect, much of the difficulties have to do with the institutions through which political representation and democratic decision-making operate in Brazil. A product of the amalgamation of old and new structures and processes, Brazil's institutional framework has several aspects that have constrained the better functioning of representative democracy and democratic government. This is the last topic to be examined in this essay.

As mentioned before, the 1988 Constitution institutionalized political decentralization by strengthening the federation and the presidential structure, and by allowing fragmentation of political forces. If this represented an important achievement as far as democracy is concerned, it resulted in a combination of factors that has led to serious imbalances between the several loci of power influencing the formulation and implementation of policies. Federalism was strengthened by the provisions of the 1988 Constitution. In fact, before that date, Brazil's federal system was based on a very centralized government at the national level. The lack of political and financial strength in sub-national government was constantly pointed out as one of the causes of government inefficiency and the gap between public policies and local needs. Under the 1988 Constitution, a new distribution of fiscal responsibilities was enforced with a remarkable transfer of tax assignments from the federal to state and local governments. This made Brazil one of the most decentralized countries in the world.[29] Sub-national governments and regional and local politicians have their own political space and their actions can considerably affect the federal government's capacity to implement policies with nationwide impact.[30] This is particularly problematic with regard to the government's attempt to tackle the fiscal crisis.

If imbalances between national and sub-national governmental relations have made policy-making more complicated, two other features of Brazil's institutional structure have added further difficulties to the functioning of the political system: presidentialism and a very fragmented party system. As suggested by Lamounier,[31] Brazil's political system is an institutional model that combines a plebiscitarian presidency with political fragmentation and many counterweights, which are typical of the so-called "consociational" democracies.[32] On the one hand, given its electoral and party systems and its federal structure, the Brazilian polity is very fragmented, so that political competition tends to lead more to the representation of minorities than the formation of ruling majorities.[33] On the other hand, counteracting political fragmentation, a powerful center of decision-making is located in the executive, whose legitimacy is based on nationwide and substantial electoral support.[34] A legacy of the Vargas era, this combination of two contrasting institutional mechanisms has important effects on the process of policy-making, not only because of the features and dynamics typical of presidential systems, but also because of the fragmentation resulting from the party system.

With respect to presidentialism, it is worth recalling some of the features of the relationship between the executive and the legislature under this system.[35] First, in spite of the fact that policy results from the interaction between the two branches of government, there is no requirement for their cooperation, since they are independent and their relationship is based on the principle of checks and balances. Second, although power is shared among different institutions and policy emerges from their interaction, the full responsibility for government policy is nevertheless borne by the executive. One of the implications is that there is not a clear commitment from a party or parties to support the president in the legislature. Apart from the fact that the legislative power is independent, the president and legislators respond to different constituencies.[36] Thus, any member of the party of the president can feel free to take a position against the executive if it is to his or her advantage. In sum, under presidentialism, party politics displays different dynamics from those of cabinet government.

There is still a second complication: unlike the North American model, Brazilian presidentialism lives with a multiparty system, which means that a coalition has to be built to support the government. The problem, however, is that under a presidential system, coalition government seems to operate differently from those of parliamentary systems. The conditions for creating an effective party coalition to back up the president, the way the coalition partners behave, and their effectiveness regarding parliamentary support for policy-making are different.

This is still more complex in a presidential system characterized by high party fragmentation, as it is the case with Brazil. In the legislature inaugurated in the year Cardoso took office (1995), none of the 18 parties represented in the Chamber of Deputies had more than 20 per cent of the seats.[37] The best evidence of the fluidity of the party system – not to mention its fragility – is the high index of electoral volatility. Pedersen's index of electoral volatility for the Brazilian Chamber of Deputies was

30.5 (between the 1986 and 1990 elections) and 16.6 (between the elections of 1990 and 1994), while the average for the European countries between 1985 and 1996 was 11.0.[38]

Party fragmentation is not a result of social cleavages. Although Brazilian society is socially, racially, ethnically, religiously, and regionally diverse, its party system does not reflect those cleavages. Among the parties that are classified as relevant (in Sartori's terms) three are placed on the right or center-right (the PPB – Brazilian Progressive Party – the PFL, and the PTB), two in the center (the PMDB and PSDB – Social Democratic Party of Brazil), three on the center-left (the PDT, PSB – Brazilian Socialist Party – and PPS – Popular Socialist Party), and two others on the left (the PT and PCdoB – Brazilian Communist Party). Apart from different locations on the left-right continuum, none of these parties can be differentiated by a special cleavage in society – be it sectoral, regional, or religious. To the extent that the party system does not reproduce cleavages in society, the parties are more fragile as channels of representation. Social interests can, therefore, be voiced by members of several parties, which form groupings that sometimes operate in a more effective way than the parties. This is still more problematic given the prominent role played by corporatist interests. In fact, a number of sectoral and regional groupings have found ways of entrenching themselves in every part of the power structure. This is an old practice that has survived the military regime and has even been reinforced during the period of democratization. With the re-establishment of legislative prerogatives, Congress became an important arena for lobbying. But interest group lobbying has not been under the control of any regulation, making its operation very effective, especially in a context in which political parties are porous.

The fragmentation of the party system is due, largely, to elite disputes at regional or local levels, resulting in political splits as a consequence of the low cost of fragmentation. The combination of proportional representation[39] with very permissive party and election legislation not only facilitates the creation of new parties but also offers no incentives for party loyalty. It is common for politicians to change their party affiliation during the legislative term, which in turn affects electoral competition.[40] Moreover, by allowing party alliances for any kind of electoral contest, which means that the most diversified electoral alliances can be formed (even in local elections), the electoral system facilitates the survival of parties that have no significant electoral support on their own. These problems have at least two important consequences.

First, as a result of fragmentation, government formation and decision-making involve building up coalitions that are normally broad and quite heterogeneous. The implication is that the ministerial cabinet is composed of heterogeneous political forces that make coordinated government action difficult, especially in relation to social policies whose implementation involves more than one ministry. Moreover, whatever policy the government is willing to implement, it has to cope with the presence of multiple sources of resistance in Congress. In order to ensure that its party coalition provides the needed parliamentary support for its policy proposals, the executive has to work systematically to keep the coalition together. This involves the use of all sorts of political resources to negotiate support, sometimes on an individual basis – clientelism being one powerful instrument. Alternatively, the executive makes use of so-called Medidas Provisórias (MPs – Provisional Measures). With their self-enforceable character, MPs have been the president's main constitutional tool to speed up policy-making and implementation: not only do they give the executive power to legislate but they also interfere in the structuring of the legislature's agenda, since MPs have to be examined by Congress within one month, so they have priority over other bills.[41] It is obvious that the centralizing nature of the MPs works against the democratization of policy-making.[42]

Second, parties are not effective actors for structuring the electoral competition. Voters have difficulty in identifying and distinguishing the parties that are contesting the elections: so many parties, so many electoral alliances, which are different from one place to the other, from one election to the other. In addition, the competition is centered much more around individual candidates than on parties. In sum, high fragmentation and the confusing nature of the party system make it difficult for the voters to fix the parties in their minds, to distinguish who is who, and to create party identities. This certainly causes serious limitations on the effective operation of the system of democratic representation.

In sum, the combination of presidentialism and federalism with a fragmented party system has produced a situation in which the process of decision-making is complicated by the presence of a multiplicity of veto powers, increasing dramatically the costs of both political negotiation and consensus building. Using the terms of Tsebelis's model, given the large number of veto players defending different policy positions, we have a context that tends much more to keep the status quo than to produce policy change.[43] This situation has also reduced political transparency and responsiveness while indirectly contributing to the centralization of decision-making. These are problems of great concern in a political system in which democratic practices and political responsiveness are not rooted in the political culture. The fact that during the military regime some mechanisms of representative democracy – such as legislative elections and Congress activities – were maintained in operation certainly made it possible for the opposition to develop some legal political activity which eventually helped in the democratization process. However, this also had a negative consequence. It allowed Congress to function ineffectively, so that its members did not need to be worried about responsiveness, since their activities as representatives were in any case curtailed; in addition, it allowed voters to keep electing parliamentarians, who, they knew, had little weight and could not do much more than dispense them some favor, give their small town a new square, or just speak cautiously against the regime. This kind of political practice may be one of the factors explaining the absence among a significant number of politicians of a sense of political responsiveness. This may also help to explain the high levels of distrust felt amongst Brazilians towards institutions such as Congress.

This examination of the Brazilian pattern of democratic transition has demonstrated the constraints under which democratization in Brazil has taken place. The historical circumstances under which democracy was constructed are a crucial factor in explaining the Brazilian democratic project. As my analysis tried to show, the foundations of democracy in Brazil were not the result of a breakdown of the previous order. In fact, throughout Brazil's history, political rupture has never been a feature of the process of change, and Bazil's current democratization has not diverged from this historical pattern. This implies that the reconstruction of the political system was the product of an amalgamation of new and old structures and practices, an amalgamation that framed the options and strategies taken by the main actors in the political process. Nevertheless, we should not underestimate the important democratic advances that are largely the product of the new political dynamics introduced by the process of democratization.

Notes

1. Samuel Huntington, *The Third Wave: Democratization in the Late Twentieth Century* (Norman: University of Oklahoma Press), 1991.
2. Most of the analytical considerations adduced in this section, as well as in the next, rely on my *Legal Opposition Politics under Authoritarian Rule in Brazil: the Case of the MDB, 1966–79* (London: Macmillan, 1988). On the Brazilian military-authoritarian regime see also Alfred Stepan, *The Military in Politics: Changing Patterns in Brazil* (Princeton, N.J.: Princeton University Press, 1973); Alfed Stepan, ed., *Authoritarian Brazil: Origins, Policies, and Future* (New Haven, Conn.: Yale University Press, 1973); Fernando Henrique Cardoso, *O modelo politico brasileiro* (São Paulo: Difel, 1972).
3. Among the measures decreed by the Institutional Act No. 2 in 1965 was the dissolution of all political parties of the 1945–64 democratic period. Later on, the military government decreed a complementary act setting the rules for the creation of a two-party system. As a consequence two parties were created: the pro-government ARENA and the opposition MDB. Cf. Kinzo, *Legal Opposition*.

4. See Bolivar Lamounier, "Authoritarian Brazil Revisited: The Impact Of Elections in the *Abertura*," in Alfred Stepan (ed.), *Democratizing Brazil: Problems of Transition and Consolidation* (Oxford: Oxford University Press, 1989).

5. See Juan Linz, "The Future of an Authoritarian Situation or the Institutionalization of an Authoritarian Regime: The Case of Brazil," in Stepan, *Democratizing Brazil*.

6. Cf. Guillermo O'Donnell, *Modernization and Bureaucratic-Authoritarianism: Studies in South American Politics*, Institute of International Studies, University of California, Berkeley, Politics of Modernization Series, no. 9 (1973).

7. The literature on the economy under military rule in Brazil is vast. My comments are based on the works of José Serra, "Ciclos e mudanças estruturais na economia brasileira do pós-guerra," in Luis e Coutinho Belluzzo, *Desenvolvimento capitalista no Brasil: Ensaios sobre a crise* (São Paulo: Brasiliense, 1982); Albert Fishlow, "Some Reflections on Post-1964 Brazilian Economic Policy," in Alfred Stepan, *Democratizing Brazil*; Carlos Alberto Longo, "The State and the Liberalization of the Economy," in Maria D'Alva G. Kinzo (ed.), *Brazil: The Challenges of the 1990s* (London: British Academic Press, 1993).

8. On the Brazilian transition see Luciano Martins, "The 'Liberalization' of the Authoritarian Rule in Brazil," in Guillermo O'Donnell, P. Schmitter, and Laurence Whitehead (eds.), *Transitions from Authoritarian Rule: Latin America* (Baltimore: John Hopkins University Press, 1996), pp. 72–94; Stepan, *Democratizing Brazil*; Bolivar Lamounier, "Brazil: Inequality against Democracy," in Larry Diamond et al. (eds.), *Democracy in Developing Countries: Latin America* (Boulder, Colo.: Lynne Rienner, 1989).

9. Alain Rouquié, *Demilitarization and the Institutionalization of Military-Dominated Polities in Latin America*, Wilson Center, Washington, D.C., Working Papers of the Latin American Program, no. 110 (1982), p. 3.

10. This was shown by the deceleration of the growth of the gross domestic product (from 14 per cent in 1973, it fell to 9.8 per cent in 1974, and to 5.6 per cent in the following year); the sharp increase in the deficit on current account (from US$1.7 billion in 1973 to US$7.1 billion in 1974); and the growth in the foreign debt (U$6.2 billion in 1973, U$11.9 billion in 1974, and US$56.3 billion in 1981). See Serra, "Ciclos e mudanças," pp. 66–97.

11. Cf. Bolivar Lamounier and Alkimar Moura, "Economic Policy and Political Opening in Brazil," in Jonathan Hartlyn and S. Morley (eds.), *Latin American Political Economy: Financial Crisis and Political Change* (Boulder, Colo.: Westview Press, 1986).

12. The PT was created by trade union leaders, social movements, and left-wing groupings, and became the most important left-wing party. Its main leader is Luiz Inacio "Lula" da Silva who has three times run for president. The PTB, though preserving the name of the old PTB, has little resemblance to what was a growing political force in the 1945–64 democratic period in Brazil. The PDT split off from the old PTB, having as its creator Leonel Brizola who was one of the main PTB leaders during the 1945–64 democratic period. On the political parties created after democratization, see Maria D'Alva G. Kinzo, *Radiografia do quadro partidário brasileiro* (São Paulo: Konrad Adenauer–Stiftung, 1993); Scott Mainwaring, *Rethinking Party Systems in the Third Wave of Democratization: The Case of Brazil* (Stanford, Calif.: Stanford University Press, 1999).

13. Certainly the political process would have followed a different path if the second course, advocated by the more radical opposition, had been taken: perhaps Brazilian democratization would have been of a different nature or perhaps an authoritarian reversion would have interrupted the liberalization process.

14. The PFL became the second largest party. Apart from its center-right position, its main feature became its closeness to all governments since redemocratization.

15. In fact, the three PT deputies who defied the party line and supported Tancredo Neves certainly have their small place in history for believing that at that moment it was their duty to contribute to the defeat of the military government's candidate, but they were ostracized by the PT and ended up leaving politics.

16. In fact, José Sarney had to be affiliated to the PMDB in order to run as a vice-presidential candidate, because the PFL, at the time of the election, had not yet been legally founded.

17. The PSDB is President Cardoso's party, founded by PMDB dissidents who left that party during the Constituent Assembly.

18. In sum, Brazil had finally got deep into the crisis of the "state center matrix," using Cavarozzi's term to describe the total disarticulation of state-society relations that followed the exhaustion of the import-substitution development model. Cf. Marcelo Cavarozzi, "Beyond Transitions to Democracy in Latin America," *Journal of Latin American Studies*, 1991; 24.

19. Cf. Maria Helena Guimarães de Castro, "Democratic Transition and Social Policy in Brazil: Some Dilemmas in the Agenda of Reforms," in Kinzo, *Brazil: the Challenges of the 1990s*.

20. Brasilio Sallum Jr., "O Brasil sob Cardoso: Neoliberalismo e desenvolvimentismo," *Tempo Social: Revista de Sociologia da USP* October 1999; 11(2): p. 27.

21. Robert Dahl, *Polyarchy: Participation and Opposition* (New Haven, Conn.: Yale University Press, 1971).

22. In the 2000 municipal elections, electronic polling machines were used in 100 per cent of the voting places. This means that the Electoral Tribunal used 345,000 electronic polling machines to register the vote. Although this does not eliminate all possibilities of electoral fraud, it certainly reduces it considerably.

23. It is worth noting that in Brazil voting is compulsory.

24. José de Souza Martins, "Reforma agrária: O impossível diálogo sobre a história possível," *Tempo Social: Revista de Sociologia da USP* October 1999; 11(2): pp. 97–128.

25. Cf. Celso Castro, "Military and Politics in Brazil (1964–2000)" (unpublished paper, Brazil Workshop, Centre for Brazilian Studies, University of Oxford, February 2000).

26. Ricardo Paes de Barros et al., "Desigualdade e pobreza no Brazil: História de uma estabilidade inaceitável," *Revista Brasileira de Ciências Sociais* 2000; 15(42): pp. 123–42.

27. Ibid., p. 134.

28. The latter is an attempt at mobilizing social organizations and volunteers in civil society together with government resources to implement a variety of programs to target severe social problems and improve life in the country's poorest municipalities. See Kurt von Mettenheim, "The Brazilian Presidency and the Separation of Powers," paper for the XXIII Encontro Anual da Associação Nacional de Pesquisa e Pós-Graduação em Ciências Sociais, Caxambu, MG, 19–23 October 1999.

29. See Celina Souza, *Constitutional Engineering in Brazil: The Politics of Federalism and Decentralization* (London: Macmillan, 1997).

30. Examining the Brazilian case in a comparative perspective, Stepan points out that the Brazilian federalism is similar to the U.S. model in the sense that it is an extreme case of "demos constraining," that is, its institutional structure obstructs the democratic majority in the federal level. Cf. Alfred Stepan, "Toward a New Comparative Analysis of Democracy and Federalism: Demos Constraining and Demos Enabling Federations," in *Arguing Comparative Politics* (London: Oxford University Press, 2001).

31. Bolivar Lamounier, "Institutional Structure and Governability in the 1990s," in Kinzo, *Brazil: the Challenges of the 1990s*.

32. On this concept see Arendt Lijphart, *Democracies* (New Haven, Conn.: Yale University Press, 1984).

33. Political competition is aimed largely at accommodating intra-elite conflict by enlarging the space for regular intra-elite electoral competition.

34. Massive electoral support results not only from Brazil's large electorate but also from the second-ballot system, that is, a run-off ballot between the two leading contenders takes place aimed to produce a substantial majority for the winner in case no candidate gains a majority in the first round.

35. This analysis relies on Maria D'Alva G. Kinzo and Simone Rodrigues da Silva, "Politics in Brazil: The Cardoso Government and the 1998 Re-election," *Government and Opposition* 1999; 34(2): pp. 243–62.

36. Comprised of a federation of 26 states and the Federal District, Brazil has different constituencies depending on the kind of election. The nationwide constituency is the electoral basis upon which direct elections for president of the Republic are held, by a system of run-off ballot between the two leading candidates if neither receives an absolute majority on the first ballot. The same system is used for the election of both state governors and mayors of the capital and other major cities. The size of their constituencies is, obviously, related to the size of the state or the city. State constituencies are also the basis for the legislative elections at both federal and state levels. Here two systems are used. Senators are elected by the plurality system while members of the Federal Chamber (as well as of the state assemblies and city councils) are elected by proportional representation.

37. According to Laakso and Taagepera's index to measure the number of effective parties. See M. Laakso and R. Taagepera, "Effective Number of Parties: A Measure with Application to West Europe," *Comparative Political Studies* 1979(12). On political parties in Brazil, see Kinzo, *Radiografia do quadro partidário brasileiro*, and Mainwaring, *Rethinking Party Systems*.

38. Cf. Jairo Nicolau, "A volatilidade eleitoral nas eleições para a Câmara dos Deputados brasileira (1992–1994)," paper for the XXII Encontro Anual da ANPOCS, Caxambu, October 1998.

39. The PR system used in Brazil has a particular feature affecting electoral competition. It is based on the open list, which means that party lists do not show candidates in previously determined order; rather, it is the number of votes individually obtained by each candidate of a given party or alliance that determines her/his position and, hence, the chance of getting elected. Thus candidates work to encourage voters to choose a particular candidate even though the law also allows voting just for a party label. The result is that competition takes place largely among individual candidates (even from the same party), thereby relegating party organizations to a less effective position in the election campaigns of their representatives.

40. See Nicolau, "A volatilidade eleitoral."

41. The executive's legislative power is not limited to the Medidas Provisórias. It also has the exclusive right to propose to Congress bills dealing with the federal budget, the creation of positions and functions in the state-owned firms and in the public administration, salaries of civil servants, changes in the administrative structure, and changes in the strength of the armed forces. And in order to speed its business, the government can have priority for consideration of a bill by requesting the Council of Leaders (a group composed of the leaders of all parties in the House of Deputies) to treat it as an urgent or extremely urgent matter, which means that it can be put to the vote without having gone through all the phases of ordinary legislative proceedings. See Argelina Figueiredo and Fernando Limongi, "O processo legislativo e a produção legal no Congresso pós-Constituinte," *Novos Estudos Cebrap* 1994; (38); and "O Congresso e as Medidas Provisórias: Abdicação ou delegação?" ibid. 1997; (47): pp. 127–54.

42. The fact that the Congress has not yet managed to approve a bill limiting the executive's use of the Medidas Provisórias is a sign of the lack of consensus among parliamentarians about the result of this change.

43. See G. Tsebelis, "Decision-Making in Political Systems: Veto Players in Presidentialism, Parliamentarism, Multicameralism and Multipartyism," *British Journal of Political Science* 1995; 25: pp. 289–325.

3

Transitions: Argentina, Bolivia, Chile, Uruguay

Marcelo Cavarozzi

This essay considers the consolidation of political systems in Bolivia, Chile, Argentina, and Uruguay during the recent transitions to democracy. This exploration is illuminated by another relevant issue – the challenges posed to the reconstruction of political communities by the exhaustion of the politico-economic model prevailing across Latin America since the inter-war years. In the first two sections, the architecture of the contemporary political systems in the four countries is analysed, paying special attention to the models of government and the format of the respective party systems. The purpose of this assessment is to determine how, after the transitions to democracy of the 1980s, the party systems have changed vis-à-vis the patterns prevailing during the state-centered period. This, in turn, will make it possible to evaluate whether or not these changes contribute to improve the governance of these societies. The conclusion analyses some factors that could adversely affect the levels of social integration and cohesion of the national communities of the four countries, and, in turn, could diminish the relevance of political democracy for contemporary South American societies.

Models of government and party systems in the age of mass politics

Our discussion should begin with a caveat. Contemporary political science, both in the Northern Hemisphere and in Latin America, has paid limited

45

attention to the analysis of twentieth-century South American political systems, and more specifically of their models of government. To a certain extent, one of reasons for this omission is the centrality achieved by the concept of the state since the 1960s. Initially this bias was related to the impact of critical Marxism à la Althusser and Poulantzas. These French authors, and some Italian contemporaries like Cerroni and della Volpe as well, brought about an *aggiornamento* of the discussion of politics in modern capitalist societies by introducing the metaphor of the "relative autonomy of the state." The concept arrived in U.S. political science twenty years later with the book published by Rueschemeyer, Evans, and Skocpol.[1] Later, the contributions of Latin American social scientists such as Cardoso and O'Donnell to the theory of the bureaucratic-authoritarian model continued to deepen the debate, but they also had a contradictory effect. On the one hand, they positively contributed to reinvigorating the analysis of the political economy of the more industrialized South American countries. On the other hand, by overstating the importance of certain aspects of the (Brazilian and Argentine) military dictatorships of the 1960s, both authors inadvertently veiled the causes of the long-term crisis of the state-centric matrix prevailing since the interwar period. And it was precisely a debate generated between Cardoso and O'Donnell around the convenience of using either the concept of "state" to allude to the bureaucratic-authoritarian syndrome, or the alternative one of "regime," which proved valuable. For Cardoso, in preferring to use the concept of "regime," began to hint at the multiple dimensions which were (con)fused under the term "state."

The difficulties in fully understanding the nature of modern South American models of government have a second source of a more empirical nature. Twentieth-century South America was not the land of neat governmental formulae, which might be orderly classified in democratic or authoritarian boxes and easily ranked in terms of degree of stability. Besides, South American societies tended to replicate the "oriental" patterns alluded to by Gramsci; civil society was comparatively weak, and the demarcation between civil society and the state was nebulous.

It seems useful to contrast South America with the patterns that were predominant in Europe. Gregory Luebbert has argued that interwar Europe witnessed the development of four political formulae: liberal democracies, social democracies, fascist regimes, and traditional dictatorships.[2] Conversely, South America was the world of ambiguity; political formulae were intrinsically hybrid. In turn, the supremacy of the state over civil society was not always detrimental to democracy. Let us examine how the post-oligarchic political systems in Argentina, Bolivia, Chile, and Uruguay developed their main attributes.

In Argentina, the 1930–83 state-centered period was defined by a pattern of military intervention and tutelage that precluded any real possibility of consolidating a democratic system of government. Six constitutional governments were removed by the armed forces in 1930, 1943, 1955, 1962, 1966, and 1976. However, the military dictatorships also proved utterly incapable of founding stable political regimes. Hence, neither democracy nor dictatorship worked as an effective model of government. How, then, was Argentina governed? During the state-centered period, Argentina's model of government was based on a pattern of collective blackmail exercised by the key social and political actors – urban and rural capitalists, the unions, the military, and the Catholic Church – against the incumbent government.[3] One of the corollaries of this style of government was the "fusion" of economics and politics. The steering of the economy was achieved through the operation of a formula that might be defined as a "political automatic pilot."[4] I use this image in order to underscore the centrality of clusters of implicit agreements reached by the different social actors around the basic features of the regulatory and welfare functions of the state. This implicit consensus was based on the implementation of the first and second stages of import-substitution industrialization, and the protectionist and redistributive bias of state regulation. The predominance of moderate inflationary rates was a decisive factor in these arrangements. It allowed the public sector to play a strategic role in the always precarious equilibrium among the relative prices of goods and services. In summary, the continuity of the basic arrangements of Argentina's political economy allowed the country to navigate the turbulent waters of chronic governmental instability and of strong antagonism generated between the major parties during the twentieth century.

As suggested above, the major economic and political actors never demonstrated the slightest predisposition to compromise on public policies. This intransigence was shared by the major parties, the Radicals and the Peronists. The two parties, which developed very strong internal subcultures, occupied the center arena of party politics but failed to agree on building shared arenas of negotiation and compromise until the early 1970s. The Radical Party, or Unión Cívica Radical (UCR), was founded in 1890 and won the presidency twenty-six years later in Argentina's first democratic elections (in which the male native-born population participated) under the new Sáenz Peña law.[5] In 1916, the Radical leader, Hipólito Yrigoyen, defeated the loose confederation of conservative parties that had controlled the presidency since 1880. Thus, the UCR became the engine, and the symbol, of the transition from the oligarchic system to democracy. However, as a consequence of both its own shortcomings and the antidemocratic behavior of its conservative adversaries, Radicalism failed to consolidate democratic rule in Argentina. Hipólito Yrigoyen was overthrown by the military during his second presidential term which had started in 1928. In turn, thirty years later, between 1945 and 1950, the Peronists promoted radical changes in social relations, and engineered a profound revolution in Argentine political culture. They successfully challenged social hierarchies both in the countryside and in the largest cities, especially by reducing the social distance between bosses and workers. Nevertheless, as had been the case with the Radicals, the first Peronist government was deposed by the military in 1955 when it was at the peak of its electoral strength.

The combination of Radicalism and Peronism, in addition to the electoral implosion of conservatism, contributed to the creation of an "impossible political game," to use O'Donnell's image. Both parties aspired to monopolize the political representation of the "people," of the popular and middle sectors. As a result of the continued strength of both political subcultures, which in the case of Peronism acquired a quasi-religious nature, Argentina failed to build a party system. It was in part paradoxical that two mostly non-ideological parties, which by and large shared the vision of state interventionism and economic nationalism, could not recognize each other as valid interlocutors in the institutional arena.

Among the four countries discussed in this paper, Bolivia was a latecomer to mass politics. Unlike their counterparts from Argentina, Chile, and Uruguay, the export-oriented tin-mining bourgeoisie failed to promote the construction of a viable nation-state during the first half of the twentieth century.[6] Traditional oligarchic rule prevailed until the mid-twentieth century, when the nationalistic and reformist 1952 Revolution effectively put an end to it. The revolutionaries also sought to promote a process of state-led development, but they failed. The party that engineered the revolution, the Movimiento Nacionalista Revolucionario (MNR), soon proved incapable of the monumental tasks it faced. It splintered and the party structure was incapable of subordinating the main actors of the revolution, labor, the military, and peasant groups. Bolivia became acutely unstable, a situation that culminated in the 1978–82 period, when seven military and two weak civilian governments ruled the country.[7]

However, and despite the poor economic performance and political instability, political parties gradually developed. Under the personalistic leadership of Victor Paz Estenssoro, the MNR and its *politicos* became the linchpin of the fragile structure. On the left, the mining unions and progressive politicians gave birth to constantly splitting parties and factions of various Stalinist, Trotskyite, and populist leanings. On the right, several military presidents, such as Rene Barrientos, Alfredo Ovando, and Hugo Banzer used their power to generate clientelistic and regionally based networks, often relying on peasant support. Their common goal was to gradually transform these networks into personalistic party machines. There were two ephemeral phenomena that did not fit the patterns described above. The first was the Falange Socialista Boliviana (FSB), a right-wing party that oscillated between profascist positions and bizarre attempts to influence military regimes. It failed both in gaining popular support and in providing stable civilian leadership to the generals. At the other end of the spectrum, a progressive general, Juan José Torres, tried in 1971 to steer a military regime to the left. He was immediately deposed, and four years later he was assassinated in Buenos Aires with the acquiescence of the Argentine military.

General Hugo Banzer, who led an authoritarian military regime from 1971 to 1978, became the most successful politician within the armed forces. Although he was forced out of power in 1978, he laid the foundations for the creation of a party, the Acción Democrática Nacionalista (ADN). A few years after Banzer's fall from power, ADN went on to become a significant political party.

In summary, although Bolivia shared with Argentina a pattern of political instability from the 1950s to the 1980s, this did not prevent the gradual formation of a party system organized around the conventional right-left ideological spectrum.

In the case of early twentieth century Chile, the political scene was shaped by the gradual transformation of the old oligarchic tripartite scheme (Liberals, Conservatives, and Radicals) into a full-fledged party system covering the whole ideological spectrum.[8] After the downfall of the "dictablanda" (soft authoritarianism) of Carlos Ibáñez del Campo in 1931, the stability of the political formula rested upon two pillars. The first pillar was the slow, and controlled, expansion of the electorate. This was made possible by the exclusion of large segments of the rural popular classes from electoral politics until the 1950s. The peasant uprisings of the early 1930s in the Central Valley further reinforced the violent opposition of large landowners to unionization and the presence of the left-wing parties in the countryside. Liberals and Conservatives succeeded in preventing the expansion of the rural electorate beyond the social segments they controlled through clientelism and fraud.

The second pillar of political stability was associated with the role played by the Radical Party. Although this party never gained more than a quarter of the votes in parliamentary elections, the balance of power centered around Radicalism from the 1930s to the early 1960s. The Radical Party had the capability of alternatively oscillating between the Left and the Right. On the one hand, until 1952 the party sought Communist and/or Socialist support in presidential elections. This strategy enabled the Radical Party to capture the presidency in three successive elections, from 1938 to 1946. It was only in 1952, when a majority segment of the Socialist Party supported the populist candidacy of the resurgent Ibáñez del Campo, that a Radical candidate lost, ending up a distant third in the presidential elections.[9] On the other hand, during the decade and a half of Radical predominance, substantive policies in economic, social and cultural matters were largely conservative. More often than not, the Radical administrations ran day-to-day affairs with the backing of right-wing congressional majorities.

During the 1950s and the 1960s the two pillars of stability collapsed simultaneously. Successive changes in electoral legislation and the gradual transformation of social relations in the countryside eroded the almost absolute control enjoyed by the right-wing parties in the Central Valley region. These changes resulted in a dramatic expansion of the electorate; beginning in 1958 this expansion opened the possibility of an electoral victory of the Left. In turn, the Radical Party experienced a rapid and irreversible political decline, and was replaced by Christian Democracy in the center of the political spectrum. As discussed extensively by Manuel Antonio Garretón, the reluctance of the Christian Democratic Party to form alliances either with the Right or the Left increased the rigidity of the political system.[10] In Garretón's words, the three segments of Chile's party system – the Right, the Center, and the Left – developed uncompromising *alternativista* visions that rendered the making of governing coalitions impossible. These two phenomena largely explained the "implosion" of the Chilean political system, a process that unfolded in several stages from 1952 to 1973. Governing coalitions became ephemeral. The coalitions supporting presidents Ibáñez and Jorge Alessandri collapsed shortly after they managed to get their respective candidates elected. Moreover, the party system developed a peculiar sort of volatility. Beginning in 1952, the structure of the presidential electoral options and the politico-ideological orientation of the winner substantially changed in each successive election, as shown in table 3.1.

Table 3.1 **Major party groupings and electoral outcomes in Chilean presidential elections, 1938–1970**

	First place	Second place	Third place	Fourth place
1938	Center-left coalition	Right		
1942	Center-left coalition	Right		
1946	Center-left coalition	Right		
1952	Ibañistas	Right	Radicals	
1958	Right	Left	Christian Democrats	Radicals
1964	Christian Democrats	Left		
1970	Left	Right	Christian Democrats	

Finally, the political game came to the dramatic conclusion of 1973. The March 1973 parliamentary elections gave an ominous warning of what was to come. Two irreconcilable coalitions confronted each other. On the one hand, the CODE (Confederación de Partidos por la Democracia – the Christian Democrats and the right-wing parties) sought to achieve a two-thirds majority in order to impeach President Allende. CODE won the election, but it failed to reach the pursued goal of constitutionally displacing the Socialist politician from the presidency. On the other hand, the Unidad Popular left-wing government continued to implement its maximalist program and it failed to seek a compromise with the Center. The outcome was the September 1973 military coup.

Unlike the three other countries, Uruguay experienced an early transition from oligarchic politics to democracy. In fact, this country became Latin America's only relatively stable democratic regime during the first half of the twentieth century, and the legacy of the nineteenth century gave Uruguay the oldest two-party system in Latin America – the generally more cosmopolitan and centralist Colorados, and the more rural Blancos (formally known as the National Party). There was a temporary exception to this pattern during the 1933–42 period. José Batlle y Ordóñez, the founder of Uruguayan democracy and of its precocious welfare state, had died in 1929, and a conservative Colorado, Gabriel Terra, led a political backlash. Under President Terra's leadership, a coalition was formed between the conservative faction of the Colorado Party and its counterpart, the Herrerista group,[11] in the Blanco Party. The coalition closed down Congress and partially banned the political activities of the more progressive factions of their own parties, the Batllista Colorados and the Blancos Democráticos. Still, democratic equilibrium was restored in 1942, and Uruguayan democracy continued to thrive until the 1960s. A major factor in explaining this outcome was that the military were effectively subordinated to civilian authority from the first decade of the century onward.

In fact, for more than five decades, the basis of the country's political stability was a somewhat ambiguous combination of two-party democracy and one-party domination of the executive. The two parties alternated electoral victories and defeats, but after the brief civil war of 1904, the different factions of the Colorado Party controlled the executive for more than half a century. Still, Colorados and Blancos contrived consociational agreements of a sort, whereby both parties shared the spoils and the management of public enterprises. Beginning in the late 1950s, the Colorados lost their predominance and governmental coalitions became extremely fragile. The political system finally broke down between 1967 and 1973 when a conservative and authoritarian wing of the Colorado Party captured the presidency through Jorge Pacheco Areco and Juan Maria

Bordaberry. The latter, after being elected in 1971, engineered a coup with the support of the military. Congress was closed down, elections were suspended, and repression of the Tupamaro guerrillas, of the Left, and of all manifestations of social and political opposition, became extremely violent. Despite the emergence of an authoritarian Right, the major factor in explaining the collapse of democracy in Uruguay was the breakdown of the patterns of political cooperation that had prevailed between the two traditional parties for more than six decades. The Left, which in 1971 had reached 18 per cent of the vote after many decades of electoral ir-relevance, did not contribute to the maintenance of democracy either, by failing to explicitly condemn the terrorist actions of the guerrillas.

Military rule lost all pretense of legality when the armed forces fired Bordaberry in 1976; however, the removal of its key civilian ally did not prevent the authoritarian government from failing to achieve any of its goals, and from ultimately becoming a major fiasco. In 1980, the Uruguayan military regime organized a plebiscite asking the electorate to support the continuity of military rule, and lost. In Bolivia, Chile, and Argentina, whether through their failures or their successes, the military dictatorships managed to generate significant changes in economic, social, and political relations. Conversely, in Uruguay, the political system and the major institutions of the welfare state survived military rule without experiencing major transformations.

Government and political parties after the transitions to democracy

During the 1980s the four countries under analysis made the transition from military authoritarianism to representative democracy. As discussed elsewhere, transitions to democracy coincided with a "second transition," this one from the state-centered matrix to an alternative socio-political matrix defined by the predominance of markets over politics and the erosion of national sovereignty as a result of globalization.[12] Here I ana-lyze how these two processes – the consolidation of representative de-mocracy and the change in the socio-political matrix – have contributed, in turn, to the reform of the models of government and the reshaping of the party systems in Argentina, Bolivia, Chile, and Uruguay.

The combined effects of democratization and the collapse of the state-centered matrix have been ambiguous. On the one hand, most of the fac-tors that nurtured the patterns of non-institutional sectoral confrontation and political instability during the state-centered period were effectively removed as a result of political learning on the part of the major actors. In addition, and especially in the cases of Bolivia and Argentina, actors who had traditionally supported non-democratic regimes, such as the military and the business sector, have, at least in part, revalued democracy. On the other hand, new problems emerged. Although most of them are not testing the stability of democracy, as in the past, they pose novel challenges to the governability of the emerging democracies. We shall now review these processes in each country and explore the evolving trends.

In Argentina, the traditional schism between Peronism and Radicalism began to be closed in 1970. In the aftermath of the military regime launched in 1966, the so-called "Revolución Argentina," the two parties, in addition to several minor forces of the Center and the Left, signed a pact of reconciliation known as "La Hora del Pueblo." However, the advances made in the early 1970s did not have positive effects until a long decade later. The reconciliation between the two major party leaders, Juan Perón and Ricardo Balbín, did not prevent an all-out internal war within Peronism that quickly permeated the different spheres of the state, drastically undermining the capability of democratic forces to govern Argentine society. In fact, despite the efforts of the opposition parties, democracy did not survive in the mid-1970s. The aftermath of the collapse of Isabel Perón's government was the return to military rule in 1976, which inaugurated the most repressive regime in Argentine political history.[13]

The authoritarian government failed both in implementing pro-market reforms and in stabilizing an authoritarian order. The military dictatorship of 1976–83 did not achieve any of its economic and political objectives. However, the launching of its contradictory maximalist policies – like the attempt to create a private capital market, the exorbitant expansion of military expenditures, and the construction of monumental works of infrastructure – fueled a skyrocketing fiscal deficit. This phenomenon contributed decisively to the definitive breakdown of the economic pillars of the state-centered matrix. Coupled with the changes that took place in the international economic system between 1971 and 1982, the hybrid military program made utterly impossible the return to the state-led and autarchic model of economic development that had prevailed since the interwar years. In the end, the military dictatorship was ultimately forced to yield power after the Argentine occupation army surrendered to the British task force in the South Atlantic war. In fact, the Argentine armed forces suffered an internal defeat that was as ignominious as the external one.

In at least two senses, the 1983 transition to democracy became a watershed in Argentine history. The military's attempt to decree an amnesty law covering human rights violations was derailed. This outcome implied that the armed forces were rendered incapable of imposing any conditions on the new democratic government of the Radical politician, Raúl Alfonsín. Moreover, the election was not only a plebiscite against the military dictatorship; it also became an open contest between the hitherto unbeatable Peronist party and the UCR. The defeat of Peronism inaugurated a new political era: not only were the major parties effectively reconciled, but the party system offered for the first time in Argentine history the possibility of electoral alternation in power.

The Peronist party regained and has maintained its position of largest minority party since the 1987 Congressional election. In the meantime, it also won the 1989 and 1995 presidential elections. But Peronism does not enjoy an electoral monopoly of power. As the 1997 and the 1999 elections demonstrated, other parties or party coalitions could also win. In fact, the 1990s introduced a significant change in the coalitional propensities of Argentine parties. In the past, political parties, and especially the two major ones, had been reluctant to form coalitions, either in presidential elections or in Congress.[14] Conversely, during the last decade both the Peronists and the Radicals, and the parties of the Left and the Right as well, have repeatedly formed and broken coalitions both in order to improve their chances of winning presidential elections and securing majoritarian coalitions in congress.

Indeed, coalition formation has been one of the consequences of the gradual articulation of a party system in Argentina. In addition to the traditional parties, both the Right and the moderate Left seem to have become relevant players. The Right is a heterogeneous mosaic with three segments coexisting within it. The most important one is the modern liberal Right, whose center of gravity has moved from the Unión del Centro Democrático (UCD) to the Acción por la República (APR). The latter party, led by Domingo Cavallo, Carlos Menem's minister of finance, has been steadily increasing its strength, especially in the city of Buenos Aires and the more economically advanced provinces. Cavallo has become a political figure of broad national projection. The second segment is the authoritarian Right, an inchoate conglomerate of local and provincial organizations led by former officials of the last dictatorship, in most cases military officers. During the early and mid-1990s, these parties were able to win a number of governorships and several mayoralties, especially with the support of the lower middle-class sectors and the urban marginals of their districts. The authoritarian Right enjoyed some popularity, stressed an antipolitical message, and proclaimed a crusade for law and order. However, the authoritarian right wing ultimately decayed. Finally, the third segment is formed by a set of traditional provincial parties of various conservative lineages. Some of these groups had belonged to the Radicals or Peronists, while others were descendants of the old Conservative Party of the early twentieth century. They do not aspire to go beyond the borders of their respective provinces, and all their attempts to create a national confederation have proved fruitless.

On the other end of the political spectrum, the 1990s witnessed the emergence of the most successful left-wing experiment in Argentina's political history. The FREPASO (Frente del País Solidario) was a confederation of various small parties and organizations, some of them having split from the Peronists in criticism of Menem's rapprochement with neo-liberalism, and some others heirs to various socialist and social Christian splinters. The two main leaders of FREPASO, Carlos "Chacho" Álvarez and José Bordón, who had earlier resigned from the Peronist party, ended up following similar, albeit bizarre, trajectories. Bordón unexpectedly succeeded in the 1995 FREPASO national primary, beating Álvarez and thus becoming the party's presidential candidate. Although he was defeated by the re-elected president (Menem), Bordón obtained a surprisingly high 30 per cent of the national vote in that year's election, relegating the Radical candidate to a distant third. A few months later, as a result of a dispute with Álvarez, Bordón resigned from FREPASO, entered into a sort of political limbo, and finally rejoined the Peronist party. Five years later "Chacho" Álvarez was the protagonist of an even more eccentric political episode that underlined the expanded horizons of the Left, but at the same time, its shortcomings.

Alongside former President Alfonsín, "Chacho" Álvarez was in 1997 one of the architects of the ALIANZA, a coalition of the UCR and FREPASO created in 1997. The ALIANZA scored two successive electoral victories against the Peronists – the Congressional elections of 1997 and the presidential election of 1999. Álvarez became vice-president on the ticket headed by Radical politician Fernando De la Rúa. However, ten months after assuming office, "Chacho" resigned the vice-presidency as a result of a dispute with De la Rúa and his close associates over a corruption case in the Senate that involved members of the Cabinet. This resignation, coupled with the turbulent interparty relationships developing thereafter, have seriously undermined the possibility that the ALIANZA will consolidate in the long run as a center-left coalition.

Despite the fragility of the coalitions of the 1990s, they strongly suggest two tendencies that are reshaping Argentina's novel party system. On the one hand, Peronism, traditionally a nationalistic and pro-labor movement, has consistently veered to the right. Their more likely partners have been the modern liberal and authoritarian segments of the Right. On the other, the more moderate and middle-class UCR has regained the national presidency as a result of its alliance with the moderate Left. Paradoxically, President De la Rúa is certainly one of the more conservative party leaders.

In addition to the formation of the ALIANZA, the defeat of the Peronists in the 1999 presidential election, as shown in table 3.2, was also helped by the strong showing of Cavallo, who running as APR's candidate obtained more than 12 per cent of the votes.

Table 3.2 **Major parties and electoral outcomes in Argentine presidential elections, 1983–1999**

	First place	Second place	Third place
1983	UCR	Peronists	
1989	Peronists	UCR	
1995	Peronists	FREPASO	UCR
1999	ALIANZA	Peronists	APR

As suggested above, the ALIANZA government did not start on the right footing. In addition to De la Rúa's patent lack of leadership, the coalition parties have not yet proved to be capable of effectively administering the dangerous economic crisis Argentina is facing. The stability of democratic institutions is not yet at risk, but the volatility of coalitions and of electoral outcomes is probably going to increase.

In Bolivia, the post-transition political process had significant similarities with contemporary Argentine developments. The first was related to the nature of the transition itself. As with their Argentine counterparts, the Bolivian armed forces had to abandon power precipitously without being able to negotiate the conditions of their extrication. The second similar factor was associated with the role played in the post-transition period by the party that had led the process of incorporation of the popular sectors to mass politics, the MNR. As discussed in the previous section, the MNR had been the linchpin of the fragile political structure of the 1950s and 1960s. After the 1982 transition, the party, still led by Paz Estenssoro, recovered its former strategic position. Like the Argentine Peronists in the late 1980s, it did so by reversing its former nationalistic and statist positions, and by leading the process of structural adjustment and reform that allowed the country to extricate itself from the hyperinflation and the deep economic crisis of the mid-1980s.

Paz Estenssoro was elected president in 1985 in the midst of extraordinary circumstances. First, the leftist coalition led by Hernán Siles Suazo had been in government since 1982, but it had imploded as a result of its internal conflicts and the virtual collapse of the economy. Thus, Siles Suazo was forced to call elections one year before his term expired. Second, the election of Paz Estenssoro was the work of Congress, because in the first electoral round none of the candidates had obtained the absolute majority required. The election came as a result of a pact between MNR and ADN, Banzer's party. The pact included a tacit condition: if in 1989 the result had again to be decided in Congress, the MNR would support ADN's candidate. Third, as was the case with Menem in 1990–91, the searing experience of hyperinflation created high public tolerance for radical reforms that deepened the recession and increased unemployment, at least in the short run. The "Nueva Política Económica" (NEP) draconian reform package – which effectively called for the swift repression of the rebellious labor unions – was accepted by the majority of the population and secured legislative backing with the support of both MNR and ADN congressmen.

The disposition favorable to forming party coalitions that had been inaugurated in 1985 became a stable feature of Bolivian politics, surviving a major test in 1989. That year's MNR presidential candidate, who had also been the architect of the NEP, Gonzalo Sánchez de Lozada, "betrayed" his partner, Hugo Banzer, and refused to support him in the second, parliamentarian round of the presidential election. Sánchez de Lozada vicariously argued that he had received a plurality of the votes in the first round, and he refused to allow MNR's parliamentarians to vote for Banzer who, in turn, had garnered the second largest share of votes. As a result Banzer opted to support Jaime Paz Zamora, the candidate of the Movimiento de Izquierda Revolucionaria (MIR), the party that had managed to regroup most of the left-wing factions surviving the crash of the mid-1980s.[15]

Paz Zamora's government turned out to be completely irrelevant in policy terms. It was permanently dependent on ADN's backing for the approval of any legislation, and it was not capable of changing any of the major features of the orthodox neo-liberal NEP.[16] However, and paradoxically as a result of its own lack of effectiveness, the MIR administration reinforced the political patterns inaugurated four years earlier: the formation of parliamentarian coalitions supporting the programs of structural reform and the concomitant predominance of multiparty cabinets. Although the MNR formally became *the* opposition, the economic policies it had devised in 1985 continued to be implemented. In turn, incumbency had a strong negative impact on the MIR. The ineffectiveness of its government, and the corruption cases in which several officials and leading party members appeared associated with known drug dealers, fragmented the party and eliminated it as a serious contender for the next round of presidential elections. Thus, Bolivia's main left-wing party became the first victim of coalitional strategies that had, in fact, the effect of making political parties look more alike, obliterating their ideological and organizational peculiarities.

In the following election, although neither party obtained a majority, the MNR was the clear winner.[17] Gonzalo Sánchez de Lozada finally became president. In addition to the partial demise of the MIR, the 1990s witnessed a phenomenon of increasing party fragmentation associated with the emergence of several small parties. Two of them belonged to the category of personalistic neo-populist parties with diffuse economic ideologies and antipolitical overtones. The Unión Cívica Solidaridad (UCS) was led by Max Fernández, a successful businessman, and Conciencia de Patria (Condepa) had Carlos Palenque, a charismatic radio and television broadcaster.[18] A third addition to the party spectrum was the left-leaning Movimiento Bolivia Libre (MBL) which joined the MNR-led coalition in 1993 together with Condepa.

Sánchez de Lozada reiterated the pattern that had been inaugurated by Paz Zamora and his MIR, albeit with less virulence. The continued implementation of the programs of structural adjustment heavily contributed to the attrition of the incumbent president and his party. This pattern was reinforced during the 1993–97 period, despite Sánchez de Lozada's attempt to offset the impact of adjustment policies with the implementation of redistributive measures under the label of "capitalismo del pueblo." It was true, anyway, that the president's arrogant style, his rather distinct foreign accent – the result of having lived for many years in the United States – and his ineffectiveness in disciplining his own party, also contributed to his decline.

Thus, it was not a surprise that the presidential election of 1997 finally opened the democratic gate to the resilient former dictator, Hugo Banzer. After almost twenty years of exclusion from power, the old general won the first plurality in the first round, and ultimately became the legitimate choice of Congress in the second round. But the ascension of the former dictator to the presidency only accentuated the pattern of party fragmentation and governmental decay. Banzer initially enjoyed strong parliamentary support with the formation of a so-called "mega-coalition" integrated by the MIR, Condepa, and the UCS, in addition to his own party.[19] However, it soon became apparent that government offices were in most cases sought solely as a means for career advancement and for access to patronage and spoils. In the late 1990s Bolivia entered on a dangerous path of economic decline, regional breakdown – which was especially acute in the province of Cochabamba and its coca-growing regions – and lawlessness. One of the apparent victims of political disintegration has been Banzer's party, ADN. During 2000, the party has de facto broken into several factions and thousands of its activists have resigned their memberships.

It could be argued that, in contrast to Argentina, the processes of bureaucratization and the decline of party differences have transformed coalition formation in Bolivia into a ritual devoid of any ideological and policy content. The predominance of coalitional strategies has thus significantly contributed to the radical fragmentation of the party system and, furthermore, to the intensification of political apathy and deinstitutionalization.

Chile, like Uruguay, was a case of negotiated transition to democracy. Unlike Uruguay, however, the rules for the transition were largely imposed by the military dictatorship. The 1980 Constitution, which had been approved in an obviously non-competitive plebiscite, included several non-democratic clauses. First, the electoral system was designed to favor the rightist representation in Congress by establishing the system of two seats per district. In this system, which only exists in Chile, the majority party is required to obtain at least two-thirds of the vote to win the two seats. As Garretón has stated, this means that "a list that obtains 35 per cent of the votes nationally could get 50 per cent of the seats."[20] Second, the Senate includes a number of non-elected senators. Third, the commanders in chief of the armed forces cannot be removed by the democratic authorities. Last but not least, the military are given participation in the National Council of Security and the Constitutional Court.

Despite loading the procedural dice, Pinochet was defeated in the 1988 plebiscite. This outcome was made possible by the fact that the Chilean democratic opposition – the parties of the Center and the Left – had undergone profound ideological and organizational changes before and during the transition. Garretón underlines the importance of the fact that most of the opposition parties, with the exclusion of the Communists, decided to transform the coalition they formed to vote against the continuity of military rule in the 1988 plebiscite into a governmental coalition, the Concertación de Partidos por la Democracia.[21] The formation of the Concertación broke several patterns prevailing within the Chilean political system during the two decades preceding the 1973 breakdown, especially the volatility of electoral options and the impossibility of stabilizing governing coalitions. It was paradoxical, anyway, that most of the Left finally opted for compromise and for forming an alliance with the Center, at the same time that the Communist Party reversed the moderate strategies it had followed between 1935 and 1980. During and after the transition, and abandoning their traditionally moderate strategies, the Communists opted to follow a more extreme course. They criticized the Concertación leadership for its predisposition to negotiate the conditions of the transition with the military, and for its acceptance of the neo-liberal economic model implemented by the authoritarian regime.

Beginning with the first elections in 1989, the presidency has always been won by the Concertación. The two first presidents were Christian Democrats, Patricio Aylwin and Eduardo Frei; both won in the first round while securing substantial majorities against the right-wing candidates. During most of the 1990s the Right was divided between two parties: the Unión Demócrata Independiente (UDI), whose leaders were closer to the openly authoritarian positions of Pinochet and the military; and Renovación Nacional (RN), which was originally oriented toward playing the role of a democratic Right.

In 1999 the Concertación parties agreed to select their candidate in a really open primary contest, and the Socialist Ricardo Lagos soundly defeated his Christian Democrat opponent.[22] However, Lagos and the right-wing candidate, Joaquín Lavín, a former mayor of one of the wealthiest neighborhoods of Santiago, Las Condes, ended up in a virtual tie in the first round of the presidential elections.[23] Despite the fact that Lagos scored a clear but narrow victory in the ballot, the 1999 election substantially altered the interparty equilibrium reached in the early 1990s. In fact, the election might have marked a watershed in Chilean post-transition politics. The traditional "three thirds" arrangement of Left/Center/Right was replaced by a political society divided into two halves. The new Right, which dissociated itself from the discredited Pinochet, expanded its electoral base while adopting a neo-populist orientation with strong antipolitical overtones. Lavín and the Right have certainly benefited from the attrition of the center-left governing coalition and the growing political apathy of vast segments of the Chilean population, especially the youth. Besides, the trajectory followed by Lavín, himself a UDI leader, has substantially altered the internal equation of the Right. The hardline segments of Pinochetismo have become fringe actors and the more reform-oriented sectors of RN have virtually lost all political leverage.

In summary, the emerging political scenario in Chile suggests a paradox. On the one hand, the erosion of the *alternativista* visions, and the stability of politico-electoral options, have removed two of the major factors contributing to the breakdown of democracy in 1973. On the other hand, these tendencies have also nurtured the weakening of political parties, the traditional backbone of twentieth-century Chilean society.

In Uruguay the authoritarian military regime was also capable of negotiating a transition, but its power of negotiation was considerably more limited than that enjoyed by Pinochet and his associates. As Alicia Lissidini has indicated, the Uruguayan military suffered, in fact, two electoral defeats in the 1980s.[24] The first was the 1980 plebiscite, in which their proposal to install a permanent authoritarian regime was soundly defeated by the electorate: 57.9 per cent voted to reject it. In 1982 the dictatorship experienced a second and equally serious setback. The regime organized internal elections in the traditional parties, the Blancos and Colorados, hoping to give a boost to the pro-authoritarian segments of each party. To make this easier, the Frente Amplio, a coalition of various progressive and leftist groups founded in 1971, which had maintained a steady electoral presence both independently and in alliance with other actors in spite of having been declared illegal, was banned from participating. Even so, the pro-democratic segments of the traditional parties scored a decisive victory; they received more than 70 per cent of the vote among the Blancos, and nearly two-thirds in the Colorado Party.[25]

The actual terms of the transition to democracy were negotiated in the so called "Pacto del Club Naval," which was the accord signed by the military chiefs and the party leaders in 1984. Since the military continued to ban the Blanco leader Ferreira Aldunate and jailed him when he returned to Uruguay that year, this party refused to participate in the negotiations. The outcome could not be more paradoxical: the historically conservative Blancos remained as the adamant democrats opposed to making a compromise with the military, while the leftist Frente Amplio signed the Pacto.[26]

Despite the initial exclusion of the Blancos, the Uruguayan transition resulted in the full restoration of democracy.[27] In this sense, Uruguay followed a different path than the other three countries. In Chile, it could be argued that the 1990 transition inaugurated a gradual re-foundation of democracy, but in Argentina and Bolivia the prior records of instability, and the predominance of hybrid political formulae involving a mix of authoritarian and democratic aspects, going beyond the civilian/military distinction, suggest that these two countries underwent processes of actual foundation of political democracy.

The definition of the Uruguayan path as one of democratic restoration does not imply that the 1985–2000 period has been devoid of political changes. In fact, four distinct, albeit related, tendencies have reshaped the party system. First, the Colorado Party has to some extent regained the dominant position it enjoyed during the first half of the twentieth century. It won three of the four elections held since 1984, and Julio María Sanguinetti has emerged as its most powerful leader while twice occupying the national presidency, in 1985–90 and 1995–2000. In a way, the Colorados have again become the "party of the state," as Liliana De Riz aptly called them. Second, the Blancos have been losing popular support, especially in the 1990s. The heir of Wilson Ferreira Aldunate's leadership, Luis Alberto Lacalle, won the presidency in the 1989 elections, but left power five years later, seriously blemished by widespread accusations of corruption. Lacalle has nevertheless been able to retain control of the party, but at the cost of eroding its traditional electoral base, especially in Montevideo. Third, the Frente Amplio has been consistently gaining electoral support, rising from 22 per cent of the vote in 1984 to 40 per cent in 1999. In fact, the Frenteamplista presidential candidate, Tabaré Vázquez, would have won the presidency in 1999, if the 1996 constitutional reform had not introduced the run-off system for the presidential elections. Last but not least, the three largest parties have tended to become ideologically more homogeneous. This tendency, and especially the drastic shrinking of the progressive factions of the two traditional parties, has increased the appeal of the Frente Amplio within the electorate. In turn, within the Frente, the hardline Communists and the sectors formerly associated with the Tupamaro guerrillas have become more vociferous. But the dominant factions – Tabaré and his Socialist Party – have increased the moderation of their programs, and also of the tone of their political discourse.

During most of the 1990s, Congressional majorities were made possible by the cooperation, however unstable, between the two traditional parties. The Left systematically increased its number of seats in both chambers of Congress, but it was effectively shut out from power at the national level. However, since 1990 the municipal (departmental) government of Montevideo has been in the hands of the Frente Amplio. Thus, the Frente controls, in a manner of speaking, half of the country's population. Perhaps the biggest cloud on the political horizon of Uruguay is the fact that the strategies of co-operation between Blancos and Colorados have excluded the country's largest party from enjoying even a minimal share of power at the national level.

Conclusion: Democracy as a socio-political movement

The four South American countries discussed in this chapter have followed different political paths since the 1980s: democratic restoration in Uruguay, democratic re-foundation in Chile, and democratic foundation in Argentina and Bolivia. These political changes are related to one of the main aspects of the contemporary transitions, that is, changes in the type and format of political regimes. In this sense, southern South America has gone through a process of consolidation, albeit uneven, of democracies as political regimes. However, there is a second aspect to the transitions that I define as a change of politics. By this I mean a change in the "place" occupied by politics in contemporary South American societies, that is, the relationships between politics and other central dimensions of society, especially the economy and culture. This place has changed altogether. In other words, the functions of politics in the economy and in civil society have been radically redefined since the 1980s. In this sense, what changed was what and how much could be resolved through political mechanisms in the economic and cultural dimensions of South American societies.

This second sphere of change is also related to democracy. However, in this sphere, democracy should be conceived as a socio-political movement whose meaning – its content and its discourse – is historically defined. In South America, during the twentieth century, democracy as a socio-political movement has undergone two stages, and it is currently entering a third one. The first two stages were respectively associated with (1) the transition from oligarchic politics to mass politics, and (2) the building of the welfare state.[28] The fiscal crisis of the state of the early 1980s – which, not accidentally, coincided, at the world level, with the end of the era of organized capitalism that had been inaugurated after the Second World War – marked the beginning of a third stage of democracy as a socio-political movement. The specific contents of democracy during this third stage, and its eventual relevance, have yet to be defined. The contemporary meaning of democracy is still largely an unknown quantity; what it will ultimately become depends on two serious, and novel, challenges that South American societies are currently facing. The first challenge is the result of the prevalent tendencies of globalization (transnational integration) and erosion of national sovereignty. Transnational integration has increased the level of social disintegration within national societies in South America, as elsewhere. Social cohesion has reached extremely low levels, and the maintenance of society itself may be at stake. In order to recover the relevance of democracy, its institutions and protagonists have to prove capable of addressing the problem of social disintegration.

In turn, the crisis of the classic patterns of state intervention, and the related breakdown of the traditional mechanisms of political action defined during the state-centered stage, have generated a second challenge. In South American societies, especially with the beginning of the era of mass politics, the cultural cement of day-to-day life was built around state actions. Political identities, and the most important redistributional conflicts as well, were shaped by the material and symbolic content of those actions. Thus, it could be argued that the foundations of social order rested upon the state. The dramatic shrinking of the state could not but radically undermine that order. The question of how to define new bases for the reconstruction of that order is still open.

Beneath the layer of political stabilization and the relatively normal operation of democratic rules and competitive elections, large segments of the population have lost interest in citizenship. This does not seem to be, unfortunately, a passing phenomenon; it is rooted in the increasing loss of relevance of the democratic political system for settling economic and social conflicts, and for influencing the day-to-day life of the majority of the population. This is the second, and most pressing, challenge faced by democracy as a social movement in contemporary South America.

Notes

1. Dietrich Rueschemeyer, Theda Skocpol, and Peter Evans (eds.), *Bringing the State Back In* (New York: Cambridge University Press, 1985).
2. Gregory Luebbert. *Liberalism, Fascism, or Social Democracy* (New York: Oxford University Press, 1991).
3. See my "De la inflación como política a la construcción de un sistema de partidos," in *Plural* July 1988.
4. For this concept, see ibid.

5. The restriction of the suffrage to native-born males was crucial in the metropolitan area of Buenos Aires (where more than half of the males were of foreign origin in 1914) and its agricultural hinterland, the humid pampas. Between 1869 and 1914, Argentine population more than quadrupled.

6. The defeat of Bolivia in the War of the Pacific (1879–1882) did not only result in the loss of territory to Chile, but also depleted the country's material resources and state-building capabilities for several decades.

7. Eduardo Gamarra, "Market-oriented Reforms and Democratization in Bolivia," in Joan Nelson (ed.), *A Precarious Balance: Democracy and Economic Reforms in Latin America* (San Francisco: ICS Press, 1994).

8. It is interesting to underline that the 1921 foundation of the Communist Party preceded the formation of the Socialist Party, in turn, an outgrowth of the short-lived 1932 Socialist Republic. This constituted a reversal of the "classical" sequence in which a maximalist wing split from a pre-existing moderate Socialism. In fact, this pattern provided one of the first clues that the Chilean left-wing parties would not follow the conventional political itineraries of their counterparts in Europe and southern South America. One important corollary was that, at least until the 1973 military coup, Chilean Communists often tended to be more moderate than the Socialist Party.

9. It was indeed paradoxical, though revealing, that the official Socialist candidate for the presidency, who was also supported by the outlawed Communist Party, was Salvador Allende. Allende, who ended fourth in the 1952 presidential elections, became the candidate of the united Left in the next three presidential elections. However, both in the 1950s and the 1970s, the most serious obstacles to the achievement of Allende's political goals within the left, were generated by his own party, i.e., Socialism.

10. See Manuel A. Garretón, *The Chilean Political Process* (Boston: Unwin Hyman, 1989), chap. 1. Garretón discusses how the tendency of Christian Democracy to conceive itself as an alternative to both the Right and the Left contributed to the breakdown of democracy in Chile.

11. The Herrerista faction was named after Luis Alberto de Herrera, the conservative leader of the party during the first half of the twentieth century.

12. See my "Politics: A Key for the Long Term in South America," in W. C. Smith, C. Acuña, and E. Gamarra (eds.), *Latin American Political Economy in the Age of Neoliberal Reform* (New Brunswick, N.J.: Transaction, 1994), and "Beyond Transitions to Democracy in Latin America," *Journal of Latin American Studies* 1992; 24(2).

13. Juan Perón was elected president of Argentina in September 1973, after forcing the first constitutional president elected that year, his former subordinate and longtime crony, Héctor Cámpora, to resign. However, Perón died a few months later, in July 1974, and he was replaced by his wife and vice-president, Isabel Perón.

14. Parliamentarian coalitions were rare because the incumbent parties often enjoyed absolute majorities in both chambers of Congress.

15. Bolivians joked about the 1989 elections, arguing that they were left with three presidents: Sánchez de Lozada, who won the largest number of votes; Banzer, who de facto "elected" the president; and Paz Zamora, who finally became president, despite the fact that he had only the third largest share of the vote.

16. In my article "The Left in Latin America: The Decline of Socialism and the Rise of Political Democracy," in Jonathan Hartlyn, Lars Schoultz, and Augusto Varas (eds.), *The United States and Latin America in the 1990s: Beyond the Cold War* (Chapel Hill, N.C.: University of North Carolina Press, 1992), I explain how the coalition led by the MIR was a good example of the broad left-wing fronts that, on acquiring political power, have failed to advance policy options significantly different from those implemented by the conservative parties that preceded them.

17. Sánchez de Lozada obtained 34.30 per cent of the vote, while the runner-up, Banzer,

only got 20.36 per cent. The two neo-populist candidates, Max Fernández and Carlos Palenque, received similar levels of support of approximately 14 per cent. Gamarra, "Market-Oriented Reforms and Democratization in Bolivia."

18. Both Fernández and Palenque died in the mid-1990s. Their parties have been losing popularity after the disapperance of the leaders.

19. See Enrique Ibáñez, "El consenso sin alternativa: Los partidos políticos en la transición boliviana," *Zona Abierta* 88–89 (1999) for a thorough discussion of the different party coalitions of the 1985–98 period.

20. Manuel Antonio Garretón, "Chile: Political Learning and the Reconstruction of Democracy," in Jennifer McCoy (ed.), *Political Learning and Redemocratization in Latin America* (Miami: North South Center Press, 2000).

21. Garretón emphasizes that the unity of the opposition was an unforeseen effect of the 1980 plebiscite: "the paradox of the plebiscite was that it institutionalized the authoritarian regime and legitimated Pinochet's leadership, but it also harbored the possibility of unleashing a democratic transition.... the opposition found that the problem of its unity was solved because no hegemony or programmatic debate was necessary to vote 'No' in the plebiscite." "Chile: Political Learning and the Reconstruction of Democracy."

22. In the 1993 primary, the rules had been heavily weighted in favor of the Christian Democrat Eduardo Frei. The candidate was largely selected through caucuses and closed elections in which party organizations and activists played a key role.

23. The 1999 elections also marked the virtual disappearance of the traditional Left represented by the Communist Party. The Communist presidential candidate received less than 3 per cent of the vote.

24. See Alicia Lissidini Dotti, "La democracia directa en el Uruguay (1917–1994)" (Doctoral dissertation, FLACSO, Mexico, 1997).

25. Lissidini underlines that the big winner in the 1982 internal elections was Wilson Ferreira Aldunate, the Blanco politician who had become the symbol of opposition to the military dictatorship. His internal party line, "Por la Patria y Movimiento Nacional de Rocha," obtained 27 per cent of the total votes cast in 1982, far outdistancing all the other Blanco and Colorado tickets. The Frente Amplio was not authorized to participate in the internal elections.

26. Liber Seregni, the historic leader of the Left since the early 1970s, was a decisive factor in the incorporation of the Frenteamplistas in the negotiations. Seregni, a progressive general who had been banned from political activity and jailed by his military colleagues, opted to negotiate against the opposition of the Frente hardliners. Paradoxically, the military also chose to make a "pact with the devil." One of the most important causes of the 1973 coup had been their objective of exterminating both the Tupamaro guerrillas and the parliamentarian Left. In 1984 the refusal of the Blancos to sit at the bargaining table forced the military to include the Left in order to give a minimum of legitimacy to the accord.

27. There was one aspect in which the post-1985 Uruguayan democracy remained feeble: the issue of punishment of the human rights violations committed during the military dictatorship was only partially solved by means of a referendum. Only in 2000 has the new Colorado president, Jorge Batlle, started to press the military to address the issues of disappearances and mass graves.

28. Our four cases did not go through the first two stages of democracy as a social movement at the same time. Argentina, Chile, and Uruguay experienced the transition to mass politics during the first third of the century, while in Bolivia a similar process was associated with the 1952 nationalist revolution. In turn, the construction of welfare states started in Argentina, Chile, and Uruguay during the interwar years. In Bolivia, the variant of the welfare state built during the 1950s and 1960s was late and limited.

4

Reforms: Mexico and Colombia

Laurence Whitehead

Introduction

This essay explores the hypothesis of a distinctive path to democratization through "reform," with its own logic and internal structure. In this volume, this pattern of democratization is differentiated from the "foundation" of new democratic regimes, and also from democratic "transitions." In the latter two scenarios the replacement of the previous power holders is a "strictly necessary" condition for democratization, but not so in the reform route. In the scenario under discussion here, they may retain control of the reform agenda, and democratic institutions may be installed or extended piecemeal, in the course of extended processes punctuated by advances and relapses. In contrast to other types of democratization there can only be very approximate indications of when the reform route begins, and no clarity about when it ends. None of these three scenarios can be expected to occur in pure form; the search for empirical confirmation of the hypothesis of a "reform" scenario, in particular, is clouded by the complexity of each historical example and methodological difficulties in analysis.

Nevertheless, the hypothesis is important, and requires careful consideration, both because of the refinements it introduces into the theoretical debate about the nature of democratization, and because of its relevance to hotly debated processes of political transformation in such prominent countries as contemporary Mexico. The procedure adopted in this essay is first to explore the hypothesis as a logical construct, to consider what it would imply in its "pure" form. Then, searching for empirical verification, Colombia and Mexico are considered as possible exemplars of this path to democratization. This second step is not uncontroversial, and must be re-evaluated in the conclusion. Although Venezuela has been suggested as a third possible example, that seems to stretch the evidence too far, and indeed Venezuela appears elsewhere in this volume as an example of democratic regression. Thus, Latin America provides only two candidates for consideration as examples of democratization through reform, and no other very plausible examples present themselves from the rest of the world. (India as the Congress Party lost hegemony seems the nearest possibility.) Yet the paths to democracy in Colombia and Mexico seem far from parallel. So we have only two examples, and they are divergent. Insofar as Colombian and Mexican politics do proceed in tandem, it is commonly asserted that the forces bringing them together have little to do with democracy (the drugs cartels, guerrillas, judicial corruption, for example). In view of these complications the essay goes on to provide a methodological digression on the use and limitations of the method of "paired comparisons." The core of the essay then follows, in the form of a paired comparison of Colombia and Mexico that draws on the logic and the methodological approach already outlined. Comparison includes contrast, and hence the key variables highlighted by the two cases that are not emphasized by the "reform" model are also discussed. Finally, the essay offers some tentative conclusions both about the proposed subcategory of democratization through reform, and about the still open-ended processes of regime change under way in the two countries.

The logic of democratization through reform ("by stealth")

This section attempts to model the logic of democratization when the starting point is neither a military authoritarian regime, nor a monopolistic one-party regime, nor a personal dictatorship, nor a system of colonial rule. In all of the aforementioned scenarios democratization would include some unambiguous break with the past, some clear-cut change in the rules about who governs, and in the political rights of the governed. In short, the principle of popular sovereignty would be first denied and then (at least in principle) affirmed. By contrast this section concerns democratization in a context where the principle of popular sovereignty is already acknowledged through such constitutional and legal provisions as an unbreakable electoral calendar, the formal separation of powers, and the rotation of office-holders in accordance with the rhythm of contested elections. In such a context the obvious question becomes: Why enquire about democratization when so much of the basic machinery of democracy (as specified by the consensus on procedurally minimual conditions) is already in place? Surely in such a setting political reform may be conceived of as the means to perfect a democracy rather than to establish one? The question cannot lightly be dismissed, and indeed in the two cases under consideration the incumbent authorities would always claim that the basics of democracy were already in place before reform began. However, it is perfectly possible to have a civilian constitutional regime with regular contested elections, but with no institutionalized uncertainty about their outcomes. If the incumbents can effectively nominate their successors, and the voters can only ratify appointments decided elsewhere, then the electoral process falls short of even the procedurally minimal requirements for a democracy. If so, then political reform becomes a question of establishing rather than just perfecting democratic procedures. Thus, what we are examining is a form of democratization. This examination can be undertaken in three stages. The first would be to further characterize the pre-democratic regime. The second would be to consider the logic of democratizing reforms in such a setting. The third (more speculative) would be to model the likely results of political reform.

First, then, the initial characteristics of the pre-democratic regime require elaboration. It will be a well-structured and durable regime, as evidenced by the fact that change comes about through reform rather than breakdown or overthrow. In formal terms the regime is constitutional, and the right to govern is reserved to elected representatives of civilian political parties. The military do not rule by fiat, and civilian incumbents are constrained by impersonal rules of the game including a pre-fixed electoral calendar. These rules of the political game are predictable, sophisticated, and widely understood. Some of the most important rules may be tacit, unwritten, informal. But there are always inescapable formal mechanisms of adjudication – through Congress, the courts, the party conventions, for example – in the absence of which purely informal outcomes would be considered provisional, arbitrary and non-binding. After each election there is a transfer of public office to new incumbents in accordance with the constitutional rules. This happens reliably, and over many cycles. No single actor or group has the authority or power to break with these institutional procedures, or to overturn the constitutional structure. But although the system is predictable and impersonal, it is not democratic, in that the electorate is not sovereign. Elite circulation occurs essentially as the result of pacts or bargains between dominant groups. Voters see themselves (and correctly so) as ratifying personnel changes decided in the upper reaches of the political elite, rather than imposing their own preferences. All participants are aware that the system was designed to limit the likelihood of a destructive conflict between rival factions in the political elite. It therefore involves a controlled bargain whereby these factions can resolve their differences without exposure to the destabilizing effects of intervention from a potentially volatile electorate. Politicians and voters assume – and experience seems to confirm – that if all else fails, the system can fall back on the device of an electoral fraud, which the regime will prefer to the more disturbing alternative of a loss of control over the process of elite circulation.

Second, from these initial conditions it is possible to deduce some implications concerning democratizing reforms. The "transitions" literature portrays a sharp discontinuity between "liberalization" and "democratization," and models the shift from the former to the latter in terms of a power struggle between "hardliners" and "soft-liners." Neither of these assumptions are applicable to democratization through reform. The liberalization/democratization dichotomy arises from initial conditions in which power is concentrated in the hands of an unaccountable authoritarian coalition. As a result of strategic calculations or power struggles within the coalition, a faction comes to the fore that seeks to bolster its position through a controlled liberalization, probably abrupt and decreed from above. So long as the ruling coalition retains sufficient control over the process it can decide the scope and limits of this opening and can indeed withdraw concessions if they are judged to risk a regime breakdown. "Liberalization" is thus a calculated strategy to prolong authoritarian rule by co-opting some potential dissenters. "Democratization" is a conceptually distinct process whereby the ruling coalition splits between those determined to preserve authoritarian rule (the "hardliners") and those who prefer the uncertainty of a democratic competition for power to the imposed certainty of regime continuity (the "soft-liners"). But the initial conditions in our model are at variance with all of this. Instead of liberalization by decree, political reforms have to be negotiated through public debates and consultative procedures (as illustrated by the 1977–78 Mexican consultations over the reform of the electoral process and the legalization of political parties, or the 1991 Constituent Assembly in Colombia). Such consultative processes arise from the constitutionalism that characterizes our pre-democratic regimes, and from the associated needs to generate elite unity and to communicate a clear understanding of the scope and limits of the proposed reforms to all participants in the political system.

Under the conditions postulated in this model, the decision to initiate a political reform involves a public recognition of the inadequacy of the existing rules of the game, and a public invitation to debate what these failings are and how they can be corrected. In short, the reforms are to be understood as a means to prolong the existing impersonal constitutional order by tackling a legitimacy deficit that has to be publicly acknowledged. Such reforms have to be explained and justified. They cannot be presented as a mere by-product of power struggles within the ruling elite. Those currently in power must consent to a debate on reform, but must not exercise too much overt control over the outcome. The counterpart to their consent and their acknowledgement of a legitimacy deficit is that this is expected to limit recrimination against them (hence democratization "by stealth").

But this discursive practice will impede the emergence of any fixed and durable division between hardliners and soft-liners. Almost all established factions have some interest in the continuity of a regime that either extends them recognition or seems capable of responding to their points of view. The official acknowledgment of a legitimacy deficit at least opens space for some kind of dialogue. In place of a fixed division between (democratizing) "soft-liners" and (authoritarian) "hardliners," competing factions all have scope to structure (and limit) the reforms in ways that may either protect or promote their specific interests. Whereas the "transitions" literature views democratizing reform as a "one-shot" game, these are iterative processes in which the incentive structure rewards selective participation, not root-and-branch reform or diehard resistance to change.

Third, then, given this underlying logic of reform, what can be said about eventual outcomes? Does democratization through reform necessarily lead to consolidated democracy, or are there other pathways implicit in the model? The ultimate outcomes are highly speculative, but on the basis of what has just been indicated, one would not expect to find a single clear-cut discontinuity separating liberalization from the transition to democracy. Since constitutional rule was always founded on an at least formal recognition of the principle of popular sovereignty, the question is not whether there has been an overt reversal of the authoritarian basis on which the pre-democratic regime was founded, but rather whether its liberal democratic rhetoric has been given a sufficiently substantive content. Within this discursive framework it is possible to debate reforms aimed at such objectives as the deconcentration of power, the rebalancing of constitutional divisions between powers, bringing politics closer to the people, widening the scope of public debate, or enlisting the political participation of hitherto excluded social groups. All of these objectives can be defended as ways of enhancing the legitimacy of the existing regime. Equally well, all are open to counterarguments based on the need to avoid destabilizing discontinuities that might break the established social equilibrium and open the way to an unbridled conflict over the distribution of power. For this reason the most plausible outcome is a succession of proposals for, and measures of, political reform, each justified by the need to fill in a legitimacy deficit, but none of them so unambiguous and transformative as to lay that need to rest. Within the model as described there can be no foundational election, no return to barracks, no defenestration of a personal ruler, no expulsion of an oppressor. So there can be no break point that can dramatize and complete the process of democratic transition. Even a constitutional revision or the establishment of an unquestionably clear electoral count may be insufficient to staunch the demand for still further political reforms. This situation makes it very difficult to convince skeptics that the latest round of reforms really is different in kind from all those that went before. Lacking a collective consensus that existing changes mark the establishment of a new (democratic) political order, each reform is likely to be followed by further expressions of dissatisfaction, and renewed demands for yet more reform in order to achieve, at last, an authentic democratization.

This completes our presentation of democratization through reform as an exercise in modeling. For empirical verification we must of course turn to specific examples that can be interrogated in the light of this hypothesis. The rest of this essay is devoted to exploring the Colombian and Mexican cases from this perspective. But before attempting to test the hypothesis in the light of the best available evidence, we need to give brief consideration to the scope and limits of the method of paired comparison, as it is developed here.

The rationale for paired comparisons: What they can and cannot tell us

Two standard social science objections to "small n" comparisons are (i) that there are too few cases to either confirm or refute any worthwhile general propositions, and (ii) that any major "lessons" or inferences from the comparisons are either consciously or implicitly predetermined by the arbitrary initial act of case selection. Nevertheless this chapter relies on the method of the paired comparison. So how can these standard objections be countered, and what can, and cannot, be learnt from such comparisons?

First, the size of the universe under consideration will depend upon the analytical issues at stake. If the issue is the probability of democratic consolidation in developing countries, the relevant universe would include almost all Latin American republics and something like an equal number of other Third World neo-democracies – say forty to fifty in total. If the issue is the contagion and demonstration effects arising from two 1970s democratizations on the Iberian peninsula (post-Franco and post-Salazar) the relevant universe would be all the twenty republics of Latin America (plus possibly Portuguese-speaking Angola, Mozambique, and

Timor). However, if the issue is the type of democratization likely to arise from liberalizing reforms within a long-standing civilian constitutional tradition of restricted or controlled electoral contestation, then the universe is far smaller. Arguably there are only two clear cases for consideration – Colombia and Mexico.[1] At a stretch one might try to include Venezuela (although the restrictions on electoral contestation were looser), or Uruguay (although the long-standing civilian tradition there was broken by a decade of military authoritarian rule in the 1970s). So, one argument for the use of paired comparisons would be that for certain issues of general interest and significance (e.g., identifying sub-types of democratization) the relevant universe may consist of only two core cases (perhaps supplemented by a few secondary examples that would not suffice to establish conclusions on their own).

Clearly this is not an argument for the use of paired comparisons to the exclusion of other comparative methods. It is an argument for allowing them to remain part of the tool kit of the comparativist, despite the suspicions of the methodological purist. How much they are used will depend upon the importance of the analytical issues they address, and the extent to which they prove effective at carrying forward that particular type of analysis. On both headings, the relevant question is how well this approach performs compared to the alternatives, such as covering law generalizations, and probabilistic distributions, which require a "large n" universe of cases.

This first defence accepts the standard social science assumptions about the purposes of comparison. A second response would be to challenge assumptions that underlie the charge of arbitrary case selection. This would make explicit the difference separating those who undertake comparisons with an area studies perspective in mind from those who only practice a universalizing variety of social science. Although many social institutions – including political arrangements – may possess characteristics that induce predictable behavioural responses wherever they occur (for example, the convening of regular and transparent elections should stimulate the formation of competitive political parties) the area studies perspective indicates that such responses cannot be fully understood without reference to the cultural contexts and traditions within which they are articulated. If shared symbolic meanings or cultural contexts make a difference to behavioural responses, then comparative explanations of behaviour may only prove adequate when bounded within appropriate cultural or regional limits. For some explanatory purposes the appropriate universe of cases may therefore be limited in time and space. Explanatory range and depth may only be attainable if, for example, we confine ourselves to contemporary Latin America. Within those geographical and temporal confines comparisons may invoke shared understandings of such key terms as "constitutionalism," "democratization," and "reform." Again, the force of the argument depends upon the particular analytical task at hand. It must always be a question of demonstration, not mere assertion or a priori definition, that the relevant universe for comparisons needs to be bounded. The effectiveness of broad, shallow comparisons in contrast to narrower and more focused ones can only be established by attempting best practice in both, and then comparing the results.

Third, and finally, paired comparisons can be justified on the grounds that their main purpose is to deepen understanding of the two individual and unique processes under consideration, rather than to uncover universally applicable general truths. To say this need not be to abandon the quest for transferable knowledge. If, for example, we are able to specify more precisely what it is about the Mexican democratization process that sets it aside from (or confirms) standard models of democratization, such findings are of scholarly value on at least two counts. The Mexican reality is of sufficient significance both to Mexicans and to others influenced by that country's example that a fuller understanding of that one case is worthwhile for itself. And whether Mexico confirms, defies, or modifies our pre-Mexican theorizations about democratization is of general importance for theory construction and confirmation. Appropriately paired comparisons can offer an incisive strategy for analysing the supposed uniqueness of particular national cases, or complex dynamic processes. Among other things, parity of esteem between cases is required when only two processes are being compared. Thus each country's apparent uniqueness has to be given careful consideration (something which tends to be screened out by "large-n" surveys). Also, appropriately paired comparisons can provide specific yardsticks of external validation by which to evaluate theories or explanations generated from within just one national experience. And, when only two cases are being considered in depth, the classificatory categories and prefabricated theorizations of the general analyst can be subjected to more thorough critical scrutiny (and possible adjustment in the light of the evidence) than when either too many examples are processed at once, or a single unique instance is considered and demands treatment as an "exception." It is just as possible that a paired comparison may reveal similarities where the initial expectation would have been for difference, as that it may demonstrate difference even though all the standard explanatory values would have pointed to similarity. In a properly constructed paired comparison there should be no initial presumption of which of these two alternatives will prevail. When social science generalists accuse the practitioners of paired comparisons of selection bias through their choice of cases, they can be answered by the counteraccusation of interpretation bias through the prefabricated choice of categories and predicted causal chains that structure most "large-n" studies.

In summary, paired comparisons cannot be expected to validate general covering laws, or to provide conclusive answers to most controversies concerning the analysis of each case taken singly. But paired comparisons can improve the precision of broader comparative analyses, for example by specifying sub-types and clarifying their scope and limitation; or by recalibrating general classificatory categories and interpretative schemes in accordance with feedback from two cases examined together. It is just as possible to guard against selection bias in paired comparisons as against interpretation bias in more general theorizing. Indeed the two should be used as checks against each other. Paired comparisons can also sharpen the insights derivable from single-case studies, for example by providing guidance on the scope and applicability of externally generated categories and interpretations; or by providing well-specified comparators that should help the analyst of an individual case to identify appropriate counterfactuals, to isolate explanatory variables, and to generalize (or to resist generalizations) on the basis of in-depth case material.

A paired comparison of Colombia and Mexico

With this model and these precepts in mind we can now consider what a paired comparison of democratization-through-reform strategies in Colombia and Mexico may tell us, both about this proposed sub-type of democratization and about these two important cases, taken individually. The starting point is to characterize the two regimes as they were before democratizing reforms began. Then the two reform processes can be outlined and compared. Third, the probable or established results of these reforms can be considered in both cases, from the standpoint of the comparative democratization literature. Finally, this provides the basis for an evaluation of this particular sub-type of democratization (democratization through reform), together with a comparison and an assessment of the distinctive problems of democratization in these two countries.

Before the reforms began

This section compares the National Front regime in Colombia (1958–74) with the "classical" PRI regime in Mexico (1946–76). The dates are indicative only. Many features of the two regimes can be traced back to much earlier periods, notably the 1886 Constitution in Colombia and the 1917 Constitution in Mexico. Although timid reforms began in the late

1970s, these regimes were not greatly changed until the early 1990s: the 1991 Constituent Assembly was a pivotal event in Colombia, and successive electoral reforms progressively tamed fraud in Mexico between 1988 and 1997. They were both "regimes" in the sense that an elaborate set of formal and informal rules of the game structured political competition throughout each system; these rules were predictable and sustained over at least a generation; and no single political actor was ever strong enough to break free from their constraints (although powerful groups and coalitions regularly sought to bend the rules in their favour, often with success). They were "civilian" in the sense that public offices rotated between elected officials who governed in accordance with legal forms and procedures, rather than on the basis of military command; the police and the armed forces remained substantively subordinate to civil authority; and only retired military officers were allowed to compete for public office. They were "constitutional" in the sense that the electoral calendar was reliably observed, and elected officials always stood down for their successors at the indicated moment (no consecutive re-election of the president was allowed in Colombia, and no immediate re-election of either executive or legislative office-holders in Mexico). Moreover, many of the outward forms of constitutionalism (executive, legislative, and judicial separation; separation between federal, state, and municipal levels of authority; some degree of press autonomy; and some rights of voluntary association and petition) were for the most part observed, albeit with tacitly acknowledged limitations: Colombia was administered under "state of siege" regulations more or less continuously from 1958 onwards. The constitution provided for the existence of multiple parties, and the electoral process required acceptance of at least token forms of organized opposition.

Yet these civilian constitutional regimes were far from fully democratic, at least in the sense that has come to prevail in contemporary discourse. In the Colombian case the December 1957 plebiscite provided for an equal division of seats in all "public corporations" (the two houses of Congress, departmental assemblies, and municipal councils) between the Conservative and Liberal parties, who would also have a monopoly of representation (equally divided) in the Cabinet, the Supreme Court, and the public administration (excluding the military). The presidency would alternate between the two parties every four years for four presidential terms (i.e., for 16 years). All this was stipulated regardless of the party preferences of the electorate, which could only choose between alternative party lists within the two ruling parties (by proportional representation). Although the Colombian system was not fully democratic it was more so than the Mexican regime, at least in the following respects: it was multiparty; voters could affect the balance of power within each of the two dominant parties;

the press was not curbed; and these restrictions on competition were time-limited. Hence some have labeled this an instance of consociational democracy. But that overstates the scope for popular sovereignty within the National Front system. This was the only "consociational" regime to have a presidential rather than a parliamentary form of government. The pillars of partisanship were not based on linguistic or religious cleavages, but were legally imposed by constitutional fiat such that, even in a unicolour municipality, rigid parity of representation would be required. The main saving grace of this system from a democratic point of view was that it originated from a popular plebiscite, and it was subject to a time limitation. It could therefore be defended as an emergency solution to uncontrolled interparty conflict and violence. But in practice it froze a historical tradition of two-party exclusivism, and provided constitutional guarantees for the perpetuation of what many analysts have characterized as an oligarchical party system.

When in 1967 Robert Dix attempted to situate this Colombian regime within a "modernization" framework, he identified seven types of modernizing regime in Latin America, of which one was exemplified by Colombia and another by Mexico. But these two distinct types were more similar to each other than most of his other proposed sub-categories,[2] and subsequent literature on Colombia contains various references to Mexico.[3] By present-day standards Mexico was even less of a democracy then Colombia at this time, in that the governing party claimed to have won not only every presidential election since its formation in 1928, but also every legislative election, every gubernational election (bar one), and every state assembly election, together with virtually all municipal elections. This (for any democracy) historically unparalleled string of electoral victories continued unbroken for 60 years (1929–89). But Dix was only reflecting the American political science conventions of his time when he labelled this a "democratic single-party mobilization regime." In reality Mexico was by then more like an undemocratic dominant party regime which specialized in demobilizing antisystem protests, as the 1968 massacre of pro-democracy students in Tlatlelolco Square was about to demonstrate.

The essential point for the purpose of this paired comparison is that in both Colombia and Mexico before the 1980s, although power circulated predictably and according to an impersonal system of rules, it derived from an elite pact to share the spoils of public office without excessive conflict. The voters may have endorsed this pact through their voluntary participation; they may even have induced adjustments to the balance of power within the elite as needed to maintain popular adhesion; and they were persistently called upon to ratify the elite circulation decisions negotiated prior to each election. But the electorate was not sovereign (or in the Colombian case its sovereignty had been suspended for 16 years under the 1957 plebiscite). It was not allowed to make party choices independent of those already agreed upon.

In the case of Mexico much more could be said about the distinctive history and rules of engagement that regulated one-party dominance. In contrast to Colombia the Mexican Revolution had promulgated a large-scale land reform. Organized workers and (separately organized) peasants and *ejidatarios* (the beneficiaries of the land reform of the 1920s and 1930s) therefore contributed to the broad social and electoral base of the ruling party. Again in contrast to Colombia, the Mexican regime was officially anticlerical, and the powerful Catholic Church was firmly barred from participation in public life. Whereas Colombian party leaders had to contend with strong factional divisions (rival Liberal and Conservative party lists vied for popularity regardless of the preferences of incumbent officeholders) the PRI was vertically structured and accustomed to strong inner party discipline always under the direct control of the incumbent president. Whereas the *violencia* that had united Colombian opinion in favour of the *Frente* was recent and even ongoing, the extreme violence of the Mexican Revolution had been largely exhausted by the time the ruling party was established, and violence remained a peripheral phenomenon for long stretches of the PRI ascendancy. So the civilian constitutional regime of post-war Mexico differed in various important respects from that of Colombia.

But these differences were not sufficient to negate the many crucial respects in which Colombia and Mexico could be bracketed together, and contrasted to the other, not only non-democratic but typically unconstitutional and de facto authoritarian regimes of the subcontinent. Although the military or civil-military rulers of Central and South America often attempted to institutionalize themselves they never stabilized such durable or impersonal regimes as in Colombia or Mexico. Often their survival depended upon the persistence of an atmosphere of crisis (as with the various "national security" regimes) or upon the personal magnetism of an authoritarian individual (a Perón, a Castro, a Stroessner). They were "praetorian situations" rather than institutionalized regimes. In contrast the strength of Colombian and Mexican constitutionalism derived precisely from the historically conditioned understanding that it was a sine qua non for the creation of stability and predictability, and for avoiding the praetorianism or indeed national disintegration that would threaten to reappear whenever regime maintenance was neglected.

The initiation of liberalizing (and/or democratizing) reforms

It has become conventional to date the so-called global "Third Wave" of democratization from the mid-1970s, perhaps taking Greece and Portugal as the forerunners. In most of Latin America authoritarian rule was in the ascendant at least until 1978 and only gradually retreated over the following decade. Both in Colombia and Mexico, by contrast, starting in the mid-1960s, it is possible to identify antecedents of what was later to become an upsurge of political liberalization and even democratization. In Colombia the winding down of the National Front system had been envisaged from its inception and the issue became more pressing after 1966, and especially after the close-shave ("fraudulent"?) presidential election of 1970. In Mexico, also, the mid-sixties witnessed an early experiment with democratizing candidate selection within the ruling party. After the shock of the 1968 student massacre it was only a matter of time before further efforts were made to broaden the legitimacy of the regime. The party and electoral reform law of 1977–78 which gave rise to more competitive midterm congressional elections in 1979 was a logical outcome of this longer-term process.

The logic of these liberalizing reforms follows from the way we have characterized the pre-existing regimes – as long-established, civilian, and constitutional. It therefore needs to be distinguished from that of liberalizing reforms instituted by de facto, military, and unconstitutional variants of authoritarian rule. Since Colombia and Mexico both had long-established constitutional regimes they were governed by impersonal rulers and were quite stable, predictable, and routinized. These precepts were also sophisticated and flexible. The same could not be said of most "national security" military regimes of the 1970s. The result was that the reforms adopted in Colombia and Mexico were more rooted in an established matrix of rules and procedures: they were presented as adjustments to a functioning system that might require amendment, but which it was important to defend. Undoubtedly these reforms, like parallel "aberturas" and liberalizing initiatives in other parts of the subcontinent, were designed to save dominant interests and to cope with short-term difficulties. But it was harder for critics of the regime to dismiss them as purely instrumental expedients, merely serving to buy time or to distract the opposition. The architects of these reforms presented them (and probably designed them) with a broader public interest objective in view. They would acknowledge that the existing system needed some re-tuning. They would debate (often quite publicly and at length) over the sources and degree of dysfunction they had encountered and over the relative merits of alternative remedies. Reform would not simply be decreed by a self-interested ruler. It would emerge through collective deliberation and negotiation. This would produce a menu of possible reforms, and even though in the end those in power might well impose the variant that suited their interests best, the alternatives were placed on the public agenda and might well be taken up later if the results of the first attempt proved disappointing.

We can compare Colombian debates in the 1970s over how to move from the rigidity of the National Front formula to a more flexible and legitimate system of representation, with the Mexican consultations of 1977–78 which gave rise to reforms (registering more parties, legalizing part of the Left, providing small minorities with better chances of representation). In both cases there was evidence of a legitimacy deficit as indicated by accusations of electoral fraud, threats to boycott certain contests, and actual or potential outbreaks of violent protest (including guerilla activities as well as civil strikes). The basic dynamics of these two reforms involved official acknowledgment of the existence of some such legitimacy deficit, which – it was assumed – could be corrected by broadening the party system and improving the machinery of electoral representation.

As modeled above, there was indeed less scope than elsewhere in Latin America for a polarizing division between "hardliners" and "soft-liners"; and much greater likelihood that most of the various strands of reformism would unite against the prospect of a destabilizing "rupture." Instead of a debate structured around the disjuncture between uncontrolled liberalization (leading to a "democratic transition") and authoritarian regression, the major disagreements concerned alternative strategies, sequences, and timings of system-maintaining reform. In an impersonal constitutional regime elite circulation is protected even when popular sovereignty is screened out. Therefore potential "soft-liners" are cross-pressured between the wish to promote rapid democratization and the need to retain enough goodwill within the ruling elite to gain access to office under the existing rules. Similarly, potential "hardliners" who find themselves being marginalized because of their hostility to reform have an incentive to come forward with alternative strategies for reducing the legitimacy deficit in order to regain a stake in the game. Whereas in game-theoretical terms, in an authoritarian situation, liberalization may be considered a one-shot move, in a constitutional regime it becomes an iterative game. In this type of game all players have some stake in the continuation of the system, since if they lose one round there remains the prospect of trying again later. By contrast, if the reform process gets out of control and the system is destroyed, none of the participants can be confident they will enjoy the same access and the same fall-back positions thereafter.

This game-theoretical formulation may seem rather abstract and ahistorical, but it can be reformulated in country-specific terms. All established political elites in Colombia and Mexico show some common interest in averting the kind of rupture or regime breakdown in which there would be a return to disorganized violence. It was the experience of this in the Colombian *violencia* of 1948–58 and in the violent decades after the 1910 Mexican Revolution that generated such elite cohesion and such sophisticated rules of elite circulation in the first place. If contemporary elites are tempted to forget that lesson, events like the assassination of leading presidential candidates (Luis Carlos Galán in Bogotá in 1989, and Luis Donaldo Colosio in Tijuana in 1994) serve to remind them of its continuing relevance.

As already indicated, there is in principle a clear distinction between *abertura* – liberalization in which an authoritarian regime opens channels to wider forms of political participation while still retaining its last-resort capacity for control – and a "democratic transition," where there is uncertainty over who will be in office, combined with certainty that the democratic process confers the ultimate choices on the electorate. But in practice this distinction is often somewhat elusive, even when clearly authoritarian regimes come to an abrupt end. In cases of democratization through reform the ambiguity goes much deeper. The constitutional regimes of Colombia and Mexico already acknowledged the theoretical sovereignty of the voters, and a succession of reforms was adopted under the rubric of giving that theoretical principle more substance. In Colombia the pattern of two-party alternation was indeed broken in 1978, when one Liberal president succeeded another, and since then the Liberal Party has continued to benefit from more electoral support than the Conservatives, although in other respects the dismantling of the National Front system has proceeded quite slowly. Critics of reform could always find plausible grounds for denying that the power holders had generally relinquished control. Since elite circulation was already the norm there was no spectacular "flight of the dictator" or "return to barracks" that could decisively vindicate one view rather than the other to the satisfaction of all. On the contrary, while both supporters and critics might be able to agree that a given reform package must count as a "liberalization," they would be almost bound to divide over whether it should be classed as a "democratic transition." This terminology would require incumbents to admit that the previous constitutional system did not merit the appellation of a "democracy," and that more than a re-tuning, it required refoundation. Neither the civilian dominant parties of Colombia nor the ruling party of Mexico had any interest in making such terminological concessions to their critics, no matter what practical points they might concede. Indeed, the Colombian reforms were debated in the context of "dismantling" the National Front, rather than in terms of democratization. Therefore, even if by some objective standard of comparison the measures included in the reform process would seem to count as a "democratization," one key element would be missing. There would be no public collective acceptance that the previous regime had been undemocratic. That is why this path of democratization through reform can also be described as "by stealth."

In Colombia and Mexico liberalizing measures were adopted in fits and starts from the mid-seventies onward. More such measures may still be in the pipeline even at the turn of the century. It is possible to isolate certain clusters of reforms as more far-reaching than the rest – such as the 1991 constitutional revisions in Colombia and the 1995–96 party and electoral reforms in Mexico – but there is no single unambiguous and consensually identified moment of "transition." Indeed, official discourse often seems deliberately confusing, seeking to combine the incompatible assertions that (i) no major discontinuity has ever been required; and (ii) right now a new surge of democratic legitimacy is reinvigorating the system. Only after a decade or more of institutional reforms had palpably failed to bridge the legitimacy deficit (which had indeed widened by the late 1980s) would reforms that amounted to a full democratization come onto the agenda as an alternative to controlled liberalization. And after a further decade in which the discourse of democracy exerted an ever-growing moral hegemony, in the late 1990s it still remained controversial whether the civilian elites of Colombia and Mexico were really surrendering to its dictates or whether on the contrary – in the style of Lampedusa – they were still expecting to legitimize a continuation in office and power behind a screen of democratizing gestures. Meanwhile, the legitimacy deficit that was supposed to have been cleared by their programmes of representational reform still remains unerased – most spectacularly in Colombia, but at least potentially still in Mexico as well.

But if the legitimacy deficit remained unerased, does that not simply mean that the institutional reforms undertaken so far were inadequate? That they were liberalizing rather than democratizing? That there was too much "stealth," and insufficient resocialization around a new normative framework? This is certainly a logical, and in important respects a justifiable, perspective on the two processes under review. It would also enable us to fit this sub-type rather neatly into the comparative paths to democratization. But that might be too neat a conclusion. There is a danger of overstressing the parallels between two somewhat dissimilar processes, or of allowing our heuristic model to explain too much, screening out other explanatory factors which fall outside its terms. Comparisons must include contrast. For example, the foregoing discussion has presented the idea of a "legitimacy deficit" as the driving force behind political reform in the two countries. It is necessary to specify both what this may mean, and whether it means the same thing in each case. Apparently neither political system had yet reached an end point where no further changes were required in order to prove the existence of a consolidated democracy. But it is a common opinion that Mexico has been moving in that direction during the 1990s, whereas Colombia has been moving away from it. Even accepting that both regimes are driven to reform by the spur of some kind of legitimacy deficit, it cannot be assumed that this necessarily takes the same form in both countries, or requires the same solution. In Mexico it may be that the legitimacy deficit originated in the PRI system of dominance, and can therefore be rectified by an appropriate political reform. But in Colombia the problem could be rooted in more profound deficiencies of state formation that can only be corrected (if at all) by much more far-reaching means.[4] The next section offers some provisional assessments of these issues.

Comparing and contrasting the outcomes in Colombia and Mexico

Most pathways to democratization are lengthy and winding. It is all too easy to take a wrong turn. There is no guarantee of ever arriving at the initially promised destination. But if the impulse for political reform is the desire or need to fill a legitimacy deficit, there can be no durable settlement until that issue has been settled. Despite substantial differences between the two regimes as regards the origins and characteristics of their respective legitimacy deficits and the remedies attempted, we have been able to identify sufficient parallels both in structure and in timing to justify systematic paired comparison. When we compare the Colombian and Mexican outcomes so far, we are comparing unsettled situations or uncompleted processes of democratization. It looks as if Colombia is straying far from the intended destination, while even before the July 2000 presidential elections which saw the defeat of the PRI, optimists and pro-government enthusiasts were claiming that Mexico was almost there. However, if we had carried out the same comparison in January 1995 the relative picture would have looked substantially different, and in January 1992 different again. All such comparisons of outcome must be regarded as highly provisional. (Table 1 shows relative ratings of Colombia and Mexico by Freedom House in various different years. Venezuela is added as a comparator).

Table 4.1 **Freedom House country scores for Colombia and Mexico, 1972–2000**

	Colombia		Mexico		Venezuela	
1972–73	2.2	Free	5.3	Part free	2.2	Free
1978–79	2.3	Free	4.4	Part free	1.2	Free
1979–80	2.3	Free	3.3	Part free	1.2	Free
1989–90	3.4	Part free	4.3	Part free	1.3	Free
1997–98	4.4	Part free	3.4	Part free	2.3	Free
1998–99	3.4	Part free	3.4	Part free	2.3	Free
1999–2000	4.4	Part free	2.3	Free	3.4	Part free

Source: Extracted from the *Annual Survey of Freedom*, compiled by Freedom House, New York.

With this caveat in mind, we shall now attempt to identify the main similarities and contrasts between the political reform processes in our two chosen countries. This section attempts to assemble comparative evidence on the scale of the legitimacy deficit currently prevailing in each country. In Colombia there is a general recognition that after important sectors of the guerrilla movement accepted the peace terms proposed by presidents Betancur and Barco, and had therefore emerged from clandestinity to register as a legal political party that would rely on state protection for the exercise of its political rights, somewhat in excess of one thousand local candidates and organizers for the resulting Unión Patriótica were assassinated. This is a complex matter, involving rivalries between different insurgent forces, and the control of drug resources, which should not be reduced to a simple failure of the government to meet its theoretical obligations. However that may be, these assumptions diminished the credibility of governmental proposals to broaden the scope of the multiparty system. Subsequently the guerrilla forces have redoubled their military efforts and no longer show much interest in disarming. They will only curtail their insurgency if granted no-go zones where they can provide for their own security.

In post-war Mexico the guerrillas were never very strong, and as a result of efficient repression in the 1970s they were virtually eliminated. The ex-guerrillas were free to organize legal political parties and unarmed organizations, and when they did so their physical security was for the most part left intact. However, after the ruling party split in 1987, and the dominant faction orchestrated at least some degree of electoral fraud in 1988, the climate became more repressive. The evidence on political assassinations is more disputed in Mexico than in Colombia, but it seems fairly clear that in the early 1990s several hundred activists and candidates for the main left opposition party died violent deaths. Some of them may have been armed, so the analogy with the Unión Patriótica is imperfect.[5] The national leadership of the Mexican party was not targeted (whereas the Unión Patriótica's top leader was among those murdered). It is credibly asserted that the Mexican military acquiesced in the 1988 fraud on the understanding that the "hijo del General" (the son of the General, presidential contender Cárdenas) would not be targeted. In the end the Mexican PRD survived and even flourished as an electoral force, despite the repression. On this basis, therefore, we could say that the legitimacy deficit was harder to bridge in Colombia than in Mexico. However, in 1994 a new guerrilla movement burst forth in the southern Mexican state of Chiapas, and other forms of subversion and insurgency have also appeared since then. In contrast to Colombia the Mexican state has not conceded any no-go areas, and the armed opposition is not making any headway, although it has also not been eliminated. Therefore, by this criterion Mexico still faces a significant legitimacy deficit, despite the successful incorporation into peaceful constitutional politics of a substantial proportion of the earlier insurgent forces.

Another source of illegitimacy is the weakness of the rule of law, and in particular the unreliability of the forces of public order, and the penetration of the state apparatus by agents of the powerful drug cartels that flourish in both countries. Although these phenomena have deep historical roots in Colombia and Mexico, they became more visible and probably more pronounced in the 1980s, and reached unheard-of extremes in the mid-1990s. There is now not much scope for dissent from this assertion, given all that is on the public record concerning the use of drug money to finance the presidential campaign of Ernesto Samper (the Liberal incumbent in Colombia in 1994–98), and the multiple scandals over the financing of the Mexican PRI during the 1994 election – including Swiss and American legal proceedings to trace the funds amassed by the elder brother of President Carlos Salinas (1988–94).

Of course it is far easier to identify broadly parallel and comparably extensive scandals than to provide precisely calibrated measurements of the degree of drug cartel penetration of the state in each case.[6] However, since we are concerned about public *perceptions* of a legitimacy deficit, as a driving force in processes of political reform, it may suffice to establish that in both countries – rightly or wrongly – such perceptions crystallized around well-grounded evidence of serious wrongdoing at the highest levels, specifically in 1994. That date is important because it was about twenty years after both regimes had seriously embarked on "liberalizing" political reforms intended to bridge what they already considered at that time, a generation earlier, a disturbing legitimacy deficit. On the face of it, therefore, these liberalizing and subsequently democratizing reforms had not achieved one of their basic goals even after two decades of cumulative development.

Although this essay has so far presented the Colombian and Mexican cases as if they were in parallel, this is not how they have been interpreted internationally. To be more specific, the U.S. president is required by law to undertake an annual process of "certification" by which he notifies the U.S. Congress which of America's international partners are or are not providing adequate co-operation in the international effort against illegal narcotics trading. During President Samper's term of office Colombia was officially "decertified" on two successive occasions, whereas Mexico under presidents Salinas and Zedillo was always characterized as highly co-operative. There is room for debate over whether this certification process provides an accurate comparative yardstick on this highly sensitive subject. Critics assert that, for geopolitical reasons, it would be unthinkable for Washington ever to decertify a Mexican government, no matter what its failings, whereas a tougher standard can be afforded against Colombia. It is undeniably the case that Washington continued to champion the personal integrity of Carlos Salinas well after this was prudent or tenable, and the DEA issued a public commendation to President Zedillo's choice of "drugs tsar" a few weeks before General Rebollo was arrested and convicted as an agent of one of the largest cartels. Nevertheless, as far as public perceptions of a legitimacy deficit are concerned, it seems clear that the United States used its very substantial influence to counter such fears in Mexico (to stabilize the Zedillo administration) at the same time that it acted with great determination to destabilize or delegitimize the Samper administration in Colombia. Since internal conditions warranted something like the same degree of delegitimation in the two cases, the major determinant of subsequent differences in perception (and outcome) may have been U.S. policies that were adopted for reasons other than the actual degree of domestic legitimacy enjoyed by each government.

A third potential source of discontent, and possible impetus for political reform, is the incidence of acute social inequality and exclusion. Where large numbers of voters are deprived of the most basic socio-economic conditions for security and subsistence, it can be argued that the presuppositions of electoral sovereignty are lacking. More particularly, where such deprivation is accompanied by large concentrations of wealth and economic dynamism in other parts of the society, it is common to hypothesize that a truly competitive and responsible political system (a full democracy) would be liable to generate socially damaging policy outcomes ("macro-economic populism" is the shorthand for this fear). Widespread and extreme social inequalities and injustices are therefore a plausible source of legitimacy deficit. This is not just because the poor may be blocked by their circumstances from the expression of their political preferences, but also because fear of what the poor might demand if more fully enfranchised may cause the rich to turn away from the risks of democratic competition.

Latin America as a whole is notorious for the inequality of its income distribution. Colombia and Mexico are in no way exceptions to this pattern, despite their long-standing civilian constitutional regimes. Indeed, one recent compilation covering the years 1980–94 ranks Colombia the second worst of the eight countries for which a full set of indicators are available, with Mexico not far behind. (The Mexican figures show a fairly stable degree of inequality over the period, whereas Colombia manifests evidence of substantial deterioration).[7] This contrast presents Colombia in an unfavourable light, but the authorities on macro-economic populism present the two cases in reverse order. Mexico is faulted for its lapses into economic populism (1970–82) and Colombia is praised for its comparative absence of economic populism.[8]

This invites brief comments first on Mexico and then on Colombia. As a result of a whole sequence of policy reforms, both economic and political (including entry into NAFTA, extensive privatization, and enhanced autonomy for the Banco de Mexico) it is fairly clear that the Mexico of today is less prone to macro-economic populism than it was in the 1970s. In this case, therefore, political liberalization and even (arguably) democratization have been possible without increasing the incidence of economic populism. On the other hand, political opening has also not led to any clear amelioration of the pre-existing social inequalities, and it has been accompanied by other policy outcomes (renewed peso collapse, followed by a public bailout of the privatized banks at a huge long-run cost to the Mexican taxpayer, etc.) which may be considered almost as undesirable as those avoided. Thus the avoidance of populism in Mexico has not sufficed to bridge the legitimation deficit attributable to extreme social inequality and insecurity. As for Colombia, its much-vaunted distinctiveness as the Latin American republic best insulated from the perils of populism looks very questionable today. If avoiding populism becomes associated with worsening inequalities, in due course populism will gain a new lease of life (as it has in Venezuela in the 1990s). In any case, from the standpoint of this section Colombia's intensified social deficit, despite the pursuit of recommended economic strategies, must have added to the perception of a growing legitimacy deficit with adverse implications for both political and economic governability.

Perhaps enough evidence and argument has now been assembled to support the view that as of the end of the 1990s, after about a quarter-century of liberalizing political reforms, the two constitutional regimes both continue to display substantial manifestations of legitimacy deficit. On several dimensions Colombia seems clearly worse than Mexico, but both share a disturbing number of common problems. In both, therefore, further institutional reforms may be required if these regimes are to generate sufficient collective consent. But which are the institutional reforms that have worked out best, which have failed, and which are the areas of future innovation most necessary to deliver an eventually legitimate regime? The major areas stressed in the literature on institutional design in new democracies are national integration; decentralization; constitutional checks and balances; the electoral regime and party system; and citizen and minority rights.

Regarding national integration, it is a standard proposition that democracy requires agreement on the boundaries of the territory, and administration by an integrated set of governmental institutions within those boundaries (a shared political identity and an agreed source of authority). Arguably neither Colombia nor even Mexico fully satisfies these basic requirements. Both countries lost outlying territories after independence, and both display pronounced regional variations, with strong ethnic and social differentiation and substantial concentrations of "Indian" populations in the poorest and most inaccessible provinces. In both countries programmes to integrate the entire national population into the republican system have been operating for many generations, and at multiple levels – road building, schooling, conscription, taxation, property titling, electrification, and more recently the establishment of nationwide broadcasting systems. When Dix classified all the various types of Latin American regime as "modernizing," this was presumably what he had in mind. Other analysts refer to these activities as "nation building." In our two countries before the state made its presence felt, the Catholic Church was a powerful agency of socialization in many rural areas, and the traditional political parties – whether Conservative, Liberal or Institutionalized Revolutionary – also developed a nationwide reach that contributed powerfully to national integration.

Nevertheless, such homogenized national identities never completely displaced more parochial allegiances, or memories of social difference. To the contrary, in remote areas many centrally promoted policies of national integration were received and experienced as external impositions. Local agents of a distant and unaccountable (albeit formally constitutional) state had latitude to act in their own interests, and against those of the local populance, under the protection of distant national authority. The downside of national integration could be the suppression of local autonomy, and the imposition of inappropriate and even oppressive standards and exactions. Micro-histories of such locations as Viotá (the longest-established Colombian *republiqueta* in Tolima) or Juchitán (the somewhat analogous Mexican leftist stronghold on the Isthmus of Tehuantepec) suggest that integration can be a contested and dialectical process, certainly not a unilinear progression from traditionalism to modernity. Not only outposts of the Left, but also repositories of conservative values (such as Aritama in Colombia and San José de Gracia in Mexico) illustrate the same point. As the nation-building projects of the 1960s have subsided in the wake of the debt crisis and international liberalization, the roll-back of the state has revealed substantial regions not of integration but of disintegration, or at best of only asymmetric and perhaps even exploitative incorporation (what Rodolfo Stavenhagen has labeled "internal colonialism"). An almost universal crisis of peasant agriculture underscores the incompleteness of national integration in these two geographically fragmented nations. In place of universalism public policies have shifted towards highly selective variants of "targeting" which leave many in the less favoured municipalities virtually unprotected. This provides the political background for the growth of insurgency and lawlessness. It also provides the context within which to appraise one major element of recent institutional reforms: the "decentralization" policies that have been attempted both in Colombia and in Mexico.

In Colombia under the Frente Nacional (indeed, ever since 1886) governors and mayors were appointed rather than elected, and were balanced by state assemblies and municipal councils in which the two governing parties enjoyed equal representation, regardless of their electoral support. In Mexico governors were effectively nominated (and not infrequently also dismissed) by the incumbent president, and they in turn exercised much influence over the composition of ruling party slates in their respective states and municipalities. Of course this is to simplify a more complex picture, but in both countries a basic principle of local government was "verticalism." Since the 1980s the emergence of more genuinely competitive electoral contests at the national level has been accompanied by a shift to direct election of governors and mayors (in Colombia) and to a search for local electoral support, if necessary in opposition to the centre (in Mexico). Democratization has also involved a shift of responsibilities and also (to a lesser extent) of resources from the centre to the localities. The Colombian decentralization came in several stages, and was prompted by a range of competitive considerations – fiscal, partisan, and counter-insurgency logics all chipped in.[9] But despite initial optimism (particularly surrounding the more wholesale reforms produced by the 1991 Constituent Assembly) experience so far seems to justify the skeptical belief expressed by some that in Colombia institutional reforms were only an attempt to distract attention from the ruling elite's unwillingness to engage in economic and social democratization. According to this argument, if introduced in isolation, and used by the parties in power as a way of de-mobilizing independent civic movements, the reforms would prove futile. A respected assessment by Jonathan Hartlyn and John Dugas, published in 1999, seemed to validate this judgment, with the verdict that in the context of a de-ideologised two-party system with low turnout and executive patronage, "decentralization has frequently enhanced clientelism, corruption and inefficiency."[10] A similarly respected and recent evaluation of sub-national politics in Mexico arrived at a parallel conclusion, as follows: "there is reason to doubt that a coherent national-level democratization project can go forward, with an archipelago of enclaves still in place, even within a much more competitive electoral system.... the record to date suggests that pell-mell deconcentration of power – without credible mechanisms for enforcing party discipline and ensuring that state and local officials can be held accountable – is just as likely to cause political decay as it is to set the stage for a durable and comprehensive democratic breakthrough."[11]

So far as constitutional checks and balances are concerned, in 1997 the lower house of the Mexican Congress came under the control of parties in opposition to the incumbent president for the first time since the 1920s. In Mexico the Supreme Court had a long record of deference to the will of the president and the ruling party, but since about 1995 its autonomy seems to have increased. However, its credibility as an arbiter between the branches of government, or as a faithful defender and interpreter of the principles of the 1917 Constitution, remains to be solidly established.

Similarly, in 1998 Colombia found itself with a Conservative president and a Liberal Congress, no longer coordinated by the parity requirement. Despite its partisan composition the Colombian Supreme Court had a long record of exercising its constitutional authority with significant autonomy from the other branches of government (indeed sometimes without co-ordination). It was not uncommon for judicial decisions to overturn legislative projects that had been laboriously negotiated through the party system. If anything such judicial activism (and unpredictability) has become still more prevalent since the 1991 constitutional revisions, but the Colombian courts are still not regarded as incorruptible defenders of the rule of law. There has been a suggestion that Mexico may be following the Colombian path to democratization in the sense that a weak and irresponsible system of constitutionalism provides ideal conditions for the construction of a "narco-democracy." This idea is heatedly resisted in Mexican official circles, and indeed the two cases both require careful assessment without the distortion of pejorative labeling. But, while the verdict remains open, there are well-grounded bases for concern in both countries.

Turning to the electoral regimes and party systems of the two countries, there is now far more public confidence than in the past in the security of the voting process and the integrity of the count. This is a major achievement in societies accustomed to partisan intimidation and elite disregard for voter preferences. It is not only a major improvement in one key aspect of public life, it also provides a firm basis for demands that the same principles of integrity be extended into other spheres. But although recent advances are impressive, they no more than coincide with similar developments throughout Latin America, and indeed the world. In fact, Mexico was a conspicuous laggard in this respect, only consolidating an impartial and trustworthy Federal Electoral Institute in 1996. The signs are encouraging that this gain will prove irreversible, but if the rest of the institutional system is not upgraded the conditions remain in place for a potential future regression. Certainly the Colombian experience indicates that a clean count is not a sufficient condition for securing electoral legitimacy.

The most likely Achilles heel of the party systems in both countries concerns the huge financing requirements of modern electoral campaigns. With increased competition candidates become more dependent than before upon their fund-raising skills. Of course this is a matter of grave concern throughout the democratic world, but it is a particularly severe danger in countries with weak rule-of-law systems where organized crime has penetrated the state apparatus. One interpretation of the drug-financing scandal in the Samper presidency in Colombia is that the 1991 Constitution provided for a second round in the event of a close contest for the presidency, and it also provided strict financing limits. The two provisions were not co-ordinated, so when Liberal candidate Samper unexpectedly found himself required to finance a second leg of his campaign, his legal funding was already exhausted. In a similar vein the political assassinations that rocked Mexico's ruling party in 1994 seem particularly to have affected those closest to the secrets of the party financing. Since neither of these episodes has been clarified to the satisfaction of public opinion, it is not surprising that many still fear that those who provided illegal funds may try again, and that the examples set in these cases may provide future encouragement for criminal groups to attempt to manipulate the electoral process, and to capture elements of the party system.

Finally, there is the question of how to promote and guarantee the citizen and minority rights that are essential to any solid democracy. Today there are hundreds of thousands of internally displaced persons in Colombia, and the state has more or less explicitly abdicated from its responsibility to administer the law in thousands of square miles of national territory. Even where its writ is supposed to run, there is abundant evidence that basic civic and political rights cannot be guaranteed. In Mexico the situation is somewhat less acute, and the Mexican state has never explicitly ceded any territory to extra-constitutional authorities. But the problem is bad enough to constitute an issue of not merely peripheral significance for Mexican democracy as a whole. Three states out of thirty-one – Chiapas, Guerrero, and Oaxaca – may be particularly affected, but such deficiencies in one region aggravate the insecurity and discrimination that are latent elsewhere.

It would be desirable to examine collective as well as individual rights in both countries, not just as they appear in the laws and statutes, but as they are experienced on the ground.[12] But the patterns are so complex, and the evidence is so mixed, that the differences between the two countries, and within each of them, preclude most generalizations. At the most general level it is possible to assert: (i) that these constitutional regimes both have extremely long and elaborate histories of attempting to tackle the issues of citizen rights; (ii) that the measures they have adopted almost invariably produce extremely heterogeneous effects, no doubt rectifying some injustices, but also creating new inequalities because they do not achieve uniformity; and (iii) that many of those who formerly lacked the possibility for exercising their theoretical rights are no longer so passive or isolated as before, and therefore they may increasingly demand what was previously just a verbal promise from above. But many generously worded verbal promises are almost impossible to fulfil across the board in societies as segmented and unequal as these two. These three propositions could suggest that destabilizing struggles over the enforcement of citizen and minority rights may continue in both countries for many years to come. There is probably no quick fix that would either generalize minimum rights acceptable to all, or eliminate zero-sum conflicts over such rights.

Democratization through reform as a distinctive sub-type of democratization

Some of the points made in the preceding section apply to the new democracies of Latin America in general, and many serve to differentiate them from the old established rich democracies, and most notably from the USA. The unevenness of national integration; the instability and lack of definition of constitutional checks and balances (including centre-local relations); the recentness of the level playing field in party competition; and the persistence of ongoing conflicts over the scope and contents of citizenship rights all illustrate these constraints. The underlying difference is between, on the one hand, democratic regimes that are routinized, in broad equilibrium, or "consolidated"; and on the other, democratizations that involve continuing experimentation, and the construction of new institutional practices. At the root of all the democratizations in Latin America (and elsewhere) there was a perceived legitimacy deficit which has inspired and is inspiring programmes of political restructuring. Such programmes are not yet complete, the legitimacy deficits are not yet perceived to have been closed, and therefore democratization has to be studied as a dynamic process rather than a static equilibrium.

Within this framework, Colombia and Mexico can be bracketed together, and compared and contrasted to determine whether they share enough common features to constitute a coherent sub-type. The paired comparisons presented in this paper in no way exhaust the possibilities of sub-classification, and alternative pairings may be appropriate for some analytical purposes. For example, it has been common to bracket Colombia with Venezuela, since these democracies were both constructed in the late 1950s as a result of pacts between previously irreconcilable political parties.[13] In a similar vein, some scholars (myself included)[14] have tried to compare the dominant party regime in Mexico with formally analogous regimes elsewhere, for example with Taiwan under the Kuomintang. The democratization of long-standing dominant party regimes might be thought to follow a logic distinct from that of multiparty regimes, founded on non-aggression pacts.[15] However, this paper has downplayed the contrasts between Colombia and Mexico, in part by arguing that the Frente Nacional regime was a centrally imposed system for parceling out public office, much as the PRI regime also did, and in part by emphasizing the commonalities of civilian and constitutional non-democratic rule. Nevertheless, the process of paired comparison has provided an extensive list of both parallels and contrasts between the two cases, and may help to isolate differences that explain why, for the time being at least, the outcomes of their respective democratizations appear to be diverging.

Notwithstanding such divergences this essay has explored the analytical utility of a distinctive sub-type of democratization – provisionally labeled "democratization through reform" (or "by stealth") – which would be exemplified by these two cases. Behind the civilian constitutional institutions that provide an impersonal framework for structuring political processes in both countries, the categorization emphasizes the guiding role of relatively closed and coherent elite groups (popularly referred to in Colombia as the "oligarchy" and in Mexico as the "revolutionary family"). Protracted periods of uncontrolled political violence served to convince these power contenders of the advantages of negotiating and enforcing rules of elite circulation that would engage most *fuerzas vivas*.[16] This was the basis both of the constitutionalism of these regimes, and of their opposition to full democratization. Although they both required a reliable calendar of elections to sanctify elite circulation, in their classical form they both repudiated popular sovereignty, fearing that unconstrained voter choices would shatter their elite pacts and reintroduce destabilizing partisanship. Hence, formal constitutional texts were insufficient to account for the actual workings of these political systems which required informal meta-constitutional reinforcements (such as the subordination of the PRI to the direction of the incumbent president who effectively nominated his successor in an apostolic succession). In their "classical" form these regimes called on voters to ratify predetermined personnel changes, and perhaps to provide a limited degree of feedback from public opinion, but the electorate was not free to exercise a full democratic choice between contending parties. Since voting was so much more to the interest of the incumbents than to that of the electors, a programmatic electorate could not develop, partisanship declined, abstentionism threatened to prevail, and clientelistic forms of voter compensation were perfected to offset the lack of electoral sovereignty.

This provides the context within which democratization through reform could emerge as a distinctive sub-type, to be contrasted with the yes/no plebiscites that brought military rule to an end in Chile and Uruguay; or the foundational elections that marked democratic transition in Argentina and the Dominican Republic; or the peace settlements that signalled a clear change of political practice in Central America; or the constituent assemblies that rewrote the constitutions of Peru and Brazil. In Colombia and Mexico the civilians had always claimed authority over the military, and so they could not demonstratively send the generals back to barracks. In Colombia and Mexico elections had always occurred on schedule and most of the contenders for power in democratic elections owed much of their prominence to their ascent via earlier undemocratic electoral processes. This precluded foundational elections, especially since the strongest parties in democratic elections would be bound to assert continuity with past electoral endeavours. Colombia in particular has attempted to legitimize new political openings by associating them with programmes of pacification, but neither in Colombia nor in Mexico have these efforts borne fruit. The Constituent Assembly of 1991 in Colombia also failed to provide the hoped-for break with the past, despite the far-reaching institutional changes it inaugurated, because elite circulation continued much as before, and major parts of the citizenry continued to experience insecurity and exclusion.

The designation "by stealth" refers to the fact that during over twenty years of reform, in neither of these countries was there been the kind of dramatic discontinuity that would provide the basis for resocializing the voters and the political class according to the norms of a properly democratic regime.[17] This missing resocialization is particularly problematic in countries with long-established, sophisticated, and well-understood constitutional regimes. In such circumstances the working assumption of nearly all political actors will be that the practices and conventions of the pact remain intact, unless something very clear-cut and striking occurs to convince them (and those with whom they must interact) to the contrary. Democratization by stealth denies this instructive discontinuity precisely where it is most needed. It may well be that the July 2000 Colombian presidential election will turn out to provide just such a discontinuity, but in the immediate aftermath of that event judgement should be reserved. After all, many Colombians believed the same in the aftermath of the 1991 Constituent Assembly.

At this point it is important to note that what began as a very elite-focused analysis (reflecting the reoccupations of the "transitions" literature) has now introduced broader questions of societal perception and understanding. In fact this was already implicit in our presentation of the initial model where attention was drawn to the importance of establishing a shared collective understanding of the logic of the pre-democratic system and the consequent need to engage in broad public debate when introducing political reforms. Indeed, an overly elite-focused analysis would not suffice to characterize either the origins of the democratization-through-reform pathway or its dynamics. The driving force is hypothesized to be the need to fill a perceived legitimacy deficit, and that perception arises in the society at large, rather than just within ruling elites. The demands for democratization are at least in part moral claims, arising from sectors of civil society, that must be incorporated into the analysis.

It would follow from this argument that this sub-type of democratization is likely to manifest its own characteristics and distinctive tendencies and limitations. In particular, even when objectively profound institutional changes are introduced, the subjective responses to them may prove disappointing. On the one hand the authors of political reform will still wish to preserve the stabilizing effects that can be derived from continuities with the past. But on the other hand they also hope to tap the enthusiasm and creativity of their citizens by projecting the image of a new dawn. In all democratizations it is difficult to achieve a satisfying balance between these two ambitions. In the case of democratizations by stealth, the second objective may be more unattainable than usual. If what drives the process of political reform is the need to bridge a perceived legitimacy deficit, countries like Colombia and Mexico may continue to face demands for yet further political reform, even after, on the face of it, all the required institutional reforms have been enacted into law. Even then critics can still argue that the reforms enacted so far have been Lampedusan in intent, and that a much more clear-cut break with the past is still needed in order to found a new "democratic" regime. In this sub-type of democratization such endemic criticisms can continually undermine the status quo, without ever sweeping it away.

Thus democratization through reform does seem to constitute a distinctive sub-type – at least, one as coherent as most paths to democratization found in the literature. It requires a series of pre-existing features of the pre-democratic regime, features that are not commonly found. Therefore it cannot be investigated by means of "large-n" studies. This essay has argued that this sub-type of democratization can appropriately be studied by the method of the paired comparison, especially given the need to probe in depth into the potentially elusive notion of an endemic legitimacy deficit. This extended comparison of Colombia and Mexico has provided a means of elaborating on that notion, investigating its specific implications in two well-defined and contrasting settings. The method does not require that both cases turn out the same, only that they can be interpreted from the same perspective. This we have established. However, we must not overlook the limitations of this method of analysis. No really existing process of democratization will correspond fully to the logic of any single model or sub-type. All cases are to some extent hybrid. Moreover, all democratizations are long-term and open-ended in character. Colombia and Mexico both remain incompletely democratized, and future developments may take them onto quite different terrain.

In particular, the democratization-through-reform model isolates and emphasizes two analytical categories – elite cohesion, and institutional innovation – that may be decisive for a while, but which are not necessarily immutable or of exclusive importance throughout the whole course of a long democratization. Elite cohesion is a product of historical experience, not a given. In Colombia and in Mexico it broke down for a sustained period, with disastrous political consequences. The memory of those traumas does much to explain why elite cohesion has subsequently proved so durable, but the history of the two countries provides no guarantees against possible future relapses, and indeed fear of such contingencies has done much to fuel the resistance to democratization. In theory, the construction of a solid structure of democratic institutions would provide the best defence against any return to untrammelled conflict or anarchic violence. But such a theory rests on the assumption that the products of democratic institutional innovation will be thoroughly binding, coherent, and durable. This is not an assumption that sits easily with the history of Latin American constitutionalism, or with current practices in Colombia and Mexico that rely heavily on informal processes of dispute settlement. Indeed, repeated experience in both countries has entrenched the expectation that formal institutions will not constrain all participants in the political process to an equal degree. The most powerful and the most determined can be expected to breach the rules that apply to the majority, and such breaches are expected to lead not to resolute enforcement of the law, but to negotiated compromises which weaken its authority.

This uncertain interplay between institutionalized rules of the game and tacit praetorianism is found throughout Latin America. In Colombia and Mexico a rather durable and well-elaborated interdependence between the two has become entrenched, which is why these regimes have persisted for so long. But the attempt to democratize them involves rewriting this complex and finely balanced system of mutual understandings. Ultimate success would produce stable and perhaps even "consolidated" democratic regimes, but repeated cycles of institutional reform, none of which establish full legitimacy or eliminate expectations of informal concessions, would tend to generate uncertainty and the erosion of elite cohesion. It therefore remains an open question whether democratization through reform, as modeled in this essay, will indeed turn out to be a reliable path to stable democracy.

Postscript

This essay was completed before Vincente Fox and Mexico's two major opposition parties defeated the PRI both at the executive level and in the legislature. It was also completed before the worsening civil conflict in

Colombia led the Clinton administration and the U.S. Congress to endorse an expensive and long-term commitment to assist President Andres Pastrana in reasserting constitutional authority under "Plan Colombia," which has a strong military component. On the face of it, then, the two republics have moved further down divergent paths. Mexico is close to completing its democratization in a context of strengthened institutionality and positive-sum negotiations; whereas Colombia still seems headed towards heightened polarization and negative-sum conflict – perhaps even leading to a regime breakdown. But despite these contrasting trends, it remains instructive to pursue a paired comparison of the two processes, and the framework proposed in this chapter retains its heuristic value. On the Colombian side neither outright military rule nor a guerrilla victory offers a credible alternative to the still-predominant formula of a civilian constitutional regime. In the long run, therefore, the essential issue for a political settlement remains the same as it has been all along and as this essay has indicated. What set of institutional and political reforms can be devised and enforced that will elicit social consensus and bring the cycle of successive challenges and evasions to an end? The current Colombian conjuncture dramatizes how difficult it may be to solve this conundrum, but it does not change the fundamental problem. The present honeymoon period in Mexico gives the clear impression that this problem has been abolished by the simple expedient of dethroning the dominant party after seventy-one years in power. A paired comparison with Colombia warns us, however, that this promising development is only one step in a long path. To stabilize the forthcoming reforms will be the fundamental challenge.

Notes

The author would like to thank Malcolm Deas, Karma Nabulsi, Francisco Gonzalez, and the contributors to this volume for help with the revision of this essay. They are, of course, not responsible for any remaining deficiencies.
1. As the number of eligible cases for comparison falls, the number of possible paired comparisons becomes more tractable. With 50 cases there are 1,225 theoretically possible pairings. With 20 this falls to 190, with 4 to 6, with 3 to 3, and with 2 to 1.
2. Dix's relevant sub-categories were (1) "The democratic single-party mobilization regime, in which one party dominates the political scene, and seeks to mobilize the society for the ends of modernization, but does not eliminate all opposition or criticism or attempt to politicize the entire society (e.g. Mexico)"; and (2) "Rule by a modernizing elite, whereby limited modernization is carried out by an elite that holds a virtual monopoly of political, social, economic, educational, and other resources, but which does not exclude a measure of inter-elite political competition (e.g. Colombia)." Robert H. Dix, *Colombia: The Political Dimensions of Change* (New Haven, Conn.: Yale University Press, 1967), p. 7.
3. For example, John D. Martz records that after 1970, under the presidency of the Conservative Misael Pastrana, the two Colombian ruling parties considered various possi-

bilities for extending their 1957 agreement. "Some proposals even projected a bi-party coalition which might in time come to resemble the single-party domination of the Mexican PRI." "Party Systems in Colombia and Mexico," *Journal of Latin American Studies* (February 1992); 24(1): p. 104.

4. We cannot assume that insufficient institutional reform is the necessary explanation whenever we encounter a persisting legitimacy deficit. Other explanations must also be considered – for example, an erosion of nation-stateness as a result of economic liberalization and "globalization"; the weakness of civil society; a loss of social cohesion; the abandonment of welfarism and/or the impossibility of guaranteeing citizen security; or at a more symbolic and "normative" level, the discrediting of the old, all-embracing ideologies and belief systems.

5. Human Rights Watch provides an annual comparative assessment that is more independent than the U.S. State Department's standard compilation. More specifically for Zedillo's Mexico see their special report on *Implausible Deniability: State Responsibility for Rural Violence in Mexico* (New York, April 1997).

6. For a recent attempt to compare and contrast Colombia and Mexico systematically on this dimension see David C. Jordan, *Drug Politics: Dirty Money and Democracies* (Norman: University of Oklahoma Press, 1999), esp. chaps. 8, 9.

7. Larry Diamond, Johnathan Hartlyn, Juan J. Linz, and Seymour Martin Lipset (eds.), *Democracy in Developing Countries: Latin America*, 2d ed. (Boulder, Colo.: Lynne Riener, 1999), p. 52.

8. See the chapter by Carlos Bazdresch and Santiago Levy (on Mexico) and by Miguel Urrutia (on Colombia) in Rudiger Dornbusch and Sebastian Edwards (eds.), *The Macroeconomics of Populism in Latin America* (Chicago: Chicago University Press, 1991).

9. On the competing logics of fiscal rationality and political legitimation underlying the 1986 municipal reform see Luis Javier Orjuela, "Descentralización en Colombia: Entre la eficiencia del Estado y la legitimación del régimen," in Dieter Nohlen (ed.), *Descentralización política y consolidación democrática* (Caracas: Nueva Sociedad, 1991).

10. Johnathan Hartlyn and John Dugas, "Colombia: The Politics of Violence and Democratic Transformation," in Diamond et al., *Democracy in Developing Countries*, p. 290. Francisco Leal's scepticism was expressed in a 1988 paper, "Democracia oligárquica y rearticulación de la sociedad civil: El caso colombiano" (Mimeo).

11. Wayne A. Cornelius, "Subnational Politics and Democratization," in Wayne A. Cornelius, Todd Eisenstadt, and Jane Hindley (eds.), *Subnational Politics and Democratization in Mexico* (San Diego, Calif.: UCSD, Center for U.S.–Mexican Studies, 1999).

12. Compare the distinction between "rights-in-principle" and "rights-in-practice" studied by Joe Foweraker and Todd Landman, *Citizenship Rights and Social Movements* (London: Oxford University Press, 1997). A key finding is that "the strongest effect of social movement activity in Mexico is to widen the gap between the rhetoric and the reality of citizenship rights leaving rights-in-practice ever less protected than might be expected from the prevailing level of rights-in-principle." Subsequent developments in Chiapas reinforce this finding.

13. A paired comparison of Colombia and Venezuela in January 2000 would be unlikely to privilege "democratization" as the conceptual linkage. An alternative perspective would be to reintroduce Huntington's old concept of "political decay," referring to a situation in which rising social demands outpace the development of what he termed "institutionalization," and therefore prompt a reversion to praetorianism. It is precisely such fears that have cemented elite unity in Colombia and Mexico in the past.

14. Laurence Whitehead, "The Democratization of Taiwan: A Comparative Perspective," in Steve Tsang and Hung-mao Tien (eds.), *Democratization in Taiwan: Implications for China* (Basingstoke Hants.: Macmillan, 1999).

15. Hermann Giliomee and Charles Simkins (eds.), *The Awkward Embrace: One Party Domination and Democracy* (Amsterdam: Harwood Academic Publishers, 1999) explores this logic with particular attention to Mexico, Taiwan, and South Africa. My sense is that the inclusion of South Africa has more of a political than an analytical rationale here.

16. Most, not all. There would always be some powerful outsiders – in Mexico the Catholic Church had to be excluded, and in Colombia it was ex-dictator General Gustavo Rojas Pinilla and his supporters, with others also subjected to discipline and exclusion over time as these regimes took root.

17. See my "The Drama of Democratization," *Journal of Democracy* Winter 1999; 10(4), for a more theoretical discussion of this question. See my "An Elusive Transition: The Slow Motion Demise of a Dominant One Party Regime" in *Democratization* Autumn 1995; 2(3), for an application of this approach to the Mexican case.

5

Foundations: Central America

Edelberto Torres-Rivas

Introduction

Recent political developments in Central America[1] must be considered against a backdrop of complex forces and dynamics. In the 1980s, the impact of the economic crisis – which effectively came from abroad in the form of the collection of foreign debt – occurred simultaneously with the effects of the political crisis, which arose from injustice in these societies. This resulted in an extreme disorganization of society that did not end until the beginning of the 1990s. This evaluation goes beyond an attempt to understand how the fratricidal conflict was brought to a conclusion. We must now think about peace and, in doing so, it is necessary to refer to other crises, in particular the authoritarian systems that gave rise to the forces that are now trying to construct democracy.

This essay is a reflection on these forces. It is divided into three interdependent parts. It begins with an introduction to the disorder that has characterized the recent history of Nicaragua, Guatemala, and El Salvador. It is a synthesis of the causes and effects of civil war and armed conflict, and of how the peace negotiations were brought to a successful conclusion. The essay goes on to analyse how the construction of a political democracy is becoming possible by means of the reconstruction of the political system, the electoral system, and the state. Finally the essay proceeds to a synthesis of the relationship of society, citizenship, human rights, and the evolving international context.

Background and consequences of war

Revolution

The internal tensions that led to the crisis of armed conflict in Central America were always radical in their political expression; struggles on the part of organized forces that sought, in marginal political spaces, the control of the state. The conflict was political and was originally intended not only as a fight for power but also as an effort to change it. The explicit and organized desire to do so was the result of a prolonged mood of general discontent that did not take shape until after the Cuban revolution.

This is the clearest explanation for the rise of the Fuerzas Armadas Rebeldes (FAR) in Guatemala, the Frente Sandinista de Liberación Nacional (FSLN) in Nicaragua, and the Frente Farabundo Martí para la Liberación Nacional (FMLN) in El Salvador. From the beginning there was a revolutionary programmatic content because organized violence confronted the defenders of the status quo through the state.[2] The state responded with more violence, which gave the discontent the opportunity to take ideological and organic form. If the state had not reacted in this way, the popular unrest would have taken another course: it was the extreme violence of the government that unchained the conflict. In the 1960s, social and political conflicts became acute at the time of greatest economic growth in the region, which occurred simultaneously with the greatest symptoms of civil disobedience.

In the beginning, the revolutionary crisis was less of an outbreak of violence than a slow accumulation of tensions. It was the result of successive and repeated failures of several generations to address two basic, complementary demands: political democracy as a means of addressing social exclusion; and agrarian reform, which in turn was a means of achieving social justice in a decidedly feudal and servile-agrarian society. Immediately following the Second World War, both demands were peacefully and publicly raised. In both cases, they were a means of challenging the political order.

The military dictatorship always had ties to the agrarian economy and the landowning class. This can be understood when one realizes that extensive control of land goes hand in hand with intensive control of the labour force. When the economic surplus is appropriated by means of this double monopoly, violence is the inevitable result. The political order becomes more exclusive and the military is needed to safeguard what cannot be maintained by democratic means. The labour market is disturbed when social inequality widens and control of the use of capital becomes even more important than control of the use of the land. In such circumstances, participation and democratic competence become possible.

A. S. Cardenal makes a distinction between fixed assets, such as land,

and liquid assets, such as capital.[3] In an economy in which land is the monopoly of a few, the political structure is a zero-sum game, and the profits of one group are the losses of the others. It is different when the intensive use of land is replaced by the intensive use of capital. Excessive dependence on land makes it necessary to control an obedient and cheap labour force and, for that reason, democracy does not follow as the preferred political system. And when there is an attempt to change that order, it is defended violently because it is perceived by the elite as a total threat.

In the context of this socio-economic turmoil, political democracy never survived as a means of government, except for a few years in Guatemala. After the Second World War efforts of various kinds were made to break the hold of the dominant military and oligarchic structures. The crisis of the 1980s – war, revolution, armed conflict – was an attempt to settle accounts in Jacobin fashion.

The revolutions in each country

In Nicaragua the FSLN led a fight by an extensive social coalition against the Somoza dictatorship whose fall created the conditions for a radical change beginning in July 1979.[4] The Somoza regime was a typical example of a weak, personalist state, resembling the sultanesque rule discussed by Weber, supported by a praetorian guard fed by personal loyalties. The Somozas controlled the National Guard, the Liberal Party, and the government; they were the most powerful business leaders in the region and they governed as a heavily armed state with no legitimacy whatsoever, for 45 years. Urban insurrections – the guerrilla uprising, the general strikes, the passive resistance – and the end of support from the United States, between 1978 and part of 1979, made this situation untenable. The flight of Somoza can be viewed as the collapse of a fragile governmental structure that opened the way for a revolution.

It was a revolution because there was a change, by violent means, in the dominant institutional forces as well as a program for the structural reordering of society. The Sandinista program had three focal points: a mixed economy, a political democracy, and non-military alignment. There were serious obstacles to the Sandinistas' success. The revolutionary regime organized the public sectors and incorporated them into certain governmental functions such as literacy, vaccination, sanitation, environmental protection, and security. This exercise, and the creation of the Popular Assembly in February 1980, made it possible to create a participatory democracy. But in October 1984, forced by international circumstances and pressure from mercenary war, the regime was forced to legitimize revolutionary power in another way – by holding elections, which the FSLN clearly won.

But the revolution wore itself out as the process continued, caught up in the inevitable difficulties found in any backward socio-economic or cultural structure in a small and fragile country. Furthermore, the renewal of a society that was so dependent on the interests of the United States could not be successfully accomplished if that change entailed confronting those interests. Thus, the mercenary war imposed by the United States beginning in November 1981 contributed in a decisive manner to the failure of the revolutionary plan.

The counterrevolutionary military forces, the contras (known to themselves as the Nicaraguan Resistance) – former Somocistas, the indigenous population from the Atlantic coast,[5] plus thousands of disillusioned peasants – became a powerful military force around 1984. The war resulted in more than fifty thousand deaths, the displacement of more than one hundred thousand persons, and the virtual paralysis of the country's weak economy. The well-financed, low-intensity strategy to wear down the Sandinista power was met by the government with a large mobilization of ideological, human, and military resources. In actual fact, the Sandinistas won the war but lost the peace in the negotiations to end the war in Sapoá (March 1989). A number of key issues were agreed upon in these negotiations: a ceasefire, the disarming of the contras, and the holding of elections that were advanced to March 1990. In these elections, at stake was not the government but rather the system itself.

In El Salvador a major civil war developed. It lasted more than a decade and had a more clearly classist content; it was based on demands for social justice resulting from the extreme economic and social polarization of this small country, the most populous in Latin America. But again, the impetus was the political factor. The electoral system lacked credibility because of frauds in the elections of 1972 and 1977, under a regime in which the military had been in power since 1932. These 48 years of uninterrupted military power were unparalleled in Latin America.

The first crack in this authoritarian structure occurred with the coup of 15 October 1979, when a civil-military junta was created to face the growing popular discontent.[6] This was the first time in almost half a century that civilians had an input into government. Successive civil-military juntas had been incapable of reducing the levels of conflict manifested since 1978 as a rising urban insurrection. The extent of violence of the civilian population increased the brutality of the military repression. The sharing of power with civilians was undoubtedly the end of the military's monopoly, but this did not in any way weaken its repressive nature. If the erosion of authoritarian power dates from this time, it also signalled the beginning of civil war.

This repression reached a critical point with the assassination of Archbishop Oscar Romero in March 1980. Months after, the FMLN was formed, and in January 1981 it launched its poorly named "final offensive." At the outset, the wide peasant support for the FMLN, as well as the strategic weakness of the national army, were evident. Unlike in Guatemala, in El Salvador two effective and permanent military forces with unified commands and territorial support bases confronted each other. The guerrillas were recognized as a belligerent force by the joint Franco-Mexican Declaration of 1981. The military capability, the repeated initiatives of the FMLN, and the control of the population constituted a true power standing over against the regime.

The virtual overthrow of the national army was prevented by the substantial assistance of the United States. This co-operation was more than just military aid, which amounted to almost 4,000 million dollars in a decade. As a salvaging operation, it increased the armed forces from 16,000 to more than 50,000 men, with plenty of modern equipment. It also aided development and kept El Salvador from falling into the abyss of economic collapse, as happened in Nicaragua.

Finally, and of greater significance in the long term, there was the socio-political dimension of the aid, which favoured agrarian reform benefiting some 22 per cent of the peasants.[7] The nationalization of banking and foreign trade, and the opening of the political arena that resulted in the holding of constituent (1982) and presidential (1984) elections followed on from this. These decisions were something more than suggestions of a diplomatic nature; they appeared as demands of the United States Senate that insisted on a legal government as a sine qua non condition of military aid.

The strength of the guerrilla movement – which sometimes held the strategic initiative – can be explained by the extensive co-operation given them by the Cubans and the Sandinistas. Towards 1986 it was clear that neither the army nor the rebels could win the war. Several attempts at dialogue without negotiation were finally advanced by the Mexico Agreement in 1989 between the government and the FMLN, which was an effective beginning to the negotiations that were accelerated in October of that year, when the United Nations named an intermediary, Alvaro de Soto. With the Geneva Agreement of April 1990 four main objectives were achieved: a political end to the conflict; the consolidation of democratic life; a guarantee to respect human rights; and reconciliation within the society. Negotiations dragged on for two and a half difficult years, culminating in Chapultepec on 15 January 1992.

In Guatemala the experience was one of a "scorched society"; a war of the state against the society, or part of it. As early as 1962, the guerrilla movement began to surface as did the counterinsurgent military power, both resulting from the effect of the accumulating tension brought on by the fall of Jacobo Arbenz in 1954. That is why this period is called the "counterrevolution." The guerrilla insurrection was started by a military group, the Movimiento Revolucionario 13 de Noviembre (MR-13), a group of young officials dissatisfied with the collaboration of the government with the United States in the Playa Girón incident. Subsequently, numerous students and workers formed the armed group known as the FAR.

The first guerrilla outbreak occurred between 1964 and 1965 and was defeated towards the end of that decade. After that there were isolated incidents, met by severe governmental reprisals. Although it never threatened the internal order, it reinforced the takeover of the state by an army that had been learning modern techniques in the fight against subversives since 1960. From approximately 1963 until the conclusion of peace in 1996, the military power of the state openly became a counterinsurgent platform. The heightened sensitivity and level of repression must be seen in the context of the Cold War and the anxiety caused by the Cuban revolution of 1959. The state punished all forms of opposition, armed or peaceful, legal or subversive, with deadly violence. For this reason, it is said that in Guatemala there was never a civil war but rather two armed outbreaks within the framework of a permanently repressive authoritarian structure. The second guerrilla wave surfaced toward the end of the 1970s and it was again defeated around 1983. After 1983, the guerrilla organizations united in the Unidad Revolucionaria Nacional Guatemalteca (URNG). They were brutally dislodged from their offensive zones, at the cost of the lives of more than 50,000 indigenous civilians who were killed in a scorched earth operation that had genocidal characteristics. The URNG continued to carry out isolated military actions without the formidable indigenous support that it had from 1979 to 1982, which gave the fight a classist and ethnic character at that time.

After 1978, the Guatemalan army fought without the assistance of the United States, which had for years been a decisive factor in the formation of a powerful counterinsurgent force.[8] With the creation of the paramilitary Patrullas de Autodefensa Civil (PAC) in 1982, the armed conflict took another form. The members of the patrols carried out surveillance and repression from inside the peasant world. At its height, the PAC numbered more than a million organized peasants, and the society reached its greatest degree of militarization. This figure corresponded to 12 per cent of the total population of the country, or almost 20 per cent of the adults of working age, who were obliged to take some time off from earning a livelihood to defend an order that they never knew.

Especially noteworthy was the dimension of political repression in the armed conflict, which explains why, out of 200,000 dead, 92 per cent were civilians. Another important characteristic was that there was no fighting in the cities; instead the fighting was in the rural areas, away from economic activity and political life. The dominant groups were not affected by the virulence of the conflict as they were in El Salvador and Nicaragua. An important aspect of civil wars is that they are not fundamentally different from other types of accelerated social change. In Guatemala this was not the case – on the contrary, the conflict seemed to freeze some of the traditional structures. The repression systematically destroyed the social movement, utilizing methods of cruelty unparallelled in Latin America.

This peace process in Guatemala was the most drawn-out in Central America because the parties did not negotiate an end to the armed confrontation until convinced of the uselessness of prolonging it. The army always kept a vision of ending repression by eliminating the need for it through the untrammelled use of military force, and hence looked inward for a military solution. The first meeting of the URNG with a government delegation including military leaders was held in Mexico in April 1991 and marked the starting point.[9] There the foundation was laid that made possible the signing of the peace that put an end to the conflict five long, difficult years later.

Let us summarize the preceding discussion. The consequences of this turbulence in Central America, characterized by economic paralysis and structural adjustment policies, together with lengthy and widespread fratricide, are not yet known, much less evaluated. There were 300,000 dead, more than 100,000 orphans, and an unidentified number of physically handicapped, plus two million migrants who "went to the North."[10] Nicaragua and El Salvador were characterized by brutal impoverishment of the peasant class, ruralization of the capital cities, and widespread growth of the informal economy. In addition to extensive poverty, intense harm was done to the emotional life of the common man and women through the "trivialization of horror."[11]

The termination of the conflicts

A number of forces and processes coalesced and led to the end of the wars between 1989 (Nicaragua) and 1996 (Guatemala). The sinuous process of negotiation, which eventually led to the transformation of the conflicts into peace agreements, would not have been possible without the positive intervention of neighbouring countries – Mexico, Colombia, Panama, and Venezuela – that formed the so-called "Iniciativa de Contadora" (Contadora Initiative). For three years Contadora developed proposals that essentially tried to surmount the background of war by means of free elections and respect for human rights. It created a spirit of expanding co-operation that opened the way for a regional presidential summit meeting that was held in Esquipulas. In their second meeting, the Central American presidents, including Daniel Ortega, approved the "Compromiso Centromericano para Alcanzar la Paz Firme y Duradera" (Central American Commitment to the Attainment of a Firm and Lasting Peace), known as Esquipulas II (1987).

The recommendations of Esquipulas II were realistic proposals to stop the internal fighting, promote the process of democratization, and seek internal reconciliation and regional co-operation. One of these proposals was the creation of national reconciliation commissions that played a decisive role in the three countries. Prominent citizens were members of these commissions, which were headed by the archbishops in Nicaragua and Guatemala. The first contacts between the governments and the insurgent forces were made by means of intermediaries. The processes took different paths and lengths of time, but the truth is that more progress was made when the Central American presidents requested the direct intervention of the United Nations.

In July 1989 the Security Council authorized the secretary-general to send his representatives who, at different times, played the role of observers and mediators. This was essential in the construction and verification of commitments between the parties involved. The San José Agreement of July 1990 on human rights signed by the Salvadoran factions was instrumental in the creation of the UN Observation Mission (ONUSAL). The Guatemalan equivalent was the Global Agreement, also dealing with human rights, signed in Mexico in 1994, which created the U.N. Mission for the Verification of Human Rights in Guatemala (MINUGUA). Both missions have been key players in the supervision of decisions that concern everyday democracy, respect for human rights, the reform of the electoral and judicial systems, the truth commissions, and the military.[12]

Thus, just as in their beginning, there was foreign intervention in the end of the conflicts.[13] This is easier to understand in Nicaragua because of the mercenary nature of the National Resistance, or in El Salvador where foreign aid gave rise to the National Army. External actors had leverage that helped to bring the parties to the negotiating table. It is less obvious in Guatemala because of the regime's suspicion of the United States and the self-sufficiency of the military. But the pressure from the United States, a necessary cause, only became a sufficient cause when local factors drove it. More than a change in the objective situation of the conflicts, what changed was the subjective perspective of the players[14] who realized that it was no longer possible to attain their objectives by military means and that a prolongation of the conflict, far from improving their fortunes, could worsen them.

The influence of Contadora and Esquipulas II, in addition to the direct dialogue between the factions with the mediation of the UN, contributed to bringing about a change in attitude on the part of the players and then, the beginnings of trust between them. Negotiation was a forced meeting point, the result of the evolution of the strategies of the factions in the conflict, of the change in the players' perceptions and those of their international protectors. Putting an end to the mistrust was a major challenge and there were moments when there was dialogue without negotiation, but beginning in 1989 the first signs of goodwill appeared and a difficult balance was maintained as mutual concessions were made.

The origins of the long civil-military conflicts are difficult to identify now that the conflicts are over. The principles that gave rise to them have generally been lost by the wayside and what Waldman recognizes as an inevitable effect, in fact happened – the violence developed its own momentum that impelled it forward.[15] The driving force was violence; in the final negotiations the flags of revolution – popular power, socialism – had disappeared.

The peace in El Salvador has been explained as a stalemate, a reflection of the balanced power of the factions. So, then, how does one explain Guatemala? Undoubtedly, the character of the negotiations was different and this is reflected in the agreements reached. But in both countries there were influential groups who were conscious of the fact that the costs of war were growing, that it was an obstacle to economic modernization and democratic development, now accepted as viable alternatives. In El Salvador the agreements were more than a ceasefire. There was a commitment to introduce institutional changes in the state and in the handling of political life, all in favour of a "new" way of living together. The army was forced to reduce its numbers by 50 per cent and create a new civil policy; a truth commission and a new socio-economic forum were formed; and the judicial system was strengthened.

In Guatemala, the commitments resulting from the peace agreements were even more important, except as concerns the army. There was an agreement to reduce the army's numbers by 33 per cent, and to create a commission to investigate human rights violations, but without authorization to name those responsible. The agreements as a whole have been considered as a proposal for national reconstruction since, if they are fulfilled, they will constitute a substantive change in the current profile of the state and the society. They involve institutional changes, the conversion of the guerrillas into a political party, proposals dealing with economic policy, and fundamental agreements concerning the rights of indigenous peoples.

It is of primary importance to note that the experience of the violence taught the dominant class in these three countries that the only way to retain power was by democratizing it. Where the conflict involved war, the nature of the oligarchy changed more and it accepted the rules of the new political game with less reticence. There was not a substitution of elites, but rather electoral competition, which is the heart of political democracy. This fact, coupled with the subjective effects of the end of the conflict and the new international climate, all favored the acceptance of democracy as the means to political power. In fact, the structural changes exhibited by the dominant class are, in the best-case scenario, changes on the surface only. A new era of contradictions is beginning in the three countries. Nothing is the same in the political arena, but the socio-economic conditions that provoked the military conflict still exist, only in a democratic setting. For how long?

The "construction of peace" is more difficult than the signing of a peace agreement. It is the difference between a negative peace and a positive one. Beginning with the recent experiences of numerous countries in Africa and Asia, the immediate threat is of a recurrence of the violence; it is imperative to ensure that the factions think of peace as something more than diplomatic goodwill. Some of the causes that provoked the conflict must be resolved immediately and others can be dealt with in the medium term. New political institutions must be created to lead the way to democracy and national reconciliation, and conditions must be established that ensure against further human rights violations. Economic reconstruction is another dimension, which presents an enormous challenge to positive peace.

In a synthesis of diverse experiences, Senghas proposes as a requisite for positive peace, the satisfaction of the requirements of his "civilizing hexagon."[16] This requires the end of conflict and the construction of a state of law within which to apply policies of social justice, democratic participation, the establishment of a "culture of dialogue," and to attain what he calls "the control of passions." As will be seen in the following, Senghas's standards were almost completely met in the three countries.

The reordering of the political system

This section will analyze the changes that occurred in the 1980s and part of the 1990s almost simultaneously in the three countries and have raised expectations of modernization. The central characteristic is the reconstruction of the political system and the transition to political democracy. Once again, the history of each country is different, but there are also common threads.

The first transition or the authoritarian road to democracy

The term "first transition" arises from the fact that the holding of elections occurred while the internal conflict was still ongoing. In contrast to most historical experience,[17] in Guatemala and El Salvador democracy preceded the attainment of peace and the end of the conflict was only achieved when there were civilian governments. The deterioration of the authoritarian structure, the first symptoms of the erosion of power, took place as part of the political crisis experienced by military regimes. The opening up of the political arena was the result of decisions made by senior government leaders and not the result of social struggles led by democratic-minded players. For these reasons, this transition is described as authoritarian.

In spite of the big differences between Nicaragua, led by a revolutionary elite, and El Salvador and Guatemala, led by forces that were reactionary in nature, there were certain common characteristics in this period of breaking away from the authoritarian order that linked war to the elections and peace to repression. The necessary conditions for democracy arose out of this confusion, and displayed a number of characteristics.

The first characteristic was the emergence of a crisis within the top echelons of government brought on by increasing popular disobedience (El Salvador), by internal struggles within the army (Guatemala), or by the results of the war (Nicaragua). In the first two cases there was a crisis within the ruling elite that resulted in the disintegration of power. Thus, there were coups d'état within the army itself: colonels and lower-ranking officers against General Osorio's government in El Salvador in 1979 and against General Lucas García in 1982 in Guatemala. In Nicaragua there a crisis of governability. In the three countries, as was mentioned above, there were electoral processes that repaired, the stability of the region by producing a legality that favoured external recognition (and aid). The reality, as can be clearly seen in El Salvador and Guatemala, was a division of power between civilians and the military.

The second characteristic of this original transition occurred when the military in El Salvador (1982) and Guatemala (1984), and the Sandinistas in Nicaragua (1984), held elections. These were not without difficulties but were free and not fraudulent, and, consequently, legitimizing, resulting in a limited pluralism to the right of center in the first two and to the left of center in Nicaragua. In all three countries, a Constituent Assembly was called for to encourage the formation of a new constituent body, to elect a president, and thus to legitimize the political order that had been disordered by the conflict. What was significant was not the holding of elections but rather the fact that they were free and that the results were respected. The results of this period were the Salvadoran constitution of 1983, and the Nicaraguan and Guatemalan constitutions of 1986, and the election of presidents Napoleón Duarte (1984) and Alfredo Cristiani (1990) in El Salvador; and Vinicio Cerezo (1986), Jorge Serrano (1990), and Ramiro de León (1993) in Guatemala.

The third characteristic, which is even more surprising, is that the holding of elections and the preparations for voting – popular movements, legitimization of political parties, electoral campaigns – came at a time when the armed conflict was even bloodier than before, although different, in each of the three countries. The changes were not a continuation of the war by political means but rather they coexisted with military conflict. Many people wonder if both the two are compatible or if one is fostered by the other. Why were elections held? There are coinciding causes but of the various answers, there is one that meets the facts of the case – that the elections were part of a counterinsurgent strategy; democracy to win the war.

The fourth characteristic of this contradictory road to democracy is that it was not driven or applied by democratic players capable of twisting the arm of the military command. On the contrary, the initiative was taken by the military and the changes were actually put into effect by forces coming from the authoritarian past, to the point that in what is described below as the "second transition" groups or leaders who clearly came from the ranks of the dictatorship were in positions of power. It is said that society as a whole lost the war, but that the peace was won by the Right. And thus it is that the final paradox appears, a democracy that was constructed and led by those who did not believe in it and had never practiced it.

The fifth characteristic is that the road to political democracy, because of its origins and the difficulties it had to overcome, clearly led through two separate transitions, the last of which only began when peace was attained. That is, there was a first transition – authoritarian and under conditions of war – and another, later transition, under new conditions established by the end of the conflict.

This hypothesis of two transitions could lead to confusion. It makes perfect sense in Guatemala and in El Salvador, but less so in Nicaragua. The first stage, noted as such because it was an attempt to substitute war for politics by authoritarian means, was the economy of violence. It did not replace conflict with democratic politics, but it did make the two compatible. As has already been said, there were free elections and the beginnings of the exercise of political rights. Political participation in the midst of the war, and probably when war was at its worst, immediately placed limits on the construction of political institutions, on the reconstitution of citizenship.

The military crisis resulted in the forced liberalization of the regime that ended with the holding of elections and the handover of power to civilians, and opened the way to possibilities for democracy. This is not only explicable by institutional means; there was an endogenous root that was structural in nature and to which little attention is given. With the war, the economic crisis, and the changes in the international arena, the interests of the agro-export oligarchy began to change. Throughout two intense decades, the landowners as economic players were faced with significant events that had a transforming effect on them in El Salvador, and to a lesser extent in Guatemala, depending on the intensity of the fighting. In Nicaragua, the typical plantation owner disappeared. In the 1980s, the landowners' economic interests were refocused in light of new marketing opportunities and the determining factors of the new international capitalism. The old agrarian export model was changed as much by the new demand for new export products as by the declining demand for coffee. More decisive changes were brought about by the expropriation of land, the decline in export production, the insecurity of economic activity (these were partly peasant wars), and the changes introduced by the new international climate, where services, trade, and finances took the lead. An ominous sign of the relative decline of coffee was the fact that remittances sent by poor migrants working abroad exceeded the income from coffee in El Salvador and were equal to it in Guatemala. The opening of markets and the crisis of the common market paralysed the secondary sector and weakened the industrialists.

The changes in the make-up of the dominant groups were almost invisible because they consisted of inner adaptations. The violence begun by the military, which at first had the open sympathy of the dominant classes, began to work against the reordering of the latter's interests. The costs of the war were greater than the price of democracy, which meant also that the alliance with the army was now questionable. During the peace negotiations, the contradictions were visible, in the economic elite as well as in the top military actors, and between them and the interests of the United States. Without doubt, there was a change in strategy, a change in players, an acceptance of other ways of acceding to and controlling power, accentuated when the leftist threat lost military effectiveness.

The second transition: Is there light at the end of the tunnel?

The second transition – the period following the successful completion of the peace negotiations – was a transition approved by the actors in conflict. The peace agreements were a bargain made in order to initiate changes in political life, concessions that the bourgeoisie agreed to in the political arena but not in the economic sphere.[18] The pacts originating in this second transition had a negative aspect to them, they were not negotiated by the political parties and the civilian sectors were pretty much invited for show. Those most nostalgic for the authoritarian period have described the peace agreements as a muddy transaction between governments without legitimacy and a gang of bandits. Several legal experts, who are caught up in the literal meaning, argue that they are governmental agreements and not commitments of the state and, therefore, not legally binding.

The transitions in each country

In the case of Nicaragua and for the purposes of this chapter, the key question is: What was the contribution of the Sandinistas to political democracy? How is their antidictatorial legacy being processed? The Sandinistas had a democratic program, an essential part of the fight against the Somoza dictatorship. "For the FSLN, democracy was measured not only in terms of politics and not limited to the participation of the people in elections. Democracy ... signifies the participation of the people in political, economic, social, and cultural affairs. To the extent that the people participate in these affairs, the country will be more democratic. Democracy begins with the economic order, when the inequalities begin to disappear, when the workers and the peasants are able to improve their standard of living."[19]

The revolution could not carry out this programme because it was weakened in its relation to the masses and society: poverty became widespread and inequalities increased. Nevertheless, the extensive and sustained organization and participation of subordinate social groups, which had never before had this opportunity, turned out to be lasting. Thus the seeds were planted for the extensive exercise of civic duties and rights that still continues. Some institutions related to political democracy were created in this decade: a law on political parties and elections, an independent electoral board, a multiplicity of parties, and opportunities for the opposition. The establishment of a popular army was a valuable support for democracy, as proved during the political crises in the 1990s that occurred in the country; it is maintained as a guarantee of democracy, a unique case in Latin America.

However, Sandinismo was an essentially contradictory experience because at the same time, it maintained a militarized vertical structure with a concentration of power and control over social organizations. The government/dominant party regime encouraged authoritarian behavior and the war against the contra mercenaries justified censorship and exclusion. The war of attrition forced the Sandinistas to hold elections in 1990, which, contrary to all predictions, the FSLN lost. In recognizing and accepting its defeat, it made a new contribution to democratic life. In the interval before the handing over of the government, the FSLN's ambiguous nature was highlighted. On the one hand, it contributed to the preparations and respected the Protocol for the Transference of the Executive Power, which facilitated the change of government. However, on the other hand, it tried to legalize the transfer of property to the revolutionary elite by Decrees 95 and 96, thereby committing a scandalous act of collective corruption.

The protocol embraced measures which benefited tens of thousands of small rural and urban landowners by legalizing their tenure. But there was also appropriation of houses, plantations, and other state assets that went to the top Sandinista leaders. The operation took on an aspect of pillage that was popularly termed a "piñata," from the children's game of taking turns to try and break up a cardboard doll or animal stuffed with candies, and scrambling to pick up the candies once the doll is broken. It was an act of corruption stemming directly from the Somoza immorality that poisoned the political life of the country during the nineties.

The elections of April 1990 were won by Violeta Chamorro, the widow of an important anti-Somoza leader, who was apolitical and without experience in politics. The second transition in Nicaragua thus began with the coming to power of the forces of the Center-Right which began a change in the political system from within the government. But the victory of the opposition, the Unión Nacional Opositora (UNO), was really a self-defeat. The UNO was an unnatural coalition of 12 parties representing every color of the ideological rainbow; all the parties had in common was that they were all anti-Sandinista. The coalition fell apart almost immediately, at which point Virgilio Godoy, the vice-president elect, broke with Chamorro and did not take office.

This episode reveals the extreme instability of politics in Nicaragua, which made democratic consolidation impossible. The greatest frustration stemmed from the behaviour of the partisan elites, fragmented and unwilling to carry out their agreements. President Chamorro was forced to govern sometimes with the Sandinistas who had 39 representatives, and sometimes with the UNO which started out with 53 seats (and 83 per cent of the mayors' offices) but lost its majority after its irreconcilable fragmentation. The government's economic policy managed to control inflation and stabilize the exchange rate at the cost of development, and an increase in poverty. The demobilization of the contras (more than 20,000 peasants) and the juridical-political problems caused by the "piñata" wore down the government.[20] Added to this were the constant demands of the poor, who in spite of the economic disaster under the Sandinistas had still received some health and education benefits.

The most serious crisis in this period came about in 1993–95 because of an initiative to reform the Sandinista constitution. It resulted in a split between the FMLN and the rest of the opposition, and by developing various alliances with the government, it turned sworn enemies into transitory allies.[21] An effort was made to modernize some of the institutions left over from the Sandinistas, such as to put an end to a "hyperpresidentialist" executive and to depoliticize the election of the Electoral Board, the Supreme Court, and other institutions. Further proof of the difficulties encountered in the construction of a modern political system.

The second elections of the second transition (October 1996) were won once again by an anti-Sandinista coalition, the Alianza Liberal, led by Arnoldo Alemán, which gained 51 per cent of the vote while the FSLN maintained its popular support with 38 per cent. In contrast to what happened in the other two countries, the army in Nicaragua remained totally apolitical and the social organizations highly activist. This activism increased in accordance with the real needs dictated by the poverty of these organizations and the strategies of the FSLN which controlled them. The tendency towards bipartisanism seemed to develop after a "dark pact" signed by Ortega and Alemán in October 1999, which modified the Supreme Electoral Board and politicized the election of the Supreme Court of Justice and the office of the Comptroller, thereby restricting the free participation of other parties in the presidential election of 2002. This agreement between caudillos has been widely rejected by public opinion of both the Right and the Left as being contrary to the construction of a democracy.

The political system was not fully established. The levels of conflict were still high, the independence of the institutions of the state was in question, and only the Supreme Electoral Board was trusted. The party system, characterized by fragmentation, tended toward a false bipartisanship because it rested upon the extreme anti-Sandinista rancour that unified the opposition; at the same time, it was affected by the division of small parties that now included leftist forces. The democratic institutions that had been in the process of being strengthened were now threatened by the Ortega-Alemán arrangement.

Together with the institutional dimension of democracy, it is important to emphasize democracy's other side, the citizens – numerous in this political culture because the revolution took care to form them. In the post-Sandinista period, the high degree of organization, the combat experience, the political allegiance of important subordinate groups – all undoubtedly contributed to a high level of democratic participation. This explains, for example, why the rate of voter absenteeism was less and political assembly and protest were more intensive and effective than in the rest of Central America.

In Guatemala, the break with authoritarianism came by way of two military coups; one in March 1982 led by General Ríos Montt and the other in August 1983 by General Mejía Víctores. After the first coup initial measures were taken to open the way to transition: a new electoral law, a new political party law, and voter registration, among others. During the period of the second coup, elections were held for a constituent assembly in which twelve parties participated in the country's first non-fraudulent elections. This assembly created a modern constitution that took effect in 1986. This was the worst period of the armed conflict; in 1981 the guerrillas took the initiative throughout most of the country and they were not defeated until around 1982–83. The military forces took the lives of approximately 50,000 indigenous people; 500,000 people were displaced; and more than 100,000 took refuge outside the country. Meanwhile, in the city, social leaders and leaders of opposition parties continued to be killed.

The army complied with the political changes by turning the government over to the civilians but it remained independent and in complete control of the resources necessary for the violence. This contradiction of free elections with indiscriminate repression increased with the creation of the PAC, which involved more than a million peasants in watching over their villages and fighting the guerrillas. Thus, an extreme militarization of rural society was underway at the time when general elections were held in 1985 and the government was handed over to the first civilian in thirty-five years, Vinicio Cerezo, leader of the Christian Democrats, the following year.

Cerezo promoted the Esquipulas initiative and created the Commission for Reconciliation, but he could not do any more to bring about peace. In the beginning there was respect for political rights, for the defense of human rights as regards those who disappeared, and freedom for the trade unions. This first government of the transition period was an example of a civilian president trapped by military power, especially after there were two attempted military coups in 1988 and 1989. The repression – not the war – continued but from the end of the 1980s, 90 per cent of the human rights violations were committed by the PAC.

President Cerezo handed over the government to another civilian in 1991, thereby beginning a good democratic tradition. In the second general elections, a political conservative, Jorge Serrano Elías, triumphed in a precarious manner. He ran instead of the leader of his party (Movimiento de Acción Solidaria) General Ríos Montt, who was prohibited by the Constitution from running because of his role in the coup. Serrano ran the country with difficulty and thirty months later, influenced by Fujimori's conduct, he went against the Constitution and proclaimed an auto-coup. The combined and decisive action of the social forces (in the absence of political parties) and of sections of the army stopped the coup.

The legal and consensual manner in which this crisis was resolved – with the election of Ramiro de León Carpio, Human Rights Ombudsman, as successor – was a step forward in this transition period. Serrano and de León decisively furthered the peace negotiations.

And, thus, Guatemala arrived at the 1995 elections, in which 29 parties participated with ten candidates. For the first time in almost forty years, a leftist group participated – the Frente Democrático Nueva Guatemala. The Partido de Avanzada Nacional (PAN) won, a party of the economic Right that campaigned on the peace issue. This brought both parties close because the new president, Alvaro Arzú Yrigoyen, from a Basque dynasty belonging to the oligarchy and a businessman who represented business interests, completed the agenda dealing with the pending issues in less than a year and signed the peace with the URNG on 29 December 1996. On this symbolic date two distinct processes, which tend to be confused because of their effects, were brought to an end. On the one hand, it ended both the armed conflict, which was in any case dying down since the guerrillas were worn out, and also an era of more than three decades of counter-insurgent power.

Arzú's government was the first in the second transition period in which, for the first time, the requirements of Senghas's civilizing hexagon were satisfied. There were no more human rights violations resulting from state policy and, for the first time, a generation lived in peace and under democratic rule. The ethnic question became a national political issue with the recognition that Guatemala was a multicultural and multilingual nation. The genocidal characteristics of the counter-insurgency at the beginning of the 1980s had a consciousness-raising effect: it gave the indigenous population the chance to identity themselves as victims/players in the bloodiest period of the conflict. The issue of multiculturalism began to be associated with the problem of the construction of a racial democracy.

In the third general elections, held in 1999, progress was made in terms of pluralism and participation. Sixteen parties competed with ten candidates, this time including the URNG as a guerrilla group transformed into a political party (which received a modest 12 per cent of the vote). The proportion of nonvoters was reduced to 43 per cent. The election was won by the Frente Republicano Guatemalteco, a motley coalition based on a strong Evangelical vote, military influence, and the support of the former PAC members, leftist sympathizers, and peasants. It was led by Alfonso Portillo, who won a clear popular victory based strongly on anti-oligarchic sentiment of a populist nature.

It is obvious that democratization in El Salvador followed the same strategy as in Guatemala, seeking the same results, but at different times and along different paths. In Guatemala, military control ended with the election of Cerezo; in El Salvador, with the October 1979 coup before the outbreak of the war. In fact, that was the beginning of the first transition, ratified by three civilian-military juntas. The last of these juntas was led by the leader of the Christian Democrats, Napoleón Duarte, who called for elections. These elections, held in March 1982, were fraught with problems, both technical (incomplete voter registration) and practical (voting in the war zones). Without support from the United States, the defeat of the Christian Democrats would have been worse, but it could not keep the extreme Right, the Alianza Republicana Nacionalista (ARENA) and the Partido Conciliación Nacional (PCN), from electing Major Roberto D'Aubuisson as president of the Assembly.[22] A conservative constitution was put into effect in 1983 and presidential elections were held in 1984, with Napoleón Duarte just barely winning a second term.

Duarte and Cerezo were similar in that they were both civilian leaders from centrist parties. They had experienced military repression in the opposition and because they initiated political change, they ended up prisoners of military power; they were not capable of introducing the changes that their limited reformist ethos called for. And although they were willing to negotiate peace, they were incapable of doing so. The Christian Democrat party in both countries ended up discredited after its time in government, and almost disappeared from the political arena, leaving the political Center vacant.

But there were a number of differences. Duarte's government had a great deal of support from the United States, to finance the war as well as to avoid the administrative collapse of the government (salaries were paid with foreign aid!). It experienced the most successful rightist opposition in the region. Beginning in 1981 ARENA became the best-structured party of the bourgeoisie in Central America for half a century.[23] In the second presidential election ARENA won, led by Alfredo Cristiani, who successfully handled the negotiations that culminated at Chapultepec in 1992. This is the date that the second transition began in this country. Again, there was a similarity with Guatemala. It was not political reformists but rather rightist businessmen in politics who were most successful in achieving peace. The difference between the two countries is that ARENA has given permanence to the political system in El Salvador, whereas PAN was defeated in Guatemala – and in that country, if a party loses the election it disappears from the political scene.

The second transition cannot be explained in El Salvador without reference to the powerful coalition of the Right that started to make political gains in 1982. It crushed the Christian Democrats starting with the 1989 presidential elections, and since then has been the strongest political force in El Salvador, although in close competition with the FMLN. Thus, in the third presidential election (1994), called the "elections of the century," ARENA won, with Armando Calderón Sol. This event is full of significance. It marked the inauguration of a new electoral board, an electoral code, and a voter register with fewer problems.[24] It was the first election in peacetime and, therefore, with the FMLN as a political party, whose strength among the masses kept ARENA's continuity from being a sure thing. It won, but in the second round; this marks the beginning of the post-war period in the country. In fact, El Salvador has the strongest consolidation in the region.

Elections are not enough

The difficult construction of the political system

In Guatemala and El Salvador the erosion of authoritarianism began among the military, which upon handing the government over to civilians created the impression that democracy was the negation of the military regime. But the transition cannot be defined by its antimilitary aspect because when the military withdrew from government, it still controlled important elements of power and a dynamic was begun that was strengthened in the electoral processes, giving the first civilian governments uncertain legitimacy because of their coexistence with war. In both countries political reform was initiated, the first juridical institutions were created, and political parties were formed that accepted the idea of democratic participation. New forces defined social and political objectives.

Thus, the political system is slowly being constructed as the result of a cumulative set of experiences. The patterns that determined the forms and channels of access to power, the space in which it was exercised, and the role of the players (some admitted, others rejected) were more clearly defined with the signing of peace agreements. The end of the conflict foreshadowed the negation of the past and, for that reason, a second transition may be spoken of. Certainly efforts were made to stop the erosion that had begun; nobody defended the dictatorship but the authoritarian players supported the climate of armed violence to maintain their control. The signing of peace weakened the forces of the past.

The party system experienced radical changes in the three countries. The traditional parties in Nicaragua disappeared with the revolution. And by forming a powerful electoral base, the FSLN, beginning in 1990, became the axis that held together an opposition formed by almost two dozen small parties. This explains the false bipartisanship on the country's political scene: the Sandinistas confronted an enemy coalition, as well as a fierce array of small groups that knew they could not win. In El Salvador, two parties came from the authoritarian period, the Christian Democrats and the Communists.[25] In the "elections of the century," out of 14 parties, 8 were founded after 1990. Bipartisanship was established between the Right and the Left – forces, now political, which emerged as players from the civil war. There were also a dozen small parties that together gathered 18 per cent of the vote in the 1997 elections.

In Guatemala, the distinguishing feature has been the volatility of the parties. The three that controlled the Constituent Assembly in 1984 have disappeared[26] and of the parties that have governed the country, one is lifeless and the other has disappeared. Half of those that competed in 1999 were formed in the 1990s and, in these elections, five of these parties disappeared legally. Another problematic characteristic is voter abstention in Guatemala and in El Salvador, where it amounts to almost 50 per cent of the registered voters.

The notion of a weak state and how to strengthen it

The most important cause of the crisis that led to war in the region was revealed in the character of the state – a weak state, infiltrated by corruption and a military dictatorship that maintained its power through the use of force. The final argument of this essay is that democratic consolidation is structurally related to the strengthening of the state. The previous history of the region has been one of a combination of weak political power with an authoritarian military structure. Furthermore, the violence and the war strengthened the military but further weakened the power of the state.

The Central American experience provides ample evidence that no plan for revolutionary change can prosper when faced with a democratic state. Political subversion is only successful when confronting weak states. No form of civil disobedience is without a response in a democratic state. A state is weak when it is not based on the will of the majority of citizens. That is to say, when it is not the result of rationalized legitimacy. The state's weakness was increased by its lack of relative autonomy, accentuated by the crisis, and expressed in the unbridled influence of big business interests. The state left the conflict with strong corporative attachments, as Stepan points out, with a strong inclusive corporativism.[27]

In general, a weak state does not change out of fear of danger from the outside or to defend its sovereignty but rather because of internal threats and challenges from within its own society.[28] When a state lacks well-structured social support, it faces a permanent crisis of legitimacy. The logic of armed force thus imposes itself on the dialectic of democracy. The contradiction that weakens the power of the armed state is that it uses violence against the opposition to "maintain order" – in effect, fighting to keep itself in power. When the threats increase, the repression increases, not because there is hope of success but because, due to the weakness of the state, it is impossible to turn to other, less violent means.[29]

The state is weak when it utilizes force as a primary resource to ensure internal order[30] – in short, when it is not a democratic state. For this reason, expressions of social discontent and popular disobedience can accompany – as in fact it is natural that they do – democratic regimes. The definition of democracy is based as much on consensus as on the ability to resolve conflicts without resorting to force. In this sense, the strong state is a power that unifies the nation, that integrates it, beginning with its regional, social, and ethnic divisions; that can apply justice and put an end to the impunity that debilitates democracy; that can collect taxes so that those who have more pay more; that is committed to national reconciliation, and the right to know the truth about serious human rights violations. A strong state is a democratic power, and modern in the sense of Habermas who postulates a power that penetrates deeply in society because, if not, there is no direction, control, initiative, or community.[31]

The relationship between state and society

There are several dimensions to a good relationship between civil society and the state. Civil society is the realm of private interests, which only become effective when they are organized in the collective sense of community, independent from the state. When they are transferred to the public arena in a democracy, they influence society and politics. It is this capacity to transform the private into the public that makes civil society so dynamic. It is a given that the boundaries between the state and society are constantly shifting; interdependence is basic.

A number of aspects of this relationship are especially important to the process of democratic transition in a foundational context. The first and most important is respect for human rights. It is a qualitative characteristic that defines a democracy in formation because of the widespread violation of human rights and even genocide committed by the state in El Salvador and Guatemala. The identity of those responsible is still unknown, although progress has been made in terms of historical clarification. But the democratic power is still not strong enough to judge and punish. It is a task that is still pending and one that, if left undone, will establish complicity between the new regime that is trying to be a democracy and the old authoritarian regime. Society demands an end to this unfinished business.

The other aspect is related to the citizenry. Citizenship implies legal recognition, the granting of a certain identity to a person as belonging to a community. But, in its active dimension, it also refers to rights and duties and to forms of political, economic, and social participation. There are many possibilities as well as an open invitation to fight for and win these rights so as to form a stronger citizenry; however, social, cultural, and ethnic differences make it more difficult. These are societies polarized by war, with many wounds and resentments left over. The guerrillas and their supporters were not accepted as citizens. The act of signing and committing to the peace achieved this recognition. The recovery of citizenship by the players in the conflict is part of the transition.

A radically negative aspect of the identity of citizens developed during the long conflict and years of repression. The dehumanization of a person is the negation of that person's identity; it is a preliminary to inflicting the worst punishment. The "disappeared person" is a non-citizen, who even when dead has no right to citizenship because of the legal and political implications. As Castro says, with the "disappeared person" a non-citizen came into being through the denial to him or her one of liberal democracy's most precious rights: habeas corpus.[32] In the new relations with the state, citizens are recovering their rights. Citizenship is respect for human rights while the state regains a monopoly on legitimate force.

The state does not only have a punitive function. When it is democratic, it has a positive role in the creation of a social order; and it has the ability to contribute to creating or guiding new political identities, of fostering citizenship. This is the challenge posed by the indigenous groups in Nicaragua and especially in Guatemala, where they constitute half the population. Upon recovering their rights, citizens are affirmed and the civilian society grows but not at the expense of the state. The expansion of the citizenry strengthens society and the state. They are not mutually exclusive or necessarily in tension.

Finally, a healthy relationship between the state and civil society requires a democratic political culture, whose emergence supports the values of respect for human rights, tolerance, and dialogue. That is to say that the new political culture must affirm the values and practices that the violence and the crisis systematically denied.

A democratic culture in this case requires moderation: the reduction of extremist demands, based on total convictions, on ideologies of rupture. It is what in game theory is known as "aversion to risk" that can be the result of a wise calculation or the wisdom of accepting the lesser evil. This is not an individual virtue but rather a collective behavior. Political moderation can be the cumulative reactive result after years of war and violence.

The political culture of the transitions requires the values of tolerance and a recognition of and respect for differences amongst citizens. Intolerance is a cultural component of authoritarianism because it presupposes a stratified universe, one that is hierarchical, patrimonial, and forced. These behaviors are fed emotionally – they are either love or hate; they do not conform to reason. There is a third component, the culture of negotiation, of dialogue. To come to an agreement is to be able to make decisions and to give in. After the parties have signed on to peace, they have had more experiences of harmony, but still others are needed in order to ensure a mutual respect on a political level or for the good of the government. To engage in dialogue is to mutually recognize one another, to accept that we are all part of the same national scenario. This means the end of the homicidal dialectic of enmity that fed atrocious forms of human rights violations.

The international momentum

Developments since the end of the crisis of war and revolution have created a dynamic of change that establishes contradictory possibilities for renovation. Of particular importance is the nature of the international situation. Central America is living in a period of rapid, multifaceted, and perhaps unprecedented change. The possibility of change runs parallel to the difficulties surrounding its success. It happens that this complexity is, apparently, the result of a clashing combination of causes and effects, of concurrent social phenomena that are only explained by periods of crisis or periods of exit from crisis.[33]

The factor that favors an understanding of these possibilities is created by the energy of the historic moment. In the actual process of global transformation, there are forces that generate change in opposing directions. One is the internationalization of the economy and the market dominance of the transnational business. Another is the reconstruction of the political system in a democratic sense. Tension is experienced, on the one hand, as an extensive involving process, which breaks down the traditional limits of the nation-state, of society, and of the region. And, on the other, the tension is also an *involving* process but an *intensive* one, that redefines locally the limits of class, ethnic groups, and community.

It is important to highlight here the involving force of the global wave of democracy that coincided, by chance, with the end of the conflicts in Central America. The international situation appeared as a legitimizing force for democracy, capable of imposing itself on the will of local players of authoritarian disposition. The end of the Cold War favored national efforts to put an end to internal wars in the same way that that conflict had earlier stirred them up, encouraged, and even directed them.[34] The wave of democracy reached the region when our "just wars" were ending.

Nowadays it is realized that democracy will be consolidated when the institutional framework promotes objectives that are legal and politically desirable, such as the end of violence, material security, and the search for social and economic equity for citizens. Most importantly, democracy is consolidated when its institutions are capable of facing – peacefully and legally – the crises that arise when these objectives cannot be achieved. We must leave behind the instrumental and reductional idea that elections are democracy or that they alone are enough to achieve it. Democracy is still being constructed in Central America. Progress has been made because the bottom had been reached. One can be optimistic even if the realization of true democracy is in the distant future.

Notes

1. This study focuses exclusively on the three countries where there was armed conflict and political crisis: El Salvador, Nicaragua, and Guatemala. For ease of presentation, however, these countries are referred to as "Central America."
2. The theory of revolution is explored in Chalmers Johnson, *Revolutionary Change* (Boston: Little Brown, 1996) and Charles Tilly, *From Mobilization to Revolution* (Reading, Mass.: Addison-Wesley, 1978).
3. A. S. Cardenal, "La guerra y los cambios en la elite dominante en el Salvador" (unpublished paper, Barcelona, 1998).
4. For the following, see, among other works, James Dunkerley, *Power in the Isthmus: A Political History of Modern Central America* (London: Verso, 1988); Joan y Sanahuja Josep Botella (ed.), *Centroamérica después de la crisis* (Barcelona: Institut de Ciencies Politiques i Sociais, 1998).
5. This region is inhabited by three ethnic groups traditionally forgotten by the central government. In their attempt to found a nation, the Sandinistas tried to incorporate them and, in doing so, committed errors that added them in part to the counterrevolutionary opposition.
6. The first junta included three outstanding civilian leaders: Guillermo Ungo; Roman Mayorga, rector of the Catholic University; and Mario Andino, a businessman. Successive crises resulted in a takeover of the government by the Christian Democrats, represented by their leader, Napoleón Duarte.
7. This was a project in three stages. The first allowed for the confiscation of property larger than five hundred hectares; and the third handed land over to peasants with smaller holdings. The second stage, which severely punished the coffee sector, was not applied.
8. The Carter administration decided to stop aid to the Guatemalan army because of the brutal human rights violations it committed. There was, however, still aid from Israel, Argentina, and other countries.
9. The dialogue began years before, but between the Commission for Reconciliation and representatives of the URNG. In Oslo in March 1990, a plan for rapprochement was drawn up that led to this meeting in Mexico.
10. In these countries, one talks about "going to the North," a generic place that is the equivalent of paradise. "The North" means Mexico and Canada and, most of all, the United States.
11. Edelberto Torres-Rivas, "Tras la violencia y el miedo, la democracia: Notas sobre el terror político en América Latina," in *Sistema* 1996; (132/33): p. 87.
12. There is an extensive literature on this topic. See, for example, C. J. Arnson (ed.), *Comparative Peace Processes in Latin America* (Stanford, Calif.: W. W. Center Press, Stanford University Press, 1999).

13. The wars in Angola, Mozambique, Cambodia, Ethiopia, Laos, and Afghanistan ended at the same time as those in Nicaragua and El Salvador, when the foreign aid to the factions was terminated. These wars were the "non-encounters" of the Cold War, the so-called "low intensity wars" or "wars of underdevelopment."

14. G. Aguilera, "Realizar un imaginario: La paz en Guatemala," in *Del autoritarismo a la paz*, (with E. Torres-Rivas (Guatemala City: FLACSO, 1998), p. 119.

15. Peter Waldman and Fernando Reinares, *Sociedades en guerra civil: Conflictos violentos de Europa y América Latina* (Barcelona: Paidos, 1999), p. 87.

16. H. Krumwiede, "Posibilidades de pacificación de las guerras civiles," in P. Waldmann and F. Reinares (eds.), *Problemas de la guerra y la paz* (Barcelona: Paidos, 1999), p. 110.

17. In the cases of Mozambique, Eritrea, Angola, Zimbabwe, Cambodia, and Ethiopia, it was first necessary to achieve peace, and democratic elections were held subsequently as a commitment that arose from the peace agreements.

18. Cristiani explicitly declared in November 1991 that the economic model was not negotiable; in Guatemala, the agreement on aspects dealing with the socio-economic arena and the agrarian situation held up the negotiations for 14 months and was finally approved with many modifications, accepted by the CACIF, the chamber of commerce of the business leaders/owners of Guatemala.

19. Carlos Vilas, *Mercados, Estados, Guerra: La experiencia centroamericana* (Mexico City: Universidad Nacional Autorroma de México, Instituto de Investigaciones Interdisciplinarios, 1994), p. 89.

20. The government's position was difficult since the army, the police force, various media, and the judiciary were in the hands of the Sandinistas.

21. There was a time when there were two constitutions in the country, one supported by the army and the other by the legislature, in which the administration of justice was paralyzed, producing total ungovernability that emanated from the top. The backdrop for this crisis and the manner in which it was settled – intervention of the creditor governments which threatened to call in the debts owing to them immediately – show the difficulties of consolidating democracy.

22. This officer founded and directed the death squads and was accused, without proof, of ordering the assassination of Archbishop Romero. Of indisputable political talent, he hastened to found the ARENA party. His premature natural death kept him from figuring more in national politics and, perhaps, in the construction of democracy.

23. D'Aubuisson founded ARENA with the members of the peasant paramilitary organization ORDEN; support was given by almost all the trade unions unified in the so-called Alianza Productiva, formed in May 1980, plus the anticommunist middle classes. ARENA displaced a military-backed party. The Partido Conciliación Nacional received financial support from the Partido Republicano and other international sources, but it was its peasant base that gave it electoral strength.

24. The biggest technical problem in the region has been the difficulty of having a system of voter registration that adequately registers eligible citizens. In El Salvador (1994) there were 2.7 million registered but only 2.3 million had their identity documents; in Nicaragua (1996) citizens voted with three different identity documents; in Guatemala (1999) about 25 per cent of those listed in the voter register could not vote because they were dead, living abroad, or unable to confirm their registration. In these three cases, any estimate of nonvoters in elections is inaccurate because it is calculated on a false basis.

25. The Christian Democrat Party and the Partido Conciliación Nacional are still today without much strength and with a history of internal fights and alliances. Cf. the original perspective of R. Zamora R., *El Salvador: Heridas que no cierran, los partidos políticos en la Postguerra* (El Salvador: Flacso, 1998).

26. These are the Movimiento de Liberación Nacional, of the extreme Right, and the Unión del Centro Nacional and Christian Democrats, both from the Center, which lost support after they left the government. In 1999 the Christian Democrats succeeded in getting a representative elected to Congress.

27. Corporativism is the answer of the elite to what it perceives as a crisis of participation and control. Attempts at inclusion are more probable when the domination of the oligarchy is beginning to erode due to pressures of early modernization or popular mobilization. A. Stepan, "La instalación de regímenes corporativos, marco analítico y análisis comparativo," in J. Lanzaro, El fin del siglo del corporativismo (Caracas: Nueva Sociedad, 1998), p. 195.

28. Joel Strong Migdal, Societies and Weak States: State-Society Relations and State Capabilities in the Third World (Princeton, N.J.: Princeton University Press, 1998).

29. David T. Mason and Dale T. Krane, "The Political Economy of Death Squads: Toward a Theory of the Impact of State-sanctioned Terror," in International Studies Quarterly 1989; 33(2): pp. 175–98.

30. It is also said that a state is weak when its resources for defending its sovereignty are inferior to those used to defend it against its own society.

31. In the countries studied here, there was never a strong state in this sense. The trade deficits are severe. The state-centered matrix Cavarozzi speaks of rightly for countries such as Mexico, Chile, Brazil or Venezuela, does not exist here.

32. J. E. Castro, "El retorno del ciudadano: Los inestables territorios de la ciudadanía en América Latina," in Perfiles Latinoamericanos June 1999; (14): p. 44.

33. Carlos Sojo, Democracia con fracturas: Gobernabilidad, reforma económica y transición en Centroamérica (San José: FLACSO-Costa Rica, 1999).

34. Thomas Reifer and Jamie Sudler, "The Interstate System," in I. Wallerstein (ed.), The Age of Transition: Trajectory of the World System, 1945–2025 (London: Zed Books, 1996).

6

Crisis and regression: Ecuador, Paraguay, Peru, and Venezuela

Heinz R. Sonntag

Introduction

During and until the end of the 1970s, the societies of the Latin American and Caribbean region were under authoritarian governments, with five exceptions: Colombia, Costa Rica, the Dominican Republic, Mexico, and Venezuela.[1] At the beginning of the twenty-first century, all countries – except Cuba – have elected governments and undergo periodical processes of legitimization through elections and thus can replace their governments by alternative ones.

The general reasons for and features of this proliferation of democracy during the 1980s (and, in the cases of Ecuador, Peru and Nicaragua, during the last years of the 1970s) are explored in other contributions to this volume. But like any general rule, the democratization of Latin American and Caribbean political systems and states during the last two decades of the twentieth century has its exceptions. The objective of this essay is to analyse both the common and the individual characteristics of the cases whose democracies are experiencing deep crises and regressions.

These cases are Ecuador, Paraguay, Peru, and Venezuela. Each is as different from the others as each society of the region is with respect to the rest – yet they share certain common patterns.[2] These differences and similarities make comparative analysis in Latin America and the Caribbean so attractive and enriching: the existence of the differences makes it difficult, though not impossible, to fall into the trap of overall generalizations that distort reality, and the similarities, interpreted with historical sensitivity, allows one to see both the forest and the trees.

This essay deals, first of all, with some common characteristics of the evolution of these societies (and the others in the region) during the last fifty years. A synthetic analysis of each of the four cases and a mostly implicit comparison between them will then follow. Finally, some preliminary conclusions will be suggested.

Zenith and fall of developmentalism and of the state of national-popular compromise: Authoritarianism and redemocratization

During the late 1940s, 1950s, and 1960s and part of the 1970s nearly all Latin American and Caribbean countries experienced what I have called the "euphoria of development."[3] The growth rates of their economies were among the highest of the capitalist world-system, and the economies became increasingly diversified, with important second (industrial) sectors and a rapidly growing third (service) sector. The structures of social classes and sectors changed radically; segments emerged that had practically not existed at the end of the 1930s, unless in embryonic form. Extreme poverty diminished due to policies of income redistribution, although the inequality of income distribution was not really modified. The political systems and forms of government adopted in most societies became more or less democratic. Even socioculturally, the societies seemed to be on the path of modernization, as they overcame the division between the traditional and the modern.[4] Only a few countries were still trapped in patrimonial dictatorships and thus excluded from these processes, particularly Haiti, Nicaragua, and Paraguay.

This modernization occurred against the background and in the context of the expansion of the capitalist world-system after World War II and implied the dialectic of internal and external factors that the dependency approach has insisted on.[5] However, it was based on conscious internal efforts of achieving development. It was inspired by the doctrine of *developmentalism* of the United Nations Economic Commission for Latin America and the Caribbean (ECLA).[6] This doctrine involved not only a set of economic policies but also, especially from its reformulation at the beginning of the 1960s on,[7] the design and execution of social policies and an attempt at political and democratic institution building.[8]

Developmentalism met the need of emerging social classes and sectors to have an ideological orientation for their collective practices. This was important insofar as they laid claim to a new hegemony, replacing that of the classes which had sustained the oligarchic-liberal republics since independence. In fact, one of developmentalism's many important achievements was the consolidation of the social classes and sectors that capitalist development had generated. The local bourgeoisies and middle sectors, the urban proletarians, and even some segments of the peasantry developed a consciousness of their roles. This made them collective actors which adopted some form of developmentalism as their societal project. In one way or another, they built coalitions or sealed pacts to make their projects viable. No sector gave up its particular interests, but they all found a common denominator of their different interests in the national development that ECLA's doctrine implied.

From this, a sort of democratic stability developed, in most societies for the first time in a fairly long period. For some years, frequently even decades, many analysts saw the pendulum swing from authoritarianism to democracy, with the old dilemma between a national community and a stable political system overcome. Developmentalism became the most influential ideology of development that had ever existed, and due in part to its links with the mainstream economics and social sciences of the industrialized countries, it was successful in changing the physiognomy of the societies of the region in a relatively short period of time. Although this did occur in a favorable economic context, the efforts of the groups involved in it were no less significant.

However, development entered into crisis. On the one hand, this was due to failures in the design and the application of policies.[9] On the other hand, these policies began to generate contradictions that slowly undermined the basis of the commitment to national development between the different classes and sectors involved.[10] This happened in some countries relatively early, such as Brazil in 1964; in others, such as Peru and Panama, in the late 1960s; in Ecuador, Chile, and Uruguay at the beginning of the 1970s; in Argentina in 1976;[11] and in several Central American countries around the same time.[12]

The exact moment of the beginning of the crisis depended on the socio-historical trajectory of each society. It was, for example, not accidental that the first military-authoritarian rupture of the national-popular state occurred in Brazil, since it was the society that had advanced most in the direction of capitalist modernization and of democratic development in the previous decades, and even earlier.[13] In all cases, these crises implied an interruption of the life of national communities and of political systems – conceived in this volume as "political societies."

Two factors in the socio-historical trajectory of each society played a major role in the determination of the moment of crisis and, more generally, in the subsequent socio-economic and particularly socio-political evolution of the societies. First was the extent to which the collective actors, particularly the hegemonic ones, had succeeded, previously to the crisis, in building politico-institutional frameworks that could guarantee an administrative continuity of the system of decision-making, independently of the form of the political regime. The negotiation of political representation was important in this process.[14] The second factor, strongly influenced by the first one, was the degree to which the emergent classes had had the opportunity to develop socio-political identities, in the sense of identification and organization of their interests, that could assure them sufficiently flexible margins of maneuver to establish the pacts they needed to foster the modernization they desired – to establish their own hegemony over the whole society. In other words, "political society" needs a tradition: it must be rooted in historical variables that can give it the bases for its development and enhancement, especially after periods of disruption.

These factors had a major impact on the reconstruction and fortifying of national communities and democratic political systems in nearly all Latin American societies and in its relative success as well as in its failures. The bureaucratic-authoritarian regimes (and their most modern form: the technocratic-authoritarian ones) were seen by some scholars and other analysts as the inevitable result of the capitalist development of Latin American societies, be it because of their dependent character, be it because of the structural incapacity of states to "manage democratically" the contradictions which resulted from the previous modernization. There were clear differences among the authoritarian systems, in terms of economic and social policies and even the role of the state. The Brazilian military dictatorship, for example, cannot easily be compared with the Peruvian one, nor are the Chilean, Argentine, or Uruguayan experiences by any means similar to those of Panama and Ecuador.

The same can be said for the processes of redemocratization in the late 1970s and 1980s. They coincided with one of the most severe economic crises that affected the societies of the region in their entire history. At the same time the political classes of the surviving democracies of Colombia, Costa Rica, the Dominican Republic, Venezuela, and Mexico began attempts to strengthen their political systems with a movement toward state reform. The coincidence with the economic crisis makes it a difficult task to interpret the relative success of the redemocratization, since historically an economic crisis has generally provoked a trend toward authoritarian regimes. The timing of the process of state reform in the surviving democracies was partially due to the fact that this reform was an integral part of the structural reforms "suggested" to the governments by the international financial organizations. But the combination of state reform with the strengthening of democracy was a result of internal social and socio-political trajectories.

As the other essays in this book suggest, the redemocratization process has seen a great deal of success in some cases, in spite of the potentially disruptive social and political consequences of the application of the adjustment policies and neo-liberalism. Nevertheless, in Ecuador, Paraguay, Peru, and Venezuela, redemocratization or reform of state and democracy failed.

The failures of democracy: Regressions and crises

In Ecuador and Peru it was the redemocratization process itself that failed because both societies had already overcome authoritarian regimes. In Paraguay, it is the democratization process itself that is at stake. And in Venezuela, the attempt at fostering democratic and state reforms not only failed but led to a profound deterioration during a period of transition which has lasted seven years and whose definite outcome is unclear. This essay will present the most important issues in each of these countries and discuss some common challenges that result from the regressions and crises for all Latin American and Caribbean societies.

Ecuador

Ecuador had a population of 12 million people in 1997, more or less equally divided between the coast (with its capital Guayaquil) and the sierra (with its capital, also the national capital, Quito, located in the heights of the Andean mountain range), and 80 per cent of whom were Native Ecuadorians and mestizos.[15]

Its political history as an independent republic began in 1809, when a first revolt against Spain took place. In 1822, Antonio José de Sucre, one of the most important collaborators of Simón Bolívar, won the final battle and incorporated the country as the "Department of the South" into the Republic of Gran Colombia (with Venezuela and Colombia, including what in 1903 became Panama). In 1830, after the breakdown of Gran Colombia, Ecuador became independent. The Venezuelan general Juan José Flores, a hero of the wars of independence, became the country's first president. But he had to stand against an upheaval of the "liberals" of the coast. The rest of the nineteenth century and the first years of the twentieth century were marked by the "conservative" dictatorships of Flores and Gabriel Garcia Moreno, and the "liberal" regimes under the leadership of Eloy Alfaro, during whose second term (1907–11) a more liberal constitution was approved.

During this period of relatively significant political instability, a conflict was present that permeated the entire political life of the country and has continued ever since: the conflict between the coast and the sierra. The ideological fronts were and continue to change, suggesting that the conflict is somewhat deeper than a class conflict or an ideological antagonism.

It is a socio-cultural phenomenon, penetrating deeply into the everyday life of Ecuadorian society, that divides the Ecuadorians into two different and often opposed factions. Some scholars have seen in this differentiation the reason that the identities of collective actors were not forged by their belonging to social classes and sectors but rather by their regional origin. This pattern has been a significant obstacle to the process of institution building and the establishment of a political society.

From the mid-1930s until the beginning of the 1970s, José Maria Velasco Ibarra was a prevailing figure of Ecuadorian socio-political evolution. He was the country's president five times, in 1934–35, 1944–47, 1952–56, 1960–61, and 1968–72. His only complete period as elected president was between 1952 and 1956; the other tenures were interrupted by military coups d'état. In 1944, he was designated by the armed forces to replace the liberal president Carlos Alberto Arroyo del Rio; in 1934, 1952, 1960, and 1968 he won the presidential elections. Originally a conservative, he later became a populist leader, in the sense of basing his electoral campaigns, his programs, and his policies on the support of changing political groups and parties. As with populists in other Latin American and Caribbean countries at various times in the twentieth century, his main objective was to obtain and then to maintain power to satisfy the interests and demands of his clientele. Sometimes, this made a continuous modernization process possible; at other times it contributed to the creation of the state of national-popular commitment.[16] In Velasco's case, the changing character of his political alliances impeded steady decision-making within the framework of a societal consensus about what kind of social order was to be aimed at, a problem that was worsened by the volatile quality of the ideological-political identities of the main collective actors and the consequent weak structure of the political parties.

The instability of the political system had its counterweight in the repeated interventions of the armed forces, which acted, as in other countries, as the institutionalized arbiter in disputes within the state or over its form of government. From 1945 onwards, there were direct military interventions in 1947 (deposing Velasco), in 1963 (overthrowing President Carlos Arosemena Monroy) and in 1972 (deposing Velasco once more) and indirect but open ones in 1948, 1961, 1987, 1999, and 2000, not to speak of the periods of emergency because of the border dispute with Peru in 1950, 1981, and 1995, when the dispute resulted in open fighting. This active role of the Ecuadorian military in politics highlights its institutional cohesion and strength, in comparison with other parts of the state (executive, legislative, and judiciary branches, and the state bureaucracy) and the elements of its political system (political parties and corporate organizations).

The most recent openly military regimes were those of General Guillermo Rodríguez Lara (1972–76) and Admiral Alfredo Poveda Burbano (1976–78). This was a "reformist" government, comparable to the Peruvian Revolutionary Government of the Armed Forces. It tried to govern on the basis of a five-year plan that stressed agriculture (including an agrarian reform), housing, and industry. In many senses, it was the most developmentalist of the Ecuadorian governments after World War II, seeking to implement a deliberate set of social policies.[17] It was helped by the fact that Ecuador was an oil exporter from August 1972 on, so that oil revenues provided the economy with foreign currency and considerable investment funds.

The transition to democracy was a negotiated one. In 1978, the military leaders began to enter into deals with politicians on a new constitution that was approved later the same year. In April 1979, Jaime Roldós Aguilera, a "populist," was elected president, and he understood his task as reinforcing democracy. After he died in a plane crash in March 1981, the Christian Democrat vice-president Osvaldo Hurtado continued his task. In May 1984, León Febres Cordero, a "conservative" of the coast region, won the presidency. His administration was constitutionally dubious and legally often arbitrary, particularly in dealing with the numerous protests against his government's measures. He had to put down various military rebellions, including one whose leaders seized him and beat him in front of TV cameras.

In August 1988, Rodrigo Borja Cevallos, the longtime leader of the Democratic Left, took over the presidency, having been elected in a ballot in May against Febres Cordero's candidate.[18] Borja Cevallos's first political measures sought to calm down a society still troubled by the experience of the previous government. His efforts to move economic and social policies away from the adjustment policies towards a more social democratic line did not succeed, because of the pressures of the external debt and the (traditional) feebleness of the actors (social classes, sectors, and groups) on whose organizations such a shift heavily depended. It is worthwhile to remember that under this government a rebellion of the Native Ecuadorians[19] succeeded in achieving constitutional recognition as "nationalities." This was perhaps the only real success of the redemocratization in Ecuador, signalized by the fact that in the 1996 election, the political movements of the Native Ecuadorians won a third of the seats in the National Assembly.

In August 1992, Sixto Durán Ballén, a conservative politician, took over. His government was bound to economic and social adjustment policies. Its ideologue and main spokesman, Vice-President Alberto Dahik, had to flee to Costa Rica because the Supreme Court found him guilty of embezzlement. In 1995, Durán Ballén lost a referendum that proposed a series of constitutional reforms and the privatization of the health and social security systems.

Looking back to the four governments that followed the transition to democracy in 1978 (Roldós-Hurtado, Febres Cordero, Borja, and Durán), it is evident that all of them failed to attack the two basic problems of the Ecuadorian state and its democratic regime. First, the volatility of the political identities of the collective actors, manifested in the erratic electoral behavior of voters and in a poorly organized and structured party system, made a continuous "rational" political life practically impossible. Second, the weakness of state institutions (the executive, legislative, and judiciary, as well as the bureaucracy) did not allow a structured decision-making based on a shared national consensus. In addition, the problem of the country's division between the coastal region and the Andean sierra was not overcome – in fact it became even more profound, since the regional origin of the presidential candidates was used as an important rallying cry in election campaigns. The deficiencies of Ecuador's political society, so evident in the period up to World War II and in the socio-political evolution after it, could not be repaired with the return to democracy, and the integration of the Native Ecuadorians made the division in the political society still deeper (although this may change).

The deficient governability and weak governance of Ecuadorian society have become even more evident with the governments that have followed. In July 1996, Abdalá Bucarám became president, a member of a coast family and political clan that had played an important role in Guayaquil for many years. Although he received massive support from the poor citizens during the campaign because of his attacks on the adjustment policies, his measures to fight inflation and budget deficits, his nepotism and the corruption of officials appointed by him to important functions made him widely unpopular within eight months. In February 1997, the Congress, its building surrounded by a crowd of many thousands and after a general strike in which two million people had participated, voted to remove Bucarám for "mental incapacity." The president of the Congress, Fabian Alarcón, took charge and tried, without much success, to make a business-as-usual government.

In 1999, Jamil Mahuad, a Christian Democrat of the party of Osvaldo Hurtado, was elected president. He did not succeed in overcoming the problems confronted by Ecuadorian society. On the contrary, lacking a majority in the Parliament, he was maneuvering just like the previous governments, knowing that the survival of the democratic system depends on the goodwill of the armed forces. In his despair over the apparently unstoppable inflation, he presented the idea of the adoption of the U.S. dollar in place of the national currency as a solution.

This led to a crisis in January 2000. Native Ecuadorians, with the support of other social sectors and groups, besieged the Congress building for several days, demanding the resignation of Mahuad. A group of middle-ranking army and police officers joined the protest movement and withdrew their troops from the presidential palace. A junta was formed, composed of the leader-spokesman of the Native Ecuadorians, an army colonel, and a former judge of the Supreme Court. Mahuad initially enjoyed the support of the higher officers, but this was withdrawn in the face of the increasing number of middle-ranking officers who refused obedience. So, the minister of defense, an active Army general, first entered the junta and later, impelled by the reaction of the U.S. and Latin American governments, convinced the vice-president, Gustavo Noboa Bejarano, to take over.

We can doubt whether this episode means the end of the crisis of democracy in Ecuador, in spite of Noboa's ability to manage a critical situation in the National Assembly and his capacity to impose the dollarization of the economy. On the other hand, the failure of this measure would intensify the conflicts of Ecuadorian society. In addition, it can be supposed that the political movement of the Native Ecuadorians will reappear in the daily political fight, after a period of "tactical withdrawal." It is probable that the rebuilding of democracy of a different type will have this movement as its main protagonist and the Native Ecuadorians as its decisive actors, also possibly leading to the strengthening of civil society.

Paraguay

One of the most astonishing facts of the late 1980s, at least for those not familiar with internal political developments in Paraguay, was the military coup of General Andrés Rodríguez in February 1989 against General Alfredo Stroessner, eight times "re-elected" president of Paraguay after July 1954.[20] It was astonishing not only because General Rodriguez had been Stroessner's loyal collaborator (and army chief) for many years and was even his son-in-law, but particularly because Latin American and extraregional scholars and political analysts, possibly including those of the CIA, had considered this dictatorship as a regime that would only die with its leader. The astonishment was all the greater when Rodríguez allowed direct, general, and secret elections (relatively "clean," according to the observers of the OAS), with an opposition candidate. Some of the intellectuals and politicians, many of whom returned to the country after long years of exile, knew that they were now confronted with an unusual challenge: the construction, for the first time in the socio-political evolution of their country, of a political society.

Paraguay has perhaps the most homogeneous population of all Latin

American and Caribbean countries: 95 per cent of its 5.15 million people (estimated on the basis of the 1992 census) are mestizos, and 47 per cent is rural. The small colonies of immigrants (of origins ranging from Spanish to Japanese and Canadian) play a significant role in economic life but not in politics, and the German immigrants are known because of Stroessner's "love for Bavaria" and the selection of his country as a refuge by former Nazi hierarchs.

Paraguay had a rather peculiar colonial history. It was the land of the Jesuit missions, the *reducciónes*. They began around 1610 and were communities in which Native Americans, converted to Catholicism and educated by the Jesuits, lived more or less according to their original lifestyles. They took advantage of the nearly complete freedom the civil and ecclesiastic authorities had granted them. It was a fascinating social experiment, particularly because of the respect shown toward the Native Americans. This may well have been the only such experiment in the entire colonial history of Spanish- and Portuguese-speaking South America and the Caribbean. It ended when the Jesuits were expelled from Spanish America in 1767, and the missions were deserted.

Pushed by the Creole economic elite,[21] Paraguay declared its independence in May 1811, a year later than its fellow colonies Argentina and Uruguay. Between 1814 and 1840, president-dictator Gaspar Rodríguez Francia applied a policy of national isolation, so not to fall into the hands of the stronger Argentina. He also tried to apply embryonic state policies of national development, by fostering some industries, trying to orient agriculture toward production for the internal market, and building strong state institutions. His nephew, Carlos Antonio López, president-dictator between 1844 and 1862, reversed this policy, encouraged international commerce, and built a railroad, whilst continuing to strengthen state institutions.

In 1865, Carlos's son, Francisco Solano López, led Paraguay into a war against an alliance of Argentina, Brazil, and Uruguay, which were first encouraged and later supported by the British. The war ended in 1870 in disaster: half of the population killed, the economy destroyed, agricultural activity at a standstill, heavy territorial losses, and Brazilian occupation (until 1876). The consequences were manifest for many decades, even in the state and its forms of regime, because no president was able to serve a full term between 1870 and 1912. This made it impossible to continue and reinforce institution building and impeded the development of political identities. A military-political elite usurped whatever had existed by way of a national community, appealing to the collective memory of the first 50 years of independence and even of the *reduccines* during more than 150 years of colonial history.

The period between the beginning of World War I and the Chaco War of 1932–38 with Bolivia was one of recovery and relative prosperity. After the war, which Paraguay won, a new constitution was adopted, the government was highly centralized, and the state was given the power to regulate economic activities. Notwithstanding these elements of modernization, democracy had little chance. The presidents were dictators, and the main political party, the Partido Colorado, was little more than the political organization of different factions of the armed forces, whose interests happened to coincide with those of the landowners and the small commercial bourgeoisie.

In May 1954 the president-dictator Federico Chávez was deposed by an army-police junta headed by General Alfredo Stroessner, commander in chief of the army and head of the Partido Colorado, who defeated the attempts of progressive forces (mainly younger officers and intellectuals) to seize power. The elections of July 1954 confirmed Stroessner's presidency, as did a plebiscite in 1958, and elections in 1963, 1968 (after the Constitution had been amended to allow Stroessner's re-election), 1973, 1978, 1983, and 1988.

Following Stroessner, General Rodríguez – also Stroessner's heir as the head of the Partido Colorado – won the elections and inaugurated the privatization of state-owned enterprises, but without overcoming the economic recession. There were few political reforms, except an opening for the opposition parties. Another Partido Colorado man, the entrepreneur Juan Carlos Wasmosy, won the 1993 elections, but with a considerable increase of votes for the opposition. He led his country in 1995 to participate in the creation of the Southern Cone Common Market (MERCOSUR).

In 1996, Wasmosy got involved in a conflict with the commander in chief of the army, General Lino Oviedo. In a kind of "dry coup," Oviedo agreed to resign only if he were appointed defence minister and thus in charge of the military police and the armed forces budget. Wasmosy accepted, fearing the possibility of a new military coup. But he reversed his decision because of protests by many citizens – perhaps the first change in a Paraguayan government's decision produced by the resistance of the embryonic political society. Oviedo announced his candidacy for the presidency in the 1998 election, but was arrested by Wasmosy's order for his role in the coup attempt and condemned to ten years in prison by a military tribunal. The Partido Colorado's candidate, Raúl Cubas Grau, originally Oviedo's running mate, won the election in May 1998. He pardoned Oviedo, against a ruling of the Supreme Court and in spite of intense protests by many citizens and even some military officers and segments of the government party.

The last events of the century in Paraguay included the murder in 1999 of the vice-president, in which the president and Oviedo are presumably involved. Oviedo escaped to Argentina, where President Carlos Saúl Menem granted him asylum, until the new government of President Fernando de la Rua cancelled it in June 2000. When Oviedo sought asylum in Brazil, the federal government put him in jail until the Supreme Court took a decision on Paraguay's demand for his extradition. Cubas Grau is also an exile in Brazil since he was obliged to resign the presidency, when evidence came to light that he at least knew of plans for the murder of the vice-president. Luis González Machi, the head of the Parliament, became the new president. At the helm of the country he was simultaneously trying to confront a deep economic crisis and the challenges of the construction of a viable democratic political system. This task is obstructed by the constraints of adjustment policies, neo-liberal ideological offensives, and "globalization," as well as the mobilization of workers' unions against their consequences.

It is evident that, under these circumstances, the process of building a national political community is extremely complicated. The transition to democracy is traumatic because there are almost no historical roots for a political system stabilized by anything other than autocratic-military institutions. In turn, the construction of social identities for the collective actors suffers from the consequences of the structural and systemic instability.

Peru

Peru has one of the highest proportions of Native Americans of any country in the region: about 47 per cent, descendants of the Incas, a warlike tribe that created one of the most impressive civilizations in pre-Columbian America. Around 1500, the empire extended from the south of contemporary Colombia to the north of today's Chile. As a civilization it was in many aspects superior to that of the conquering Spaniards,[22] except in its military technology and organization. So colonial domination in Peru became a Gramscian one early on, characterized by the use of ideological-religious mechanisms by the conquerors with hegemonic purposes, as in New Spain in the territories of the Aztec and Maya empires and civilizations. In both areas hegemony was accompanied by extreme physical repression and the usual economic exploitation, not only through the robbery of precious metals but also by the use of the indigenous population as a slave labor force. Native Americans were systematically used as intermediaries between the central colonial administration and the local communities of indigenous populations. Even so, there were numerous rebellions in the viceroyalty of New Granada, the most famous being that of Tupac Amaru in 1780–81.

As in all colonies of the Spanish crown, the rich Creole families (of *hacendados* and merchants) led the movements for independence. On the one hand, they wanted free trade; on the other, they were inspired by the ideas of independence of the United States and the French Revolution. They perceived independence as liberation from the monopolistic restrictions Spain had imposed on the export of their goods overseas and even to other parts of the region, at least till the second half of the eighteenth century, but also as a kind of "national liberation" *avant la lettre*. So they financed the armies that defeated the Spaniards in a long and bloody war. Most of these armies' generals were also descendants of the Creole oligarchy.

Two Latin American heroes of the wars forged the independence of Peru: the Argentine José de San Martín, liberator of Chile, and the Venezuelan Simón Bolívar. The first occupied Lima and declared independence, together with the local forces, on 28 July 1821. The second guaranteed it with his victories in the battles of Junin (6 August 1824) and Ayacucho (9 December 1824).

After Bolívar's departure for the north – in 1826 he made his way to Gran Colombia – the first 20 years of independent political life were chaotic. Successive military caudillos, all of them former generals of Bolívar, seized the power of the (weak) central state. Neither they nor the Creoles had any specific concept of a political order that they wanted to build, let alone a social one.[23] This only began to crystallize under the presidencies of Ramón Castilla (1845–51 and 1855–62): a liberal constitution was adopted in 1860, slavery was abolished, and railroads and other infrastructural facilities were constructed. The economy became more integrated into the world system with the beginning of the exploitation of guano and nitrate resources. However, two wars – one won against Spain between 1864 and 1866 and one lost to Chile between 1879 and 1883 – meant severe economic regression and more than 20 years of dictatorial domination. In contrast to Ecuador and Paraguay, however, the local economically leading class acquired a self-consciousness that made it independent from the state. Nevertheless, it took advantage of its relationship with the armed forces, gaining through this "game" a strong influence over the military's policies.

Finally, in 1908, President Augusto Leguía y Salcedo instituted economic reform by adopting business methods "imported" from the developed countries, particularly from the United States and Britain, and by establishing long-lasting contacts with representatives of the international financial and business community. Between 1919, when he came to power for the second time by means of a military coup, and 1930, when he was overthrown by a new coup, he introduced modernizing reforms in the state machinery and continued the construction of the material infrastructure for the economy.

It is worthwhile to remember that exiled Peruvian intellectuals under the leadership of Victor Raúl Haya de la Torre founded in 1924 the APRA (Alianza Popular Revolucionaria Americana). Although the movement was immediately banned by Leguía's government, it became the most influential political party in the country until the elections of 1990, in spite of the permanent repression it suffered under successive governments in the following years and decades. It was the first of the so-called populist parties in Latin America, a multiclass party whose main ideological ingredients were anti-imperialism and the priority given to state policies for economic and social development. Organizationally, it emphasized a strong vertical hierarchy with eventually one leader at its top. Politically, it showed a high degree of flexibility in adapting to changing political situations.[24]

The foundation of the APRA was also the culmination of the discussion between two of the most important political theoreticians, certainly of Peru but also of Latin America and the Caribbean: Haya de la Torre and José Carlos Mariátegui. Haya choose the way of reformist pragmatism. Mariátegui was the first Marxist thinker who dared challenge the credo of Lenin and the Comintern on behalf of the "colonial and semi-colonial countries." He emphasized the original character of Latin American socialist revolution in the context of the world revolution.[25]

The 1930s and 1940s were decades of political unrest and economic advance. Some president-dictators, such as like Oscar R. Benavides, were particularly harsh in the exercise of power, and other (elected) presidents like Manuel Prado and especially Luis Bustamante y Rivero introduced liberal reforms, frequently under pressure from the APRA: it was a typical pendulum movement between authoritarianism and democracy.

During the 1950s, the pendulum continued to swing under dictator-president Manuel Odría and elected president Manuel Prado, although their governments maintained developmentalist economic policies with considerable success. 1968 was one of Peru's most chaotic years: presidential elections, denial of their results by the armed forces, quarrels among different factions within them, the substitution of one dictator by another, a call for new elections, and a civilian president's takeover as the winner (Fernando Belaúnde Terry). His was an especially incompetent government. Its numerous faults and failures increased inflation, causing devaluation of the currency and slowing the industrialization programme. In addition, in August 1968 Belaúnde "settled" a dispute with Standard Oil of New Jersey over claims of one of the company's branches in a way that not only inspired the opposition of nearly all sectors of Peruvian society but also led to the resignation of the Cabinet. Under these circumstances, on 3 October, a military junta under General Juan Velasco Alvarado, head of the Joint Chiefs of Staff, took power in a bloodless coup, silently approved by the majority of the Peruvian people (with the exception of and against the resistance of the political parties, particularly the APRA). The officers who headed the coup designed the Plan Inca. It was strongly inspired by reformists, civilian and military, of quite different ideological backgrounds – from an ex-leader of the guerrilla Movimiento de Izquierda Revolucionaria (Movement of the Revolutionary Left) Hector Béjar, to intellectuals formerly identified with the APRA, like the anthropologist Carlos Delgado. These reformists had been teachers of the officers at the Military Academy, more a "subversive" think-tank of the armed forces than a mere military school.

The "Gobierno revolucionario de las Fuerzas Armadas" (Revolutionary Government of the Armed Forces) immediately revoked the agreement regarding the oilfields and expropriated the assets of Standard Oil. A series of additional reforms were initiated, all of them based on a radical interpretation of ECLA's developmentalism: agrarian reform, including nationalization of foreign-owned land; nationalization of the fishing industry; price controls on goods and services; customs protection for local industry; and state investment in industrial diversification. At the same time, social policies were applied and a broad social mobilization set in motion, centered on a new institution called SINAMOS – Sistema nacional de movilización social (National System of Social Mobilization).

The initial popular support for the government withered away when the economic situation became more and more difficult. Dictator-president Velasco Alvarado fell ill, and following some weeks of strikes and demonstrations, he was deposed on 30 August 1975 and died shortly thereafter. He was replaced by General Francisco Morales Bermúdez, the most moderate of the high officers originally involved in the coup.[26] He began negotiations with the civilian politicians and their organizations and promised a return to democracy within five years, but many of the economic and social reforms of the Velasco era were halted or reversed.

During this period, a Maoist guerrilla movement, Sendero Luminoso (Shining Path), became increasingly active and important. Born in the late seventies in the south of the country, particularly in the University of Ayacucho – its leader Abimael Guzmán, "Chairman Gonzalo," had been a philosophy teacher there – it extended throughout Peru, but above all in the Andean mountains. Its attacks against villages and small towns were often highly cruel and bloody, and the armed forces reacted with widespread and undifferentiated repression.

In July 1985, the first APRA president in the history of the country took charge: Alan García Pérez. His campaign was a populist one, with promises to improve the material conditions of the Peruvians, to stop the violence, and to overcome the economic decline, and not to pay more than 10 per cent of the state's income from exports to service the external debt. But Garcia Pérez could hardly accomplish his program – his initially good image became tarnished, corruption grew, the economic and political situation became worse and worse, the 10 per cent limit for the payment of the external debt was never really respected, the violence increased considerably, and inflation soared.

In the 1990 presidential elections, Alberto Fujimori, an agricultural economist who had been rector of a private agricultural university, defeated Mario Vargas Llosa, the famous novelist and candidate of the Right with a clearly neo-liberal program. Fujimori's promises were vague, except for his undertaking to stop the violence. During his first eighteen months, he began to apply adjustment policies and, as it seems from information that has recently come to light,[27] to build up the intelligence and secret services he needed for what he planned. His main adviser, Vladimiro Montesinos, became a kind of Rasputin of the regime. In April 1992, a little more than one year after taking over, alleging that the country had become "ungovernable," he dissolved the Congress, suspended the Constitution, sent home the judges of the Supreme Court and other judicial bodies, and took full control of the state, obviously with the approval of the armed forces. He then imposed a drastic program of adjustment policies, reduced inflation, and had impressive victories in the fight with Sendero Luminoso (whose *lider maximo* Guzmán was captured in September). The parties and groups that supported Fujimori – the leftist ones had already withdrawn their backing – won a solid majority in the November legislative election. In October 1993 a new constitution was proclaimed. It increased presidential power and diminished the Parliament's control functions. In fact, it was the legal cover for a total restructuring of Peruvian society, its political system, and its state.[28]

In 1995, Fujimori won a second term with an overwhelming majority, obviously because of his successes on the economic front (where record growth rates were reached and inflation was eventually eliminated), against the guerrillas, and in re-establishing "external confidence" in the country, as well as in giving assistance to the poor. All of this was achieved against a background of scandals; incredible concessions to the military – recall the amnesty in June 1995 for all human rights abuses committed by military and police forces between 1980 and 1995; electoral frauds – recall the "loss" of millions of votes in the 1995 legislative elections; widespread corruption of Fujimori's immediate entourage – including an annual salary of US$600,000 for Vladimiro Montesinos; and the eventual destruction of society – given the way in which Fujimori won control over the most significant mass media. None of these "episodes" – of which only a small number has been mentioned – really damaged Fujimori's system and he continued to enjoy high popularity.

During the year 2000, Fujimori once more ran for president, although his own constitution allowed only one re-election. The Supreme Court decided that his first term had begun after the approval of the new Constitution in 1992, and the three judges who dissented were dismissed. As in previous elections, Fujimori discredited his opponents by unscrupulous use of the mass media, deceptive ads, and the political mobilization of the poor and "marginalized" urban sectors, particularly against Alejandro Toledo, an economist of indigenous origin who had quickly climbed in the polls. In the first round, Fujimori remained 0.14 per cent short of the necessary 50 per cent. For the second ballot, Toledo decided not to run, although legally he could not withdraw his name. Fujimori won with somewhat more than 55 per cent of the vote, and his victory was recognized some days later by the military commands. The increased and much more combative opposition tried to impede his "illegal and illegitimate" inauguration ceremony on 28 July, but its peaceful demonstrations were transformed by probable agents provocateurs, probably of Montesinos's secret service, into violent confrontations with the police and acts of vandalism in the center of Lima. In August, Fujimori began his third tenure with a kind of business-as-usual attitude.[29]

Thereafter, the events were somewhat surprising.[30] In mid-September 2000 a videotape was shown by one of the few independent television channels that had survived, showing Montesinos giving an opposition parliamentary representative a bribe of fifteen thousand dollars to switch to the government party. The date shown on the recording was 4 May, that is, this happened even before the run-off. The scandal was enormous, indeed disproportionate: Peruvian political circles knew for sure that similar things had happened earlier, conscious as they were of the perverse network between politicians loyal to Fujimori, the secret service under Montesinos, the high military command, and a mafia of more or less obscure businessmen, drug traffickers, and even arms merchants. Two days after the release of the video, Fujimori announced his intention to dissolve the secret service, and called new elections for president, in which he would not be a candidate, so as to allow the inauguration of a new head of state on 28 July 2001. He did not involve Montesinos, who flew in the meantime to Panama, where he waited three weeks for a decision on his demand for political asylum, supported by the secretary-general of the OAS, the presidents of several Latin American and Caribbean countries, and the U.S. government. Fujimori travelled to the United States and got both the OAS's and the State Department's approval for his plans. Shortly after his return, Montesinos came back as well, and went underground. In a nationwide televised search, Fujimori (heading a team of high-ranking army and police officers) tried to find him, without any success.

Throughout these events negotiations were being conducted between the government and the opposition, supervised by the OAS. They were difficult because it seemed on the face of it that the whole political system and the state structure created by Fujimori, Montesinos, and the military command had to be destroyed before a new democratic beginning became possible. In addition, there was growing uncertainty about what Fujimori really planned, which was fostered by himself with his announcement of his possible candidacy in the elections of 2006. Thus the initial euphoria of the opposition after Fujimori's original election announcement withered away, and confrontation became more frequent than eventual agreement in the negotiations. In addition, the opposition succeeded in changing the Parliament's president, helped by the votes of members who had deserted the Fujimori group.

Fujimori left the country, ostensibly to attend the summit of the Asian countries in Brunei. When the summit was over, he stayed in Japan and sent a fax with his resignation from the presidency. But the Parliament did not accept, deposing him because of "moral incapacity" to be president. Vicente Paniagua, the speaker of the Parliament, a moderate politician without any connection to the regime, was designated president, and he took the first steps toward cleaning up the mess: he dismissed a dozen high military officers appointed under Fujimori (putting some in jail); established a commission for the investigation of human and political rights violations; dissolved the different secret and information services; and tried to reestablish political rules of legality and morality so as to make a "new beginning." In April 2001, new elections were held. Alejandro Toledo and, surprisingly, Alan García won the first round and Toledo finally gained the presidency by a very slim margin. Whether this apparent normalization is sufficient remains to be seen, particularly because Toledo's economic program is quite similar to Fujimori's and some time is needed for the mafia-like net of the previous ten years to be broken up – a process in which Montesinos, captured in Venezuela and handed over to the Peruvian government, could play a role.

An important task of all social and political collective actors and their organizations will be the constitution of a national community, in the sense that the particular interests of economic and social groups and classes become subject to the general interest of the nation. This is a major challenge. The collective identities of social actors, except the dominant segments, had never reached a stage of class and political consciousness capable of allowing them to pursue what could be called a common destiny, so that the corresponding party system remained relatively weak, except for APRA. The state bureaucracy never won sufficient autonomy to defend itself against abuses by dictators and "democratically legitimized" presidents. As in Ecuador, the armed forces are the only institution that is strong enough to defend its own interests, and hence its role as a "reformist" or "reactionary" force within the ups and downs of Peruvian politics. It is still problematic to characterize the military generally as "the armed branch of the dominant class," as the traditional Left still tends to do, yet there has never been any doubt about their position in favour of Fujimori as a part of the perverse network he created.

Mariátegui's dream of a nation whose base was the Native Americans – the Incas – and their forms of organization has not become reality until now, and Haya de la Torre's desire for Western-style modernization with a social democratic profile has collapsed in many truncated modernizations that never reached modernity as such. As in Ecuador, it can be supposed that the political movement of the Native Peruvians will appear in the daily political struggle, as soon as the conditions imposed on them by the Fujimori government are abolished. If their agenda is not addressed, and if they are capable of constructing their own political movement, it is not impossible that the rebuilding of society, and thus democracy, of a different kind could have such a movement as its main protagonist and the Native Peruvians as its decisive actors.[31]

Venezuela

The regressions and crises of democracy in Venezuela are perhaps the most curious and emblematic in the context of the region. Sometimes, the success of democracy there has been attributed to the country's oil riches, as if the availability of foreign currency were a guarantee for the survival of democracy. Scholars and analysts who have made such an assumption forget that the construction of Venezuelan democracy was a conscious and laborious effort that took more than two decades of heavy political struggle.

Venezuela has a territory of approximately 920,000 square kilometers. Its main export product is oil; estimated reserves are about 700 billion barrels. The country had an average annual rate of growth of 5.9 per cent between 1900 and 1996, the highest of all the Latin American and Caribbean countries.[32] The population is 22.5 million, estimated on the basis of the 1990 census. 67 per cent are mestizos or mulattos, 21 per cent white, about 10 per cent African Venezuelans, and a little more than 1.4 per cent Native Venezuelans. More than 80 per cent of the people live in cities and towns.

As in other Latin American countries, the movement in favor of political independence began at the end of the eighteenth century when the burden of the commercial monopoly of the Spanish metropolitan companies was increasingly perceived by the Creole economic elite as too heavy and disadvantageous. This elite did not believe in the seriousness of some reforms introduced by the crown in the 1760s. In addition, the elite was, as were those of other societies, strongly influenced by the ideas of the Enlightenment and by the independence of the United States. The elite had contacts with Europe. Francisco de Miranda had visited the major European countries, and his letters and reports were widely debated in the social, intellectual, and political circles of Caracas. Simón Bolívar had visited Spain and afterwards France at the time of the coronation of Napoleon I. There were also some intellectuals in Caracas with a surprisingly independent vision of the region – most notably, Simón Rodríguez – who had been the tutors of young people like Bolívar.

The process of separation from Spain began in April 1811 when the Cabildo of Caracas declared independence, but it took until June 1824 for the process to become sealed by the victory of Bolívar's troops against the Spaniards in the Battle of Carabobo. As already stated, Bolívar also fought for the independence of Colombia and Ecuador, participated in the liberation of Peru, and founded Bolivia. The state Bolívar considered his most important creation, Gran Colombia (today's Colombia, Ecuador, Panama, and Venezuela), fell apart in 1829–30, and revealed to him the loss of his political support and the end of his dream. He retired in 1830 from state affairs and died of tuberculosis on the way to Cartagena, Colombia, at the age of forty-seven.

As in other countries, the first years of Venezuelan independence after Bolívar's retirement and death were a period of political turmoil: his generals fought as caudillos for the maintenance of their power, based on the domination of their regions. The central state was relatively powerless, a kind of booty of whichever caudillo proved to be stronger than the others in these struggles. In spite of the existence of a constitution and a republican state structure, with separation of the executive, legislative, and judicial branches, neither stable institutions, nor mechanisms for the formation of political identities of collective actors, nor a sense of national community could arise. The omnipresent caudillos exercised power in the regions they dominated and in the central state when they conquered it. The power of each of them appeared and disappeared in a seemingly endless game, but none of them could reach a compromise that assured the ascendancy of the general interest of society over the particular interests of the generals, not to speak of the small segments of *hacendados* and merchants who were their financiers. The existing political parties – as in all parts of the region, Liberals and Conservatives – were weak, ideologically imprecise, and without a definite view of the kind of social and political order that they sought to create. The social forces that had supported the heroic deed of independence had little idea of the trajectory they wanted to give to their society. In this political situation, it is not surprising that an open civil war broke out. Between 1857 and 1864, the caudillos became warlords, some popular leaders like Ezequiel Zamora arose, the many battles were cruel and bloody, and the country suffered terribly.

The first attempt to establish a lasting political order (though not a national community) was that of Antonio Guzman Blanco, a dictator-president for several periods between 1868 and 1890, exercising power through proxies when he was not president. *El Americano Ilustrado* ("the Enlightened American" – one of his numerous titles) succeeded in maintaining a relative calm by negotiating with the caudillos and their heirs; in constructing state institutions, particularly an educational system; and in fostering some economic "progress." Nevertheless, after his retirement to Paris the turmoil began once more, and lasted for a decade until Cipriano Castro and Juan Vicente Gómez completed the construction of the oligarchic-liberal republic with Castro's "Revolución Restauradora" (1899–1908) and Gómez's dictatorship (1908–35).

In December 1908, when Castro was on his way back from a health trip to Europe, his vice-president and *compadre*[33] Juan Vicente Gómez stopped him aboard a passenger ship in Curaçao and "suggested" that he not return. A week later, Gómez was sworn in as the republic's president, a job he did not give up. Gómez was aware of the opportunities the oil discoveries meant to the country. He succeeded in a relatively short time in paying the external debt. Then he began to establish the bases of a nearly 30-year-long domination of the state.

The first step was the elimination of the caudillos: he bought or confiscated their lands and became the country's biggest landowner. He co-opted their sons as military "deans" of the president and eliminated the power of the *jefes* of the regional states, reserving for the president the right to designate the governors. They became completely, including financially, dependent on the central power of the state's president. Parallel to this, through the administrative reforms of his finance minister Román Cárdenas, he built up, from 1916 on, a serious state bureaucracy (in which even many of his adversaries served, particularly in diplomatic ranks). And finally, he centralized the armed forces: since he had eliminated the caudillos and their bases of regional power, he succeeded within a relatively short time in centralizing the command of the military and in subordinating the armed forces to the state (that is, to himself).

The exploitation of oil was in the hands of the transnational companies that dominate this business. However, Gomez used a mechanism that helped him to assure the loyalty not only of the part of the economically dominant class that took advantage of the growing oil boom, but of broader sectors of that same class and of people linked to him. He distributed oil-rich land to establish links of dependency and favour, but in such a way as to ensure substantial revenue for the state.

Oil exploitation had a deep impact on the economic and social structure of Venezuela. It eventually undermined agriculture and cattle raising as economically and socially relevant activities, enriched the importing sector of the bourgeoisie, created a small proletariat, and fostered a middle sector – both of the latter two being social groups that soon would play an important role in politics. Indirectly, oil therefore created the conditions for political change.

Gómez died in December 1935, General Eleazar López Contreras, his minister of defense, took over, and "Venezuela entered the twentieth century."[34] The president decided in February 1936 upon reforms that represented, as quickly became clear, a rupture with the ancien régime. Various pressures were behind this change: from the middle sectors and some segments of the bourgeoisie, but also from the unions, secretly formed during the years after a defeated student rebellion in April 1928, and after big street demonstrations. Reforms gave Parliament power to legislate and to control the government, allowed an opposition, introduced universal, direct, and secret male suffrage in local and congressional elections, and granted limited political rights: freedom of opinion and expression, of political association (except for the Communists and those who were denounced as such), and of political assembly.

In those years the process of construction of democracy began. The local bourgeoisie and the middle sectors had developed two social-political projects that could have been complementary but were in opposition until 1954. Both sought modernization, the middle sectors via political modernization (democratization), and the bourgeoisie via economic modernization (industrialization and diversification). The former organized themselves in political parties, notably the Acción Democrática (AD), founded formally in 1941; the latter trusted more to corporative organizations like the Federación de Cámaras de Industrias, Comercios y Bancas (FEDECAMARAS).

AD extended its influence during the following years under López Contreras's successor, General Isaias Medina Angarita. Its leaders, particularly Rómulo Betancourt, got in contact with young officers of the armed forces who were dissatisfied with the military policy of the government. On 18 October 1945, this coalition overthrew Medina and installed a civilian-military junta under the presidency of Betancourt. For the moment, the project of the middle class was victorious; but the local bourgeoisie stayed hostile to the "revolution."

The experience of the next three years, which Venezuelan scholars call the *trienio*, was important for all social actors, but especially for the AD leaders. The junta called for elections to a Constituent Assembly that had an overwhelming AD majority and drew up a new constitution. This guaranteed human and political rights to all Venezuelans, gave voting rights to women and the illiterate, assured free education up to university level, gave the state broad rights to intervene in the economy, and subordinated the military to civilian power. At the same time, AD and its unions, including the peasants' league, engaged in a program of politicizing and organizing the whole population. That gave rise to political unrest, since the expectations of the "dangerous classes" (including a considerable part of the middle sectors) were raised but not always met. The first presidential elections with universal, secret, and direct voting were held in December 1947, with a victory for AD's candidate, novelist Rómulo Gallegos. All of this caused growing concerns amongst the bourgeoisie and the officers. Both groups tried to convince the president to stop the unrest, if necessary by repression, but Gallegos resisted the pressures. As a result, the officers overthrew him on 24 November 1948, and installed a military junta that governed, with the Constitution suspended, till December 1952 when its chief, General Marcos Pérez Jiménez, made himself "elected" president. The bourgeoisie's project of modernization had won.

Finally, in 1954, both projects merged. The bourgeoisie, in a conflict with the dictator over ownership of the basic industries, withdrew its support from the regime and began negotiations with the political leaders, exiled in the United States, on the possibility of a deal. The result was, three years later, what some scholars have called the "silent pact" or the "commitment of the elites," which led directly to the overthrow of Pérez Jiménez on 23 January 1958, with the installation of a civilian-military junta.

The pact led to two formal agreements in 1958. The first was an agreement among the most important political parties ("Pacto de Punto Fijo") and as such involved four points, which had already been present in the "silent pact":

• respect for the results of the presidential and congressional elections of December 1958;
• the commitment to draw up a new constitution that guaranteed a representative-democratic form of regime with the political parties as the privileged channels for the citizens' participation, as well as the strict subordination of the military to the civil power;
• a system for distributing oil income (incentives for economic development, financing of social policies, building of infrastructure, and so on); and
• agreement that socio-economic development would follow the pattern of ECLA's developmentalism with import-substitution industrialization, based on a combination of private initiative, market forces, and state intervention.

The second agreement was between entrepreneurs and workers (*Adveni-*

miento obrero-patronal), signed shortly after the political agreement. It established that disputes between employers and employees had to be resolved by "pacific means," that is, negotiations without strikes and lockouts.

The elections were won by AD and its candidate, Rómulo Betancourt, the principal architect of the "silent pact." The pact was codified in the Constitution of 1961, which was eventually approved by an overwhelming majority of all parties in Congress and all social actors. It showed considerable strength during the following years. A number of developments demonstrate this:

- the defeat of attempts at military coups by right-wing officers in 1959 and 1960;
- the increasing incorporation of all socio-political collective actors (including the officers of the armed forces, the high state bureaucrats, the union leaders, and the hierarchy of the Catholic Church);
- the identification of the represented with the parties that claimed to represent them and hence, the consolidation of a functioning party system; and
- the political and subsequent military defeat of alternative left-wing projects, such as the guerrilla war between 1961 and 1964/67.

Thus the silent pact succeeded. The economy grew and diversified considerably. Social policies confronted poverty through direct income redistribution, creating a relatively modern public health system, reforming and fostering education at all levels, and forming a net of social security. In political terms, a civic culture was born, visible in high rates of electoral participation and in the active and dynamic interaction in both directions between the leaderships of the political parties and the members and the people they represented. This was particularly true of the two "big parties": the social democratic AD and the Christian Democrat COPEI (Comité organizativo para elecciones independientes, later Partido Socialcristiano COPEI).

As can be seen, oil income helped make the silent pact viable, but it did not create it. The building of democracy was an achievement based on a conscious collective effort. The different classes and groups, especially the middle sectors and the local bourgeoisie, played a major role by coordinating their interests in a project of national community. And that is why it survived for more than twenty years and was emblematic in the context of Latin America and the Caribbean.[35]

The slow breakdown of the "silent pact" began in 1974 with the project of "La Gran Venezuela" of President Carlos Andres Pérez (1974–79). As a direct consequence of an increase in oil income in October 1973,[36] Pérez and his advisers saw the necessity of changing the development model: instead of an equilibrium between the private sector/market forces and state intervention in the economy, they decided to foster state capitalism. This meant more restricted (though still enormous) profit margins for the local and international bourgeoisie and its organizations, more power for the state's technocracy to the detriment of its bureaucracy, less socio-political participation for the middle sectors and their organizations, and the eventual exclusion of negotiation and thus of representation for the working class and its unions.

These contradictions did not allow a recovery of the essence of the "silent pact." On the contrary, they made state policies increasingly inconsistent and eventually "populist" (in the worst sense of the word). Thus the deterioration of the mechanisms of the pact and of political practices during the governments of Luis Herrera Campins and Jaime Lusinchi (1979–84 and 1984–89) became manifest in many ways, beginning with the devaluation of the Venezuelan currency on 18 February 1983. The blindness of the leadership to the demands of the social groups, sectors, and classes, as well as to growing corruption, led to an increasing crisis of representativeness of the parties, i.e. their loss of credibility for their members, and of the legitimacy of democracy. This became evident in higher electoral abstention, citizen apathy, and the discrediting of the parties.[37] At the same time, a decrease in oil income, combined with the spending of funds on merely "populist" projects, reduced the state's capacity to answer the demands of society, in spite of a last-minute attempt to foster a reform of state and democracy from 1985 on.

It was during this period of deterioration of democracy that Hugo Rafael Chávez Frías and his military comrades received their political education. Having entered the Military Academy in 1973, they began to forge a "secret lodge," Movimiento Bolivariano Revolucionario 200 (Bolivarian Revolutionary Movement 200), from 1982–83 on. It was supposedly founded on the political thinking of Simón Bolívar, but this was only partly the case. It mainly served the fight for independence in various aspects: pan–Latin American nationalism; republicanism vs. militarism; centralism vs. federalism/decentralization; "revolution" as the transformation of the politico-institutional bases of the state and not as socioeconomic change (which Bolívar did not push forward during and after the wars of independence); and democracy when possible and dictatorship when necessary. This thinking had been frequently followed by military or civilian caudillos of the nineteenth and twentieth centuries.[38] The Comacate movement (of "Comandantes, Mayores, Capitanes, Tenientes" – "lieutenant colonels, majors, captains, and lieutenants") incorporated these elements into its own politico-ideological principles. It added later, already under Chávez's hegemony, the somewhat mythical thesis of an obscure Argentine sociologist, Norberto Ceresole, on the "unity between the armed forces and the people" and "the necessity of a strong leader to foster [this] unity."[39] It integrated a kind of "leftist" technocraticism promoted by the Movimiento Antonio José de Sucre (Antonio Jose de Sucre Movement) of professionals, mainly employed in the state-owned industries.

The Movimiento Bolivariano Revolucionario 200 played a significant role within the armed forces from 1989 on. That year, Carlos Andrés Pérez began his second presidency. He had been elected in a campaign in which he presented himself as the candidate who guaranteed both the continuity of the "populist" Lusinchi government and a return to prosperity. Two weeks after taking over, he announced the signature of a letter of intent with the IMF and a drastic program of adjustment policies. On 27 February 1989, the long-lasting and accumulated frustrations of the people resulted in a popular rebellion. The president called on the armed forces to calm down the situation. This had two serious consequences. Firstly, the crisis of legitimacy of the existing democracy became even more obvious and widespread. Pérez's government, for example, never recovered from these events. Secondly, the officers of the armed forces, not only those of the MBR 200, felt that they had been used to exercise repression against the people on behalf of politicians who had not been able to manage the country; thus, consciousness of a new "mission" began to arise, a fertile soil for the acceptance of Chávez's leadership some years later.

A first dramatic expression of this new climate within the armed forces was an attempt at a military coup on 4 February 1992, followed by a second attempt nine months later on 27 November. Although unsuccessful, both attempts showed that one of the main principles of the "silent pact" – the subordination of the military to civilian authority – was weakening, and with it democracy.

Rafael Caldera won the 1993 presidential elections. He had been the *líder máximo* of the Christian Democratic party COPEI and president between 1969 and 1974, but following the events of February 1992, he broke with his party and presented himself as an independent candidate, supported by relatively small center-left and left parties. Two features of this election are worth noting: the increase of electoral abstention to 38 per cent, in a society in which participation had been traditionally high; and the fact that Caldera and the candidate of Causa R (Causa Radical, a small political party) gathered more than 54 per cent of the votes, which was a clear signal of the beginning of the end of the "really existing democracy" under the hegemony of AD and COPEI.[40]

One of Caldera's most attractive campaign promises had been that he would design and put into practice a new model of development and democracy. For different reasons, mainly the financial crisis at the very beginning of his government, this was impossible. The rest is well known.

Chávez decided in November 1996 to run in the 1998 presidential elections. He built up his Movimiento Quinta República (MVR), which called for a Constituent Assembly to draw up a new constitution as the basis for a major political transformation. With an abstention rate of about 36 per cent, he won the election in December 1998 with 56 per cent of the votes. He began immediately with his project and pushed it through in two referenda and one election during 1999 (with abstention varying between 63 and 52 per cent). The new constitution was even more presidentialist than the previous one, the control of the military by the civil power was eliminated, the Parliament's functions of control over the executive branch were reduced, and basic social rights (employment, health, education till graduate studies, housing) were guaranteed. In the "relegitimization election" of 30 July 2000, with an abstention rate of 47 per cent of the registered voters, Chávez won 60 per cent of the votes, and the parties that support him (besides MVR, above all the Movimiento al Socialismo [MAS]) have a two-thirds majority in the National Assembly. Since then, Chávez has toughened his authoritarian grip on society and continued to militarize the state. He is also trying to occupy all public spaces, for example through the constitution of a new workers union, the Frente Bolivariano de Trabajadores (Bolivarian Workers Front). Without any doubt, he is building up a new hegemony, whose main ingredients are vast segments of the urban popular sectors and of the deteriorated middle sectors. His political style is aggressive, with a high degree of intolerance in his unlimited use of the mass media which apparently approaches Carl Schmitt's scheme of "enemy-friend" as the essence of polity.[41] The lack of an opposition with a project capable of reaching an echo in Venezuelan society has helped Chávez in his authoritarian (perhaps totalitarian?) transformation of Venezuelan society.

It is worthwhile to note that economic policies under Chávez have not changed. Most of them are the same adjustment policies of previous governments. They have been accompanied by rhetoric against "savage neoliberalism" and devoted declarations in favor of a "humanist economy." In the meantime, the increase of oil prices allows the Chávez government a certain – though artificial – economic recovery by high public spending.

In addition, like Bolívar, Chávez seems to be little interested in the socio-economic transformation of the society. His is a political revolution, which recalls the ideas of a "conservative revolution" at the end of the Weimar Republic in Germany.

The Venezuelan case at the turn of the century seemed more than emblematic: it was paradigmatic, in its successes and its failures. The efforts of collective actors between 1936 and 1979 were extraordinarily successful in the shaping of a democratic system. Although this relied too much upon representation and negotiation through the political parties and offered little space to the citizens to develop independent political activity, it assured a way of political life that established a national community and an institutional framework, both of them strong enough to make up a political society. But in the long run, socio-political trajectories seem to be stronger than the will and capacity of actors to introduce drastic changes. So the authoritarian embrace, the destruction of democracy during the last two years of the twentieth century, could count on two decisive elements: the apathy of a considerable part of society vis-à-vis the political system and the pressing needs of democracy; and a nostalgia for the "strong man" and the consequent denial of the necessity of the permanent and conflictive construction of social order.

Conclusion

The crises and regressions analyzed in this contribution allow some specific conclusions.

1. A new concept of development is required that is less technocratically influenced than both developmentalism and neo-liberalism, and more adapted to the idiosyncrasies of the people of the region – not just oriented to "globalization." This implies the necessity to foster research and thinking on the cultural elements which nourish our societies' own modernizing processes.

2. The adjustment policies (already questioned by their original preachers) have to be modified, since they not only have not achieved what they presumably could have reached – economic growth – but have actually harmed the economies of the region by reverse diversification and industrialization. This implies the necessity to return, in research and thinking, to the possibility of inward development, to understand the process of development once more as a totality, and to overcome the immanent limitations of neo-liberalism.

3. Social policies must be designed and executed that do not rely on assistance but on the active inclusion of citizens. This implies the necessity of research and thinking on new socio-institutional designs that aim at structures and agencies in which the societies have a high profile.

4. The processes that lead to marginalization and social exclusion have to be looked at from different perspectives. Clearly, those processes are inherent in the system to which the four societies – as well as all other Latin American societies – belong. It has to be asked to what degree these processes have become increased in the present period of bifurcation and continuing polarization.[42] It also has to be asked whether some of the processes are transforming into resistance movements, others into new forms of organizing production, distribution, and con-

sumption, and others also into elements of new definitions of citizenship. Here, too, much research and thinking must be done to prevent the segregating reality of the socio-economic "order" undermining the possibilities of participatory democracy.[43]

The trajectories that have characterized Ecuador, Paraguay, Peru, and Venezuela during the democratization processes of the last 20 years are not an exception to the Latin American and Caribbean rule: all societies have failed, in one way or the other, in constructing a strong political society. From the perspective of this volume, such a society would be characterized as a strong national community with historically deep-rooted and vigorous institutions that are independent of the dominant state regimes, and with the societal capacity of allowing the collective actors to establish and reinforce their identities in a framework of representations and negotiations that allow peaceful political transitions and/or ruptures between one regime and the "next." In other words, if our comparative analysis had been directed toward the study of a successful case and a critical one, it probably would have shown that those components of political society involved had, at the beginning of each process, the same chances to become successful or to fail. If and when these components failed, as in the cases examined here, this was because their historical trajectory, and thus the political societies that they constituted, had made them particularly weak, but that can be pure coincidence and does not have to be historical-structurally determined. In any case, historical-structural determinations are relative constraints on the action of human beings, not absolute ones. There is always the possibility of choice.

Notes

1. This essay covers developments up to October 2000, with the exceptions of Peru and Venezuela where more recent data have been included. In accordance with the scope of this volume, the Dutch-, English-, and French-speaking countries and territories of the Caribbean and the Central and South American mainland are not considered in this essay.
2. One of the clearest and most innovative approaches to the singularities and simultaneously general characteristics of Latin America and the Caribbean is still CENDES–Equipo Sociohistorico, *Formación histórico-social de America Latina* (Caracas: Ed. de la Biblioteca de la UCV, 1982).
3. Heinz R. Sonntag, *Duda–Certeza–Crisis: La evolución de las ciencias sociales de America Latina y el Caribe* (Caracas: Nueva Sociedad/UNESCO, 1988), pp. 52ff.
4. Gino Germani, *Política y sociedad en una epoca de transición* (Buenos Aires: EUDEBA, 1961).
5. Cf. Fernando Henrique Cardoso and Enzo Faletto, *Dependency and Development in Latin America* (Berkeley: University of California Press, 1976; the first Spanish edition was published in 1969 by Siglo XXI Editores in Mexico).

6. The Caribbean was originally not part of ECLA's official name. Only in the eighties did the Caribbean became recognized as a region in its own right. Developmentalism was "founded" by Raúl Prebisch (1908–87). In a famous document of 1948 for the UN secretary-general, he theorized upon and systematized the experiences of Latin American economies that had developed "early capitalisms" at the end of the nineteenth century, and thereby created the initial body of developmentalist doctrine.

7. José Medina Echavarria's works on the social consequences of economic development during the early fifties, notably *Las consecuencias sociales del desarrollo económico en America Latina* (Santiago de Chile: ECLA, 1954), were especially significant for this shift.

8. Fernando Henrique Cardoso, "The Originality of a Copy: CEPAL and the Idea of Development," *CEPAL Review* 1977; 1(22): pp. 7–40.

9. There is a vast literature on why the developmentalist project finally failed, a good part of which blames developmentalism's emphasis on state intervention in the economy. The Hegelian "irony of history" has produced, after two decades of market-oriented (neo-)liberal adjustment policies at the behest of the international financial organizations, a new emphasis by these same agencies on the importance of the state for the performance of developing economies.

10. A good example is the reorientation of the local bourgeoisies. The internationalization of capital in the sixties turned them away from the idea of national development and fostered their association with foreign capital. Cf. Fernando Henrique Cardoso, "Las contradicciones del desarrollo asociado," *Cuadernos de la Sociedad Venezolana de Planificación* 1974; (113–15): pp. 3–28.

11. In Argentina the period between 1955 (Perón's overthrow) and 1976 was one of permanent political crisis. However, different (democratic and not so democratic) regimes represented the typical state and the typical political system of the region; cf. Marcelo Cavarozzi's contribution in this volume.

12. The exception was Guatemala. There, a CIA-inspired coup d'état in 1954 aborted not only the possibilities of democracy but also the application of ECLA's policies for economic and social development.

13. Thomas E. Skidmore, *Brazil: Five Centuries of Change* (New York: Oxford University Press, 1999).

14. Claudia Jean Elliott, "The Negotiation of Political Representation: Crisis and Democratization in Latin America" (Ph.D. diss., Brown University, 1999).

15. This fact is important, as will be seen below, because of the socio-political impact it had during the process of redemocratization in the late eighties.

16. In a few cases, the populism of one leader could even create conditions which allowed both socio-economic modernization and political stability, for example Cárdenas in Mexico and Vargas during his first government in Brazil; cf. Elliott, "The Negotiation of Political Representation," and Skidmore, *Brazil*.

17. It should be noted that this was not a new feature in military governments. For example, the junta that took power in 1963 had been also reformist, like others before it.

18. Perhaps one of the symbols of Febres Cordero's lack of respect for democratic rules, norms, and customs was the fact that he did not attend his successor's swearing-in ceremony during a plenary session of the Parliament.

19. Unlike other indigenous movements, the Ecuadorian one succeeded this time in overcoming the Creoles' policy of keeping the different tribes and groups divided. It brought those of the sierra together with those of the Amazonian flatlands in one organization.

20. On Ecuador, I have relied on Peter Lambert and Andrew Nickson (eds.), *The Transition to Democracy in Paraguay* (Basingstoke, Hants.: Macmillan; New York: St. Martins Press, 1997); and on Riordan Roett and Richard Scott Sachs, *Paraguay: The Personalist*

Legacy (Boulder, Colo.: Westview Press, 1991). In addition, I am deeply indebted to the Centro Paraguayo De Estudios Sociológicos and its director, Domingo Rivarola, for their help in providing information and interpretations.

21. Creoles were people of Spanish descent but born in America. Their privileges were considerably less than those of the officials of the colonial administration and others who spent only relatively short periods in America before returning to Spain.

22. This is also true for the Maya and the Aztec civilizations in Mexico and the northern parts of Central America. It is frequently an emblematic feature of the relations between European conquerors and conquered societies during the expansion of the European world-economy from the sixteenth century on. Cf. Immanuel Wallerstein, *The Modern World-System*, vol. 1 (New York: Academic Press, 1974).

23. Peru shared this characteristic with nearly all the countries that won independence at this time, with the possible exceptions of Mexico and Brazil.

24. These features were present in other populist movements and parties, such as the MNR in Bolivia with its revolution in 1952, the Acción Democrática (AD) in Venezuela with its radical reforms between 1945 and 1948, Perón's original "justicialism" in Argentina till 1955, the PRI in Mexico from 1928 on, Getulio Vargas's movement in Brazil in the thirties, Jose Figueres's Liberación in Costa Rica from 1948 on, or Juan Bosch's PRD in the Dominican Republic after the murder of the dictator Trujillo in 1961. However, Latin America's populism is such a multifaceted phenomenon that it is difficult to generalize. In addition, these parties changed greatly over time, although they maintained some features such as organizational verticalism, an ideological emphasis on their multiclass character, development policies, and flexibility in coalition building. This makes it extremely risky to define populism as a historical-political phenomenon: the many populist trees in the political landscape make it nearly impossible to visualize the forest. The enemies of populism commit the opposite error: they see the populist forest but cannot distinguish the trees.

25. Marc Becker, *Mariátegui and Latin American Marxist Theory* (Athens: Ohio University Press, 1993). The most distinguished intellectual in Mariátegui's tradition is the Peruvian sociologist and political thinker Anibal Quijano; cf. Anibal Quijano, *Reencuentro y debate: Una introducción a Mariátegui* (Lima: Mosca Azul Editores, 1981).

26. The period 1968–75 has been interpreted in different ways. Some have seen it as a modernizing military regime: Darcy Ribeiro, *The Civilizational Process* (Washington, D.C.: Smithsonian Institution Press, 1968). Others have viewed it as a kind of Latin American Nasserism: Julio Cotler and Heinz R. Sonntag, *Der Fall Peru* (Wuppertal: Peter Hammer Verlag, 1971). Yet others interpret it as a new façade for a pro-imperialist regime: Anibal Quijano, *Nationalism and Capitalism in Peru: A Study in Neo-Imperialism* (New York: Monthly Review Press, 1971). It was similar to Torrijos's regime in Panama between 1968 and 1981 and to the Rodríguez Lara/Poveda dictatorship in Ecuador from 1973 on. None of these regimes were "traditional" military dictatorships "at the service of the dominant classes," as the orthodox Communist and leftist movements called them.

27. Two Internet information services (idl.org.pe and alai-amlatina.ecuanex.net.ec) have been publishing recently a growing amount of information which has become public since the first round of the general elections in April 2000. I make use of this information without indicating each time the exact source.

28. In this sense, Fujimori was different from what some scholars have called "delegative democracy." His project went also quite beyond the adaptation of populism to the necessities of the adjustment policies and even neo-liberalism, as was arguably the case with Carlos Andres Pérez in Venezuela and Carlos Saúl Menem in Argentina. It is implausible to categorize Fujimori together with these, as does Kenneth Roberts, "Neoliberalism and the Transformation of Populism in Latin America: The Peruvian Case,"

World Politics 1996; 48(1), given the existence in Fujimori's case of an overwhelmingly powerful social and political transformation project supported by a no less mighty alliance (with a mafia-like inner circle) of military officers, the monopolistic local bourgeoisie, probably drug traffickers, and middle-class sectors that had been seduced into giving their support.

29. The role of the OAS, previous to the elections highly committed to the democratization of its member Peru, became limited, due to the decision of the assembly at the beginning of June 2000 in Windsor, Canada, for a "friendly appeal" to Fujimori to allow some democratic reforms and to permit the establishment of an advisory committee for negotiations with his opponents.

30. An excellent account of them is Clifford Krauss, "Fujimori's Fall: A Nation's Lion to Broken Man," *New York Times*, 3 December 2000.

31. The strong resistance of indigenous people in Bolivia against governmental adjustment policies and the prohibition of coca cultivation during the last months of the year 2000 seems to confirm their growing presence in Latin American political life.

32. Rosemary Thorp, *Progress, Poverty and Exclusion: An Economic History of Latin America in the Twentieth Century* (Washington, D.C.: IDB; Baltimore: Johns Hopkins University Press, 1998), p. 318.

33. The *compadrazgo* is an important institution in Venezuelan society. A *compadre* is a man who has been designated by a father as a godfather of his child (or one of his children), but the latter's obligations go far beyond those that a godfather normally has, and cover also the physical, economic, and psychological protection of the child's (or children's) whole family.

34. Manuel Caballero, *Gomez, el tirano liberal: Vida y muerte del siglo XIX* (Caracas: Monte Avila Editores Latinoamericana/Banco de Maracaibo, 1993).

35. Luis Castro Leiva gave a masterly exposition of this fact in his speech to Parliament on 23 January 1998, the fortieth anniversary of the overthrow of Pérez Jiménez.

36. The price per barrel grew from US$3 to nearly US$11, and the national budget quadrupled from US$3 billion to US$12 billion.

37. Cf. Heinz R. Sonntag and Thais Maingon, "Las elecciones en Venezuela en 1988 y 1989: Del ejercicio del rito democrático a la protesta silenciosa," *Revista Mexicana de Sociología* 1990; 52(4): pp. 127–54.

38. Cf. Luis Castro Leiva, *De la patria boba a la teología bolivariana: Ensayos de historia intelectual* (Caracas: Monte Avila Editores, 1991); German Carrera Damas, *El culto a Bolivar: Esbozo para un estudio de la historia de las ideas en Venezuela* (Caracas: Instituto de Antropología e Historia, Universidad Central de Venezuela, 1969).

39. Norberto Ceresole, *Caudillo, ejército, pueblo: La Venezuela del Comandante Chávez* (Madrid: Estudios Hispánicos Arabes, 2000), pp. 12–13.

40. Heinz R. Sonntag and Thais Maingon, "The Crisis of Democracy in Latin America: The Case of Venezuela," *Latin America Report* 1993; 10(2): pp. 2–16.

41. Carl Schmitt, *Der Begriff des Politischen* (Berlin: Duncker & Humblot, 1932), passim.

42. Cf. Immanuel Wallerstein, *The End of the World As We Know it: Social Science for the Twenty-First Century* (Minneapolis: University of Minneapolis Press, 1999), pp. 2ff.

43. Immanuel Wallerstein has frequently argued that *egalitarian* and *democratic* cannot be separated from each other: "A historical system cannot be egalitarian if it is not democratic, because an undemocratic system ... distributes power unequally, and this means that it will also distribute all other things unequally. And it cannot be democratic if it is not egalitarian, since an inegalitarian system means that some have more material means than others and therefore inevitably will have more political power." Ibid., p. 3.

Democracy and the (re)construction of political society

7

Social dimensions: Ethnicity

Rodolfo Stavenhagen

Social dimensions of democracy

The debate on the links between political democracy and social and economic issues is as old as democracy itself. However, it has re-emerged
in recent years in the framework of what has been called (perhaps over-
optimistically) a third wave of democratization in the twentieth century.
In this process, two world regions have stood out in the latter decades of
the century: Eastern Europe and Latin America, where the problems and
struggles of building democratic societies have challenged the imagina-
tion and analytical skills of scholars.

Most Latin American countries have been formal democracies since
the beginning of their independent existence in the nineteenth century,
but they have never been able to achieve the stature of fully democratic
polities including equal rights for all citizens, governmental accountability, an independent judiciary, and a widely shared democratic political
and civic culture. As military dictatorships and authoritarian regimes
began to crumble in the 1980s a number of Latin American societies attempted earnestly to build up their democratic institutions and institute
credible and participatory electoral mechanisms. Some have been more
successful in this than others, while in some states there have been wor-
risome reversals. At any rate, it soon became clear that electoral politics
alone could not resolve the fundamental issues of democracy. Indeed, the
justifiable concern over the transition to, and consolidation of, political

democracy may have led to the neglect of a number of other important problems, such as the economic, social, and cultural rights of populations; the challenges of equitable and sustainable economic development; and the questions of personal liberties, collective goods, distribution of wealth and resources, social justice, and regional inequalities. In addition, the issue of national and ethnic identities as well as the often strained and sometimes violent relationship between the political center (state, government, power elites, ruling classes) and the culturally diverse segments of the population, particularly Latin America's indigenous peoples, have been a key challenge.

The concept of democracy is multidimensional and there is no clear and widely accepted meaning of the term. While a competitive electoral system and regular free elections of government authorities seem to be essential – minimal – ingredients in any definition, other characteristics may vary according to historical circumstances and to different theoretical approaches used by scholars in various disciplines.[1] The social dimensions of democracy are usually linked to issues such as interest groups and their articulation, effective popular participation and representation, human rights, income inequalities, social mobility, political paternalism, and clientelism and corruption. These concerns are not usually taken much into account in considerations of formal political and electoral democracy, but as many observers have noted, they are essential elements for a fuller analysis of how democracy functions at the practical level.

A recent comparative study of democratic transitions in the "new" democracies of Eastern Europe and Latin America has led to some interesting conclusions. The authors find that "what makes democracies sustainable, given the context of exogenous conditions, are their institutions and performances. Democracy is sustainable when its institutional framework promotes normatively desirable and politically desired objectives, such as freedom from arbitrary violence, material security, equality, or justice, and when, in turn, these institutions are adept at handling crises that arise when such objectives are not being fulfilled." Attention must then be given to various kinds of institutions: economic, political, and social. The authors acknowledge that "culturally heterogeneous societies present particularly difficult problems in the design of institutions that would channel conflicts into the framework of a rule-governed interplay of interests."[2] While their assessment was influenced especially by the situation in Eastern Europe in the early 1990s, the need to establish adequate institutional arrangements in order to manage ethnic and cultural diversity as a safeguard for sustainable democracy applies also to Latin America. At one level, the issue of cultural diversity relates to the problematic relationship between a political center concerned with territorial integrity and sovereignty, and the centrifugal forces of regional autonomy or even independence based on real or imagined, historical or recently constructed ethnic and national identities. But it is more than this. Cultural heterogeneity is a challenge for most of the social and political institutions of the state: the educational system, the media, the judiciary, the military, the civil service, and the mechanisms and priorities whereby economic policies are carried out. Most of all, cultural diversity relates to the effective exercise of citizenship which is an essential ingredient of sustainable democracy. If modern citizenship entails a bundle of predictable and enforceable rights and obligations for every member of the political community, we do indeed "face a new monster: democracies without an effective citizenship for large sections of the political community."[3] As we shall see in this essay, the monster is alive and well in Latin America, for large sections of the population, namely the indigenous peoples, lack effective citizenship and have been excluded from the political community for most of their history. What this implies and how it is changing, is the subject of this essay.

The re-emergence of indigenous peoples

In January 2000 the Indians of Ecuador mobilized, as they had done on several previous occasions, to make their organized strength felt on the critical political situation in their country. In alliance with other groups, they succeeded in forcing the resignation of a democratically elected but highly unpopular president. The Confederation of Indigenous Nationalities of Ecuador (CONAIE), which represents the country's four million Indians, organized what it called an "indigenous uprising" – the first national "uprising" had taken place in 1990 followed by two others – which included blockading highways and a march on Quito by at least 10,000 Indian people. After several days of confrontation, a civil-military junta, including an indigenous leader, ousted the president and after two days of political negotiations handed over power to the country's vice-president. Demanding profound structural changes in the country's economy, the Indians disbanded.[4]

The Ecuadorean crisis is a clear example of the difficulties facing indigenous peoples in the process of democratization. In order to take part more actively in the electoral process, the well-articulated and consolidated indigenous organizations decided to create a political party, the Movimiento Pachacutik. They were also involved in building a national popular alliance with other social movements, without, however, losing the specificity of their indigenous demands. This difficult balancing act was undone during the January 2000 crisis, but the principal elements of the situation are still present and will most likely erupt again in the future.[5] The Ecuadorean Indian movement also underlines an important shift in indigenous movements over the years: the transition from the demand for civil and ethnic rights to an open challenge to the hegemonic political and economic model from which Indians have been traditionally excluded.[6]

The Mapuche people of southern Chile have long protested against large-scale projects in their region that would severely damage their environment and livelihoods.[7] The military dictatorship had been hostile to Indian demands, and after the return to free elections, the new Chilean government was more favourably inclined towards indigenous rights and participation. This opening did not last long, however, and new tensions and conflicts arose between the Mapuche and the national government, mainly over the issues of land and resources. The Socialist president Ricardo Lagos, elected in January 2000, decided to open negotiations with the Indians and appointed a special commission to deal with these issues on a priority basis. Similar protests mobilized the U'wa people in Colombia against oil prospecting on their lands by transnational petroleum companies supported by the national government. In Chiapas an armed conflict pitting the Mexican government against the Zapatista National Liberation Army began in 1994 and was still unresolved six years later (see below). A proposal to amend the Guatemalan constitution to include an agreement on indigenous rights and culture, which the government had signed with guerrilla forces after a thirty-year-long civil war, was roundly defeated in the Congress in 1999. These are just a few of the more recent incidents involving the relationship between the state and indigenous peoples in Latin America, a conflictive relationship that is rooted in history and which bears significantly on the issues of democratization and citizenship.

According to census returns and estimates, the indigenous inhabitants of Latin America numbered around 40 million in 1990, approximately 10 per cent of the region's total population. They are distributed quite unevenly, being concentrated in the Andean countries as well as in Mexico and Central America. In two states – Bolivia and Guatemala – the indigenous are the majority of the national population, while in two others (Ecuador and Peru) they make up more than one-third. Mexico has the largest absolute number of Indians, who account for around 12 per cent of the total population. Elsewhere, as in Brazil and Argentina, they make up only a small percentage of the population.[8] Except for Uruguay, indigenous peoples are present in all Latin American countries. They are mainly rural dwellers but in recent decades, due to internal migrations, their presence has grown significantly in urban centers. Within the various countries, higher concentrations of Indians are found in certain areas and very low densities or none at all in others. This is due to the historical process of settlement and to the population policies of the colonial and independent governments over the centuries. In southeastern Mexico, for example, the indigenous represent a higher percentage of the population than the national average, whereas they are almost absent in some northern provinces.

Estimates also vary regarding the number of distinct indigenous peoples. Taking mainly linguistic criteria (whether they speak a specific indigenous language), we are dealing with around four hundred different ethno-linguistic groups, which are in turn divided into many thousands of local communities. Some indigenous-language speakers – such as the Maya and the Quechua – number in the millions, whereas others – such as numerous Amazon tribes – are on the verge of extinction. To the extent that scholars do not agree among themselves and that countries adopt different criteria to classify their populations, some Indian languages are subdivided into smaller linguistic communities, whereas others may be variants of larger linguistic families. In Colombia eighty-two distinct indigenous peoples have been counted – the latest group, the nomadic Nukak-Makú, having been identified as recently as 1988 – with a population of less than 600,000 altogether, representing only around 2 per cent of the country's total. There are no clear rules of identification, because the census bureau uses linguistic criteria (64 Indian languages are counted) but the self-perception of "being Indian" is also used increasingly.[9] Numerous methodological and conceptual problems are involved in efforts to estimate or actually count the number of Indians and indigenous groups. In Ecuador, for instance, the census bases its calculations on people living in Indian communities, thus leaving out Indians who live in other villages not so identified or in cities. This leads to the official underestimation of Ecuador's Indian population. Numbers, of course, have political consequences. In general, in Latin America, the indigenous populations are growing in absolute numbers but declining in relative terms. Governments may be interested in understating the numerical importance of the indigenous for a number of reasons. Ruling elites of European stock used to deny that there were Indians in their countries at all, and this racist attitude was reflected in the way the national census was set up. Others try to show that their assimilationist policies have been successful, in order to reduce specific budgetary allocations for Indians and channel limited resources into other areas considered of higher priority. Moreover, by undercounting Indians, governments try to counteract growing pressures from indigenous peoples for greater participation in national affairs. The Indians, on the other hand, who have become politically mobilized over recent decades, find strength and arguments in numbers, and they feel that under-representation in the census means greater political and social marginalization. Some authors have actually referred to these manipulations as "statistical ethnocide."[10] When faced by census takers or survey field workers, many Indians who would in earlier times deny an identity which they carried like a stigma, nowadays are proud to signal their ethnic ancestry and belonging. The change in attitude reflects the changing political importance of indigenous peoples who have emerged in recent decades as new social actors at the national, regional, and international levels.

Despite such methodological difficulties in defining and quantifying indigenous individuals and groups, social research over the years has been able to draw a fairly accurate picture of the situation of indigenous peoples in Latin America. First, there is no denying that Indians represent a specific ethnic and cultural segment of the total population. Indian ethnic identity is expressed at various levels and in different domains. Indians speak their own vernacular languages which are mostly derived from those spoken in pre-Columbian times.[11] Except for a number of isolated areas (the Amazon basin, for example) most speakers of native languages, above all the males, are bilingual in Spanish or Portuguese. National educational efforts over the years have achieved the progressive decline of the use of Indian languages, though recent tendencies may reverse this. Indian migrants to urban areas also have difficulty in maintaining their languages, even though almost all known Indian tongues are spoken in the cities as well.

A second distinctive element of Indian cultures is community participation in social, economic, and religious affairs. Most Indian communities have a strong sense of ethnic identification and their membership is clearly defined in corporate terms; individual members must acquit themselves of community obligations and participate in community life, and this applies very frequently to migrants as well. Endogamy is often the rule. The economic and political changes of recent years have weakened traditional communal bonds and numerous observers suggest that this is an irreversible process.[12] Indian spokespersons, however, maintain that the reconstitution of their communities is one of their major aims. A crucial ingredient of cultural identity is the self-recognition and self-identification of people as members of a specific ethnic group which is distinct from the rest of the population. To the extent that such subjective identification is held to a greater or lesser degree, cultural identity becomes an ethnic marker with implications in determining the relations between Indians and the rest of society.

A further characteristic that sets indigenous peoples apart from the rest of society is their strong roots in a peasant way of life and the crucial importance that attachment to the land and a specific territory represents for the social and cultural reproduction of the group.[13] Traditionally Indian communities have been peasant societies, and while there are also numerous non-Indian farming communities in Latin America and increasing numbers of Indians have been forced to emigrate from the rural areas, the Indian peasantry has been emblematic of Latin America for centuries. Indeed, the peasantry has been so much identified with Indian cultures that for some scholars it is difficult if not impossible to separate these two concepts. For decades the anthropological literature has presented us with studies of Indian peasant communities, their traditions, their transformations, their conflicts, so that it has been difficult to conceptualize the Indians outside of a peasant context (particularly in the Andes and Mesoamerica). Indians in a non-peasant environment still appear to some as exceptional if not downright abnormal. This has led to continuing theoretical arguments between scholars. Are Indian cultures and identities linked to the social class position of their members, or do ethnic characteristics transcend class? Will class-consciousness override ethnic identifications, and under what circumstances? Are ethnic groups in turn divided into social classes, and are class issues influenced by ethnic divisions? How does all of this impinge upon the collective consciousness and how does it influence social agency and political strategy?[14] I will attempt to answer some of these questions below, but others must await more thorough treatment elsewhere.

What is undeniable is that because of their cultural distinctiveness, Indians have been marginalized and discriminated against, and because of their position in the rural class structure they have been and are exploited and oppressed. After being victimized by European colonialism for three hundred years, throughout much of the last two centuries Indians have remained locked for the most part in a rigid structure of internal colonialism.[15] The combined effect of this ethnic class structure maintains indigenous peoples overall in the lower ranks of the social stratification. As a result they are now among the poorest sectors of society, and at a time when the international development agenda demands a massive effort to alleviate and reduce poverty worldwide, this situation presents a special challenge to the countries of Latin America.[16]

Poverty is the bane of Latin America at the turn of the century. Recent data show that between 1980 and 1990 the number of poor increased by 60 million, reaching a total of 196 million Latin Americans with an income of less than two dollars a day; in other words, 46 per cent of the total population is unable to meet its basic needs. At the same time, the extremely poor population, with an income of less than one dollar a day, increased during the decade from 19 per cent to 22 per cent or 94 million people. This means that one out of five Latin Americans does not have sufficient income for him or her to consume a diet which would satisfy minimal nutritional requirements – they go hungry or are regularly undernourished, a situation which affects women and children in particular. While some progress in alleviating poverty was made during the 1990s, Latin America is the world region with the largest income inequality, and the gap between the upper and the lower strata appears to be increasing.[17]

Not surprisingly, at the lowest level of poverty we find the indigenous populations. "Poverty among Latin America's indigenous population is pervasive and severe," concluded a World Bank study in the early 1990s. In Bolivia, while more than half of the total population was impoverished, over two-thirds of the bilingual and almost three-quarters of the monolingual indigenous population was poor. In Guatemala 87 per cent of all indigenous households were below the poverty line and 61 per cent were below the extreme poverty line, a proportion that was way above the national average. In Peru 79 per cent of the indigenous were poor and more than half were extremely poor. The *municipios* with the highest indigenous density were also the poorest in Mexico. The study found that, closely related to poverty status, the living conditions of the indigenous population were generally "abysmal" and their health problems were "severe."[18]

Nation building without Indians

While the roots of this situation are to be found in the colonial history of Latin America, the social and economic structures which gave rise to today's indigenous problematique emerged during the nineteenth century, after political independence had been achieved, as the ruling elite was faced with the daunting challenge of building new nations and constructing national identities. In this cause it enlisted the emerging intelligentsia to formulate the nationalist ideologies that would guide it in its search of legitimacy. To many observers, at that time the Latin American countries were not yet national states at all, but rather a series of loosely knit regional units, based on a partially self-sufficient agrarian economy.[19]

However, a persistent rift existed along class lines, between the small ruling groups, owners of the land and the mines, and the majority indigenous peasantry. Class cleavage was also a cultural cleavage. The subordinate Indian populations had been incorporated by the Spaniards as servile labour into the colonial economy, and a rigid system of stratification and segregation kept them effectively outside the political process. After independence, slavery and serfdom were abolished and legal equality of all citizens was proclaimed. In fact, the subordination and exploitation of the Indians continued, mainly through the operation of the landholding system.

The concept of the nation-state and of national culture was developed by the upper classes: the white descendants of the European settlers, the landholding aristocracy, the urban bourgeois elements. The model of the modern nation which evolved together with the expanding capitalist economy was that of the Western liberal democracies on the French, British, and American patterns. The elites considered themselves as part and parcel of Western civilization; by religion, language, and cultural ethos. Once independence had been obtained by force of arms, under the leadership of the "Liberators" – Bolívar, O'Higgins, Hidalgo – the rulers of the new states were faced with the daunting task of building new nations. It was no small matter to forge viable polities that might serve the interests of the new ruling groups out of the fragmented remains of the Spanish empire, particularly in view of the highly stratified and hierarchical nature of the social system inherited from the colonial period and the ethnic and racial diversity of the population. Well known are the words of Simón Bolívar, the "Liberator of America," who realized the difficulties of creating unified nations out of such mixed populations, and warned in 1819:

We must keep in mind that our people are neither European nor North American: rather, they are a mixture of African and the Americans who originated in Europe. It is impossible to determine with any degree of accuracy where we belong in the human family. The greater portion of the native Indians have been annihilated; Spaniards have mixed with Americans and Africans, and Africans with Indians and Spaniards. While we have all been born of the same mother, our fathers, different in origin and in blood, are foreigners, and all differ visibly as to the color of their skin: a dissimilarity which places upon us an obligation of the greatest importance.[20]

Bolívar was not alone in expressing qualms about his ethnic identity and his place in "the human family" (he himself was of mixed origin, though a prominent member of the dominant Creole class). Others, such as the Argentine writer and president F. D. Sarmiento later in the century, also doubted that civilized nations could emerge at all from such diverse racial and ethnic backgrounds. So it became necessary to create and invent nations, to construct national identities, which was the task that the intellectuals set for themselves in the nineteenth century. By some accounts this task has not yet been completed, for the search for national identity is still a principal concern of Latin American intellectuals to this day.[21]

By the beginning of the twentieth century the majority of the population in numerous countries – mainly in the Andes, Central America, and Mexico – still spoke an Indian language and lived in closed, semi-isolated village or tribal communities according to their ancestral customs. This did not, however, alter the national self-perception of the dominant classes. Though lip-service was given to the indigenous roots of modern society, the cultural and political leaders of the region were reluctant to recognize the native Indian peoples as part of the new nations in the making. Indeed, the Indians were explicitly rejected and excluded from the polity and the "national projects" that emerged in the nineteenth century. As elsewhere in the world, it was the ruling class and the intelligentsia who imagined and invented the modern Latin American nations, trying to shape them in their own image. Indigenous groups have ever since remained in the background, shadowy figures which, like Greek choruses, step into the historical limelight on certain occasions – revolutions, rebellions, uprisings, such as in Chiapas, Guatemala, and Ecuador – only to recede again into a forgotten world.

While the indigenous peoples were recognized as distinct and separate cultures, neither their languages nor their social, religious, and political institutions were incorporated into the dominant mode of governance. Indian cultures were at best ignored, and at worst exterminated. They were considered an obstacle to national integration and therefore as a threat to the rightful place which the national elites considered to be theirs among the civilized nations of the world. The principal intellectual leaders of the nineteenth century were openly contemptuous of the Indian cultures and considered them to be inferior to the dominant civilization of the times. It was common to refer to the Indians as "degenerate" races as a result of their humiliation and oppression by the Spanish conquerors in earlier times.

The major ethnic fact of the twentieth century was the rapid growth of the mestizos, the biologically mixed population. The mestizos also occupied the middle rungs of the social and economic stratification system and they were increasingly identified with the growing middle classes. Originally marginal to both the Spanish and the Indian cultures, the mestizos lacked a coherent identity of their own, a problem which preoccupied intellectuals, psychologists, and sociologists for a long time. The Indians were rejected outright as passive, dependent, fatalistic, docile, stupid, incapable of higher civilization, lacking in emotions and sensitivity, impervious to pain and suffering, unable even to improve their miserable conditions of living, and therefore generally a major obstacle to progress. The mestizos, in contrast, were said to embody the worst elements of both their ancestries: they were hot-headed, violent, unreliable, dishonest, opportunistic, power-hungry, lazy, and generally considered less than ideal to rule and run their countries. But times changed. The mestizos did in fact come to occupy the occupational slots and the economic and social space which neither the reduced Creole upper groups nor the Indian peasantries were able to control. With the capitalist expansion of the economy and the growth of cities, trade, services, and industry, the mestizo soon became identified with the national mainstream, the driving force of economic and social development, as well as eventually political progress.

The earlier doubts about the mestizo's biological and pyschological capabilities vanished, except among some diehard Creoles and foreign observers who still conveyed the old stereotypes well into the twentieth century.

By that time, the mestizos had developed their own distinct culture; they became the bearers of truly nationalist sentiments. Moreover, the mestizos became identified with the burgeoning urban middle classes, and thus with progress, change, and modernization. An ideological reversal had occurred. Mestizo intellectuals themselves sang the virtues of *mestizaje* not only as a biological process, but rather as a cultural and political condition leading to economic development and political democracy. "Por mi raza hablará el espíritu" ("The spirit will speak for my race"), proclaims the slogan of the National University of Mexico, coined by José Vasconcelos, minister of education in one of the post-revolutionary governments and standard bearer of the mestizos as a new "cosmic race" in Latin America. In Peru the *mistis* became power brokers between the Indian communities and the world of the whites when the local elites, the *curacas*, who had represented Indian interests at the seat of government, were eliminated by the colonial authorities after the famous failed Indian rebellions at the end of the eighteenth century.[22] Nowadays, the recently urbanized Indians known as *cholos* occupy this ambiguous role as a new ethnic category in the Andean countries. In Guatemala and parts of Mexico Indian identities contrast with those of the locally powerful Ladinos, so-called because they speak a Latin language, and at midcentury social scientists thought they observed an inevitable and irreversible process of ladinoization taking place, meaning that Indian communities would change through a process of acculturation and also that individual Indians could become upward-mobile by adopting a Ladino cultural identity.

Shunned and despised at first, by the middle of the century the mestizos were considered to have incorporated the best features of the two original races (the white and the Indian) which combined in their make-up. The rise of the mestizo, now extolled in literature, social science, and political discourse, coincided with the growing political presence of the middle classes. The identification of the mestizo population with national culture, the middle classes, and economic progress soon became the ideological underpinning of various kinds of government policies designed to strengthen the unitary nation-state and the incorporation of the "non-national" elements, namely, the Indian peoples.[23]

The nineteenth century brought independence and a new legal and political system in which Indian populations in most countries were recognized as citizens. Nevertheless, the expansion of agrarian capitalism and the modernization of the economy did not bring benefits to the Indians. On the contrary, numerous indigenous communities lost their lands and were forced into servile labor on the large estates. Despite holding legal citizenship rights, they were excluded from equal participation in the economic, social, and political system; the Indians, like other members of the popular classes, were only "imaginary citizens."[24] Indeed, these unequal relationships have often been described as a "caste system" in which the indigenous peoples occupied the lowest strata of the social pyramid. Special legislation often placed indigenous populations at a disadvantage in relation to the rest of society, even when some laws were of a protective and tutelary nature. While formal citizenship to all nationals was granted in most countries shortly after independence, in others members of Indian communities were treated as minors and as legally incompetent until very recently.

Indian cultures were thought to be backward, traditional, and not conducive to progress and modernity. Furthermore, the existence of a diversity of Indian cultures, distinct from the dominant, Western, urban culture of the elite, was considered to undermine efforts towards national unity and development. Thus, the solution found by governments and social scientists in the twentieth century was to further what has variously been called acculturation, assimilation, incorporation, or integration. For this purpose, the state set up specialized institutions and followed specific policies in the educational, cultural, economic, and social fields designed to integrate the Indian populations into the so-called national mainstream. Whereas in some countries indigenous affairs departments had been set up earlier, the parting shot of continental *indigenismo* was sounded at the First Inter-American Indianist Congress held in Mexico (1940), which established the Inter-American Indianist Institute to coordinate *indigenista* activities on the continent and laid down the general principles of this policy: to further the social and economic development of Indian communities, promote respect for their cultures, arts, and languages, and facilitate their integration into national society.[25] The prevailing thinking at the time was that the "Indian problem" was basically one of economic backwardness and that by promoting productive activities and community development at the local level, indigenous cultures were bound to disappear through a process of progressive modernization. This vision, promoted by mestizo intellectuals, was considered to be in the national interest and was to be actively pursued by government policy.[26]

To the extent that for several decades indigenous populations declined, it may be said that *indigenista* policies were successful, but as we have seen before, indigenous poverty and marginalization remain a crucial problem everywhere. *Indigenismo* helped the process of assimilation (which was going on in any case because of the changing economic and social circumstances), but it was unable to set in motion any kind of meaningful economic development leading to an overall improvement of standards of living among Indian communities. On the contrary, accelerated capitalist development in recent decades has been generally harmful to indigenous peoples.[27] It could be argued that as Indians move out of poverty and marginalization they become acculturated to the mestizo society and therefore are no longer counted as Indians, but this implies that the only way out of poverty for the indigenous is to cease being Indians, and it ignores the fact that much poverty and extreme poverty is now also an urban phenomenon.

Poverty and economic inequality explain much of the indigenous problematique, but there is a much deeper problem, and this is racism and discrimination. Racism is not so much based on perceptions of biological superiority and inferiority, inasmuch Latin America's population is becoming increasingly mestizo. What we are speaking about mainly is cultural discrimination, and this occurs because the prevailing dominant idea of the nation-state is based on Western values which ignore, deny, or reject the indigenous components of the national culture.[28]

To their economic backwardness and to social and cultural discrimination, must be added political exclusion. Despite enjoying formal citizenship, indigenous peoples did not have much of an opportunity to participate qua Indians in the political life of their nations until recently. They were expected to assimilate and in fact to disappear as culturally distinct entities and were not recognized as collective political actors. To achieve this objective was the purpose of the school system, religious missionary activities, as well as the various social policies designed to address what used to be call the "Indian problem." The school system, inspired by Spanish and French educational philosophies, was designed to impart national values and homogenize the population, from the schools that taught "Argentine national" identity to the children of immigrants and Indians (when the latter went to school at all), to the "socialist education" of the Mexican revolutionary governments in the 1930s. Indian schools were the transmitters of national culture and their task was to transform Indians into citizens. Native languages were not allowed in the school system, and "castellanización" became the declared objective.[29] Missionary activity in the process of Indian deculturation or ethnocide is also significant. Whereas Catholic missionary schools were determined to wipe out all indigenous culture, Protestant missionaries who began coming to Latin America in droves after the Second World War, mainly from the United States, used more sophisticated methods. In fact one notorious missionary institution, the Summer Institute of Linguistics from the USA, trained linguists in the use of Indian languages and proceeded to spread the word in native language texts. Protestantism has made considerable inroads in Latin America over the decades and is challenging the hitherto hegemonic position of the Catholic Church.[30]

As late as the 1960s scholars and politicians were still largely convinced that indigenous peoples and cultures would sooner or later disappear. In fact anthropological research was carried out to "retrieve" as much ethnographic information as possible while it was still out there and to document the changes leading to the progressive transformation of Indians into national citizens. The fashionable academic theoretical orientations of the times supported this view. On the one hand, theories of modernization and the sociology of development predicted the demise of the traditional Indian societies, deemed unsuitable for progress, and the accelerated transformation of Indians into members of the mestizo population. On the other hand, various strands of Marxist ideology considered Indians as unfit for revolutionary pursuits, and actively promoted their transformation into militant members of the oppressed working class. Indeed, Marxist analysts often denied the existence of ethnic issues at all, which they considered as "reactionary," and in this Marxist theory by and large coincided with the view of the "bourgeois" sociologists of development. This neglect sometimes spilled over into the practical strategic analyses of revolutionary movements with traumatic political and human costs for those who were unable or unwilling to recognize the social and cultural realities of their countries (the most dramatic examples in recent years are Guatemala, Nicaragua, and Peru).[31]

Indians become political actors

During the last half-millennium there have been numerous indigenous revolts and uprisings in Latin America that are not usually mentioned in official history books, perhaps because they ended in failure and repression. As scholars now acknowledge, Indian opposition to domination took the form of passive resistance, of turning inwards, and building protective shells around community life and cultural identity. This is what enabled so many indigenous cultures to survive into the twentieth century, though countless others did indeed disappear. To the surprise of many observers, the Indian peoples reappeared on the national scene in the 1970s and in less than a decade became newly organized social and political actors that states and national societies have been challenged to deal with. The factors which led to this emergence are many and complex, and the history of the diverse Indian movements and their impact remains to be written.

As the indigenous peoples became the victims of renewed assaults upon their lands, resources, and cultures in the latter half of the twentieth century, they began to adopt new forms of resistance and defense. Beginning in the seventies (though there were scattered initiatives before that), various types of indigenous organizations expressed claims about

Indian rights that had before been stated only occasionally and unsystematically. Some of these were local associations; others became regional in scope; and national coalitions and federations followed. Finally international organizations were set up. Congresses were held, manifestos were published, and the media and the politicians took notice. As in other forms of social and political mobilization, factionalism, divisions, and rivalries appeared. Grassroots organizations sprang up in different areas; local groups merged to structure organizations along ethnic-group lines; there were signs of alliances with peasant organizations, trade unions, teachers, and students, as well as political parties.

One of the earlier efforts at indigenous organization took place in Ecuador. Since the 1920s the militant Federation of Ecuadorean Indians (FEI), linked to the Communist Party, organized struggles around agrarian issues. It was soon followed by other associations, which concentrated their activities around peasant class-based demands. As social conflict over agrarian and trade union issues increased in the following decades, the mobilization of Indians became more common. In the eastern lowlands, the major issues were not land reform because there was no traditional peasantry linked to an exploitative landholding system. Rather, Indian territories came under attack from the expanding agribusiness and oil-prospecting interests. In this region, as in others, indigenous organization took on the form of the defense of a threatened ethnic homeland, and demands were phrased more in ethnic than in class language. In 1980 the various organizations came together in a first national congress of Indians and peasants, and formed the umbrella organization CONAIE, which came to play an increasingly political role by massive social mobilization, culminating in the failed attempt to stage a coup jointly with a group of army officers in January 2000.[32]

Indigenous social and political participation has taken various forms in different countries, even though it can usually be traced back to agrarian issues and peasant struggles over land. Indeed, by the mid-1960s, calls for agrarian reforms to eliminate unjust land tenure systems and provide landless peasants with access to land and resources, echoed across the continent. In the Peruvian highlands Indian peasants staged massive land occupations of large privately owned estates, led by radical political militants. This may be one of the reasons why Peruvian highland rural social movements have taken on much more of a "class" identity than an ethnic one. But indigenous organizations have become quite heterogeneous: some have an occupational basis, such as indigenous plantation workers, bilingual schoolteachers, traditional healers, and Indian lawyers. In some countries, such as Bolivia and Guatemala, attempts were made to set up indigenous political parties, whereas in others "indigenous sectors" of existing parties appeared: the PRI in Mexico organized a National Council of Indigenous Peoples but its fortunes have been rather unimpressive. The indigenous political party Movimiento Katarista Nacional was able to elect an Aymara schoolteacher as Bolivia's vice-president in 1993 in alliance with a traditional party, the Movimiento Nacionalista Revolucionario, but on its own its electoral showing has been poor.[33] A number of organizations, particularly at the national and international levels, were structured from the top down. In contrast to the 1960s, when no more than a handful of indigenous associations existed, by the beginning of the 1990s there were hundreds if not thousands continent-wide.

An interesting question has bothered analysts over the years. Why is it that in Bolivia and Ecuador ethnicity played an important role in recent indigenous mobilization but in Peru, which is also an Andean country, this did not take place? Why did the guerrilla group Sendero Luminoso appear solely as a class-based and not an ethnic movement, even though it was made up principally of indigenous peasants? Degregori argues that while ethnicity is certainly present in Peru, it is but one of several levels of identity, and that social unrest and peasant resistance are expressed through non-ethnic channels and organizations, such as *campesino* federations. Indian identity has always been stigmatized in Peru, and the state was able to process peasant demands in agrarian reform legislation and at the same time carry out a programme of "national integration." Massive migration from the Andes over a period of three decades turned Indian peasants into urban squatters in the Lima metropolis, where new identities have been fashioned in the process of "cholification" (*cholos* is the local name for cultural mestizos). Finally, the ideological impact of Marxism on political leaders and social militants emphasized class rather than ethnicity in political organization. Thus Sendero Luminoso was able to alienate a large part of the Indian population of the Andes, by attempting to force a "class identity" on Indian communities.[34] During the 1980s, peasant communities in several parts of Peru formed their own rural self-defense associations known as *rondas campesinas*, which were later recognized as legal entities by the state.[35]

Through the activities of their organizations the indigenous peoples have acquired a new awareness of their past and present situation and have become political actors in their own right. There is not one single model of such ethnic organizations, but rather different types of associations that reflect different kinds of circumstances. Thus we may find indigenous sections of wider trade union organizations (as for example, the Guaymí in the banana workers union in Panama). In addition, Indian ethnic groups have dominated some organizations, such as the Shuar Federation in eastern Ecuador (actually, one of the earliest Indian organizations in Latin America) and the National Mapuche Federation in Chile. There are also multi-ethnic regional organizations, such as the Consejo

Regional Indígena del Cauca (CRIC) in Colombia or the Consejo Regional de Pueblos Indios (CORPI) in Central America, as well as multiethnic national-level organizations such as the União de Nações Indigenas (UNI) in Brazil, now defunct, which included over one hundred different groups, and the Unión de Indígenas de El Salvador (UNIS). Such organizations may expand and consolidate over time, but often they are only short-lived and disintegrate as a result of attrition and internal factionalism. Thus it is a daunting task to list even the principal indigenous organizations in Latin America at any one time.

The activities of these organizations also vary considerably. Three main kinds of orientations may be distinguished. First there are organizations which are basically motivated by economic concerns such as struggling for trade union benefits or land rights, and which include ethnic and communal grievances and petitions in their negotiations with the state. Secondly, there are the strictly ethnic movements, which develop integral communal projects and demands. Yet another type of organization is principally political, usually made up of a small group of motivated intellectuals and activists, who develop and promote the ethnic ideology of "Indianity" in its various guises.[36]

Many of the indigenous organizations received early support from outside sympathizers, who were at times instrumental in their emergence. Christian missionaries were particularly active in the 1960s and 1970s in establishing some of these organizations. Yet as time has passed, local leadership has taken over and external advisers have become secondary. Occasionally, governments have fostered and tried to control such organizations, basically in order to pre-empt possible oppositional activity. More commonly, however, governments have tried to fragment these movements and in more than one case they have suffered severe repression at the hands of the military. Colombia, Chile, and Guatemala during the 1970s and 1980s are cases in point. Overall, the traditional political parties of Latin America have not seriously concerned themselves with indigenous problems, and while there are numerous indigenous members of political parties of various tendencies, and some of them have been elected to Parliament or Congress while others occasionally occupy token Cabinet positions, indigenous demands have hardly become an electoral issue in any country.

Frustrated by traditional party politics and often exasperated by the slow progress that national governments are making in dealing seriously with their demands, a number of indigenous movements have sought alternative ways of political action. The best known example is surely the uprising of the Zapatista National Liberation Army in south-eastern Mexico in 1994. The Zapatistas, a ragtag group of indigenous peasants in one of Mexico's poorest regions, rose up in arms against the national

government in January 1994, demanding the recognition of their peren-
nially denied rights, solutions to a large number of agrarian and social
problems, a change in the government's neo-liberal policies which had
affected them quite negatively, and effective democratic participation in
the national political system.

After ten days of fighting with several hundred victims, a ceasefire was
declared and laborious peace negotiations began which extended for many
months. A first agreement between the Zapatistas and the government was
signed in February 1996. This accord focused on indigenous rights and
culture, one of the six items to have been discussed (the other five items
on the agenda were not taken up). Among its provisions it included recognition of the need for new national legislation setting up some kind of
local and regional autonomy for indigenous peoples. Whereas this provision appeared to have been accepted by official negotiators at the beginning, the government later backed away from its commitment, arguing
that autonomy would threaten the territorial integrity of the state and
national unity, and that the recognition by the state of the customary laws
of indigenous communities would be in violation of the national constitutional order. Scholars and others pointed out that such an interpretation of the accords was unwarranted, but six years later the national
authorities had not budged on this issue.[37]

In the meantime, the local situation in Chiapas deteriorated markedly.
While the ceasefire was holding up, to the extent that no direct military
confrontation took place, local violence and human rights abuses were on
the increase. Observers accused the government of adopting a strategy of
"low-intensity warfare" and other counter-insurgency tactics, such as the
arming of paramilitary groups in several regions of the state which are
known to intimidate and harass Zapatista sympathizers and grass-roots
organizations. This atmosphere of tension led in numerous communities
to acts of violence between Zapatista supporters and other groups close
to the government. In December 1997 one such paramilitary group at-
tacked an unarmed gathering of people sitting in a prayer meeting and
killed 45 men, women, and children. As a result of the expanding violence in areas not directly under the control of the Zapatista army, many
thousands of indigenous families have become internal refugees. Human
rights organizations the world over have monitored the situation in
Chiapas.

Here as in other areas of confrontation involving indigenous peoples, a
newly emerging indigenous intelligentsia has played a fundamental role,
aided by Indian advocates from the social sciences, the churches, and a
number of political formations. In earlier years, the intelligentsia would
have been siphoned off and assimilated into the dominant society. While
this is still an ongoing process, indigenous professional people, intellec-

tuals, and political activists are increasingly adopting a conscious ethnic identity and providing leadership to their communities. The new leadership is also displacing the more traditional kind of community authority which has played such a fundamental role in the period of passive resistance and retrenchment when, as anthropologists would have it, Indian peoples lived in closed, corporate communities. As Indian communities are also becoming internally differentiated according to socio-economic criteria, so the new indigenous leaders often reflect different interests in the community itself. Whether this leadership represents the interests of the indigenous ethnic groups at large, or only those of an emerging "indigenous bourgeoisie," is being widely debated currently. Guatemala provides a good example of the rise of a new, widely encompassing ethnic identity. Mayan intellectuals have built up over the years a Pan-Maya cultural movement, which poses serious challenges to the dominant view of the nation-state and at the same time refuses to play the game of the political parties of the Right and the Left. It has contributed to changing the self-perception of the Indians as well as of the Ladinos (the non-Indians) in the Guatemalan state, but its long-term impact on the nation is still an open question.[38]

Democracy and the indigenous: Some tentative conclusions

The expansion of Indian movements and their demands can be seen as a process of increasing empowerment of indigenous peoples in Latin America, which coincides with similar phenomena in other parts of the world. What are their principal demands? Why are they occurring at this time, and how do they relate to other important changes in the region?

The indigenous agenda that has developed over the years includes a number of crucial issues for the future democratic evolution of Latin America. High on the list is the right to land and the recognition of their own territories, a concept that is not easily accepted by governments. Many of the Indian organizations demand the recognition and demarcation of these territories as a necessary step for their social, economic, and cultural survival. In Panama, the San Blas Kuna have obtained constitutional protection of their territory; so have the Yanomami Indians in northern Brazil. The Mapuche of southern Chile and the Miskitos of Nicaragua, among many others, have been in the forefront of these struggles in their countries. The Colombian constitution of 1991 recognizes the traditional homelands of a number of indigenous groups and assures them of legal protection.

The right to their own culture and to bilingual and intercultural education has also emerged as an insistent demand, and in a number of countries, as in Bolivia for example, bilingual and multicultural education is constitutionally stipulated. In others it is being practiced with varying results. More problematically, indigenous organizations have been raising the banner of local autonomy, self-determination, and political representation. Though governments reject the claim because of its possible international implications, the right of peoples to self-determination is understood by indigenous organizations mainly as the right to local and regional autonomy, and has never been interpreted as implying secession or separation from an existing state. Some Latin American states are more open towards these demands, whereas others, such as Mexico, are deeply suspicious of them. Indigenous spokespersons insist that self-determination and local or regional autonomy are essential features of a democratic polity.

It is clear that the emergence of the Latin American indigenous movements as an expression of resistance happened during a period of political closure and increasing economic and social exclusion in a number of countries, at the same time that ethnic and nationalist demands were also coming to the fore (for other reasons perhaps) in other parts of the world. However, the indigenous movements expanded rapidly and were able to articulate their grievances and demands, as well as build links and networks to other organizations, during the period of transition to more democratic polities. Simultaneously, indigenous populations became particularly vulnerable to the negative effects of globalization and so-called structural adjustments, including the retreat of the state from the active promotion of social development, within the framework of privatization and neo-liberal modernization. Moreover, it is no coincidence that the emergence of an indigenous political presence happened during a period of transition (the 1980s principally) in which some Latin American countries overcame the heavy burden of military dictatorships and authoritarian regimes and returned to a semblance of civilian and democratic rule. By the 1990s the old Cold War confrontations had begun to fade and earlier rigid ideological positions became more flexible, while Latin American societies searched for more democratic governance. As numerous observers noted at the time, the traditional party systems and exclusionary political regimes were in deep crisis and in their attempt to re-establish democratic legitimacy, the political elites, spurred on by opposition and popular movements, embarked upon state reforms and constitutional transformations in a number of countries, which were designed, among other things, to broaden the basis of political representation, consolidate the rule of law, modernize state institutions, and further governmental accountability.[39]

In a wave of constitutionalist fervour numerous Latin American states reformed their constitutions during the 1980s and 1990s, and many of them included, some for the first time, the issue of indigenous rights and representation in their new legal texts. In some cases important secondary legislation on indigenous issues was adopted. This activity coincided with the drafting of new international legal instruments in the field of indigenous human rights, such as the UN Declaration on Indigenous Rights (still stalled in the UN Human Rights Commission at the beginning of 2001), and the adoption of Convention 169 on indigenous and tribal peoples by the International Labor Organization in 1989.[40] In fact, the issue of indigenous rights coincides with the emergence and expansion of a vast and assertive human rights movement in Latin America involving many disparate social groups and segments, which has been instrumental in turning the tide against authoritarianism and promoting democratic transformations, even as it opens the doors to greater participation by civil society in the political process.[41]

One of the earlier and more remarkable constitutional changes was undertaken in Brazil. The Brazilian indigenous movement arose during the 1970s in response to the military government's attempt to accelerate the Indians' "integration" into national society by eliminating existing, if hardly efficient, tutelary mechanisms and allowing private interests to usurp traditional Indian lands. The mobilization of Indian groups became a rallying cry for democratic opposition forces to the military regime. By 1987, after a return to civilian government, a public groundswell for a new political constitution had taken hold in which Indian organizations and their many advocates and sympathizers, especially the Catholic Church, played a major role. Indians were active participants in the Constitutional Assembly in 1987, and the discussion concerning Indian rights in the new constitution became the object of intense public debate. Formally adopted in 1988, the new Brazilian constitution contains a chapter on Indians which recognizes their rights to land and natural resources as well as their capacity for legal action (which had been denied them in earlier legislation in which they were treated as legal minors). One of the difficulties of implementing the new constitution is that the indigenous represent less than 0.2 per cent of Brazil's population but occupy vast areas of the Amazon and central Brazil (some estimates mention over 9 per cent of Brazil's surface), territories that powerful private transnational interests, and millions of poor landless squatters from the coastal areas, have long coveted. Soon after the constitution was adopted, the vested interests organized to prevent its implementation in the Indian areas, generating numerous conflicts that have now been diverted into judiciary channels, and thwarting the adoption of a new statute for the indigenous peoples.[42]

Perhaps of more lasting significance are the constitutional reforms undertaken in countries where the indigenous represent a larger part of the total population. Such reforms were adopted in Argentina (1994), Bolivia (1994), Colombia (1991), Ecuador (1998), Guatemala (1986), Mexico (1992), Nicaragua (1987), Paraguay (1992), Peru (1993), and Venezuela (1999), countries whose indigenous peoples make up over 90 per cent of the total indigenous population of Latin America.[43] All of these constitutional transformations occurred within a span of little more than a decade, a period characterized by the retreat of military dictatorships, intense social mobilization, and in some cases, violent civil strife. While the extent of constitutional reform regarding indigenous peoples varies from country to country, the long-term implications will have to be judged by the effectiveness of implementation and the nature of the accompanying secondary legislation. A number of elements are common to most if not all of these transformations: the specific cultural identities of indigenous peoples; their rights to land and territory, and sometimes to natural resources; the right to education in their own languages; the (occasional) recognition of their customary legal institutions and local authority structures; the obligation of governments to respect their values and identities; their right to be consulted and heard by government authorities over decisions affecting their livelihoods (including development projects); and their eventual participation in public and political affairs. States are explicitly or implicitly obliged to respect cultural and ethnic diversity and to carry out bilingual and intercultural educational policies.[44]

More than an expansion of indigenous rights is at stake here. In fact, the new debate between the state and indigenous peoples challenges some basic notions concerning state and nation. The Ecuadorean Indians who staged an uprising in January 2000 demanded a complete reformation of the state and the establishment of "radical democracy," but were unable to obtain the political support of the wider society.[45] The Maya associations in Guatemala are more than a cultural movement; they propose an entirely new national project based on the recognition of ethnic diversity and multicultural citizenship.[46]

Indeed, two centuries after their emergence as independent states, a number of Latin American nations are faced with the challenge of reformulating their national projects, which relates to the burning issue of redefining citizenship and the nature of democratic polities. In Western democracies which are based on solid liberal principles current debates have noticed the "boundaries" and "limits" to classical notions of citizenship.[47] The emerging concept of multicultural citizenship may also find useful application, *pari passu*, in Latin America's multiethnic societies.[48] As I have written in another context,[49] multicultural citizenship in Latin America, as far as indigenous peoples are concerned, includes their recognition as peoples with clearly defined legal status and possessing the rights to self-determination, to indigenous communities as legally recognized entities in public law holding autonomous rights, to Indian languages as national languages, to the demarcation of their own protected territories, and to handle their own resources and development projects. It also involves respect for their internal norms of governance and their customary legal systems, freedom of religion and culture in community with others, and political participation and representation at the regional and national levels. Multicultural citizenship as far as indigenous peoples are concerned must have two essential reference points: the unity of the democratic state and respect for individual human rights within the autonomic units that may be established. Neither pure liberal individualism nor the corporativist structure of the state respond to the needs of a multicultural citizenship: this can only be built upon democratic practice, within the framework of dialogue, tolerance and mutual respect, in which indigenous peoples may finally find the dignity and recognition they have been denied for so long, and where the long struggle for their human rights may finally be rewarded.

Notes

1. Takashi Inoguchi, Edward Newman, and John Keane (eds.), *The Changing Nature of Democracy* (Tokyo: United Nations University Press, 1998).
2. Adam Przeworski et al., *Sustainable Democracy* (Cambridge: Cambridge University Press, 1995), p. 107.
3. Ibid., p. 34.
4. "We don't accept the presidential succession," said Indian leader Salvador Quishpe. "Mr. Noboa [the new president] wants to take advantage of our people's fight to keep helping the same people as always, the corrupt bankers. We will defend our historic fight." He was later charged with sedition. CNN, 23 January 2000; *La Jornada* (Mexico) January 24, 2000.
5. In fact, a new "uprising" took place early in 2001 (after this essay had been finished).
6. Diego Iturralde, "Lucha indígena y reforma neoliberal" (unpublished manuscript, 2000).
7. Projects such as a hydroelectric dam on the Bio-Bio river were promoted without regard to the rights of indigenous inhabitants by the Pinochet dictatorship, and have been implemented by government-supported private enterprises. The dam directly affects the livelihoods of more than seventy Pehuelche families, and their cause has been taken up by many national and international indigenous rights advocate organizations.
8. Alexia Peyser and Juan Chackiel, "La población indígena en los censos de América Latina," in CELADE, *Estudios sociodemográficos de pueblos indígenas* (Santiago de Chile: CELADE, 1994); Rodolfo Stavenhagen, "La situación y los derechos de los pueblos indígenas de America," *América Indígena* January–June 1992; 52(1–2): pp. 63–118; Mary Lisbeth González, "How Many Indigenous People?" in George Psacharopoulos and Harry Anthony Patrinos (eds.), *Indigenous People and Poverty in Latin America: An Empirical Analysis* (Washington, D.C.: The World Bank, 1994), pp. 21–39.
9. Magda Ruiz Salguero and Yolanda Bodnar Contreras, "El carácter multiétnico de Colombia y sus implicaciones censales," in CELADE, *Estudios sociodemográficos de pueblos indígenas.*

10. Luz María Valdés, *El perfil demográfico de los indios mexicanos* (Mexico City: Siglo XXI, 1988) p. 39.

11. Hundreds of Indian languages have disappeared since the sixteenth century. Some have only a handful of native speakers, while others number in the millions. Many languages have several variations and dialects. A number of distinct languages actually emerged after the Conquest as a result of linguistic contact with African and European populations (such as Garifona along Central America's Atlantic coast). Others, such as Quechua in the Andes and Guaraní in Paraguay, became vehicular languages for larger populations during the colonial period.

12. On Mexico see Frank Cancian, *The Decline of Community in Zinacantan: Economy, Public Life, and Social Stratification, 1960–1987* (Stanford, Calif.: Stanford University Press, 1992); David Frye, *Indians into Mexicans: History and Identity in a Mexican Town* (Austin: University of Texas Press, 1996).

13. For a Colombian case study see Herinaldy Gómez and Carlos Ariel Ruiz, *Los paeces: Gente territorio, Metáfora que perdura* (Cauca: Universidad del Cauca, 1997).

14. Ricardo Pozas and Isabel H. de Pozas, *Los indios en las clases sociales de México* (Mexico City: Siglo XXI, 1971); Carlos Vilas, *State, Class and Ethnicity in Nicaragua* (Boulder, Colo.: Lynne Rienner, 1989); Philippe I. Bourgois, *Ethnicity at Work: Divided Labor on a Central American Banana Plantation* (Baltimore: Johns Hopkins University Press, 1989).

15. Rodolfo Stavenhagen, "Classes, Colonialism, and Acculturation," in *Studies in Comparative International Development* 1965; 1(6).

16. The World Bank, *Poverty Reduction and the World Bank: Progress and Challenges in the 1990s* (Washington, D.C.: The World Bank, 1996).

17. BID, CEPAL, and PNUD, *Informe de la Comisión latinoamericana y del Caribe sobre el desarrollo social 1995* (Santiago de Chile: CEPAL, 1995).

18. Psacharopoulos and Patrinos, *Indigenous People and Poverty in Latin America: An Empirical Analysis.* The bank fixes the poverty line at an income of two dollars a day, and the extreme poverty line at one dollar a day. The data are based on household surveys, and the poverty line is fixed according to the cost of a basket of goods (mainly food) required to meet a person's basic material needs.

19. These paragraphs are adapted from Rodolfo Stavenhagen, "The Culture of Resistance in Latin America: New Thinking About Old Issues," in Selo Soemardjan and Kenneth W. Thompson (eds.), *Culture, Development, and Democracy: The Role of the Intellectual* (Tokyo: United Nations University Press, 1995), pp. 155–79.

20. Simón Bolívar, *Discurso de Angostura*, in *Latinoamérica 30: Cuadernos de cultura latinoamericana* (Mexico City: UNAM, 1978). English version in Vicente Lecuna and Harold A. Beirck (eds.), *Selected Writings of Bolivar*, vol. 1 (New York: Colonial Press, 1951), p. 181.

21. Pablo González Casanova (ed.), *Cultura y creación intelectual en América Latina* (Mexico City: Siglo XXI, 1979); Hugo Zemelman (ed.), *Cultura y política en América Latina* (Mexico City: Siglo XXI, 1990); Leopoldo Zea, *The Latin American Mind* (Norman: University of Oklahoma Press, 1963).

22. Carlos Iván Degregori, "Identidad étnica, movimientos sociales y participación política en el Peru," in *Democracia, etnicidad y violencia política en los países andinos* (Lima: Instituto de Estudios Peruanos, 1993).

23. Magnus Mörner, *Race Mixture in the History of Latin America* (Boston: Little Brown, 1967); Richard Graham (ed.), *The Idea of Race in Latin America, 1870–1940* (Austin: University of Texas Press, 1990); Agustín Basave Benítez, *México mestizo* (Mexico City: Fondo de Cultura Económica, 1992).

24. Fernando Escalante, *Ciudadanos imaginarios* (Mexico City: El Colegio de México, 1992).

25. Alejandro D. Marroquín, *Balance del indigenismo* (Mexico City: Instituto Indigenista Interamericano, 1972).
26. Gonzalo Agruirre Beltrán, *El proceso de aculturación* (Mexico City: UNAM, 1957).
27. The Zapatista Liberation Army in southeastern Mexico stated this very clearly in its first published document, *Declaración de la Lacandona*, in which it justified its armed uprising in 1994. Other indigenous gatherings continent-wide have underscored this as well. See the Web site www.ezln.org.
28. Alicia Castellanos Guerrero and Juan Manuel Sandoval (eds.), *Nación, racismo e identidad* (Mexico City: Editorial Nuestro Tiempo, 1998).
29. Gonzalo Aguirre Beltrán, *Teoría y práctica de la educación indígena* (Mexico City: SepSetentas, 1973); Shirley B. Heath, *La política del lenguaje en México: De la colonia a la nación* (Mexico City: Instituto Nacional Indigenista, 1977).
30. David Stoll, *Fishers of Men or Founders of Empire?* (London: Zed Press, 1982); Soren Hvalkof and Peter Aaby, *Is God an American?* (Copenhagen: International Work Group for Indigenous Affairs and Survival International, 1981). See also David Stoll, *Is Latin America Turning Protestant?* (Austin: Texas University Press, 1988). The Summer Institute of Linguistics was invited to come to Mexico in the 1930s by President Cárdenas to help in the government's effort to create Indian language alphabets for schooling in native tongues as a step towards the acquisition of Spanish as the "national language." The SIL was accused during the Cold War of "spying" for the CIA and was later expelled from various Latin American countries where it had established its missions. In Mexico the government broke its contract with the institute but did not actually expel its missionary-linguists from the country. See also Mark Münzel, *The Aché Indians: Genocide in Paraguay,* IWGIA Report No. 11 (Copenhagen: International Work Group for Indigenous Affairs, n.d.), and by the same author, *The Aché: Genocide Continues in Paraguay,* IWGIA Report No. 17 (Copenhagen, International Work Group for Indigenous Affairs, n.d.).
31. One comparative political scientist wrote in the mid-seventies: "The availability of the mestizo channel of mobility is crucial and distinguishes the Latin American setting from most culturally plural environments.... No Latin American political movement has ever operated on the national level through the mobilization of Indian racial or ethnic solidarity." Crawford Young, *The Politics of Cultural Pluralism* (Madison: University of Wisconsin Press, 1976), pp. 458–59.
32. Interestingly, CONAIE was formed as a non-political organization, but it soon became involved in the country's politics, and some of its member associations fielded candidates at election times. Several prominent indigenous leaders now occupy crucial positions in Ecuador's parliament. See Diego Iturralde, "Movimientos indígenas y contiendas electorales (Ecuador y Bolivia)," in Miguel A. Bartolomé and Alicia M. Barabas (eds.), *Autonomías étnicas y estados nacionales* (Mexico City: Conaculta, 1998). For a study of the early stages of Indian organization see Alicia Ibarra, *Los indígenas y el estado en el Ecuador* (Quito: Ediciones Abya-Yala, 1987). Also, Melina H. Selverston, "The Politics of Culture: Indigenous Peoples and the State in Ecuador," in Donna Lee Van Cott (ed.), *Indigenous Peoples and Democracy in Latin America* (New York: St. Martin's Press, 1994).
33. Xavier Albó, "And from Kataristas to MNRistas? The Surprising and Bold Alliance between Aymaras and Neoliberals in Bolivia," in Van Cott, *Indigenous Peoples and Democracy in Latin America.*
34. Degregori, "Identidad étnica, movimientos sociales y participación política en el Peru"; also María Isabel Remy, "The Indigenous Population and the Construction of Democracy in Peru," in Van Cott, *Indigenous Peoples and Democracy in Latin America.*
35. Ana María Vidal, "Derecho oficial y derecho campesino en el mundo andino," in Rodolfo Stavenhagen and Diego Iturralde (eds.), *Entre la ley y la costumbre: El derecho*

consuetudinario indígena en América Latina (Mexico City: Instituto Indigenista Interamericano and Instituto Interamericano de Derechos Humanos, 1990), pp. 141–53; Orin Starn, *Nightwatch: The Politics of Protest in the Andes* (Durham, N.C.: Duke University Press, 1999); Raquel Irigoyen, "Un caso de pluralidad jurídica en Perú: Las rondas campesinas de Cajamarca," in José Luis Dominguez (ed.), *La joven sociología jurídica en España* (Oñati: International Institute for the Sociology of Law, 1998).

36. On indigenous intellectuals in Mexico see Natividad Gutiérrez, *Nationalist Myths and Ethnic Identities: Indigenous Intellectuals and the Mexican State* (Lincoln: University of Nebraska Press, 1999).

37. For views on the peace negotiations see Cynthia Arnson and Raúl Benítez Manaut (eds.), *Chiapas: Los desafíos de la paz* (Mexico City: ITAM, Woodrow Wilson Center, Porrúa, 2000). For a blow-by-blow account of the uprising and its aftermath to 2000, see John Ross, *The War Against Oblivion: The Zapatista Chronicles* (Monroe, Maine: Common Courage Press, 2000). After a new administration took power in Mexico in December 2000, the Zapatistas organized a peaceful caravan to Mexico City to press their claims, and the legislative branch of government considered a bill on indigenous rights and culture which had been drafted on the basis of the earlier accords signed by the Zapatistas and the previous government.

38. Kay B. Warren, *Indigenous Movements and Their Critics: Pan-Maya Activism in Guatemala* (Princeton, N.J.: Princeton University Press, 1998).

39. Terry Lynn Karl, "Dilemmas of Democratization in Latin America," *Comparative Politics* 1990; 23(1): pp. 1–21; Scott Mainwaring, Guillermo O'Donnell, and J. Samuel Valenzuela (eds.), *Issues in Democratic Consolidation: The New South American Democracies in Comparative Perspective* (Notre Dame, Ind.: University of Notre Dame Press, 1992).

40. Activity in the UN system concerning indigenous peoples began in the early eighties and received further support by the declaration of an international year of indigenous people in 1993 and an international decade of indigenous people in 1995–2004. On indigenous peoples' rights see Rodolfo Stavenhagen, *Derecho indígena y derechos humanos en América Latina* (Mexico City: El Colegio de México and Instituto Interamericano de Derechos Humanos, 1988); and Rodolfo Stavenhagen, *Derechos humanos de los pueblos indígenas* (Mexico City: Comisión Nacional de los Derechos Humanos, 2000).

41. Kathryn Sikkink, "The Emergence, Evolution, and Effectiveness of the Latin American Human Rights Network," in Elizabeth Jelin and Eric Herschberg (eds.), *Constructing Democracy: Human Rights, Citizenship, and Society in Latin America* (Boulder, Colo.: Westview Press, 1996), pp. 59–84.

42. Maria Teresa Sierra, *La lucha por los derechos indígenas en el Brasil actual* (Mexico City: CIESAS, 1993); Silvio Coelho dos Santos, "Pueblos indígenas de Brasil: Derechos constitucionales, tierras y luchas presentes," in Miguel A. Bartolomé and Alicia M. Barabas (eds.), *Autonomías étnicas y estados nacionales* (Mexico City: INAH, 1998) pp. 215–29.

43. The recognition of indigenous collective rights and territories is also established in Panama's Constitution of 1972, a special case in Latin America. Whereas Guatemala's 1986 Constitution gives perfunctory recognition to its indigenous population (the country's majority), the basic issues were taken up in the peace accord between the Guatemalan government and the guerrilla forces (UNRG) in 1995, but a referendum to amend the Constitution accordingly was defeated in 1999.

44. Cletus Gregor Barié Kolb, "Los derechos indígenas en las constituciónes latinoamericanas contemporáneas" (unpublished thesis, National University of Mexico, 1998); Donna Lee Van Cott, *The Friendly Liquidation of the Past: The Politics of Diversity in Latin America* (Pittsburgh: University of Pittsburgh Press, 2000).

45. "El movimiento indígena había propuesto una crítica radical a la democracia ecuatoriana, pero no había sustentado esa crítica con un proyecto creíble y legítimo de cambio social al mediano y largo plazo." Editorial in *Boletín Rimay* (Quito, Instituto Científico de Culturas Indígenas) 13 April 2000; (13).

46. Demetrio Cojtí Cuxil, *Políticas para la reivindicación de los Mayas de hoy: Fundamento de los Derechos Específicos del Pueblo Maya* (Guatemala City: SPEM-CHOLSAMAJ, 1994); Jesús García Ruiz, *Hacia una nación pluricultural en Guatemala: Responsabilidad histórica y viabilidad política* (Guatemala City: CEDIM, 1997).

47. Spinner argues for pluralistic rather than liberal integration in the state, whereas Soysal notices the new idea of "postnational" membership in European societies. See Jeff Spinner, *The Boundaries of Citizenship: Race, Ethnicity, and Nationality in the Liberal State* (Baltimore: Johns Hopkins University Press, 1994); and Yasemin Nuholu Soysal, *Limits of Citizenship: Migrants and Postnational Membership in Europe* (Chicago: University of Chicago Press, 1994).

48. Will Kymlicka, *Multicultural Citizenship* (Oxford: Clarendon Press, 1995); Charles Taylor et al., *Multiculturalism* (Princeton, N.J.: Princeton University Press, 1994).

49. Rodolfo Stavenhagen, "Derechos humanos y ciudadanía multicultural: Los pueblos indígenas," in Emma Martín Díaz and Sebastián de la Obra Sierra (eds.), *Repensando la ciudadanía* (Seville: Fundación El Monte, 1999) pp. 77–107.

8

Reconciliation

Edward Newman

The ghosts of the past, if not exorcised to the fullest extent possible, will continue to haunt the nation tomorrow.

– José Zalaquett[1]

A pervading challenge has accompanied (re)democratization in many Latin American countries: how to balance the needs of justice, truth, and reconciliation in a viable and progressive democratic project. The manner in which (sometimes fragile) democracies have dealt with a history of human rights abuse and dictatorship – amidst a plethora of political and social tensions – is a major theme of democratic transition and consolidation.[2] This challenge is central to the processes of (re)democratization – and for some people, even the concept of citizenship – in the region. The legacy of brutality and human rights abuse has left its mark not only upon the dynamics and terms of democratic transition but on public life. This legacy is thus central to the nature of transition.

The modalities of dealing with a past of human rights abuse – the possibilities for achieving justice and accountability – are conditioned and in most cases constrained by the terms and pace of democratic transition. Moreover, the manner in which political elites and society in general deal with this legacy is central to the democratic project. Thus, even when democratic transition and consolidation are no longer jeopardized or threatened by regression in the search for justice and accountability – in countries such as Chile, Argentina, Uruguay, and Brazil – this does not mean that the public modalities of dealing with the past do not have an impact upon the quality of public life and democratic institutions. The deficiencies of dealing with the past, of achieving truth, justice, accountability and transparency – the elusiveness of "reconciliation" – may not threaten the "procedural minimum" of democracy.[3] Yet these deficiencies continue to impose constraints upon democratic institutions, upon a sense of reconciliation, upon unity of purpose in an inclusive progressive democratic project as the legacy of the past continues to divide society and bring into question the legitimacy of democratic institutions.

This issue is thus central to the (re)construction of political society in many Latin American societies coming to terms with a history of division and human rights abuse. Beyond this, reconciliation is not only a restorative project of dealing with past abuses of human rights, but also one of reconciling disparate visions of progress and democracy and overcoming social and ethnic divisions that lay behind conflict in the past and continue even though the conflict itself may have ceased. This essay will therefore (1) explore the modalities of reconciliation, of dealing with past abuses of human rights, in the context of different trajectories of democratic transition and consolidation; (2) consider the successes and deficiencies of dealing with the past and the promise of achieving genuine reconciliation, which has often left an ongoing struggle for the truth and accountability; and (3) offer some comparative observations between "national" attempts at reconciliation – such as in Chile, Argentina, Brazil, and Uruguay – and "international" efforts to the same end – such as in El Salvador, Guatemala, and Nicaragua – which reflect a greater prominence of transnational norms of humanitarian conduct and governance. The essay will consider if the growing prominence of transnational forces – reflected in a growing body of international law and an increasing recourse to international tribunals and courts that have a humanitarian remit – is changing the balance of power of transition in favour of accountability and justice, and challenging the pragmatism of trade-offs and impunity that earlier appeared to necessarily be the price of democratic transition and stability.[4] Thus, the formulas of "balancing ethical imperatives and political constraints" and "settl[ing] a past account without upsetting the present transition"[5] may be evolving in the context of international norms and laws that impose expectations of accountability.

Dealing with the past: The perennial challenges

As democratic forms of government replace authoritarian regimes and civil conflict, a central issue in the success of this transition is the management of past human rights abuses and crimes against humanity. A sense of justice and accountability for the past is integral to sustainable democracy and to installing a sense of confidence and trust into public life. Moreover, this is not just a historical issue: "disappearances" from the past continue to impose intolerable cruelty upon family members and human rights abuses continue to occur, even after the establishment of democratic political procedures. Conversely, the appearance of impunity for past crimes undermines confidence in new democratic structures and casts doubt upon commitments to human rights, which are integral to successful consolidation.

Simultaneously, however, the search for the truth and for accountability can be destabilizing and can prolong, even obstruct, the transition to and consolidation of democracy. In many cases the transition from authoritarian rule depends upon the co-operation of actors and individuals directly involved in human rights abuses in the past. This has involved a delicate balance. The victims' demands for justice must surely be addressed, but the participation and support of all major actors – including the perpetrators of crimes and their supporters – in the democratic system is sometimes essential for its short-term sustainability. The lack of support of some actors for democratic institutions – again, sometimes including the perpetrators of crimes and their supporters – clearly challenges the stability and credibility of democracy. Reconciliation has thus been difficult. Amnesty – even immunity – has been a necessary component but inevitably it has been difficult to forget, much less forgive, the suffering which has occurred. Many countries have sought a middle course – supported by judicial procedures and international monitors – which has been politically realistic but which has not satisfied large sections of society.

There is a paradox to be solved. Justice is necessary in order to move forward; it is integral to the democratization process. But stability and the inclusion and support of all actors make the search for truth and justice difficult. How are Latin American countries managing this dilemma? With what degree of success? To what degree, and with what effect, does the management of the past condition democratic politics? How are the lessons learnt from earlier experiences applied to more recent cases?

The framework

The legacy of human rights abuse is never far away from politics in many Latin American countries, although experiences vary very widely. The parameters for dealing with former abusers of human rights have in almost every case been determined by the dynamics and pace of transition, and in particular the balance of power at work within the transition. (Now that transition is accomplished, however, we are witnessing a different set of dynamics at work – for example in Chile and Argentina – which offer different opportunities for accountability.) It is commonly observed, for example, that different outcomes (in terms of seeking redress and dealing with past human rights abuse) often accompany different models of transition. We can offer a fourfold typology: where the transition from military/authoritarian government was a negotiated transition on terms laid down, at least partly, by the military; where the transition followed the collapse of the regime and/or the military; where the transition to democracy followed civil war and a restoration of government; and where foreign intervention conditioned the process of transition. In the context of this volume, the difference between *foundational* and *transitional* democratization is instructive.

Reconciliation involves many processes. It involves achieving social cohesion and unity of purpose in overcoming and coming to terms with the divisions, abuse, and conflict of the past. It involves learning from the past in embracing the future by addressing wrongs within the framework of a national project that is both political and social and integral to the process of democratization. It involves symbolism. It involves giving meaning to human rights in the present by addressing the security of people in their everyday lives, even though the political polarization of the past may be over and violence is not necessarily ideological any longer. Beyond the banners of accountability, truth, and justice, it also involves addressing the roots of conflict and division that lie behind abuse.

Patterns of abuse

The extent of abuse is very well documented and understood within and outside the region. It is necessary only to remind ourselves of that here with some illustrative examples. Readers already familiar with the historical background of human rights abuse in the region may wish to pass over this section. A number of social and political patterns arose across much of the region as the backdrop to repression. In the Cold War context, socio-economic change and development radicalized a clash of social and political forces in many countries in the 1950s to 1970s, leading to a violent reaction on the part of the establishment forces.

In Argentina, after the 1976 coup that deposed President Isabel Perón in the midst of violent social and political instability, a succession of military leaders pursued a "dirty war" against purported left-wing subversives that led to the extrajudicial death, disappearance, torture, and intimidation of tens of thousands of people; according to some estimates the number of killed or disappeared was 30,000. Whilst "excesses" were cynically acknowledged by members of the armed forces, the military remained defiant, maintaining that the brutality was somehow justified by the necessity of defending national security or Western, Christian values.[6] International condemnation, growing domestic opposition, and economic deterioration were compounded by the Argentinian military defeat by the British in the Malvinas/Falklands war. Efforts to deal with the abuses of the authoritarian period between 1976 and 1983 in Argentina have proved to be a microcosm of the tensions and dilemmas of these issues throughout the region.

It is widely argued that the military's weakness following its defeat in 1982 allowed a particularly wide margin of action by the first civilian president who came to power the following year, Raúl Alfonsín. In fact, the process of accountability and justice was constrained and finally suffered a partial reversal. Upon entering office, Alfonsín appointed a National Commission on Disappeared Persons under the leadership of Ernesto Sabato. What happened subsequently is well known. The final report, *Nunca Más*, was widely read and recognized as being authoritative. The "Law of National Pacification," an amnesty granted to the military by itself, was repealed and prosecutions were begun against officials of the first three juntas on charges of mishandling the Falklands/Malvinas war and abuses of human rights; five men were convicted and sentenced to prison. Following the junta trials the courts addressed violations by other personnel. The armed forces strongly resisted this and, beginning in 1986, staged a number of minor rebellions to demonstrate their recalcitrance and unity in opposition to any purge.

Under intense pressure, the government sought to limit the trials by imposing a "Full Stop Law," a two-month deadline for processing criminal complaints against military officers by members of the public. This speeded up the filing of complaints and antagonized the military further. The result was a rebellion at Easter 1987 as the tensions between accountability and democratic consolidation erupted into a dramatic standoff. Alfonsín met with the rebels and made a number of concessions, in particular the "Due Obedience Law" which was passed in June. By essentially exonerating all military personnel on the basis of the principle that those involved in human rights abuses had been obeying orders, further prosecutions were effectively halted. The power of the military – some six military coups had occurred since the 1930s – was pervasive. Alfonsín was thus forced to compromise on his determination to challenge the history of impunity in the country, later arguing that punishment is only morally justified if and when it is effective in preventing society from suffering further harm.[7] Alfonsín's successor, President Carlos Menem, took this pragmatism further – too far, many would say[8] – in granting pardons to 39 officials convicted of or charged with human rights abuses, alongside a few hundred leftist guerrillas. In 1990, Menem pardoned the junta leaders who had been convicted.

The 1992 law that provided financial compensation to victims of abuse and the families of those who had died has not buried the past. The balance between stability, moving forward, and justice has not been satisfactorily reached. Tensions continue to be present in politics in Argentina, spurred by reminders of past atrocities and international as well as regional developments. The struggle, mainly headed by civil society groups and fueled by occasional disclosures of brutality, refuses to go away. In March 1998, the anniversary of the military coup, the Chamber of Deputies voted to derogate – though not annul – the two amnesty laws. Moreover, criminal charges have been brought against former military officers for crimes not covered in the exculpatory laws. Whilst these laws still largely obstruct a meaningful project of accountability, they do not prevent the continuing search for the truth.

Chile reflected similar patterns of brutality and context before and during the years of dictatorship between 1973 and 1990, and also tensions and constraints during democratization. Social, economic, and political turbulence, exacerbated by the Cold War and U.S. intervention, dogged the government of Salvador Allende in the months before General Augusto Pinochet seized power in a violent coup. The aftermath was particularly repressive. Again, in the context of political polarization between Left and Right that had built up in the years preceding and during Allende's presidency, the army waged a war against perceived enemies of the Right. Thousands – close to 3,000, according to the Report of the Chilean National Commission on Truth and Reconciliation[9] – were murdered or disappeared as a result of state repression. Many thousands more were tortured, persecuted, or driven into exile. The campaign of terror hid behind the façade of "saving" the country from communism or instability, or "saving" the economy from chaos and bringing it into the safe harbour of neo-liberalism. The only crime of most victims was the most tenuous connection with associations, professions, or political parties deemed to be threatening to the new authoritarian order and its backers. Irrespective of guilt, these acts were conducted extrajudicially and in secret. The impact of this intimidation was felt far beyond the immediate victims and has thus left a deep wound upon the psychology of certain sectors of Chilean society and continues to be divisive. The Pinochet years have been embedded into a polarized and politicized interpretation of history.

Whilst the search for truth has been admirable, reconciliation efforts have been obstructed by a deeply recalcitrant political/military establishment, the persistence of authoritarian "enclaves,"[10] and political/legal factors that made a full accounting of the past difficult. The legacy of impunity continues to condition – to sour, if not to limit or constrain – democracy. The post-authoritarian government under Patricio Aylwin supported an extensive fact-finding exercise, realizing that the truth would be a poor but necessary substitute for justice and accountability. Pinochet had imposed a number of conditions upon his withdrawal that severely constrained Aylwin's government in its attempts to disclose the truth and serve the needs of justice and accountability, and thus build reconciliation. The 1978 amnesty prevented prosecution of officials for human rights abuses from the time of the coup in 1973 until early 1978. The 1980 Constitution preserved military autonomy; General Pinochet remained commander-in-chief of the army until 1987; much of the judiciary had been appointed by Pinochet; the Senate retained a strong pro-Pinochet composition; and Pinochet was made senator for life following his stepping down as commander-in-chief.

Following the example set by Argentina, Aylwin appointed a National Commission on Truth and Reconciliation. This commission was drawn from a diverse background and had just nine months to investigate and make recommendations on past abuses. The report represented a major milestone in the country's redemocratization and had a major impact upon politics. President Aylwin issued a televised acceptance of the commission's findings, at which time he apologized on behalf of the state, and upon the recommendation of the commission, an extensive reparations program was created. Yet the legacy of authoritarianism and the social and political divisions have remained; the unrest and polarization ignited by Pinochet's arrest under extradition procedures in Britain in May 1998 demonstrated that the Pinochet years continue to divide society. Many observers believe that justice and accountability have not been achieved, and that therefore neither has reconciliation. Before these dramatic events there were a number of standoffs that showed that the official acceptance of "truth" had not overcome a volatile political and institutional struggle.

In the early 1990s General Pinochet publicly warned the new government not to attack the army or challenge the 1978 amnesty law. The Aylwin government suggested that the disappeared persons constituted a crime that was ongoing – and thus outside the amnesty law – and Pinochet effectively threatened a repeat of 1973. In 1990 and 1993 the army was put on alert on the instructions of Pinochet, to demonstrate that the military would not accept humiliation and that its concerns still held sway. This represented a genuine threat to democracy; not necessarily that the military would move in as they had in 1973, but that the wishes of a democratically elected government were being blatantly threatened by the forces of authoritarianism; symbolism, even when not a physical threat (although some would argue the threat of a coup was real) can undermine a fledgling democracy. In response to this, in August 1993 Aylwin proposed to make the 1978 amnesty permanent and give anonymity to military defendants in cases involving past abuses. A public and party political outcry caused him to withdraw the proposal. Authoritarian attitudes were also not only a thing of the past; "enclaves" remained. Indeed, despite the amnesty law of 1978, Aylwin favoured investigation, but the judiciary interpreted the amnesty law as prohibiting even this. Nevertheless, there are some who suggest that the limitations on dealing with past human rights abuses were not only a condition of the dynamics of transition. Indeed, a number of people believe that the successor governments, whilst bemoaning the constraints they worked within, in fact preferred to reap the benefits of the socio-economic programme begun under authoritarianism.[11] In September 1998 the Chilean Supreme Court for the first time revoked a military court's upholding of amnesty and reopened a case involving a 1974 disappearance.

Whilst the transition from authoritarianism in Brazil was quite different from other cases – most notably in being relatively prolonged – the human rights abuses reflected a pattern common to a number of Latin American societies. Again, the historical and social context – at both national and international levels – provided the backdrop of social and political polarization and instability that led to violence, repression, and reactionary responses to a welfare agenda. The Brazilian armed forces overthrew President João Goulart in 1964, in part as a response to a strengthening leftist movement and the social and political instability that was accompanying economic and social change, exacerbated by the polarizing environment of the Cold War. Military rule lasted until 1985, until which time the military ruled by decree whilst allowing a superficial degree of local and national parliamentary activity. Political participation – in terms of both the public and organized parties – was severely curtailed and the use of repression was widespread, although much less so than in other countries, such as Chile and Argentina. Torture is well documented, and the number of dead and disappeared was approximately 300. Thousands suffered persecution, lost their jobs, or were forced into exile for their political views. A gradual *abertura* or political liberalization began around the middle of the 1970s with a dialogue between military and civilian actors and there was a gradual improvement in political rights. However, earlier human rights violations were still unpunished.

In 1979 President General João Figueiredo succeeded in passing an amnesty bill covering both sides of the equation: those imprisoned or exiled since 1961, politicians barred from activity, and members of the security services. The political process was further opened, including a questioning of human rights abuses; simultaneously the military remained adamant that its record would not be scrutinized. In the context of serious economic problems electoral opposition was given recognition in the early 1980s and in 1985 Tancredo Neves was elected the first civilian president; it is generally assumed that he conceded to the military that there would not be an official inquiry into human rights abuses of the past. The relatively long period of transition – as opposed to the dramatic changes in Argentina and perhaps Chile – also contributed to a weak political movement in favour of accountability and a full disclosure of truth; new civilian governments thus chose or were compelled to let sleeping dogs lie. Civil society was determined not to accept this and the Catholic Church led a coalition of civil society actors in conducting its own investigation and producing *Brasil: Nunca Mais*. The publication was very popular and indicated the desire for official truth and justice.

Uruguay displayed all the characteristics of abuse, whilst its transition to democracy was both dramatic and "managed." The historical context again conformed to the regional patterns. A polarization of political attitudes and recourse to extremism on both the left and the right accompanied social and political divisions and ideological militancy. In response to a revolutionary movement the government suspended many liberties and used the army to enforce domestic security. In 1973 the army dissolved the parliament and until 1985 there was military rule with varying levels of repression. The nature of human rights abuse in Uruguay was somewhat different from that in other Latin American cases. In the late 1970s Uruguay had one of the world's highest proportions of political prisoners; thousands were detained or interrogated, hundreds disappeared or were tortured. The repression permeated society, but especially in education and labour, where the pressures to conform to state ideology were overwhelming. In 1980 a referendum was held, which rejected a draft constitution that would have formalized the role of the armed forces in national government. Subsequently, the military engaged in negotiations with the major political parties on the framework and terms of transition. The result was the famous – or infamous – Naval Club Pact of 1984, which paved the way for presidential and congressional elections in that year and a new government in 1985. It is widely felt that, in return for the co-operation and willingness of the military to accede to this transition, the parties to the pact agreed not to seek prosecutions of government agents for previous human rights abuses, although the possibility of private prosecutions was left open. The new president, Julio Maria Sanguinetti, is closely associated with this trade-off, and he proceeded to liberalize the country within this context, freeing prisoners and facilitating the return of exiles through a commission.

In March 1985 a Law of National Pacification was passed, which granted an amnesty to most political prisoners but more significantly, obstructed legal proceedings against forces accused of human rights abuses. However, civilian courts did proceed with human rights cases, against the military's resistance. In December 1986, a law nullifying the state's claim to punish certain crimes – the Ley de Caducidad – passed, which confirmed the amnesty for security personnel. The law provoked a national debate that resulted in a 1989 referendum on repealing it; 58 per cent of the votes were in favour of retaining it. Nevertheless, in a 1992 decision the Inter-American Commission on Human Rights decided that the amnesty violated the country's obligations under international law, and particularly the American Convention on Human Rights. The government's desire to take a pragmatic approach made it unwilling even to thoroughly investigate past abuses. Not unlike in Brazil, therefore, this was left to civil society: a non-governmental organization, Servicio Paz y Justicia (SERPAJ), investigated the abuses and produced *Uruguay Nunca Más* to add to the regional chorus of "Never Again."

Guatemala is the most recent country to have confronted similar issues, although the patterns are somewhat different to those outlined above. The country was racked by a destructive civil war between 1954 and 1996; the peace process continues to be fragile. Some estimates reach 200,000 dead or disappeared as a result of the conflict, the great majority of them civilians. During this conflict a string of right-wing military governments sought to bolster their political power and wealth – and that of their sponsors – and stave off the attempts of a militant opposition and an increasingly aware working/peasant class who resisted their subservience to the post-colonial oligarchy. The Cold War context was clearly present – indeed, the involvement of the United States in supporting repressive governments "had a significant bearing on human rights violations," according to the report of the Commission for Historical Clarification, published in February 1999. Yet the ideological dimension, the struggle between Left and Right, should not obscure the social and ethnic roots of the conflict which was as much about control of natural resources and land as it was about doctrine. The UN Commission was mandated to "Investigate human rights violations and acts of violence which caused suffering to the Guatemalan people connected to the armed conflict." It found that "the majority of human rights violations occurred with the knowledge or by the order of the highest authorities of the state." Alluding to the history of social and racial division, the commission stated that approximately 90 per cent of victims were Indian or Ladino. Moreover, the commission came to the conclusion that agents of the state of Guatemala, within the framework of counterinsurgency operations carried out between 1981 and 1983, committed acts of genocide against groups of Mayan people.

The peace agreement was characterized by the pragmatism and trade-offs that are common throughout the region. For the sake of peace, and a transition to something that resembled democracy, the military had to be embraced and this made accountability unfeasible. A general who was in power during the most oppressive period in the early 1980s, Efraín Ríos Montt, remains a prominent opposition politician. Society continues to be polarized – and in some ways traumatized – the military remains recalcitrant and unrepentant, and the government seems unwilling or unable to make serious steps towards accountability on the basis of the commission's recommendations. Indeed, some groups dispute the commission's findings. A separate initiative, the Project to Recover Historical Memory, begun by bishops in 1994, produced a report entitled "Guatemala: Never Again." Bishop Juan Gerardi, who oversaw this project, was murdered two days after the report was issued. Controversy still surrounds this murder and it would be presumptuous to come to a conclusion, although there are many who would point the finger at groups that have an interest in obstructing accountability. Reconciliation is far from achieved, politics is entrapped within a prison of retribution and bitterness, and the legacy of the repression still leaves its mark in the form of violence, both political and casual.

El Salvador reflects the scope of conflict and the socio-political context of Guatemala. A landowning oligarchy shared power with the army for much of the twentieth century. In the 1960s and 1970s the working class and peasantry – often through the efforts of the Church and other civil society groups – became increasingly politically aware, partly as a result of the hardships imposed by neo-liberal economic policies. In response to this potential opposition, which had become politicized by the Cold War, the army and death squads murdered hundreds of church leaders. This further radicalized and mobilized the opposition to the point that a full-blown civil war raged in areas of the country in the 1980s with the opposition Frente Farabundo Martí para la Liberación Nacional (FMLN) taking the lead amongst the revolutionary opposition. In response governments became increasingly hardline beneath the façade of electoralism and reform.

The rightist government in Washington, given its Cold War perspective on Central America which was heightened by the leftist revolution in Nicaragua in 1979, reinforced the repression in El Salvador to the tune of $2 billion during this period, often giving direct assistance in the fight against guerillas. The fight was brutal and engulfed thousands of innocent people. The political Right in El Salvador formed the Alianza Republicana Nacionalista (ARENA) which was associated with the death squads. The "election" of the first civilian president in 54 years (Christian Democrat José Napoleón Duarte), could not obscure the reality of a vicious civil war. ARENA won power in 1989 under Alfredo Cristiani. As a result of a reduction of U.S. support and international pressure to find peace, stalemate in the military situation, and a general feeling of exhaustion, ARENA and the FMLN entered into negotiations within a UN framework. Under great international pressure historic peace accords were signed in January 1992 and seemed to presage the peaceful settlement of conflict throughout Central America. As usual, however, this peace accord embraced a number of compromises and balances that left a huge task in terms of reconciliation; accountability and justice have been tempered by reality. Following the peace accords a limited amnesty was passed.

A regionwide characteristic during and after the years of oppression has been the role of civil society in resisting oppression and struggling for justice, especially when organized political parties were outlawed or constrained, or when successor governments were more concerned with political expediency than with achieving accountability for the past. In Chile, human rights organizations such as the Vicariate of Solidarity, founded in 1976 by Silva Henrique, worked from the relative safety of the Church to record abuse. There was also the Chilean Human Rights Commission and the Defence Committee of People's Rights.

Managing the past: Options and constraints

The question of past abuses of human rights has been integral to (re)-democratization in Latin America. The nature and pace of the transition has, in most cases, defined the parameters, opportunities, and constraints within which democratic successor governments have been able to seek truth, accountability, and justice. At opposite ends of the spectrum, a distinction is most commonly made between, on the one hand, transitional, negotiated democratization – where authoritarian actors dictate the pace and nature of change – and on the other, revolution and upheaval. The former model, most common in Latin America, typically ties the hands of the successor government, and policy options for accountability for past crimes are limited because the actors implicated in these crimes defined the terms of transition. In contrast, the model of revolution or upheaval tends to offer greater opportunities for seeking accountability and redress. However, this rather mechanical correlation fails to consider the manner in which successor governments – of all political persuasions – are often content to forget the past whilst claiming that their "hands are tied."

Nevertheless, these different paths have had a strong bearing upon the progress of societies towards democratic consolidation and reconciliation. The outcomes have varied, however, according to a number of variables: the political, institutional and legal framework left over by the authoritarian regime and conditioned by transition; the electoral and party balance of the successor government; the position and power of authoritarian actors after transition; the decision-making and leadership of the successor government; and the level of public consciousness and mobilization, amongst others. To deal effectively with past abuses of human rights so as to consolidate democracy and achieve reconciliation requires that certain abstract principles or values be achieved to the level "expected" in the context of the process. These values are accountability, truth, justice, compensation, restitution, and deterrence. In the social and political context of a democratizing country, these must be achieved alongside other values: democratic consolidation, stability, reconciliation, economic development, and (re)building national institutions, amongst others. A number of so-called policy "options" exist for transitional societies in coming to terms with past abuse of human rights, and this has been a favourite subject of political scientists, sociologists, and comparativists for many years.[12] A common point is that dealing with the past is both essential to building a healthy democratic society, but can also, in the immediate post-authoritarian context, endanger this process. Thus, there can be a tension between these values.

Within this frequently observed dilemma, a number of abstract policy options exist, depending on the nature of the transition. If we consider these options in isolation from the context, they include: prosecution of all abusers; prosecution of the most horrendous human rights abuses; partial or complete amnesty; concentration on truth and reconciliation; forgetting; and compensation to victims. Perhaps the major division of opinion is between (1) seeking accountability and justice, including criminal prosecutions; and (2) a more pragmatic approach, often involving amnesty, forgiveness, and emphasis on the need to move forward, and in general, flexibility in the interests of stability and democratic consolidation. In conceptual terms, one could make a distinction between the search for absolute justice as an abstract ideal irrespective of political, practical, legal conditions; and the need for societal justice, that is, approaching reconciliation within the limits and opportunities presented in a particular context, in the interests of society. This is often presented as a dichotomy or a tension between justice and pragmatism, or justice and stability, especially in volatile or post-authoritarian situations.

A further theoretical and practical challenge is the concept of reconciliation itself. The concept is ambiguous at best; some see it as prosecution of past crimes, others as amnesty or forgiveness. It is argued here that it is not prosecution or amnesty that necessarily leads to reconciliation or lack of reconciliation, but the dissipation of conflict, the recognition that evil has occurred and that society as a whole – and most importantly the perpetrators of abuse – unite in condemning abuse and in facing the future.

The issue of whether to "punish or pardon" is often presented as a dilemma, a conscious decision, and a clear choice between two opposites. The challenge is often presented as striking a balance between a "whitewash" and a "witch hunt."[13] It is in fact rarely the case that such policy options are laid out as a simple choice with equal feasibility; the options are a condition of a number of constraints and political balances that will be discussed below. Thus, to ask the question whether to punish or pardon, or how to deal with a legacy of human abuses, is quite meaningless in an abstract sense; policy options cannot be considered out of context, and each context is different. Hence the distinction between abstract justice – the ideal situation – and societal justice, based on the exigencies of reality. Before discussing what is possible, it is worth considering the issues at stake together with the various conditions that may impact them, and how different contexts allow greater relevance to certain options than others.

Justice and accountability above pragmatism

When an authoritarian regime collapses or gives way to a democratic form of government the instinct is to support a process of legal accountability and justice that may involve prosecution, where justice is weighed heavier than expediency and political considerations. There are a number of abstract arguments in favour of pursuing justice and accountability to the full, even to the extent of legal prosecution. A society does not (re)-democratize without a collective memory, and hence perceived injustice, if not addressed, will continue to have a negative societal impact. A number of implications stem from this. A thorough, and if necessary forceful, accounting with the past is necessary in order to draw a line under the past, to make a fresh beginning, to give the new democracy – its institutions and ethos – confidence and credibility. The effect is not always tangible: not to deal effectively and fairly with the past does not necessarily threaten the structures and procedures of transitional and consolidating (re)-democratization, but it can undermine the quality and substance of democracy. Moreover, a policy of justice and accountability is surely more likely to insure against future repression; conversely, a climate of impunity is not conducive to the foundation of a democratic society or regime.

Democracy involves many norms and values: above all, the security of the individual against arbitrary arrest, torture, and extrajudicial execution are fundamental. For a democracy to have meaning these principles must have meaning.[14] The rule of law is integral to democracy, and thus, within the framework of the law, accountability is essential both for the justice that is owed to victims and the families of the victims, and so that society and the institutions of democracy can be purged of repressive elements. In this context justice and accountability involve the reform of institutions. A person involved in Alfonsín's government has argued that "democratic governments are morally bound to proceed against the military even at the risk of a military rebellion."[15] Whilst impunity survives – especially where the memory of abuse is so fresh, as in Guatemala – and whilst the perpetrators of injustice remain prominent in public or private life, democracy can have little meaning. Whilst impunity remains, social divisions remain open and volatile; it is as if the state has not granted a public acknowledgement of the wrongs of the past, which constitutes a continuing affront to society. This is not just an intangible issue of ethics. In the absence of justice and accountability repressive institutions are unreformed, and whilst there may be democratic regime change, human rights abuse can continue, albeit under a different ideological guise. Perceived lack of justice in dealing with the past in Chile underscores a latent social and political division never far from the surface; the 1999 detention of Pinochet Britain clearly demonstrated this. According to this perspective, the failure to deal with these issues inevitably comes back to haunt society.

A rigorous accounting of the past is also important for the formal restoration of the dignity of victims and an acknowledgement of wrongdoing by the state. The value of this is immensely important and expressed by the testimony given to the Chilean Truth and Reconciliation Commission. Justice is not only part of national and social reconciliation; it is important to the healing and in some cases the grieving process of individuals. If past abuses are committed, if a loved one is killed illegally, whilst no comfort can possibly be gained, at least one's pain and anguish can be slightly assuaged by the knowledge that the people responsible for perpetrating the abuse have had to pay for their crime. Secondly, the official acknowledgement that such an abuse was indeed a *crime* – rather than some expediency or excess that was somehow historically justified by the circumstances prevailing at the time – is fundamental. At a societal level, a thorough accounting for the past is obviously important from the perspective of excluding certain elements from public positions in the new democratic regime. The continuing presence of unreformed or recalcitrant individuals and institutions in public life can be damaging in the intangible sense of souring democracy, but also in a more substantive manner. Indeed, former officials of repressive regimes are likely to be the least supportive of new democratic institutions, and there is thus a risk of undemocratic or antidemocratic activity amongst such groups. In this sense the pursuit of justice and accountability is not only an issue of the past. It is indivisible from human rights standards in the present.

True, from a philosophical point of view, forgiveness is better than punishment for reconciliation; but forgiveness is a positive action – and amnesties preclude forgiveness. As Hannah Arendt observed, "men are unable to forgive what they cannot punish."[16] Forgiveness is a transaction between the forgiver and the forgiven, a shared acknowledgement of past wrongdoing, an acknowledgement of appropriate punishment, and a demonstration that contrition and repentance have been met by mercy.[17] Contrition must be supported by positive restorative steps by the forgiven: reparations, community service, compensation. And in its pure form, forgiveness is a voluntary act by an individual – not an imposed policy for a whole society, or a "legislated forgetting" imposed for political reasons, irrespective of the wishes or needs of those touched by suffering.[18] It can hardly be said that "reconciliation" in most Latin American societies is based upon this ethos. The restorative meaning of forgiveness – a concept of reconciliation based upon repairing relations – is undermined when it is faced with recalcitrance, lack of information, and disputes about wrongdoing. The pattern of blanket amnesties in Latin America, if compared to South Africa, appears to be more political than in the interests of reconciliation or morality. In South Africa, "accountable amnesty" – in contrast to "blanket amnesty" – is awarded on condition that individuals testify and tell the *truth*, in a "third way" between the extremes of summary trials on the one hand and forgetting the past – between "Nuremberg and national amnesia."[19]

A further aspect is that prosecution may be necessary under international law covering violations of human rights, and particularly crimes against humanity, genocide, and torture; there are limits to the discretion of states in terms of punishment and clemency.[20] The Universal Declaration of Human Rights of 1948, and subsequently the International Covenant on Civil and Political Rights in 1966, codified the internationalization of human rights and placed certain rights within a transnational, rather than merely domestic, context. This movement has strengthened in recent decades, placing significant limitations upon the ability of governments to grant amnesties and clemency or recognize immunity, and sometimes overriding national statutes of limitations. Articles VI and V of the Convention on Prevention and Punishment of the Crime of Genocide hold that perpetrators of genocide shall be punished irrespective of position or office, and that international mechanisms for pursuing justice shall be used if necessary. The Convention on the Non-Applicability of Statutory Limitations to War Crimes and Crimes against Humanity, and Article IV of the Convention against Torture and Other Cruel, Inhuman or Degrading Treatment or Punishment, support this principle. In many cases in Latin America, therefore, legal proceedings should have been the responsibility of the successor governments in the context of international law.

In a regional context transnational human rights regimes have also had effect. In 1992 the Inter-American Commission on Human Rights determined that Uruguay's 1986 Ley de Caducidad violated Uruguay's obligations under the American Convention on Human Rights. In a quite different context, but invoking a similar principle of obligation to transitional human rights and criminal law, Augusto Pinochet was placed under house arrest during a trip to London following an application for extradition to Spain for human rights abuses. This extradition application, and the legal decisions taken by the highest British court, went against the wishes of the Chilean government, although the court gave recognition to the amnesty law of 1978.[21] Considering the array of legal instruments in effect across Latin America, one observer has suggested that "arguably, none of these amnesties is valid under international law."[22] The Inter-American Commission on Human Rights has consistently held that many such amnesties violate states' obligations under the American Convention on Human Rights.[23] The criticism by the Inter-American Commission on Human Rights in December 1999 of the amnesty law that allowed the killers of six priests in El Salvador – in addition to many other known killers – to go free is a further example of pressure against impunity that may earlier have been seen as politically pragmatic, but is increasingly seen as morally unacceptable. In the wider context of increasing internationalization of legal and political norms and the strengthening of international humanitarian law, these norms are steadily intruding into "national" forms of dealing with the past. The option of a country coming to terms with its past, and making whatever trade-off and balances it feels necessary and legitimate within its own political, social, and legal context, is being slowly eroded by international forces and norms. The impact of this movement upon the achievement of reconciliation is a crucial and relatively new perspective to this debate.

In terms of social benefit, but also in the interests of individual justice, judicial findings of wrongdoing carry more weight in condemnation of certain activities, institutions, and individuals, than mere disclosure of information. Hence the importance of a rigorous legal accounting for past human rights abuse. It could also even be argued that whilst prosecutions can destabilize democratization – or even prevent it proceeding in negotiated transitions – they can help the military adapt to new democratic systems. Indeed, if prosecutions are limited to certain commanders or categories of abuses this can have the effect of purging the most authoritarian and "political" elements, showing the ranks that the direction has truly changed. When the most senior officers are not disciplined – and especially when they flaunt their position and remain recalcitrant – the ranks follow their lead and close ranks.

The pattern of pragmatism and impunity

There are a host of arguments that challenge the thesis of accountability in the interests of absolute justice. These usually reject the concept of abstract, absolute justice as idealist and unfeasible, and invariably argue that there is no universal model which democratic successor governments should follow in dealing with former authoritarian actors. This argument offers a utilitarian alternative as a moral and practical option: the route of absolute justice may not be feasible, but it may not even be in the interests of democratic consolidation and reconciliation. It is important to consider the distinction between these arguments.

Firstly, it may not be feasible or physically possible to confront human rights abuses in a just manner when it may jeopardize democratic transition or consolidation. Thus, whilst not dealing with the past may sour democracy, to deal with it may actually threaten democracy. Therefore, the principal obstacle to accountability in a transitional situation, may be that the actors upon whom democratic transition depends upon for its success – often the military – are the same actors responsible for human rights abuse in the past. A negotiated transition will invariably involve compromises on past human rights abuses, and in many cases outright amnesties or immunities. The corollary is that a rigorous treatment of past human rights abuse may provoke instability, a coup, or authoritarian regression. There are many examples of this tendency in Latin America. In Chile, "the transition to democracy was controlled from above."[24] Pinochet blatantly warned the Aylwin government not to pursue the military or attempt to nullify the 1978 amnesty law, and staged a number of threats in the 1990s to back up this recalcitrance. As late as 1995, with the conviction of General Manuel Contreras for the Washington murder of Orlando Letelier in 1976, the army made a public show of support for one of its own, in clear defiance of civilian authority. Whilst a military coup was doubtful, it is clear that the military threat was real, and had a bearing upon the limited extent of legal justice in Chile, the lack of co-operation of the military in the National Commission on Truth and Reconciliation, and the unwillingness of the military to accept the findings of the commission report and repent for its violations of human rights.

It was also the balance of power that resulted in constitutional arrangements allowing undemocratic, authoritarian elements to remain in a number of national institutions – such as the Senate and the judiciary –

and the continued public role for Pinochet for years after the end of the military regime. The cumulative effect of these and other factors has left the impression of a state divided between a progressive civilian government and an unrepentant and recalcitrant military that flaunts its strength in public. Whether it is reality or not, the message many people read into this is that the civilian government had, and perhaps has, to compromise on past human rights abuse because it did not have the power to achieve accountability. This has been a source of social unease and has continued to taint political discourse, leaving a state of "incomplete democratization."[25] Nevertheless, courts are increasingly willing to authorize investigations of human rights abuse during the Pinochet regime.

The more prolonged transition in Brazil shows a similar pattern. During the gradual liberalization of the political situation and the transfer of power to civilian authorities the military sought to avoid accountability for abuses in the 1960s and 1970s. In 1979 the president succeeded in passing an amnesty bill covering both sides of the equation: those imprisoned or exiled since 1961, politicians barred from activity, and members of the security services. Tancredo Neves was elected the first civilian president and the general assumption was that he conceded to the military that there would not be an official inquiry into human rights abuses of the past. The military remained prominent in public life and in politics, having dictated the pace and conditions of change; a classic "managed transition" that imposed severe constraints upon the ability of democratic governments to hold former government agents accountable for past human rights abuses.

Uruguay reflected similar dynamics. After the 1980 referendum the military authorities had a major stake in the conditions and terms of transition. It also had the power to impose these conditions to a large extent. It is widely believed that behind the Naval Pact lay an agreement that the military's acceptance of democratic transition was conditional upon the new government not pursuing legal prosecutions of military officials for human rights abuses. The implication and corollary of this is that the military would have obstructed democratic transition or physically resisted criminal prosecution within its ranks if these conditions had not been met. President Sanguinetti subsequently passed the 1986 Ley de Caducidad. Shortly afterward, Sanguinetti preferred to present this as an issue of reconciliation rather than political pragmatism or necessity: "Looking back to find culprits – which without doubt there were – will not revive the dead nor relieve the pain of those who suffered torture. Looking forward, we can build a better country that will have banished forever terror and violence."[26] Elsewhere he is presented as being much more politically pragmatic: "What is more just – to consolidate the peace of a country where human rights are guaranteed today or to see retroactive justice that could compromise that peace?"[27]

In Argentina the military was clearly in a weaker bargaining position, having lost a great deal of credibility as a result of its defeat in 1982. This opened greater space for the civilian government to bring former junta members to trial – to a greater extent than anywhere else in the region – and revoke the amnesty law. But it clearly did not give the government a free hand. When it came to prosecutions in the ranks, the army resisted – in fact rebelled against – the Alfonsín government, reminding the new government that it had seized power six times since 1930. In a dramatic standoff at Easter 1987 a major uprising occurred which the president had to deal with directly. Subsequently, the Due Obedience Law was passed, establishing the principle that only the most senior officers were liable to prosecution; the rest were merely following orders. Menem went further, but for more political reasons. A human rights adviser to President Alfonsín has described how the government's determination to challenge impunity was moderated by the reality: "It was our view that trying the military perpetrators of the worst crimes would contribute to the consolidation of democracy by restoring confidence in its mechanisms [but with time] the fear that a military coup could bring the country back into another dark period moved President Alfonsín to send a draft law to Congress to put an end to future criminal proceedings against the military."[28] Alfonsin himself conceptualized this as the reality of "social morality," in contrast to absolute justice.[29] The problem is that this has not exorcized the ghosts of the past: the "Daughters and Sons for Identity and Justice against Forgetting and Silence" are an enduring reminder of this. The series of legal cases – for example the conviction of former officers for stealing babies during the dictatorship – that is laying siege to the amnesty laws demonstrates that concrete progress is nevertheless underway.

In Guatemala the civil war situation made the transition quite different from that in Chile, Argentina, and Uruguay. The peace agreement was characterized by political compromises and balances that were reflected in the institutional and legal arrangements that were created for the democratic successor government. In order for peace – which was obviously a prerequisite for democracy – the military had a strong influence upon the terms of transition, and obviously resisted a thorough accounting for past abuses of human rights. In 1996 the Law of National Reconciliation created a partial amnesty but stated that "crimes of genocide, torture, and forced disappearance" were not covered. Yet the UN Truth Commission agreed not to publish names. A general who was in power during the most oppressive period, in the early 1980s, Efraín Ríos Montt, remains a prominent opposition politician. Society continues to be polarized, and in some way traumatized; the military remains recalcitrant and unrepentant; and the government seems unwilling or unable to make serious steps towards accountability on the basis of the commission's recommendations. Many human rights organizations were unhappy with the composition of the official Historical Clarification Commission, seeing it as a compromise inevitably tied into the peace negotiations. In 1995 the Guatemalan Catholic Church began its own project for the Recovery of Historical Memory, which presented its report in 1998.

In El Salvador as in Guatemala, the international dimension of the peace agreement appeared not to have significantly increased openings for accounting for past abuses. The peace accord embraced a number of compromises and balances that left many serious obstacles in the way of accountability and justice; reconciliation is therefore some way off. To attempt a rigorous pursuit of the military during the negotiations to end the civil war would have prolonged the conflict; to have attempted proceedings after a peace agreement would have seriously risked regression. Even if there was not a coup, former offenders could resist and elude prosecution or punishment, and despite the attempt to achieve justice, this can be damaging to the credibility of the new government and possibly even worse than not doing anything at all. A failed attempt can expose the inadequacies of fragile democratic regimes; perhaps this consideration figured in Sanguinetti's pragmatism in Uruguay. According to Huntington, "the efforts to prosecute and punish in Argentina served neither justice nor democracy and instead produced a moral and political shambles."[30] One of the members of the UN Truth Commission in El Salvador, Thomas Buergenthal, recalled that even in trying to uncover the truth – let alone punish perpetrators – "it was obvious to us that the military had built a defensive wall to protect itself. As we interviewed more officers, this wall appeared to be becoming more formidable.... All of them, moreover, seemed to have great faith in the ability of the system to cover up, to protect them, and to punish those who talked."[31]

The Truth Commission was far-reaching in its condemnation of human rights abuse, implicating a number of people and institutions in illegal behaviour and recommending various sanctions, including removal from office of those named in its report, provision of compensation to victims and their relatives, rehabilitation of victims, and a number of institutional and legal reforms.[32] On 20 March 1993, just five days after the report was issued, a broad amnesty law, ruling out both criminal and civil action, was passed by the Legislative Assembly. Various groups challenged the amnesty law, but the Supreme Court ruled in its favour.

In addition to the obvious physical threat posed by the military in certain circumstances – and the risk of instability and authoritarian regression –

there is also the argument that a thorough accounting for the past can prolong consolidation of democracy and reconciliation, by maintaining enmity in public life and not allowing the wounds of the past to heal. Thus, the utility of any such action must be judged according to its social usefulness. According to this view, the politics of "resentment" against the people and images of the old order is not constructive for an emerging democracy.[33] This has a familiar ring to it: we cannot change the past, we cannot even be sure of the facts of the past, so move forward, concentrate on the future. Thus, reconciliation is preferable to retribution, and the latter does not serve the former.[34] As retribution tends to focus on the offender, it also lacks a restorative dimension from the victim perspective. Fundamentally, reconciliation cannot be founded upon retribution. A "different kind of justice,"[35] one based on restorative justice rather than retribution, is more conducive to reconciliation.

There are also practical problems to prosecution: it is rarely possible to prosecute everyone responsible for human rights abuses. Thus, the decision on how and whom to prosecute cannot be fair, if pursued on a basis of absolute justice. In most democratizing societies efforts are arguably best channeled into national recovery and development. The time and expense of prosecution are also a practical challenge. Moreover, prosecution can hinder or indeed conflict with the search for truth, which is arguably just as crucial for society as justice in a legal sense. People – particularly perpetrators – are less likely to disclose information if it would implicate them legally. It may be worth compromising on justice in order to achieve truth – a trade-off practised by the Truth and Reconciliation Commission for South Africa. And whilst it might be argued that legal truth is the most irrefutable truth, it takes much longer to establish. If one considers the time allowed under the Chilean commission's terms of reference – less than a year – then legal procedures would have been impossible. In that and other cases, the speed with which a report could be issued was critical.

Finally, people who counsel against a rigorous accounting with the past sometimes put events into a historical context: they see the past as a struggle where both sides did bad things in a polarized and exceptional context. To move beyond that, forgiveness is more conducive to reconciliation than punishment and retribution. There is also often the moral and legal argument that soldiers followed orders and should therefore not be held accountable for illegal orders, especially when to resist such orders would put their own lives in peril.[36] The general political argument in favour of "looking forward instead of backward" declares that mistakes were made on all sides and that complete justice and accountability are elusive – and perhaps illusory – so that the energies and resources of society would be best put into progress and development, rather than mired in the past or in witch hunts. Moreover, a rigorous pursuit of accountability could be in danger of appearing as "victor's justice."

Sanguinetti observed that reconciliation is inevitably a political, not a moral process: "The bottom line is that either we're going to look to the future or to the past."[37] Finally, there is the argument – certainly seen in Eastern Europe – that people are simply not interested in these issues and are preoccupied with bread-and-butter issues of day-to-day living, or else they see the issue of "dealing with the past" to be mostly a game amongst political elites. They often deny that the future need necessarily be founded upon a just settlement of the past.

Conventional wisdom

The conventional wisdom of political scientists is that the policy options – what is politically feasible – are determined by the dynamics of transition within a delineated political community. Because authoritarian actors often play a role in guiding and negotiating transition – and certainly in Latin America – they are able to imbue the terms of transition, and the successor framework, with self-protection. Justice and morality are normative issues and inhabit a quite different sphere of discourse. To fail to recognize this is to be "naïve."[38]

Samuel Huntington presents such a viewpoint: arguments for and against punishment or prosecution may well be moral or legal, but the practice has been largely conditioned by political issues, the distribution of political power before and during transition, and the nature of the democratization process. Thus, many transitions were guided by the authoritarian actors themselves – specifically the military – who precluded or obstructed attempts to achieve accountability.[39] In such a situation – which was common to Chile, Brazil, Guatemala, El Salvador, Uruguay, and to a lesser extent Argentina – "the political costs [of attempting to prosecute and punish] will outweigh any moral gains."[40] The result will always be compromises and trade-offs, and the cases in Latin America appear to support this view.[41] The conventional wisdom of political and comparative scientists is that justice – as well as accountability and truth telling – will necessarily be secondary to pragmatism and political balance in achieving a transition.

How well has the conventional wisdom served the cause of reconciliation? To what extent has this facilitated the process of "healing the wounds and calming the soul?"[42] Is the conventional wisdom being challenged? To what extent has this achieved genuine social reconciliation and reconciliation between the state and citizens? It is here that the moral weakness of the conventional model is clear. Many observers in the region would argue that the pattern of pragmatism that secured transition – including amnesties – has failed to achieve reconciliation, and that this continues to taint democracy, perpetuating a sense of injustice amongst large sections of society. With the passage of time, in countries such as Argentina and Chile, memories of the abuse fade amongst the wider population. But the divisions are never far from the surface, as the Pinochet issue has demonstrated. The manner in which his arrest in Britain triggered demonstrations in Chile, and debate elsewhere in the region, suggests that there has been a reawakening of the issue, a reawakening of a dormant desire for justice that was not achieved by the compromises and pragmatism of the transitions in many cases in the past. New cases in national courts, and international extradition requests and warrants, suggest that this is a substantive development. Yet, the time when decisions were made has also passed, making it difficult to recreate the opportunities that existed at the time of the transition. Many voices argue that democratization has not been completed. The fact that Pinochet's case continues to "disturb social peace" suggests an unclosed chapter in Chile's history.[43]

True reconciliation rests upon a number of tenets: justice, repentance, forgiveness. These are value-oriented concepts. If the institutions of society have officially *acknowledged* the abuses – which is something more than merely establishing *knowledge* of them[44] – and brought about reforms, then this is a framework within which society can make a fresh start. "A nation has to confront its past by acknowledging the wrongs that have been committed in its name before it can successfully embark on the arduous task of cementing the trust between former adversaries and their respective sympathizers, which is prerequisite for national reconciliation. . . . The wounds begin to heal with the telling of the story and the national acknowledgement of its authenticity."[45] A truth and reconciliation commission is, in principle, an integral part of this process; indeed, in Chile and Argentina the processes, as well as the publication of the reports themselves, were therapeutic to the victims and those touched by tragedy, and also to society as a whole. Yet, as an alternative to more forceful measures towards justice and accountability, truth commissions have an element of compromise that is unsatisfactory. The varying degrees of recalcitrance demonstrated by the government or military in Argentina, Chile, El Salvador, and Guatemala, clearly weaken the cleansing value of the truth, when it is not accepted by all sectors of society, when there is in fact no consensus on the truth or history. At worst, this betrays a social division that belies "reconciliation"; at least, it shows that unreformed or recalcitrant "enclaves" continue to play a role in public life. The denial of justice is not confined to the past; it continues to condition justice and form an element – albeit often latent – of social instability. In some cases, such as Argentina and Chile, this is not a threat to democracy; it merely challenges the inclusiveness of democracy as a vehicle of social justice. In other countries, such as Guatemala and El Salvador, it is certainly a threat to democracy – not necessarily its institutions, but its substance and spirit. The latter point is worth emphasizing because in El Salvador and Guatemala reconciliation is not just an issue of dealing with the past; the anti-democratic forces of past abuse are still present and active in resisting democracy and accountability, and are forming new political and economic spheres of influence through legal or illegal means. Human rights abuses continue.

Transnational forces

Within the mass of academic research on these issues, the constraints on and opportunities for dealing with the past have been seen as a condition of the dynamics of transition in each particular case. As we have seen, these dynamics have tended to be represented as a pattern of pragmatism and political trade-off, with transition rather than justice as the principal objective. An important and relatively new dimension to this debate concerns the internationalization of norms of transition and political morality which have increasingly impinged upon "national" or "communitarian" attempts to come to terms with the past.

In various political, social, and technological fields, the boundaries between the "domestic" and the "international" are increasingly blurred in a number of areas relating to governance and socio-economic organization. Democratic transition, including the modalities employed to deal with past abuses of human rights, is no exception. International legal and humanitarian conventions, international tribunals and courts, the role of foreign governments and international organizations in assisting processes of transition, extradition processes, the issuance of international arrest warrants, the sending of expert assistance, and even the organizing and hosting of truth commissions and the holding of elections, are all manifestations of this. Regional human rights instruments are central to this process across the world. The Inter-American Commission on Human Rights has clearly had influence in regionwide promotion of justice in Latin America; the statute of the International Criminal Court is a landmark in both the ethos and the process of internationalization of humanitarian law.[46] The cumulative effect is that the modalities of dealing with the past – the constraints and possibilities and indeed responsibilities – and the balance between justice and pragmatism that characterize every such society, are no longer a condition of the dynamics of transition within a particular society. This is also a characteristic of recent democratic transition, as demonstrated in Argentina and Chile, where international norms and processes have intruded upon (unsuccessful) national attempts to deal with the past.

In Argentina, Uruguay, and Chile the emphasis was on a communitarian process of a society coming to terms with its own past; overcoming the past together, and finding answers from within. Indeed, in the case of Chile, the report of the Truth and Reconciliation Commission was notable for the manner in which it preferred to present the crisis of the early 1970s as a culmination of social and political tensions within the country; little mention was made of the U.S. role or the Cold War, or of Operation Condor, the network of repression amongst the dictators of the Southern Cone. In contrast, more recent transitions in the region, such as those in El Salvador, Guatemala, and Nicaragua, have been characterized by a very high level of international involvement. The norms and values of the processes have reflected international legal and moral standards to a greater extent. In turn, the older transitions in Argentina and Chile have been revisited. The transition in Guatemala, including the report on past human rights abuse, was under a United Nations mandate and took place under the aegis of an international consensus on norms and values. This has clearly had a bearing upon the outcome of the truth commission's report, which has called for accountability. The commission in El Salvador was notable in avoiding any nationals amongst its members.

The case of Chile also raises interesting dimensions here. The transition had been a rather "communitarian" process: the norms, values, solutions, and institutions invoked to deal with democratization and the issues of the past were national constructions. The record is still widely debated in the country. The arrest of Pinochet in Britain pending a Spanish extradition request re-ignited a debate about the efficacy of this communitarian approach,[47] and triggered a movement across the region in favour of revisiting past solutions, measuring them against the standard of justice rather than of pragmatism. For some in the region, this reawakening reflects a substantial movement in favour of revising the (a)morality of pragmatism that characterized transition in a number of countries.[48] A number of conflicting logics appear, which are not fully answered by classical transition scholarship. Clearly, the restoration of democracy imposes limitations upon the pursuit of justice. Yet the Pinochet case, and others, highlight a clash between sovereignty/communitarian approaches and emerging transitional – perhaps even global – norms of justice. The fact that the impulse for legal proceedings against Pinochet was from outside Chile does not detract from the debate that the process has stirred within the country.

Those who supported the proceedings against Pinochet argued that justice had finally caught up with him, that the "national" solution had been inadequate in failing to offer any accountability, and that the law should take its course. Obviously, justice would have been better had it been achieved within Chile, but the moral imperative was such that justice overrode national and sovereign privileges, especially when justice had not been served by them.[49] In the House of Lords ruling against Pinochet's immunity, Lord Nicholls declared that "International law has made plain that certain types of conduct, including torture and hostage taking, are not acceptable conduct on the part of anyone. This applies as much to heads of states, or even more so, as it does to everyone else; the contrary conclusion would make a mockery of international law." Here we see the absolutist ethic again: legal justice must be pursued irrespective of context. The debate that Pinochet's arrest re-ignited in Chile and perhaps elsewhere in the region appeared to demonstrate Zalaquett's observation that "the ghosts of the past, if not exorcised to the fullest extent possible, will continue to haunt the nation tomorrow." It refocused attention upon and challenged pragmatism, political trade-offs, and amnesties – impunity – throughout the region. Whatever the merits of the case, the Spanish move does demonstrate that the question of reconciliation in Chile is no longer purely domestic. The release of Pinochet on health grounds did nothing to alter this. This principle has spread to other countries, so that a number of movements have arisen seeking accountability, questioning the policies employed during transition, and contesting the "national" approaches and pragmatism that characterized the earlier transitions.

The internationalizing of the reconciliation issue has had a number of effects. Clearly, international laws, norms, and standards of expectation have conditioned the modalities of dealing with the past in transitional societies. There are some positive effects. This means that concepts of justice and morality are likely to be more prominent (at least in theory) than if the transition is governed by local political dynamics and compromises. International laws and norms can theoretically be more impartial than purely local solutions, which are more likely to be conditioned by local power balances than by concerns for justice. Moreover, society is often polarized, and local approaches will inevitably be accused of bias. The approaches taken in El Salvador and Guatemala and the intervention of international law in the Chilean case with the arrest of Pinochet, reflect this influence of transnational norms and standards. In support of this, one might argue that transnational standards or expectations establish a minimum level of behaviour that transcends the tendency for transitional societies to fudge the issue of justice in the interests of political trade-off. Clearly, it is possible that without a UN presence in Guatemala, the indigenous peoples who represented the vast majority of the victims would not have received the recognition that they did, given the social and ethnic dimensions of the conflict. Clearly, the victims in Chile can argue that without the extradition process against Pinochet and the measure of justice that his arrest has afforded to them, he would have largely escaped any form of accountability. Moreover, it could be argued that impartiality in the process of acknowledging the truth of the past and establishing the terms of reconciliation is best brought by people and actors from outside. In El Salvador, it was thought that no one from the society could win the confidence of the populace in establishing a basis of truth from which to move forward; none of the commissioners on the truth commission were citizens of the country.

A number of countervailing arguments are also compelling. From what can be described as a communitarian perspective, social values, norms, and rights can never be universal or abstract. These values grow out of a particular society's social processes, history, and culture. As an extension of this, the socio-economic, legal, and political organization of a particular society, and the manner in which it confronts problems and challenges, can only come from within. Democratic transition, and dealing with past human rights abuse, must be seen within this context. Solutions cannot be imposed from outside. The values and tools employed to deal with these challenges, if they are to be effective, must be an extension of this ethos. The opportunities and constraints of transition are a product of this, and if this means that accountability is conditioned by expediency and the need for a trade-off, then so be it. Ultimately, external actors cannot change the destiny of a community; this change, if it is to be sustainable, must come from within. Intervention cannot fundamentally work. There are also more practical objections: members of a particular society know the society best, can best formulate the modalities of dealing with the past, and can most easily win the confidence of society, across all political divisions. Argentina and Chile are notable examples: whatever the weaknesses of the processes of reconciliation, the truth and reconciliation commissions won a high level of legitimacy and confidence from the people, and this was reflected in the high degree of acceptance of these commissions' reports, and the cathartic value of the commissions' work.[50]

In terms of weighing up strengths and weaknesses of the transnational forces that are having an impact upon reconciliation, the evidence is mixed, perhaps inconclusive. Methodologically, whilst it is certainly possible to identify patterns in the manner in which these issues are addressed in the region, it is difficult to directly compare cases. If one considers Argentina as an example of a "national" approach to reconciliation, and Guatemala as one conditioned by international norms and standards, this cannot constitute a comparison of the relative merits of the different approaches, for the circumstances and societies are vastly different. Nevertheless, a number of general observations may be possible. The increasing prominence of international law, political and ethical norms – and perhaps even solidarity – may impart a stronger likelihood of justice and accountability.[51] Certain responsibilities and expectations in dealing with the past extend beyond borders in many transitional societies, especially following particularly oppressive and violent circumstances. Legal standards and obligations, international supervision of elections and in the reconstruction of national institutions, dealing with past human rights abuse, are increasingly characterizing transition around the world. Yet it appears that domestic political and social forces continue to hold sway in Latin America, and the dynamics of transition largely continue to define the modalities of approaching the challenges of reconciliation. The fundamental dynamics of transition – in particular, the distribution of power – and the social complexion of a society, cannot be readily altered. But more than that, the attitudes and perceptions of the people, upon which the chances of reconciliation finally rest, cannot be fundamentally changed by outside intervention.

Revisiting the issue of dealing with the past has presented an unavoidable truth: reconciliation can mean different things to different people, and the path to reconciliation is not based upon consensus. For some it is forgetting the past, forgiving the past, and moving forward. Justice is the price paid for pragmatism. According to this view, reconciliation is necessarily based upon compromise. For others, "restorative" reconciliation must be based upon justice, and this justice must be based upon the perception of society, but also of individuals, and most importantly, of those individuals violated by abuse.

Conclusion

Politics rarely offers simple choices between right and wrong. Still less do these choices result in solutions that satisfy everyone. No democracy has a pure past, based entirely upon justice. Latin America is no different from anywhere else in this respect. Yet the historical proximity of recent human rights abuses sours democracy, albeit without threatening it. The arguments over how to deal with the past are often moral or legal, but the reality has been largely a product of political dynamics. Thus, there are a number of points of tension: between justice and stability, between justice and pragmatism, between absolute justice and social/utilitarian justice, and perhaps even between truth and justice. Developments that have taken place long after democratic transition have indicated a number of patterns common to societies in the region, straining to strike the right balance amongst these values. The pattern of impunity has not been conducive to consolidation and an inclusive democratic public sphere. Those sectors of society estranged by the tendency of "imposed forgetting and forgiving" are, however, not easily assuaged. The struggle for justice, spurred by movements inside countries such as Chile and Argentina and by transitional forces, has not gone away. The ghosts of the past may well yet be exorcised.

Notes

1. José Zalaquett, 'Balancing Ethical Imperatives against Political Constraints: The Dilemma of New Democracies Confronting Past Human Rights Violations,' in Neil J. Kritz (ed.), *Transitional Justice: How Emerging Democracies Reckon with Former Regimes*, 3 vols. (Washington, D. C.: United States Institute of Peace Press, 1995), 1:205.
2. A number of excellent volumes have been written or compiled in this area of "transitional justice." See, for example, Kritz, *Transitional Justice*; A. James McAdams (ed.), *Transitional Justice and the Rule of Law in New Democracies* (Notre Dame, Ind.: University of Notre Dame Press, 1997); Naomi Roht-Arriaza (ed.), *Impunity and Human Rights in International Law and Practice* (New York: Oxford University Press, 1995). The journal *Ethics and International Affairs* 1999; 13, has a number of interesting contributions to the debate: David Crocker, "Reckoning with Past Wrongs: A Normative Framework"; David Little, "A Different Kind of Justice: Dealing with Human Rights Violations in Transitional Societies"; Susan Dwyer, "Reconciliation for Realists"; and Margaret Popkin and Nehal Bhuta, "Latin American Amnesties in Comparative Perspective: Can the Past Be Buried?"
3. The basic definition of liberal (representative) democracy is an open competition for political power and collective decision-making within a legal framework that ensures accountability, transparency, equality, and participation; but also individual rights of privacy, freedom of speech, and property rights. See Robert A. Dahl, *Polyarchy: Participation and Opposition* (New Haven, Conn.: Yale University Press, 1971), pp. 1–9.
4. Guillermo O'Donnell and Philippe Schmitter, *Transitions from Authoritarian Rule: Tentative Conclusions about Uncertain Democracies* (Baltimore: Johns Hopkins University Press, 1986), wrote of "coaxing the military out of power and inducing them to tolerate a transition toward democracy," cited in Kritz, *Transitional Justice*, 1:64. Samuel P. Huntington, *The Third Wave: Democratization in the Late Twentieth Century* (Norman: University of Oklahoma Press, 1991), p. 231.
5. Zalaquett, "Balancing Ethical Imperatives and Political Constraints"; Luc Huyse, "Justice after Transitions: On the Choices Successor Elites Make in Dealing with the Past," in Kritz, *Transitional Justice*, 1:114.
6. "Far from expressing any repentance, they continue to repeat the old excuses that they were engaged in a *dirty war*, or that they were saving the country and its Western, Christian values, when in reality they were responsible for dragging these values inside the bloody walls of the dungeons of repression." Ernesto Sabato, prologue, *Nunca Mas: The Report of the Argentine Commission on the Disappeared* (September 1984), in Kritz, *Transitional Justice*, 3:6.
7. Raúl Alfonsín, "'Never Again' in Argentina," *Journal of Democracy* 1993; 4(1): pp. 380–81.
8. Luis Moreno Ocampo, a prosecutor in the trials of perpetrators of state violence in Argentina, wrote that "With a stroke of his pen, Menem erased years of fighting for justice." "Beyond Punishment: Justice in the Wake of Massive Crimes in Argentina," *Journal of International Affairs* Spring 1999; 52(2): p. 685.

9. *Report of the Chilean National Commission on Truth and Reconciliation, English trans-lation* (Center for Civil and Human Rights, Notre Dame Law School, 1993).

10. A concept explained and elaborated by Manuel Antonio Garretón in "Chile 1997–1998: The Revenge of Incomplete Democratization," *International Affairs* 1999; 75(2).

11. Tuomas Forsberg and Teivo Teivainen, *The Role of Truth Commissions in Conflict Resolution and Promotion of Human Rights: Chile, South Africa and Guatemala* (Research report prepared for the Department of Cooperation of the Ministry of Foreign Affairs of Finland, 1998, forthcoming).

12. The definitive three-volume collection on this topic is Kritz, *Transitional Justice.*

13. Neil J. Kritz introduction to Kritz, *Transitional Justice,* 1:xx.

14. Amnesty International argues that "Impunity negates the values of truth and justice and leads to the occurrence of further violations"; *Oral Statement by Amnesty International before the United Nations Commission on Human Rights, Sub-Committee on Prevention of Discrimination and Protection of Minorities* (Amnesty International, International Secretariat, August 1991), reprinted in Kritz, *Transitional Justice,* 1:220; Human Rights Watch, *Special Issue: Accountability for Past Human Rights Abuses,* no. 4 (New York: Human Rights Watch, December 1989), holds a similar position in rejecting the pragmatist argument of transitional circumstances, calling for the rejection of amnesties, even when applied to rebels or anti-government forces, and argues that popular disinclination to hold abusers accountable does not negate the duty of governments: "it is not the prerogative of the many to forgive the commission of crimes against the few"; reprinted ibid., p. 218.

15. Jaime Malamud-Goti, "Transitional Governments in the Breach: Why Punish State Criminals?" in Kritz, *Transitional Justice,* 1:192–93. He observes that "the very ceremony of the criminal trial supports democracy. It depicts those who previously subjugated others as currently being subjugated themselves by institutions that apply to everybody" (ibid., p. 201).

16. Hannah Arendt, The *Human Condition,* 2d ed. (Chicago: Chicago University Press, 1998), p. 241.

17. Little, "A Different Kind of Justice," p. 71.

18. Popkin and Bhuta, "Latin American Amnesties in Comparative Perspective," p. 108.

19. Desmond Tutu, *No Future without Forgiveness* (London: Rider Books, 1999).

20. See, for example, Zalaquett, "Confronting Human Rights Violations Committed by Former Governments: Principles Applicable and Political Constraints," in Kritz, *Transitional Justice,* 1:14–17. See also Diane F. Orentlicher, "Settling Accounts: The Duty to Prosecute Human Rights Violations of a Prior Regime": "The threat of instability is minimized when prosecutions are backed by unambiguous international law whose requirements are confined within principled limits" (in Kritz, *Transitional Justice,* 1:412). See also the response to this: Carlos S. Nino, "Response: The Duty to Punish Past Abuses of Human Rights Put into Context: The Case of Argentina," in Kritz, *Transitional Justice,* vol. 1.

21. Thus, the decisions of the House of Lords were based upon offences allegedly committed after 10 March 1978, the period of Pinochet's rule not covered by the amnesty.

22. Aryeh Neier, "What Should be Done about the Guilty," in Kritz, *Transitional Justice,* 1:178.

23. See Popkin and Bhuta, "Latin American Amnesties in Comparative Perspective."

24. David Pion-Berlin, "To Prosecute or to Punish? Human Rights Decisions in the Latin American Southern Cone," in Kritz, *Transitional Justice,* 1:89.

25. See Garretón, "Chile 1997–1998."

26. Letter from President Sanguinetti to Amnesty International regarding the Ley De Caducidad, 31 March 1987, reprinted in Kritz, *Transitional Justice,* 3:601.

27. Lawrence Weschler, *A Miracle, A Universe: Settling Accounts with Torturers* (Pantheon Books, 1990), reprinted in Kritz, *Transitional Justice*, 2:399.
28. Malamud-Goti, "Transitional Governments in the Breach," pp. 189, 192. Nino, "Response: The Case of Argentina," argues that Alfonsín did "all that could be morally required under the circumstances" (p. 434).
29. Alfonsín, "'Never Again' in Argentina."
30. Huntington, *The Third Wave*, p. 221.
31. Thomas Buergenthal, "The United Nations Truth Commission for El Salvador," in Kritz, *Transitional Justice*, 1:303.
32. See Popkin and Bhuta, "Latin American Amnesties in Comparative Perspective," pp. 103–8, on El Salvador's attempt to "bury its past."
33. Juan J. Linz and Alfred Stepan (eds.), *The Breakdown of Democratic Regimes* (Baltimore: Johns Hopkins University Press, 1978), p. 42. Herman Schwartz considers the divisive impact in a different context, in "Lustration in Eastern Europe," in Kritz, *Transitional Justice*, vol. 1.
34. Little, "A Different Kind of Justice," weighs up the relationship between retribution and reconciliation, and argues that in most transitional situations a kind of justice should be pursued that is "less conventional and vindictive, and more experimental and restorative" (p. 67).
35. Ibid.
36. Jeanne L. Bakker, "The Defence of Obedience to Superior Orders: the *Mens Rea* Requirement," in Kritz, *Transitional Justice*, vol. 1, discusses the moral and legal difficulties of the due obedience argument.
37. Cited in Weschler, *A Miracle, A Universe*, in Kritz, *Transitional Justice*, 2:407.
38. Buergenthal, "The United Nations Truth Commission for El Salvador," p. 313.
39. Huntington, *The Third Wave*, pp. 114–17.
40. Ibid., p. 231. Huntington later declares: "the least unsatisfactory course may well be: do not prosecute, do not punish, do not forgive, and, above all, do not forget" (ibid.).
41. See, for example, O'Donnell and Schmitter, *Transitions from Authoritarian Rule*, in Kritz, *Transitional Justice*, 1:61.
42. "Cerrar las heridas … calmar los espiritus." Former human rights worker from Costa Rica, correspondence with the author, 23 November 1999.
43. "Pinochet continua siendo el elemento disturbador de la paz social." Ibid.
44. Margaret Popkin and Naomi Roht-Arriaza, "Truth as Justice: Investigatory Commissions in Latin America," in Kritz, *Transitional Justice*, 1:276.
45. Buergenthal, "The United Nations Truth Commission for El Salvador," p. 325.
46. Geoffrey Hawthorn describes this as "new international law," and "new international politics," in "Pinochet: The Politics," *International Affairs* 1999; 75(2).
47. See, for example, Alexandra Barahona de Brito, "Getting Away with Murder?" *The World Today*, December 1998, arguing that in Chile there was a successful policy on truth but a less successful policy on justice.
48. Former human rights worker from Costa Rica, correspondence with the author, 23 November 1999.
49. Garretón, "Chile 1997–1998," p. 263.
50. For a useful outline of the role and politics of truth commissions see Popkin and Roht-Arriaza, "Truth as Justice"; and Priscilla B. Hayner, "Fifteen Truth Commissions – 1974–1994: A Comparative Study," *Human Rights Quarterly* 1994; 16(4).
51. Popkin and Roht-Arriaza, "Truth as Justice," make a tentative conclusion that national commissions may be more conducive to reconciliation, and international bodies may be more conducive to accountability.

9

The new socio-political matrix

Manuel Antonio Garretón M.

Some analytical orientations

This essay will begin by indicating some of the analytical principles that are relevant to the study of particular socio-political processes, within which democratization processes find their place.[1] First, it is necessary to go beyond a structural determinism according to which particular or national histories are merely illustrations of general laws. Likewise, it is necessary to overcome the vision of an essential and abstract correlation between economics, politics, culture and society; in other words, the idea that to a given economic system there must necessarily correspond a determined political or cultural form, or vice versa. This is not to deny that there are interactions between these spheres, but the scheme of interactions is a flexible one. There is no universal interaction or relationship between these dimensions, which are in any case impacted by globalization processes that act differently according to each context.

Second, it is necessary to emphasize the autonomy of social processes in relation to their "structural base." It is not the task of the social sciences to construct a "natural history" of social structures and their dynamics, but to understand their meaning; and this cannot be done without introducing the concept of "social actor" or "social subject." The central challenge in the social sciences lies in describing how a structural situation or category interacts with actors/units, and how actors constitute themselves and interact within a historical and institutional context that they themselves contribute to produce and reproduce. The concept of actor-subject refers to the bearers of individual or collective action that invoke principles of structuring, conservation, or transformation of society – they are involved in societal projects or counter-projects. In other words, actors are subject to tension between specific and particularistic economic, socio-demographic, cultural, and psychosocial characteristics, and their projects vis à vis society.[2]

Third, the meaning of the struggles, and more generally of the collective action, of actors is not univocally given by the struggle against "domination" in general, or by social projects ideologically determined outside of its own orientations. The autonomization and interrelation of diverse social dimensions – which before seemed to be subsumed mainly in the economy and politics – create diverse conflicts, struggles, and social movements, and, therefore, diverse teleologies of those struggles, as well as diverse utopian principles. Systems of domination within societies result from a combination of diverse axes or systems of action (involving the economy, social organization, culture, politics), and are not the reflection of only one of them, even if one or more of them may be predominant. In each axis or system of domination there is a confrontation around the principles and instruments that define its orientation and destiny. Thus there is not one single subject of historical action, but several. Even when, in moments when a society's historical problematique is concentrated in one of the principles or axes of domination, there may be one privileged actor-subject, this will always be the case in a manner restricted to that precise struggle or conflict. In this orientation, utopia as the architecture of a type of society with which history ends – "modern," or democratic, or socialist society – disappears, and gives way to partial utopias pointing towards the provisional realization of only some of the principles that define a society. There is no ideal society around the corner; there is always struggle and process.

Fourth, a society is not defined on the basis of a structure or system of values, but of the particular configuration of the relationship between (a) the state, (b) the political regime and parties, and (c) civil society/social actors. This historically defined relationship is what allows one to speak of a "socio-political matrix." This concept refers to the relationship between the state, the system of representation or political party structure, and their socio-economic and cultural bases that constitute the moment of participation and the diversity of civil society. The political regime is the institutional mediation between these three components, called upon to solve the problems of who governs and how, the definition of citizenship, and the way in which demands and social conflicts are institutionalized.[3]

Fifth, the political model or system of a society that is referred to in this paper is composed of the state, the regime or institutional mediations between state and society, the actors-subjects that intervene in politics in the name of social projects that define the historical-structural problematique of each society, and the particular political culture or style of relations between these elements. In this perspective, democracy is, strictly speaking, no more nor less than a political regime characterized by certain principles and mechanisms: popular sovereignty; universal human rights guaranteed by the state; free election of government by universal suffrage; and political pluralism, whose main but not exclusive expressions are the parties, the principle of alternation in power, and respect for majorities and minorities. Between democratic principles, institutions, and mechanisms there is always a tension.[4]

As we will see, the study of political regimes and changes of regimes – with exceptions in the case of revolutions or democratic foundations to which we will refer – can be done with a certain autonomy from the analysis of the dimensions of social transformation. These transformations may be left as hypothetical dimensions of democratic consolidation or deepening, to be examined in each historical case.

It is within this field of conceptual orientations that we may analyse the new historical context in Latin America, within which the democratization processes are inserted.

The new historical-structural context

The great transformations

In the last decades, at different times and in different degrees depending on the context, Latin American societies have been living through profound transformations.[5] The first is the rise to dominance of political-institutional models of consultation and conflict, replacing the dictatorships, civil wars, and revolutionary modalities of previous decades. The second is the exhaustion of the model of "inward development," the loss of dynamism of the public and industrial-urban sectors, and their replacement with formulas of adjustment and stabilization that seek new forms of insertion into a world economy that is characterized by phenomena of globalization and transnational market forces. The third is the transformation of the social structure, with an increase in inequality, poverty, and marginality and precarious education and labor systems. This has produced a restructuring of the system of social actors and a questioning of the traditional forms of collective action. Finally, we can observe a crisis of the model of modernity associated with Western modernization and the North American mass culture predominant in Latin American society – or at least among the leading elites – and the rise of indigenous and hybrid formulas of modernity.

Hidden by these transformations is deeper change that affects the wider world and in a specific way Latin America. The fact is that we are facing a shift away from the basic referential societal type in contemporary Latin America as a result of globalization and an expansion of the principles of identity and citizenship. This means a disarticulation of what was the predominant societal type, the national-state industrial society, although in different degrees according to particular situations. This type was organized around labour and politics – especially the latter in Latin America – and around processes of social change defined as modernization, industrialization, and development; and its fundamental social actors were classes, parties, and social movements related to both.

It is not a question of a passage from one societal type to another, but rather a combination in each particular case of the national-state industrial society with a societal type that we could call "globalized post-industrial." This type of society is structured around consumption and communication, and its main actors are publics, networks, NGOs, and de facto powers – that is, a wide variety of forces on the margins of the democratic game, ranging from local or transnational economic groups to armed forces, that have gained de facto power beyond their legal authority. To different degrees and in different forms, Latin American societies never completely achieved a national-state industrial type of structure; they were less defined by that type as such, than by their change and movement towards it – a process of change that was called "development" and "social integration." But these societies were always torn between their national-state industrial society projects and a fragmented, hybrid blend of different civilizations/worlds within each society. The transformation away from the would-be national-state industrial society to a globalized post-industrial one redefines the roles of politics and states, the central actors of social change. And this has, as we will see, important effects on the democratic issue of the future in the continent.

The future of the Latin American countries is tied to their ability to confront four challenges or, stated differently, to simultaneously engage four dynamic processes which redefine the basic concept of development centered upon economic growth and its causes or effects in other spheres of society. The first is the construction of political democracies, which constitutes the main topic of this paper. The second process is what we call social democratization. This has different meanings, ranging from the redefinition of citizenship beyond classical rights, to the overcoming of new forms of exclusion and the restructuring of social actors or reinforcement of civil society. The third process involves a definition of the model of economic development. The classical model of "inward" development, based on the state as agent of development, had been replaced by the reinsertion of the national economies into the process of globalization and transnational market forces. This meant a greater autonomy of the economy compared with the inward development model, but has left society entirely at the mercy of transnational economic forces, as the predominant mode in which the transformation has been effected has been adjustment or structural reforms of a neo-liberal kind.[6]

But neo-liberal modalities have meant only the partial insertion and new dependency of certain sectors, so that a society of a dual type has been again configured and the issue of a new model of development raised. Put another way, the neo-liberal model has constituted a rupture and demonstrated its inherent failure to become a stable and self-sustaining development. The concept of "transition to a market economy" was also an ideological instrument that identified a particular way of adjusting the economy in times of crisis to a new and alternative development model.

The fourth process could be considered a synthesis of the others, but it has its own dynamics. It is one of definitions of the kind of modernity that these countries will generate and live by. Modernity is the affirmation of subjects, individual or collective, builders of their own history – the way in which a society constitutes its subjects.[7] The particular form of Latin American modernity, configured around the national-popular matrix, is in crisis as it faces the model of modernity identified with specific processes of modernization in developed countries, and in particular the North American consumption and mass culture model. In opposition to this is the vision of a Latin American modernity identified either with a "profound" Latin America of indigenous roots, or one with a social base that is racially mixed and with a particular subject that is the Catholic Church.[8]

Modernity can no longer be defined by identifying it with historical models of modernization or with only one of its sources, be it the most rationalist or instrumental one, the most expressive, or simply the historical memory of a national identity. Each society combines these three dimensions in a different way and "invents" its own modernity. The question for Latin America society is whether it will be able to construct its model of modernity, at the country and regional levels, in order to enter autonomously into the globalized world.

The changing socio-political matrix

This ensemble of processes and transformations redefines the very concept of development.[9] They point towards a transformation of the matrix or constitution of society, or the socio-political matrix that constitutes society – the socio-political matrix – in Latin America. This socio-political model existed in a historical-structural context characterized by the contradictory confluence of nationalist, developmental, and modernizing processes. Industrialization was oriented towards the internal market with a central role given to the state,[10] the leading oligarchic and middle-class components, and intense processes of popular mobilization in which politics constituted the main axis.

In this context, Latin American societies privileged a socio-political matrix that defined a relationship of fusion, subordination, or elimination of some of the elements in this relation between the state, the system of representation, and social actors. Thus, in some countries the fusion between these elements was achieved through the figure of the populist leader, and in others through the identification between state and political party or through the articulation between social organization and political party leadership. In some situations the party system fused all social groups, or corporate organizations monopolized the totality of collective action, without leaving room for autonomous political life.

This has often been called a "politically centered matrix." It can also be described as "national-popular," having gone through diverse historical expressions of populism and even certain forms of militarism or authoritarianism, surviving for long decades through very different types of political regimes. In this classical matrix, the state played a central role in all collective actions, whether development, social mobility and mobilization, redistribution, or the integration of popular sectors. But it was a state with a weak autonomy from society and upon which weighed all pressures and demands, both internal and external. This interpenetration between state and society gave politics a central role. Aside from exceptional cases, this was more a mobilizing than a representational politics, and the institutions of representation were, in general, the weakest part of the matrix. The "statist" principle present in the whole of society was not always accompanied by institutional autonomy and effective capacity for action of the state.

Directed against this matrix and this type of state were the revolutionary movements of the 1960s – which criticized its elitist aspect and its inability to satisfy popular interests – as well as the military regimes that began in the 1960s in Latin America. In the 1980s and 1990s the processes of political democratization and of structural adjustments and economic reforms, in turn, coincided with the acknowledgement of the void left by the disarticulated old matrix. This was not replaced by another stable and coherent configuration of the relations between state and society. Different substitutes tended to install themselves into this void, making impossible the strengthening and complementarity between the components of the matrix (state, regime and political actors, social actors or civil society), either eliminating one or two of them, or subordinating them.

Two tendencies attempted to replace this dissolving matrix. On the one hand, an attempt to deny politics on the basis of a distorted vision of modernization, expressed in an instrumental politics that substitutes technocratic reason and the market logic for collective action, seemed to crush any other dimension of society. The main expression of this tendency is neo-liberalism. Here, the state is seen only in its instrumental dimension. For this reason, the priority becomes above all a question of reducing it, turning public spending cuts and privatizations into a synonym for state reform. Paradoxically, no transformation made in pursuit of this vision has been able to do without very strong state intervention, increasing its coercive capacity. On the other hand, there is a tendency towards the negation of politics that comes from a kind of irrationalism that replaces collective action with identitarian refuge, or by moral or religious action.

Populist, clientelist, or corporativist nostalgias, and in cases of extreme decomposition neo-populist leaderships, may arise between these two poles, but except in Venezuela, they have lacked the wide-ranging appeal of great ideological projects that effect mobilization with a strong integrative capability. The fundamental issue is whether or not, beyond the democratic transitions or the passage to an economic model based on the forces of the transnationalized market, we are witnessing the emergence of a new societal type, this is, a new socio-political matrix.

Most probably, the Latin American countries will follow different routes in this respect. Some will suffer a long process of decomposition without the emergence of a new matrix. Others will attempt the recomposition of the classical matrix. Others again may lean towards a new matrix of an open type, characterized by the autonomy and complementary tension of its components, combined with subordinate elements of the decomposing classical matrix and redefining classical politics and cultural orientations.

This last hypothesis describes some tendencies already occurring, but also defines a normative orientation. Thus, it is possible to affirm that the future of democratic regimes depends on the consolidation of a new matrix, characterized by this triple strengthening of state, party system, and civil society; and on the establishment of a relationship between them, no longer of fusion, but of autonomy and complementary tension. In the absence of this, the political framework will most probably be merely formally democratic. It is difficult to be sure of whether such democracies will be effective and operative or whether they will be to a great extent replaced by diverse de facto powers lacking general legitimacy.

The redefinition of politics

The starting point of new relations between state and society is the recognition of the historical fact that no contemporary national development, especially in countries of late development such as the Latin American ones, has been able to do without a predominant role of the state. Perhaps the epoch to which this applies – characterized by "inward" national developments in which the mobilizing state was the unquestionable and uncounterweighted agent – is ending, and we are confronting the emergence of developments inserted into transnational market forces. This does not mean the loss of significance of the state, but the modification of its forms of organization and intervention and the redefinition of its relationship with other actors in society.

If one examines the insertion of the state into a new socio-political matrix, this is far from involving the elimination of the principle of "statism"; rather, in some cases the issue is creating it, and in others, that of strengthening it. This creation or strengthening, value-normative in regard to the principle of autonomous statehood, and institutional-organizational in relation to the role of the state as an agent of national unity and development, demands the elimination of its most bureaucratic tendencies, associated to forms of the past, as well as the strengthening of the levels of representation and participation of society. This implies a transformation of politics and demands the reinforcement and proliferation of civil society and social actors autonomous from the state and the system of parties – that is, a redefinition of the meaning of politics in democracy.

Politics had a double meaning in the social life of these countries. On the one hand, given the role of the state as the central motor of development and social integration, politics was seen as a way of gaining access to the state's resources. On the other, politics played a fundamental role in giving meaning to social life through the projects and the ideology of change. Hence its more mobilizing, ideological, and confrontational character, compared to other contexts.

In the new scene generated by the social, economic, and cultural transformations we have referred to, which decompose the unity of the polis-society, the exclusive centrality of politics as the expression of collective action tends to disappear. But it acquires a new centrality, for it must engage and articulate the diverse spheres of social life without destroying their autonomy. Thus, there is less room for highly ideologized, or totalizing projects, but there is a demand on politics for a "meaning" that market forces by themselves, the media, the particularisms or mere calculations of individual or corporate interest, are not able to give.

If the risks of classical politics were the extremes of ideology, polarization, and even fanaticism, today's risks are banality, cynicism, and corruption. With the exhaustion of classical politics as well as the attempts at its radical elimination, and in the light of the insufficiency of present-day pragmatism and technocratism, the great task for the future is the reconstruction of the institutional space, the polis. Politics can be meaningful again in this polity as the articulation between autonomous and strong social actors and a state that recovers its role as agent of development, in a world that threatens to destroy national communities.

Democracy and democratization

The redefinition and revalorization of democracy

Historically, democratic practice and thought in Latin America were characterized by the mutually reinforcing relationship between political democracy and social democratization. The authoritarian or military dictatorships in the Southern Cone and elsewhere were a landmark that provoked a mutation in political life and theoretical reflection on this relationship. In these circumstances, the elemental idea of ending the dictatorships arose – even if that did not solve other problems, nor change other maladies of society – because these regimes appeared as the negation of human life and were an evil in themselves. In other words, what mattered was the end of a particular form of domination, regardless of the fact that this would not end all ills. That is the basic foundation of human rights: a regime in which those human rights are valid and where no one with power can eliminate them or violate them with impunity.

Democracy, then, is separated from other dimensions not directly related to its ethical principles, and becomes a particular and irreplaceable point of reference of the ideal society, that is, the political regime. Democracy becomes the ideal political model worthy of struggle, regardless of whether or not other ends are satisfied or other benefits obtained, however important they may be. Opening up the ethical, intellectual, and political space to think democracy as a regime, and not as a type of society, restricts the concept, of course, but not the strength of its ethical principle.

A political regime is a very particular sphere within society. What we call a political regime can change, progress, and relapse, independently from, although in connection with, the mode of production, the value system, and the social structure. Democracy is a particular type of regime. It is a concept, not a theory, even though diverse theories may be established about the conditions that allow for its constitution and development or regression, and its relationship to the other spheres of society.

Studies of political democratizations

One can study, with reservations that we will mention, how a society passes from one political regime to another, be it from nondemocratic regimes to democratic ones, or from these to other types of regime. To say that there is legitimate intellectual and scholarly room for such a study does not imply approval of any particular theory or ensemble of theories – for they may all be wrong – but only the recognition of the validity of the object of study – namely, democratizations, inadequately called "transitions to democracy," but which we prefer to call "political democratizations," for reasons we will examine next.

The validity of a study of a change of regime requires at least three conditions equally applicable to the other examples of changes, passages, or transitions that we mentioned. The first is to adequately and rigorously define the points of departure and arrival. The second is to avoid any kind of teleological analysis of ongoing processes, or explanations that predetermine the results – in other words, to avoid the evolutionist type of thought in which the script is written beforehand and all actions are explained through it, leading to a determined objective, to depart from which would constitute a "deviation." The third is to avoid making of the process of political democratization the only fundamental process that affects society, and making all the others dependent on it without recognizing their autonomy, just as before the autonomy of the processes or changes of regime was disavowed.

In fact, in approaching the study of political democratizations, one of the main risks was to study them with the same attitude that influenced Latin American social sciences in the study of earlier processes. This would mean to give to democratization processes the role of leading on to the ideal society. Democracy, like politics, cannot solve all problems of society. But in that irreplaceable realm of society that is specific to it, democracy solves problems better than any other regime, and for this reason it is a value in itself. Therefore, it would be a serious error to turn what have been called "democratic transitions" – or rather "political democratizations" – into the only new area of social theory, and their theorization into the new sole paradigm of social phenomena. They must be considered a thematic focus, but only a partial one: a question of passing from an authoritarian society to a democratic one, which does not, however, imply that the political regime defines the whole of society.

Without doubt, that was one of the main problems to be confronted at the beginning of these studies. Given the reality of general oppression by the dictatorships, and facing the crisis of the categories in which the upheavals and frustrated revolutions were lived and thought, there was a temptation to think that political democratization was "the" new problematique that replaced that of development, socialism, and revolution, and "the" new theoretical-analytical paradigm that replaced that of modernization, dependency, or the global capitalist system. Continuing to approach the new realities with the old attitude entailed the risk of slipping from theoretical analysis into ideological discourse.

We can no longer think of the issue of political democratization as "the" general solution, as "the" new global paradigm. The diverse processes in our countries would each require, at least, its own paradigm. As we have noted, a number of sometimes contradictory developments have occurred with the construction of democratic political regimes: social democratization as social integration and cohesion and the overcoming of inequalities and exclusions; the reinsertion of Latin American economies into the world economy with national and regional models of development; and the definition of a model of modernity different from the classical Western variant. All of them are present in one way or another, and face regressions, advances, and also mutual effects, but they are not unidirectional processes, nor can they be effected by one single predominant actor. Among these processes there are interrelations, tensions, contradictions, autonomies, and specific dynamics.

There is not, then, "one" subject, "one" basic or unique process, "one" theory of global change, because today the very concept of social change no longer follows a single guiding thread. Now, what did the studies of the processes of political democratization, wrong and inadequately called "the theory of transition" or "transitology," consist in, and what did they contribute?

First, these theories contributed to the understanding of how democratic institutions were generated and established, replacing non-democratic regimes or authoritarian institutions. Second, they departed from all-embracing paradigms, from global theories of social change, and from determinist theories in which one structure is the consequence and reflection of the other, and which make of political democracy an irrelevant object of study. Third, they differentiated the processes of political democratization. This last point is highly important, to avoid confusions that speak about "waves" and consider all the Latin American democratizations of the last decades as belonging to the same type and at the same time as part of a cycle that includes cases from other socio-historical contexts. In this sense, one of the contributions of the study of political democratizations in Latin America is that it allows for the understanding of processes that are very different, such as foundations, transitions, and reforms.

Democratic theory and the change of society

Beyond the analysis of democratization processes, Latin America demonstrates the weakness and problems of democratic theory in general. This is because classical democratic theory grew out of one type of society, the polis. A polis-society is a space where an economic system, a political organization, a model of identity and cultural diversity, and a social structure correspond to one another, even if in a contradictory way

– that is, they are historically shared by a population. This means that it is also the space in which a political community and a centre of decisions is defined for those inside such a polity, called the national state. This is what we call a "country" or "society." This type of society is defined around labour, economy, and politics. It possesses institutions and its actors, positioned around production and around politics, debate, compete, and struggle over the general orientation of society.

Today, this polis finds itself undermined by processes of globalization that diminish the margins for maneuver of states, conditioning and penetrating societies, and modifying identities. New principles or identities appear here to compete with the classical principles of class identity or nation, educational or income level, political or ideological views. Identity that does not depend on choices but is "received" – such as age, colour, or sex – and comes to play a significant role by imposing itself on, or at least combining itself with, the acquisitive identities which derive from work, education, or ideology, for example. Seemingly, the classical predictions that affirmed a passage from societies of ascription to societies of acquisition, from particularism to universalism, were doomed to failure.

This makes for a state relatively severed from society, and actors split between their universal belonging to a socio-cultural category and their belonging to a local, regional, and above all, national state space, of which they still feel a part. We are today in a societal type different from the one we lived in during the greater part of the twentieth century, which is characterized by combining the former with another, which we have called globalized post-industrial. The institutions that are appropriate for the national industrial dimension are not necessarily adequate for the globalized post-industrial dimension. One must therefore envision a theory of democracy for a society that combines both of these dimensions, because the democracy that we know, its mechanisms and its theory, were conceived for a type of society that no longer exists as the only referent.[11]

This is aggravated in Latin America by two circumstances. First, as we have said, these societies never fully achieved the national state industrial society. Secondly, the urgency and pressure for ending the dictatorships or civil wars privileged reflections and strategies about democratization and not about the nature of democracy. This debate was postponed at the risk of uncritically accepting a model of democracy taken from other historical contexts.[12]

Achievements and deficits of recent political democratization

When we speak of political democratization we are referring to those processes that depart from a historical situation characterized by the presence or dominance of a political regime in which democratic institutions are non-existent or minimal.[13]

Foundations, transitions, and reform

The construction of democratic institutions which we call political democratization has followed three main directions in the region. The first is that of democratic foundation, of the type classically analyzed by Moore or Rustow.[14] This refers to societies or countries that have not experienced democratic regimes and that install democracy for the first time. This process implies deep and widespread change in society, such as happened with the original democratic installations in European countries or the United States. In the last decades, this process of democratic foundation in Latin America has taken place above all in Central America. These are situations in which a democratic regime is constituted for the first time, or the political system is entirely refounded, after processes of confrontation through civil wars or revolutions.

This type of political democratization presents three important characteristics, linked to this aspect of civil war, revolution, or global change. On the one hand, the construction of democratic institutions fuses with a process of pacification, reconciliation, and national reconstruction. On the other hand, that means we are in the presence of negotiations in the aftermath of war, witnessing the complicated conversion of warriors and combatants into political actors. The issue is how those who sought to eliminate their enemies turn into actors that have to engage in conflicts and negotiations within a shared institutional frame, in order to govern and reconstruct a country. The warring forces have to suffer a complex metamorphosis into political parties, confronting tendencies towards the maintenance of paramilitary or insurrectional forms. Finally, the other characteristic of foundations is that, depending on the level of the confrontational situation, the weight of foreign actors and mediation is fundamental. This has been visible in the Central American case, where the roles of the churches, international institutions, North American policy, European social democracy, and mediating Latin American countries, have been highly significant. The generation of democratic institutions in the case of foundations has been extremely slow, and in it, governments oscillate between a conservative restoration of previous forms of domination under precariously democratic conditions, and effective democratization.

The second type of political democratization – which at some time tended to be identified as the only one – is what we will call "transitions." Leaving semantic discussion aside, we will define this as the passage from a formally authoritarian or military regime to a basically democratic regime, although it may be incomplete or imperfect. That is the case with countries like Spain, from where the analytical criteria for Latin America were taken, and with South America, especially the Southern Cone in a broad sense.

In the case of transitions, there is no internal defeat of the military, even though there is a sort of political defeat for the military nucleus that holds power. All of them are characterized by complex processes of negotiation and by the definition of an institutional arena for ending dictatorship, be it a constituent assembly, a plebiscite, elections, or a combination of these. The influence of the authoritarian or military institution at the first moment of democracy depends upon the nature of the political defeat of the military nucleus in power and of the existence or nonexistence of an institutional frame for the future democratic regime bred by the authoritarian regime. For the military institution, it is a question of maintaining its prerogatives in order to operate as a power factor, defending what they consider their "work" and covering up and/or ensuring impunity for the crimes committed during the dictatorial period. In cases where some level of guerrilla or insurrectional activity is maintained, this gives the military a pretext to recover part of their influence and power that were lost during the transition.

Even though in transitions there is no defeat of the military, nor even an actual overthrow of power holders – as often happens with foundations – there is an attempt to displace or change those holders with the purpose of generating democratic institutions. And this differentiates transitions from the third type of political democratization, namely democratic reforms.

This third road for political democratization – sometimes called "opening" – involves a broadening or extension of democratic institutions from regimes that are not formally military or authoritarian, but operate instead under the dominance of autocratic or semi-authoritarian forms, or in the form of restricted or exclusive democracies. The Mexican or Colombian cases reflect some such characteristics, which might also be present in the decomposition of Venezuela. With many differences amongst these cases, all of them are cases in which the point of departure is not a formally authoritarian regime or a military dictatorship, but instead processes take place in which the protagonists are the government or the party or parties in government.

We are not referring to just any type of political or democratic reform or some extension or broadening of a democratic regime already in place. For example, the extension of elections to certain spheres, or of the vote to certain social categories excluded before could no doubt be part of the reforms we refer to. But, when we speak of reform as a type of political democratization we are referring to a deliberate process of transformation of political institutions to make them democratic. These processes of political reform imply an institutional transformation, either to incorporate sectors excluded from the democratic game, or to configure an effectively polyarchic and multiparty system, or to eliminate obstacles to the exercise of popular will, or to control de facto powers at the margins of the regime, or to combine all these dimensions.

Political reforms can, in the long run, be more profound or more radical than transitions, but they are not the same. We know when transitions start and when they end, but democratizing reforms have much less clarity about when they begin and no clarity about when they end. They consist in extremely lengthy, complex, and progressive processes of installation and creation, with advances and relapses, of democratic institutions by the regime and, in general, by the previous holders of power, without their elimination or replacement being strictly necessary, as in the other two types of political democratization. It is impossible to single out and celebrate "the" moment of democratic inauguration, as happens with foundations and transitions. Obviously, this democratization "from the top" is always activated by pressures and mobilizations from below, for it involves a dialectic between the conservation of power and the incorporation of new sectors or actors, which implies, at the same time, a redistribution of power and maintenance of a certain political-institutional continuity.

It can be noted that these three processes, of a different nature even though all are oriented towards political democratization, are not historically pure. There are components of each one in the others, so that at determined moments they face common problematiques. For example, in the case of Argentina, the fact that a government has for the first time democratically succeeded another is a foundational component within a typical process of transition. In the Colombian case, the reform process at the beginning of the 1990s evolved towards the decomposition of the state and the political system, and was pervaded by elements of pacification and national reconstruction that brought it close to being a foundation. In the Chilean case, the transition in a strict sense ended a long time ago, but there is not a complete democratic regime. A process of political reform is still underway to democratize institutions inherited from the military government.[15] It is evident that this is not the case with Mexico, for in the Chilean case the holders of power, the military, were replaced from the outset in order to usher in a democratization process. But both cases have common aspects like, for instance, transformations of the political constitution and the institutional framework to eliminate the authoritarian legacy.

Foundations, as well as transitions from military dictatorships or authoritarian regimes to democratic regimes, seem to have ended, or at least do not seem to be the central political processes any more. Put otherwise, the great crises of authoritarian regression or decomposition seem to have died down, with very few exceptions. An indicator of this is that in all the cases where there have been very diverse situations of crisis or possible regressions, like the Alfonsín-Menem succession in Argentina, or phenomena like Collor de Mello in Brazil, Bucaram in Ecuador, Oviedo in Paraguay, Chávez in Venezuela, and Fujimori in Peru, the solutions have not been the restoration of formally military or authoritarian regimes. A different situation is presented by reforms where the democratizing tendencies are continually combined with partial regressions, so that the process as a whole is slow and not so coherent and it is dubious to consider it finished.

In any case, and with the reservations noted, the existing formally democratic regimes seem to be consolidated. It may be the case that we are so far beyond transitions and consolidations that it is equivocal or confusing to continue to use the name "transition" for the task of completing democracies by overcoming the inherited authoritarian enclaves that coexist with the full functioning of other democratic institutions. To say that in Chile the transition has not ended, for instance, because authoritarian enclaves persist or because of Pinochet's presence as commander in chief or, later, as senator for life, seems analytically and politically less adequate than accepting that what is called "transition" is already over, but its result is an incomplete democracy.

In other words, political democratizations, in the sense of specific processes of establishment of a minimal nucleus of democratic institutions, in any of their forms and in the majority of the cases, seem to have ended in the sense that they are no longer the central dynamic that defines all the behaviours of the actors involved. But this does not mean that they have necessarily been successful. Their pending tasks will have to be fulfilled in the context of social and political processes that cannot be meaningfully defined as transition.

Thus, the crucial question is twofold. First, what type of democracy is emerging in the continent?[16] Second, what transformations must these democracies undergo in order to consolidate with regard to the challenges that will define Latin American society or its gestating socio-political matrix? Concerning the first question, we are facing, with some exceptions, incomplete or weak democracies, but even if a very fluid situation exists in some countries, it is possible to draw a very preliminary balance. In some cases a post-authoritarian regime seems still not to be consolidated or the proper transition is lacking, as in Peru and Paraguay. In other cases they are regimes that, while being basically democratic, maintain certain traces of the prior regime, or what we have called "authoritarian enclaves" (Chile, Mexico, and Guatemala, for example). In other cases, the composition of the system of representation in the democratic regime is still under way, as in Venezuela. There is also a group of countries where the political system as a whole is in disarray, or in which the de facto powers do not submit to the rules of the institutional game or the citizenry is not able to constitute itself as such, which makes democracy relatively irrelevant for the fulfillment of the tasks inherent to every regime, as in Colombia and in some aspects Peru and perhaps Ecuador. Finally there are cases of successful political democratization and others that are consolidated democracies but with serious problems of representation and quality of their regime, as Brazil, Bolivia, and Argentina.[17]

The authoritarian enclaves and de facto powers

When we talk about authoritarian enclaves, we are not referring merely to any problem inherited from the previous military or autocratic regimes, but to those elements that by definition belong to that former regime and that subvert the democratic regime that succeeds it, preventing it from becoming a full political democracy.[18] They are problems or pending tasks of the transitions and foundations, and constitute part of the essence of the processes of reform that have to be confronted under the post-authoritarian regime.

There are four types of authoritarian enclaves in these countries, whose existence and relative strength depend both on the nature of the previous military regime and on the type of transition.

First are the institutional, constitutional and legislative elements that prevent or limit the exercise of popular will, the principle of representation and the effective government of the majority, or that maintain the prerogatives of the armed forces above the political order.

Second is the ethical-symbolical enclave, that is, the effects upon society of the violations of human rights under military dictatorships or situations of civil war. Here there is also an institutional dimension, such as the laws of amnesty or the inability of the judicial institutions to achieve justice.

Third is the actorial enclave. This consists of persons and groups that constitute themselves as social actors who, not content with defining themselves in terms of the democratic present and future, either seek to project the principles and orientations of the preceding dictatorship onto the circumstances of the democratic regime, or maintain the struggle for power through confrontations that can be military or simply extra-constitutional.

Fourth, in the case of democratic foundations or reforms that follow long-standing authoritarian regimes or prolonged situations of extra-institutional confrontation, we also find the cultural enclave. This is the ensemble of habits and styles among the elites, but also among middle and popular sectors, that conspire against the principles and rules of the democratic game: corruption, clientelism, and apathy, among others. The rejection of electoral participation in some countries, could be due, precisely, to the manipulative use that the authoritarian regimes made of it.

Historical analysis of all the experiences of political democratization leaves two main lessons regarding authoritarian enclaves. The first is that they must be confronted at the beginning of the democratic regime or at the moment of pacification, taking advantage of the moral strength and legitimacy enjoyed by the government that succeeds the dictatorship or confrontation, in order to reach a national agreement on the matter. To let what has been called the "state of grace" pass, and be late in posing these issues, makes them enter the game of immediate political interests, generally electoral, of all the actors involved.

The second, even more important lesson is that, because of their nature, these enclaves are interconnected and cannot be treated in isolation. They must be the object of a general strategy; each one has an ethical or democratic minimum and a political maximum possible, and the combination of both can only be resolved by their joint treatment. An optimal solution in each of them is impossible, and the best solution – and the only one that is both ethically acceptable and politically viable – is that of tackling and overcoming the enclaves. This is the only way possible to complete the pending tasks of transition and of national reconstruction and reconciliation.

However, as we have noted, the presence of authoritarian enclaves is not the only product of transitions, foundations, or incomplete reforms and weak democracies. There are also, above all in the case of reforms and democratic extensions, situations in which the institutionalization and legitimization of democratic power cannot be achieved, and in which society is left to the mercy of de facto powers that may or may not be connected with the preceding regime or situation. These situations have provoked some partial regressions or unstable balances in which a democratic regime is not consolidated, there being instead a combination of "situations," authoritarian as well as semi-democratic.

By de facto powers, which play a crucial role in the cases of greater decomposition of the political system in the region, we mean entities or actors that process the decisions pertaining to a political regime – that is, political power, citizenship, and demands and conflicts – at the margin of the rules of the democratic game. They can be extra-institutional, such as local or transnational economic groups, corrupt elements and drug traffickers, insurrectional and paramilitary groups, foreign powers, corporate organizations, and the media. But there are also actors that constitute de jure or institutional powers, which acquire autonomy and assume political powers beyond what is legitimate, thereby becoming de facto powers, as may happen with presidents, judicial authorities, constitutional courts, and the armed forces themselves in many cases.

The presence of the past: Human rights and reconciliation

A major legacy of the military regimes as well as of the confrontations and civil wars was the massive and systematic violation of human rights.[19] Thus, the human rights issue constitutes, as we have said, one of the authoritarian enclaves present in the newborn democracies. Other essays in this book refer to this, so we will limit ourselves to some quick observations. Considered in absolute terms in regard to their orienting principles, truth and justice – the solutions to this problematique – cannot but be partial and insufficient. In no country has the problem been satisfactorily solved in terms of ethical perspective, social legitimacy, or purely political solutions. Everywhere, two logics confronted each other. On the one hand there was the ethical-symbolic logic that demanded the whole truth, the maximum of justice, which meant nothing but punishment for all those guilty, and the greatest possible reparation to the victims. On the other hand, there was the reason of state which placed the problem of human rights within the broader context of the process of democratization or pacification. This logic therefore accepted the ethical principle but combined it with the political criterion of avoiding destabilization on the part of those guilty of human rights violations. It was in the space between both logics that the deliberate actions of the military organizations, and often the judicial power, operated, extorting amnesty or impunity as the price of political stability.

If the issue of the violations of human rights under dictatorships or in situations of civil war has not been, and cannot be, fully resolved under the democratic regimes, the dilemma for these is either to let the issue of human rights die or close it off in the present state of affairs, or re-address it acknowledging the precariousness of the solutions devised. It is no doubt possible, in many cases, to substantially improve the solutions that have existed until now. In this sense, one may think of the derogation of the amnesties granted to itself by the military power, or of the explicit acknowledgement by the armed forces of their repressive action. As examples of this, one can consider the South African case, where the Truth and Reconciliation Commission learned from the Sabato Commission in Argentina and the Rettig Commission in Chile and overcame their defects. But this re-addressing of the issue should find a culmination in the reform of the two institutions that made the violations of human rights possible under authoritarianisms or dictatorships, the military power and the judicial power: in other words, in a drastic revision and reformulation of the state's coercive dimension.

Two central issues appear in considering the balance of human rights issues in the processes of political democratization in these countries. The first, regarding the past, points toward the reconstruction of the national community after the processes that divided it very deeply: this is the issue of reconciliation. The second, looking to the future, refers to the ethical validity and expansion of the principles of human rights.

Regarding the first, it is necessary to find a meaning for the concept of reconciliation that avoids the confusions and ideological uses with which it has been invested until now. Beyond religious or moral language, the issue of reconciliation in societies emerges when great national breaches have been produced. Historically, reconciliations are implicitly achieved with the passage of time or, explicitly, with an act or precise moment in which people decide it is better not to kill one another and to coexist, recognizing each other as members of the same community, as is the case with pacifications or national reunifications. Reconciliation is, thus, a process of recognition of the field of coexistence, understanding and co-operation, of managing conflict and struggle. In other words, it is something that is never finished, and which requires the existence of institutions and rules of the game valid for all.

Thus, on a national plane, after great divisions, reconciliation points towards the reconstitution of basic national unity without eliminating struggles and conflicts. This national unity, so far as political democratizations exclusively are concerned, demands the overcoming of two great cleavages or fragmentations. The first has to do with historical unity and continuity, with the history and ways of life of the country, so that reconciliation points towards the past. This implies coming to terms with history, acknowledging the value of every period in which there has been an attempt at collective creation and of the social sectors that incarnated them, and disavowing the periods of war and massive repression. Without collective memory there is neither country nor common history.

The second division to overcome is a political one, based on the perception of the other as enemy. This division or fragmentation of society tends to be deeper than others, such as those of a socio-economic type, to the extent that here there are no degrees of separation but a tendency to be total. The other was eliminated – by war, executions, exile, imprisonment, torture, kidnapping, and disappearance – or is denied. This cleavage springs from a process in which there were victors and vanquished.

The central issue at stake when speaking of reconciliation is the creation of institutions where the different persons, sectors, or actors recognize each other as part of the same society. This requires a basic recognition, in the case of the armed forces, of their responsibility for the brutal massive repression. Without such acknowledgement, they will remain severed from society. On the other hand, without a basic act of recognition, truth, justice and reparation, the problems of the past will always prevent the adequate treatment of the great challenges of the future. So it is, for example, that all discussion of defence policy, or of restriction of military spending, or of future redefinition of the judicial power, is contaminated by the role of the military institution in the past repression or "dirty war," and of the judiciary in dealing with human rights violations.

The second issue regards the role of human rights in democracy, beyond the treatment of the violations that occurred in the preceding regimes or situations. Here there are at least three dimensions involved. First is the issue of the right to life and physical integrity – reformulated in terms of demanding from the state protection against physical violence coming from urban, criminal, familial, and other sources. Second is the extension of human rights to all of the population, that is, its practical universalization, including the problems of education, work, poverty, inequalities, and access to justice. This involves, at the same time, a problem of transformation of the quality of that access. Finally, beyond the extension and deepening of human rights, there is the problem of the human rights of people as part of such specific social categories as age, gender, and ethnicity, which constitutes a revolution in the classical concept of human rights. Many of these issues point towards another, future dimension of reconciliation, namely the formulation of a new national consensus, which can often have constitutional implications.

A provisional balance sheet of political democratization

The balance sheet of political democratizations cannot avoid being contradictory. On the one hand, and with a few significant exceptions, electoral participation in the region has not decreased in the last decade and reaches over two-thirds. Likewise, according to public opinion polls, the acceptance of democracy as the best political regime to live under has not diminished and remains relatively high. To this, we can add the regularity of elections, and, with the noted exceptions, stable political participation, the relative formalization and institutionalization of political processes, and the emergence in almost all the countries of a system of parties and coalitions that tends to ensure a fair degree of governability.[20]

On the other hand, the characteristics of processes where negotiation plays a determining role, as well as the limitations on democracy emanating from the authoritarian enclaves, the absence of institutionality, and the dominance of de facto powers, explain, in part, the frustration and disenchantment of vast sectors of society. Thus, we meet with the view that although there is advancement in freedoms, democracy has not at all changed the lives of people and for them things remain the same. Although the institutions pertaining to democracy are valued, there is also a rather radical critique of those actually existing in each society and their functioning.[21]

Summing up, beyond the intrinsic problems of political democratizations, and overlapping sometimes with them, the main challenges for democracy in the region can be best defined today in terms of three main challenges. The first is that of deepening and extending the ethical principles and mechanisms of the democratic regime to other realms of social life. Second is the challenge of enhancing the participation, representation, and satisfaction of the citizenry in decision-making processes at the local, regional, and central levels. The third challenge is that of enhancing the relevance of democracy to solving the issues pertaining to a political regime. These are the issues that will determine the stability of the regimes, their possible disintegration, and the possibility of new waves of authoritarianism.

The future of democracy in Latin America

The reconstruction of a socio-political matrix

The democracies under discussion here now face the challenge of completing the remaining tasks of an incomplete democratization and also of deepening and enhancing democracy's quality and relevance. What will the existence of democratic regimes in the future depend upon? This question cannot be answered, as in the past, by pointing to the determinism of the structural factors that will make democracy possible, because sometimes there can be democratic regimes simply because people want them. If one had to set forth a hypothesis that does not make of democracy a purely dependent variable but an active factor in the construction of a society, and which does not again fall into reliance upon ideological or structural determinisms, one would affirm that the future of democracy in Latin America will fundamentally depend upon constructing a legitimacy of politics that allows for states, parties, and strong social actors, autonomous from but complementary to one another.

This hypothesis gives us a criterion by which to evaluate political action. Today, concrete political projects, politics, and policies within a democratic framework make sense if they are capable of giving meaning to, and improving the quality of, personal and social life. That, in present circumstances, depends less on their content, which can be very diverse for the different actors and visions, than on the capability of individual and collective action to intervene in their own and national destinies. Which implies asking oneself, every time, if the projects or policies strengthen at once the state, the system of representation, and the social actors.

At the basis of this hypothesis is the central issue of the reconstruction of a polis-society where democracy can have roots and sustenance. For the reconstruction of a polis-society means precisely the construction of a system of relations between state, system of representation, and strong actors at very different levels: at the local and regional level of each country, at the national level, and also at the supranational, regional and global level.

At a moment when the transit from authoritarian or semi-authoritarian regimes to regimes with a democratic tendency seems to be assured, this appears to be the only way of answering the main problem that political democracy faces from now on in Latin America: making it an effective regime that is not left to the mercy of de facto powers, from the past or from the future.

Strengthening the state

We have noted that a new socio-political model in Latin America that replaces the national-popular one and the neo-liberal or authoritarian formulas that have been tried, no longer involves the formal installation of a political democracy, but its quality, deepening, and relevance. This is linked to the triple strengthening of the state, the system of representation, and the social actors. Beyond foundations, transitions, and democratic extensions, these are the new tasks of political democratization. The state was dislocated from society for a number of reasons, amongst which were the processes of economic transformation, authoritarianism, and political polarization.

The anti-state visions fashionable in the 1980s and 1990s emanate from two contradictory viewpoints. One affirms the market as the universal panacea. This conflicts with social demands and the very tendencies of globalization, which, rejecting the bureaucratic and inefficient states, demand of it an active role as an agent of redistribution and as a principle of national unity. The other viewpoint affirms the existence of an inherent confrontation between civil society and the state. This conflicts with the present weakness of social actors, to which we will return.

What is needed, then, is not the reduction of the state, but its transformation – its modernization, decentralization, and participative reorganization, in order to perform its function as a key agent of development. While there have been processes tending to a minimal reconstitution of the state after the dismantling of the so called "structural adjustments," an integral reform that accounts for the new socio-economic realities and redefines its role in society and development, has been, in general, postponed. This reform should be directed towards strengthening the state's capacity to promote development. If one examines the serious problems of public security, development, infrastructure, and communications, re-insertion into the globalized economy, environment, education, and health, to name a few, a strong investment in the state seems essential. This requires an emphasis upon efficiency and an increase in human and economic resources, perhaps balanced by a decrease in some areas, like the military. Likewise, it requires decentralization and strengthening of local and regional authority in the allocation of resources, as well as administration, management, and participation by actors at the social basis.

There is doubtless a paradox in the functioning of the state according to a new socio-political model. If one can no longer think of a state that is the exclusive unifier of social life, neither can one do without an intervention of the state directed at the constitution of spaces and institutions that allow for the emergence of significant actors, autonomous from it, and the protection of individuals. But a strong state requires political and social control, through the system of representation and the political parties and civil society or, better yet, the social actors.

The crucial role of the parties

The nature of parties and party systems has been very diverse in Latin America.[22] Military authoritarianism attempted to destroy all forms of political action, and had as a central target the political parties and organizations. Although it did not succeed, and indeed parties became a key actor in democratization, the construction of strong party systems remained a pending task. In some cases, where the party system was pulverized, there is an attempt to build parties; in others, the main task is to build party systems that break the monopoly of the hegemonic party or the traditional two-party system; and in still others, the main issue is the reconstruction of the relationship between society, its actors, and the parties. Each country has a different problem, but all are in some way in the midst of a complex process of attempting to strengthen the party system so as to enable it to control a strong state.

In general terms, there are at least three issues that will have to be addressed regarding parties, to ensure that they perform their task of mediation between the people and the state. First, the diverse functions of the parties (representation, assembly and public debate, civic education, the conduct of government or opposition, recruitment for public office) demand a legislation that supports and finances them, but at the same time establishes adequate public control over them. This requires an internal reform of the party system that ensures internal democracy and technical capability.

The second problem concerns the representation of new kinds of divisions and conflicts in society that are represented by the parties. In order for the party systems to effectively re-elaborate the expression of social demand and its diversity, it is necessary to be innovative in the constitution of institutional spaces where they can meet with other manifestations of social life without absorbing them or making them irrelevant to the participation of the citizenry.

A third question that will also define the future of the political parties will be the capability of forming majority governmental coalitions. When competitive multiparty systems are established, it is very unlikely that there would be any single party capable of constituting itself as majority on its own to ensure an effective and representative government. This is already a central issue of party politics in Latin America, and will remain so in the next decades. But the formation of governing coalitions of parties does not have institutional incentives, given the presidentialist systems current in Latin America. Rather, the incentives encourage irresponsible oppositions and minority governments. This is a basic issue in the reform of existing political institutions. There is also a need for change in political culture, not only among the leaders or elites, but also among activists and clienteles, accustomed to see the other only as an adversary to defeat or absorb, or a partner with whom to sign electoral agreements without programmatic compromise.

Reinforcing social actors

Both a strong state and a system of strong parties have to be controlled by the citizenry, and this presupposes strong actors and social networks. In this way, the third element of the new socio-political model or matrix, to be strengthened and endowed with autonomy so as to permit an effective control of the state and the parties, is what is called "civil society."[23] This poses a very difficult problem in societies that have been impacted by the disarticulation of their classical actors, the erosion of the state referents for collective action, new forms of massive exclusion, and a weak structuring of the social basis for new public issues and affairs.

The new waves of liberal economic reforms raised the profile of entrepreneurs, but this is not enough. A socio-political matrix of a classical or national-popular type tended to correspond to a type of collective action centered on the state and politics, and a type of social movement that fused developmental, modernizing, integrative, popular, and nationalist dimensions and orientations. Its epitome was the workers' movement, to which all other movements should be subordinated or "allied," even when in fact it was the party or the political movement that took up the conduct of social action.

Authoritarianism, the demands of negotiated political democratization, and the economic transformations of recent decades resulted in the dismantling of this type of action. Under authoritarianism, the constitutive issues of social actors centered upon the struggles against this form of domination and against the structural transformations it promoted. In the processes of democratization, there was a repoliticization of social life, yet the socio-economic transformations under the aegis of the so-called "structural adjustments" deeply weakened the material bases and the spaces of constitution of social actors.

The socio-economic transformations of the last decades and the political and cultural changes have profoundly modified the panorama of social actors. Classical actors have lost part of their social significance and have tended to become corporate. The actors that have emerged around the new post-authoritarian issues have not succeeded in constituting themselves as stable actors or a body of citizens. In situations like these, social actors tend to be replaced by sporadic mobilizations and fragmentary and defensive actions – sometimes in the shape of social and other networks which are significant but which possess low political institutionalization and representation – or by individual reactions of a consumerist or withdrawal type. On the other hand, the aggregation of individuals takes center stage, through the phenomenon of public opinion measured by means of polls – conducted not by mobilizing or representative organizations, but by the mass media.

There are elements here that harm the quality of democratic life, eroding the incentives for collective and political action on the one hand, and subjecting the political game either to intense pressures and negotiations by corporate actors, or to blackmail by mass opinion or the mass media, on the other. Still, there is the potential for allowing a redefinition of citizenship and a new way of conceiving collective action. What is pending is the relationship of these manifestations with political life – the reason that the institutionalization of spaces where classical forms express themselves together with emerging forms seems indispensable.

The dismantling of the classical matrix and the end of democratic transitions generate a situation in which a unifying principle of social action disappears and in which, on the contrary, the different principles become diverse and even in some cases contradictory (environment versus growth, to name just one example), each expressing itself through different dynamics.

The complexion of actors can no longer be thought of in the styles of the past. One must recognize that it is almost impossible to find one single social or political subject or actor, around which a single field of tensions and contradictions is generated, that articulates the different principles and orientations of action springing from the processes of social modernization and democratization. While it is true that it will no longer be possible to return to traditional collective action, the paradox lies in that this can only be effected from politics and its actors, however problematic that may be and in spite of seemingly navigating against the current.

Conclusion

The main conclusions that emerge from our analysis can be summarized as follows. First, the existence of democratic regimes demands the existence of a polis. Today, we find ourselves in the presence of an explosion of this concept that defines the locus, the site, and the territorial space where the phenomena of power take place. This forms the locus of the problems of globalization and the outburst of identities.

Second, political democratizations wholeheartedly endorsed democracy as a political regime. While these are specific processes limited to the political realm and do not solve other problems of society, they are the most visible part of a deeper social change and cannot be understood without relating them to it.

Third, this change involves the end of an era of which authoritarianism, and then the processes of economic adjustment, were the moment of rupture. We have summarized this transformation as the rupture of the national-popular socio-political matrix and the attempt to replace it with new relations between state, politics, and social actors.

Fourth, the successes, failures, and limitations of democratic transitions, reforms, and foundations can be better understood if we place them in this broader historical context or problematique of a change of epoch and of the type of articulation between state and society. Alongside the political democratizations, we must understand processes of reformulation of the model of development, social integration, and modernity.

Fifth, political democratization means not only completing the pending tasks of foundations, transitions, and incomplete reforms, but also reconstructing the polis and the political systems, and articulating a new form of relation between state, politics, and social actors. The future of political democracy in the Latin American countries will depend to a great extent on the strength, autonomy, and complementarity of these components of the socio-political matrix.

Notes

1. This essays draws upon and elaborates on other works of the author on the new socio-historical problematique and sociological perspectives: *Hacia una nueva era política: Estudio sobre las democratizaciones* (Mexico City: Fondo de Cultura Económica, 1995); and "En qué sociedad vivi(re)mos? Tipos societales y desarrollo en el cambio de siglo," in H. González and H. Schmidt (eds.), *Democracia para una nueva sociedad: Modelo para armar* (Santiago, Chile: Editorial Nueva Sociedad, 1997); *La sociedad en que vivi(re)mos: Introducción sociológica al cambio de siglo* (Santiago, Mexico: Ediciones LOM, 2000).

2. For this concept of actor-subject, see F. Dubet et M. Wiewvorka, Penser le sujet: Author d'Alain Touraine (Paris: Fayard, 1995).

3. Besides the works cited in note 1, see the most recent definition of "socio-political" matrix in M. A. Garretón, Política y sociedad entre dos épocas: America Latina en el cambio de siglo (Buenos Aires: Ediciones Homo Sapiens, 2000).

4. This is why the idea of a minimal or procedural definition of democracy is inadequate. See Guillermo O'Donnell, "Democratic Theory and Comparative Politics" (paper, Notre Dame University, July 1999).

5. P. H. Smith (ed.) Latin America in Comparative Perspective: New Approaches to Methods and Analysis (Boulder, Colo.: Westview Press, 1995); Raquel Sosa (ed.), America Latina y el Caribe: Perspectivas de su reconstrucción (Mexico City: ALAS, UNAM, 1996).

6. On the economic transformations and new model of development, C. Acuña, W. Smith, and E. Gamarra (eds.), Latin American Political Economy in the Age of Neo-Liberal Reform (Miami: Transaction Publishers, 1994).

7. On modernity, see J. Beriain (comp.), Las consecuencias perversas de la modernidad (Madrid: Anthropos, 1996).

8. The best-known work from the Catholic point of view is P. Morandé, Cultura y modernización en América Latina: Ensayo sociológico acerca de la crisis del desarrollismo y de su superación, Cuadernos del Instituto de Sociologia (Santiago: Edit. Pontificia Universidad Católica de Chile, 1984).

9. See PNUD, Informes sobre desarrollo humano (Madrid: Cedial, 1993; Mexico City: Fondo de Cultura Economica, 1994; Mexico City: Harla, 1995).

10. A. Hirschman, "The Political Economy of Import-Substituting Industrialization in Latin America," Quarterly Journal of Economics February 1969.

11. For theoretical discussion of democracy, see Alain Touraine, Qu'est-ce que la democratie? (Paris: Fayard, 1994); Norberto Bobbio, El futuro de la democracia (Mexico City: FCE, 1986).

12. For a criticism of the political democratization processes and studies in this sense, see C. Franco, Acerca del modo de pensar la democracia en América Latina (Lima: Friedrich Ebert Stiftung, 1998).

13. On transitions and political democratizations, both in Latin America and in general, see J. Linz and A. Stepan, Problems of Democratic Transition and Consolidation: Southern Europe and Post-Communist Europe (Baltimore: Johns Hopkins University Press, 1996); C. Barba, J. L. Barros, and J. Hurtado (comps.), Transiciones a la democracia en Europa y America, 2 vols. (Mexico City: FLACSO, Universidad de Guadalajara, Editorial Angel Porras, 1991); G. O'Donnell, Ph. Schmitter, and L. Whitehead (eds.), Transiciones desde un gobierno autoritario 4 vols. (Buenos Aires: Edit. Paidos, 1988); S. Mainwaring, G. O'Donnell, and S. Valenzuela (eds.), Issues in Democratic Consolidation (Notre Dame, Ind.: University of Notre Dame Press, 1992). A balanced and updated revision is Jonathan Hartlyn, "Contemporary Latin American Democracy and Consolidation: Unexpected Patterns, Re-elaborated concepts, Multiple Components," Forthcoming in a volume edited by the Latin American Program, Wilson Center, Washington, D.C., 2000. For my own view, see Hacia una nueva era politica.

14. B. Moore, Los orígenes sociales de la dictadura y de la democracia (Barcelona: Eds. Peninsula, 1976); D. Rustow, "Transitions to Democracy: Towards a Dynamic Model," Comparative Politics April 1970; 2(3).

15. A. Menéndez-Carrión and A. Joignant (eds.), La caja de Pandora: El retorno de la transición chilena (Santiago, Chile: Planeta/Ariel, 1999).

16. F. Weffort, Cual democracia? (San José, Costa Rica: FLACSO, 1993).

17. For another balance sheet, see Hartlyn, "Contemporary Latin America."
18. I have developed the ideas on authoritarian enclaves, relevant democracy, and de facto powers in *La posibilidad democratica en Chile* (Santiago, Chile: FLACSO, 1988).
19. E. Jelin and E. Herschberg, *Constructing Democracy: Human Rights, Citizenship and Society in Latin America* (Boulder, Colo.: Westview Press, 1996).
20. D. Zovatto and J. Rial (eds.), *Urnas y desencannto politico: Elecciones y democracia en America Latina (1992–1996)* (San José, Costa Rica: IIDH, CAPEL, 1998).
21. Latinobarometro, *Encuesta latinoamericana, 1998*.
22. On Latin American parties and problems of representation, see Scott Mainwaring and T. R. Scully, *Building Democratic Institutions: Party Systems in Latin America* (Stanford, Calif.: Stanford University Press, 1995).
23. See the conceptual discussion on civil society in J. Cohen and Y A. Arato, *Civil Society and Political Theory* (Boston: MIT Press, 1992).

10

The transformation of political culture

Amparo Menéndez-Carrión

Introduction

A major study of democracy and neo-liberalism in the Central Andes published in the mid-1990s began with the statement: "No single word was used more than *crisis* to describe the state of Latin America in the 1980s."[1] Three years later an edited collective volume addressing politics, social change, and economic restructuring in the region stated at the outset that "social, economic, and political practices and institutional arrangements in Latin America are undergoing a profound *transformation.*"[2] Such a choice of rubrics to set the tone and lead the framing of research questions illustrates one of the noteworthy shifts taking place at the dawn of a new century in approaches to the region's problematique, from the question of "crisis," its dynamics and consequences, to the question of "transformations."[3]

Clearly, the question of transformations – if this rubric is to suggest a scope and depth of any consequence – brings culture and politics to the forefront. Within mainstream social science in Latin America the issue of "politics and culture" leads into the realm of "political culture" and the values, attitudes, and orientations – understood as the "contents of culture" – presumed to have a bearing on the shape of societal structures. Some analysts, however, equally interested in politics and culture though not necessarily working within the confines of mainstream notions of the relationship, frame the "transformations" question within the "politics of culture" narrative. Here, the deployment of culture as strategy and the idea of culture as site for action take center stage, with quite different analytical implications. That this latter approach to politics and culture has recently become available is not only a reflection of ongoing theoretical searches. It simultaneously reflects the profound transformations such searches seek to unravel.

With these points in mind, this essay addresses the question of politics and culture, acknowledging it from the start as a concrete realm of experience, as a contested field of knowledge, and as a key point of entry for reflecting upon the question of "transformations." A basic premise of the essay is the acknowledgement of the interplay between politics and culture as a strategic and open-ended terrain occupied by concrete actors in concrete situations and contexts. The analytical emphasis is placed throughout on shifting practices, shifting narratives, and shifting terrains for deploying culture as it interacts with and transforms the realm of the political – shifts regarded here as central to envisioning the (re)construction of political society. The focus is placed on three interrelated queries: (i) How has the relationship between politics and culture in Latin America been portrayed in the past two to four decades? (ii) What can be said about the meaning of "politics as lived and experienced" in today's Latin America? And (iii) what implications emerge from those ruminations for grappling with the question of political culture, for portraying the interplay between politics and culture in the region's increasingly complex milieux, and for envisioning the (re)construction of political society?

Within this framework, the argument is set forth that at the turn of the century what frames the problematique in the four scenarios identified in this volume – regardless of the diversity of conditions, situations, and moments they portray – is the combination of two major factors. These are the quality – weakening, disowning – and the texture – corrosive, eroding – of the myriad encounters of persons and collectivities with the "stuff" on the basis of which they conceive and experience politics; and the seemingly unyielding gulf between the durability of civilian regimes ("democracies of regimes") and "polities of citizens," within the context of increasingly unsettling environments for both polities and citizenship as organizing principles of public life.

I also endeavor to suggest that the transformations taking place at the politico-cultural sphere represent disturbing tendencies, not just toward the fragmentation of society but also toward dislocation of the polity. The changes in the socio-political matrix explored by Garretón in this volume are inextricably associated with the manner in which meaning is being constructed through increasingly dispersed sites and contexts of experience, remapped along the local/global axis. This renders the polity – as site of encounter between increasingly differentiated publics – more complex than ever in the past. In some cases, the sites for "learning" about the meaning of the polity are being eroded, while in others, the socialization processes they introduce run counter to the attribution of meaningfulness to the political system. The problem goes well beyond the question of malaise, "disenchantment with politics," or "discontent with democracy." It signals tacit "secession" from the polity for some and disjointed contexts of experience for the majority – at the same time that a dynamic process of empowerment takes place at new sites, for new transnational publics. Within this framework, the dilemmas for the (re)-construction of political society seem overwhelming in magnitude.

The essay is organized in four sections. I start by reviewing how the relationship of politics and culture has been portrayed in the past two to four decades and provide a reading of contending approaches and their relevance. I then make my own conceptual choices explicit. Within this framework, a portrayal of the problem is then offered. Finally, some reflections are offered on the implications of this commentary for envisioning the re(construction) of political society.

Political culture? The politics of culture? Politics and culture? Differing views and some implications for framing the question of "transformations"

The insistence of some prominent late nineteenth- and early twentieth-century Latin American thinkers on searching for, capturing, and depicting the "essence" and "intrinsic character" of Latin America[4] – endlessly replicated in literary writings throughout the century – has not been alien to social scientists thinking about the "political culture of the region." Within the international political context of that period the essentialist views of the early thinkers – as well as their calls for regional unity, integration, and self-reaffirmation of Latin America vis-à-vis the United States – were framed within explicit political projects. Thus, and in spite of their often times grandiose claims to certitude about the (superior) "nature and culture" of Latin Americans, such reflections are beyond methodological reproach, for preoccupations with "systematicity" and "rigor" were alien to the explicit logic of their thinking. The claims of social scientists in depicting the "political culture of Latin America" stand in stark contrast and are part and parcel of the trajectory of the notion as conventionally applied to the region.

Here I endeavor to outline relevant moments in the trajectory of the politics and culture question within the shifting analytical terrain of the past two decades. I also attempt to suggest how the contributions of studies that recuperated the notion in the 1980s and 1990s from fresh theoretical perspectives have made available a much more textured knowledge of the complexities involved in the interplay between politics and culture in the region than the mainstream political culture perspective allows.

From the 1960s to the mid-1980s the relationship between politics and culture was predominantly approached through attempts to characterize "the political culture of Latin America" or the "national political culture" of Mexico, Peru, Argentina, and so forth. For some time to engage in such endeavors meant to remain virtually unchallenged as the study of political culture was dismissed by many analysts. Because the political culture perspective was associated with attempts to characterize national ethos, some analysts discarded it based on the importance they attached to acknowledging the region's internal diversity (along class, ethnic, regional lines, and so forth).[5] In other cases the dismissal of the political culture perspective rested on methodological considerations such as the importance attributed to structural considerations vis-à-vis the individual realm of attitudes and values.

In the resulting intellectual terrain, approaching the region from a political culture perspective also meant that the problems of "underdevelopment" – one of the leading emphases framing the region's problematique throughout the 1960s and 1970s – were associated with the patrimonial and authoritarian culture attributed to the "Iberian heritage." Within such a framework, the features of the famed "civic culture" – as conceptually formulated by Almond and Verba[6] – were regarded as either structurally or ideologically alien to the region. Within such narratives Latin America appeared as "condemned" by its political culture.[7]

The determinism – and condescension – inherent to such visions[8] would remain unchallenged until the 1980s. Since the 1970s significant transformations began to be recognized in politics and culture as realms of experience in Latin America. In complex interaction with those transformations the portrayal of their interplay would begin to undergo significant shifts which, taken together, render the conventional political culture perspective quite shallow or wanting.

First came the extensive field research of the 1970s to the mid-1980s on the "urban poor." Searching for how mature or immature, developed or underdeveloped a political culture might be was rejected by that literature as analytically unwarranted. Such research eventually demonstrated that neither "passivity" nor "apathy" nor "conformity" were features of the political culture of the urban poor.[9] Study after study was successful in documenting dispositions to engage and participate. The problem of participation of the urban poor was not their political culture but the nature of their context and the structural constraints. Clientelistic practices – one of the recurring concerns of that literature – were the product of structural conditions and not of some sort of ingrained mentalities, outlooks, and dispositions.[10]

That literature introduced an additional shift, namely, approaching political culture from a microperspective. The focus on the *barrio* and its most immediate context, the city, allowed the problematization of the complex interactions between the macrolevel context (national politics) and emerging political arenas (the urban milieux) for understanding the culture of politics, establishing the significance of the microlevel settings for the construction of concrete political meanings and practices. Another important shift that these studies introduced was the methodological relevance granted to focusing on concrete practices and what they revealed about the culture of "survival" politics. As this research lent solid basis to portraying the urban popular sectors as "grounded" in their immediate local scenarios, the national culture perspective was weakened from the inside – that is, by scholars who were not rejecting the notion of political culture per se but its conventional use to encompass macrolevel (national) culture.

Until the mid-1980s the overriding concern in looking at the political culture of the urban popular sectors was exploring the operation and mechanisms of social and political control. The complex linkages between micro and macro politics would be first problematized within the framework of that literature and its debates. The question of "agency" was emphasized but structures still weighed heavily as "determinants" of political practices and culture. In addition, the site for the interplay between culture and politics was still overwhelmingly located in articulation with the political system – and through parties and political machines. Subsequent shifts were soon to occur in thinking on society and politics of Latin America that signalled, among other things, the erosion of previous determinisms and the emergence of views now willing to envision the nature of change as an open-ended process.[11]

The "new social movements" literature of the mid- to late 1980s clearly illustrates these shifts. As has been pointed out, the attention of that literature to identity and culture and "its insistence on placing the question of power beyond institutional behavior, provided important antidotes to the structural rigidity that had characterized the studies published in the seventies."[12]

The portrayal of culture was part and parcel of that shift. As the empowerment narratives gained momentum, particularly with the emergence and increasing visibility acquired by ethnic movements and women's movements throughout the region, the re-evaluation of culture as a field of inquiry and as strategy for action would take place, with significant implications for our purposes, namely, for the theoretical place granted to the question of identity, meaning, and their strategic deployment.

Within that narrative, power and culture were "constructed" and the relevant questions became how people negotiate within parameters of power that they do not themselves create but which they do not necessarily accept passively, and how in the process they modify the structures of power and meaning through agency.[13] Within the new narratives the static visions of culture as "condemnation" through historical legacy appeared anachronistic. In addition, new concerns about the relationship between the public and the private spheres arose, and linkages of day-to-day practices (lo cotidiano) and micro-scenarios with national (macro-level) politics came to the forefront. The portrayal of the urban popular sectors would increasingly be framed within the empowerment narrative as well – in what would also signal, incidentally, a major shift in the very framing of la cuestión urbana in Latin America.

Through the research of political scientists, anthropologists, and sociologists in the new thematic fields of the 1980s (first the urban poor, and then the new social movements) the assumptions of the "national" political culture perspective would come into question and increasingly lose ground. Meanwhile, significant shifts were taking place in the treatment of political culture at the macrolevel of the nation-state. The literature on Mexico is illustrative. In Claudio Lomnitz-Adler's Exits from the Labyrinth[14] the construction of hegemony through nationalist and localist ideologies, and their tense coexistence as the myths of revolutionary nationalism lost ground, are what frame the author's concerns. Posed this way, "culture as content" did not appear as a simplistic reduction of "the national traits of the Mexicans" but allowed, rather, for the discussion of cultural complexity at the national level. In addition, it provided elements directly relevant to portraying transformations, rather than endless discoveries of resilient features of culture in the Mexican context. Thus framed, the theme of national identity – in this case of Mexico – could be posed in terms of "Many Mexicos,"[15] and culture as content appeared not in terms of essentialist searches for the "soul" or "national character" of the Mexicans but in terms of the configuring and reconfiguring of "the national" as a legitimating myth.[16]

In general, over the past four decades the analytical landscape has seen culture brought from the sidelines to center stage. From the study of "cultures in conflict" in Peru to research on emerging transnational identities[17] since the mid-1980s, culture has been "rescued" as a source of fresh theoretical perspectives for exploring the myriad faces of the region's political problematique.[18] To be sure, the "Iberian heritage" school is still alive and well, as is cultural determinism in its "national character" mode.[19] The endless search for the "soul" of the Latin Americans is found in the literature as well. Be that as it may, the aforementioned analytical shifts – taken together – suggest the significant transformations of the research terrain opened in the past two decades. Not one (national) political culture but many ways of constructing the meaning of politics; not one type of encounter (with the political system or institutional politics) but myriad encounters of relevance to learning about things political – including the "rejection" of traditional political sites and the emergence of new sites for thinking and enacting politics[20] – are among the most relevant of those transformations. Within the resulting intellectual terrain the conventional political culture perspective is no longer unchallenged as the sole repository of wisdom on the articulation between politics and culture, as it was in the past. The existence of this research terrain also suggests the methodological relevance of keeping open the searches for alternative ways of framing the region's politics and culture problematique.

Thinking politics and culture: Concepts and assumptions

Here I will introduce some premises and conceptual choices, as follows:

(1) Culture is a key point of entry for exploring the transformations that bear on the political as realm of experience. The notion of culture is understood here as meaning and meaningfulness of relations, arrangements, institutions, and things.[21]

Within the realm of culture the appropriate place of "content" is not regarded here as individuals' reported opinions, attitudes, and values aggregated by calculating, adding, and subtracting percentages and claiming these as "captions" of "political culture." The realm of culture as content may operate and create sediments, resilient features, and stubborn obstacles to change. Nevertheless, in order to frame and visualize "transformations" it is important to focus upon the milieux and situations within which meanings are practised and lived, paying special attention to exploring the learning and unlearning, casting and recasting of meanings about relations, institutions, arrangements, and things. Important, that is, if exploring major transformations rather than conjunctural proximity or distance to regimes, institutions, or mood swings of public opinion – the stuff of public opinion surveys – is the aim.

Furthermore, regardless of how "democratic" or "authoritarian" the aggregate values of individuals are found to be in specific cases at any point in time, this does not necessarily mean that the outcome – even in the middle to long run – will be, say, the strengthening (if more people are reported to hold more democratic values) or erosion (if the authoritarian "mentalities" are more weighty in numbers) of democracy. It is, rather, the complex interplay and outcomes of the interactions among a diversity of power struggles, situations, and events in the global/regional/local arenas that produce or deny the conditions of possibility for the realm of attitudes and orientations to eventually become relevant. Positive attitudes towards democracy in general may not matter much in the face of long-standing political positons of the elites and the international environment as salient factors in the production of outcomes in regime types – as such attitudes may not be for precluding the operations of "uncivil movements" either.[22] Regime dynamics have other salient paths and vectors.[23] The place of "content" is the concrete contexts and the features or textures of interaction and quality of interaction these contexts tacitly allow or discourage. Thus, the questions considered relevant here are more along the lines of "is the texture and quality of abc milieu more or less closed or open, facilitating or precluding of xyz meanings and identities from configuring along x valued dimension(s) of a healthy coexistence" rather than "are the people of abc more or less authoritarian or democratic" in their outlooks and values.

(2) For purposes of this essay politics is regarded as a field of socialization and learning about the meaning of encounters with others in tacitly shared contexts – that is, the environment of experience in encountering "the collectivity," be it the neighbourhood, the workplace, the city, or the larger polity. Thus, classical approaches to political socialization, involving the internalization of social values or "induction" to norms and rules such as "civic values," designed to "create" citizens or subjects through civic education as institutional/formal practice, are not what I have in mind. Here I am not interested in looking at socialization processes as fields for the creation of consent. The perspectives of normalization and disciplining (Foucault), construction of hegemonies (Gramsci), or conformity (Durkheim) are paramount for analyzing central aspects of the problem of consent. But for the purposes of this essay I want to emphasize that whether or not consent results; regardless of what is learned; and above and beyond the success or failure of any mechanism of induction to specific "contents," politics as lived and experienced is a school. The basic question then, becomes: What do people learn from that "multifaceted portrait of encounters"[24] that configures their terrain of socialization about "their" place and that of others in tacitly shared contexts, and thus the meaning they confer on politics through their encounters with institutional arrangements, formal and informal settings and situations, as well as through their day-to-day experiences?

(3) Today's political milieux are characterized by the presence of systematic contradictions of identity and by the multiplication of appeals to individual and collective subjectivity by all kinds of actors, forces, and movements.[25] Thus, perspectives that attempt to place culture as the manner of "thinking" or "believing" that may characterize a specific

nation-state or "society," or for that matter, that attempt to place cultures and identities as "national" in character, are no longer useful – if they ever were.

(4) The "transnational" evokes the very manner in which human agency is building new exchanges and sites of experience and meaning which transcend or circumvent state-centered channels and which operate through circuits of multiple impact and direction (at the micro-, meso-, and macrolevels in whatever way we may wish to understand them, as the subnational, local, supranational, interlocal or global-local levels, and so forth). That transnational phenomena are salient in the contemporary world is hardly a statement of any novelty at this point.[26] It is of interest, however, to underscore the realm of the transnational as a basic feature of today's transformations that calls for the theoretical reframing of the relationship between politics and culture.

(5) This essay acknowledges the increasing complexity of the milieux and situations that require attention as we seek to examine the relationship between politics and culture. That is not to suggest the loss of interest or relevance and much less the disappearance of the long-standing sites of the modern era – the nation-state, most notably.[27] Yet as we attempt to understand the interplay between politics and culture, it is important that we not tie our frameworks a priori to any assumption about specific sites. In other words, no territories – "real," imaginary, or virtual – should be taken as givens. This means not only to acknowledge as no longer warranted the privileging of the nation-state as site; but, further, to regard as unwarranted the assumption that the polity or the state are sites that "contain" "their" society or frame "their" culture.

This point goes beyond the mere acknowledgement of the impact of centrifugal tendencies associated with "globalization."[28] The facts that the state has lost centrality as site, and that the notion of society has begun to make some sociologists uncomfortable,[29] suggest that the "trans-," the "intra-," and the "sub-"national in multiple combinations must be examined. The new sites resulting from the transnationalization of circuits of action are relevant. But the articulation between micropolitics and macropolitics at the level of the nation-state is relevant as well. The milieux and situations will vary depending upon concrete conditions which should be regarded as problems to be researched rather than as assumptions about the loss of relevance of the nation-state, or about the increasing relevance of any other site or combination of sites as units of analysis.

This is suggested, for example, by the politics of ethnicity in Latin America since the mid-1980s, as indigenous movements have defined their own repertoires of action placing them simultaneously in the countryside, the city, the national scene, and the regional and global stages. Far from a rejection of the traditional sites for "doing politics," these practices suggest, rather, a novel appropriation of the idea that all available spaces may be acknowledged as sites for action, from formal institutions of politics and electoral games to the configuration of transnational networks. As these diverse sites are traversed, the meanings of politics and the culture of politics are transformed for all the actors concerned – from government officials to political parties, to NGOs to the public at large.

Thus framed, the basic path for reflecting upon the articulation of politics and culture for purposes of this essay may lead through the following basic set of questions: What are the sites within which people are deriving meanings about public life, about the nature of the polity, and about their own place and that of others in the polity? How are the encounters (sites of identity and meaning, both individual and collective) being defined? What kind of political learning do the quality and texture of such encounters suggest? What do people learn on the basis of their multiple encounters with institutional arrangements, situations, and things?

(6) A core element is needed, however, to complete the framing of such questions. For purposes of this essay the core element is provided by "citizenship" and "public space." Envisioning the (re)construction of political society is the salient concern of this collective volume, which sooner or later brings us to the question of democracy. Though my specific concerns here are not framed in terms of this question, an idea that does frame the essay is that envisioning "democracies that matter"[30] requires the acknowledgement of culture as a key dimension of the polity. For some analysts this means that democracy requires "a host of cultural practices – habits of mind, rituals of participation, forms of dialogue between rulers and ruled – that make large numbers of people across generations believe in the meaningfulness of basic democratic principles."[31] Nonetheless, if this essay is premised on the centrality of culture as the point of entry for understanding politics and its transformation, it is also premised on the assumption that the relevant questions are not so much related to the construction of "a democratic culture" but, rather, to the acknowledgement of citizenship as a key feature for a healthy polity. I thus pose as a more fundamental premise that democracy requires citizenship[32] and that a reasonably healthy polity requires access to democracy *as field of experience* and thus as site of value for persons and collectivities.

The notion of citizenship has been at the basis of historical debates and concrete struggles from classical Greece to the present, within a context of meanings as diverse as "conquest" and "expansion" of individual and collective rights; senses of "belonging" and "community"; and "restriction" (insiders/outsiders) or "closure" (national/alien), among others. The complex itinerary of the notion is linked to the strategic questions it evokes. Regardless of the contents attributed to it or the dimensions emphasized to define it (legal, territorial, functional, moral, and so forth) the idea of citizenship provides frames of reference within which different ways of understanding, defining, and "resolving" the place of persons and collectivities within complex environments becomes possible – in order to regulate, confront, or transform those environments.

My understanding of the *notion* of citizenship takes as premise its fluid and changing emplacement. I do not understand "changing" in cumulative terms. I find it analytically relevant, instead, to emphasize the discontinuities in the practices and values included under the rubric of citizenship, and to underline the plurality of meanings of the notion, both across time and within the same time period "despite all the attempts to codify it within a single definition."[33] Citizenship is regarded here as "an avatar for all parts of the spectrum ... an open technology, a means of transformation ready for definition and disposal in dispersed ways at dispersed sites."[34] Citizenship can also be regarded – borrowing from Roberto Alejandro – as "a space of fluid boundaries within which there is room for diverse and even conflicting understandings of individuality, commmunity, and public identity."[35]

The *problem* of citizenship is premised here on the acknowledgement that, in general, citizenship changes in the manner in which different conceptions "resolve" questions as fundamental as the place of individual and collective identities, and the meaningfulness of institutions, norms, and policies. In more specific terms, citizenship changes in the manner in which different conceptions regard the nature, meaning, and value of the public sphere.[36]

From this perspective, politics is rendered meaningful through practices of "civic discovery" and through the production of public issues and public spaces. Issues can be wide-ranging: from the election of governments to the distribution of valued resources; to the defence against racial, gender, or any other form of discrimination; to the observance of human rights; to the battle against censorship; to the defence of religious freedoms; to the demand for quality public services; to the respect for non-conventional life styles; to the envisioning of conviviality among strangers. From this perspective, the narrowing and/or erosion of the production of issues, practices, and public spaces is regarded as harmful to a healthy polity. It is from a basic concern with the quality and texture of public life thus understood that the problem of politics and culture and their transformations in Latin America will be read below. The citizenship corollary to the above question is, therefore, the following: How is politics as realm of experience linked to the presence, absence, erosion, or loss of citizenship in concrete contexts and arenas?

Politics, culture, and their interplay in Latin America: What kind of problematique?

Throughout the 1990s concerns with politics and society in Latin America – whether framed within the question of the changing relations between state and civil society, or in terms of polyarchy,[37] the dilemmas of citizenship, and so forth – have situated the "transformations" question within the context of globalization and economic restructuring. Typically, the transformations that have been emphasized are the weakening of the role of the state in development and in the regulation of the socio-economic sphere as well as the consequences of the retrenchment of the state in terms of the redefinition of the relations among the state, the market, and civil society. The following passage is illustrative of widespread views on such transformations and their connection to the interplay between politics and culture in the Latin America of the 1990s:

The devastating effects of the so-called "lost decade" contributed to eroding the loyalties and expectations of assistance and redistribution placed on the parties and on the state, until then [understood] as the organiz[ing] [factors] of economy and society. In addition, the crisis of Marxism and the demise of socialism also contributed to undermining nationalist, populist, or revolutionary identities as well as ideological certainties centered on the state. Together, they [account for the surge] of critical attitudes and the [shift] away from such political and cultural [points of] reference; as a consequence ... the disarticulation of the institutional and normative edifice that parties and the state had erected ensued. The discredit of political institutions in Latin America has been the basis for references to a divorce of society from politics and the state. At the same time, the relative dissolution of the linkages of integration that politics and the state used to provide have contributed to creating a feeling of "value crisis" and of social "anomie," particularly among the young. The most visible expressions of this [become evident] in the assimilation of values and practices of 'unsolidarity' and the growth of delinquency ..."[38]

In addition the perspective of "the global" has permeated the treatment of culture since the 1980s with the pre-eminence of the market as site for the construction of meaning; and the impact of the information era has become paramount in studies of the transformation of contemporary cultural experience, including the Latin American context.[39]

Without taking issue with those perspectives, in what follows I endeavour to outline my own reading of the interplay between culture and politics in the Latin American milieux. This seeks to transcend the confines of state-centered perspectives without falling into the temptation of dismissing them *tout court*. Instead, I shall seek to ponder how the old sites and the emerging sites intersect; and will emphasize these intersections as the basic features of the transformations that merit consideration. The following elements define the contours of the problem.

Moving beyond the traditional repertoires of disaffection with politics

The lack of interest and "motivation," and the discontent that Latin American polyarchies exhibit – regardless of their proximity to or distance from a "functioning polyarchy"[40] – have been a leading concern over the last decade. The problem of civic disengagement is scarcely a novelty in the Western tradition, however. At the same time, the (implicit) emphasis of the "malestar con la política" theme – unless explicitly placed within the narrative of the postmodern malaise, which is not usually the case in the problematization of discontent with democracy in Latin America – is the conjunctural/temporary nature of the problem.

The problem of disaffection is best placed today beyond the traditional repertoires of discontent with politics and *políticos*; lack of participation and passivity; or lack of "fit" between civil society and its increasing complexity, on the one hand, and institutional political arrangements, on the other; and cyclical, conjunctural, or "pendulum" tensions. The problem should also be placed well beyond the issue of constructing "senses of belonging." Senses of belonging are being sought and found through clientele networks that are alive and well today not as legacies from the past, but as functional technologies to glue together otherwise excluded publics at selected moments, and through the selective presence of the state or its formal and informal agents.[41] There are also "parallel polities" ranging from "urban tribes" to international-domestic networks and so-called "transnational communities" providing contexts for the enactment of "solidarity." Disaffection is not a problem of lack of empowerment initiatives either, since depoliticization and collective empowerment of selected publics may be found coexisting in any and all countries of the region – in environments as different as Santiago, Bogotá, Cuenca, Buenos Aires, or Lima. The problem is best seen as signalling the dislocation of the polity as lived and experienced by those whose lives it is supposed to frame – be they *barrio* dwellers, peasants, college students, workers, or elites.

The politics of disjointedness

This term refers to the quality and texture of the present Latin American milieux – this as a basic effect of three simultaneous tensions linked to (a) the usual sites of the modern era (symbolized basically by the governmental sphere); (b) the impact of emerging transnational modes of interaction in reconfiguring sites, identities, and meanings; and (c) the dislocations that operate within and through both sites. This suggests the analytical interest of defining the contextual terrains framed by the inertias of civilian regimes, on the one hand, and the impact of "the transnational" on the other, as the two (interactive) poles engaged in the restructuring of today's modes of experiencing and understanding public life. This produces multiple combinations of milieux which have as a common feature the day-to-day enactment of situations, events, and learning experiences that trivialize citizenship practices and introduce strong tendencies not just towards "civic disengagement" as in the past but towards dislocation and decentering. This configures societally disjointed milieux and – to borrow from Sandel[42] – introduces the possibility of tacit "secession" for those who have no reason to worry about the public and command the kind of capital required to "buy their way out" of public space.

When people "learn to live without their governments" ... and civilian regimes learn to live without a citizenship that matters

The discredit of political institutions in Latin America – political parties, most notably, but also executive power, parliaments, and public institutions in general – has been a leading theme throughout the 1990s.[43] It is a sufficiently established point that stands in no need of reiteration here. Rather, what is worth emphasizing is that the effect of the cumulative experience of the encounters of the people at large with their political institutions in the past two decades has resulted in disturbing kinds of learning experiences.[44]

One of the basic lessons of these encounters is that neither the discredit of formal politics, nor the rejection of *políticos* and their ways of doing things, nor the crisis of political parties, nor the deepening of the "obscene"[45] socio-economic inequality in the region, necessarily affect the durability of regimes, or the routinization of "politics as usual," nor do they threaten these routines or lead to their altering in fundamental ways. The "socialization processes" made possible by the experience with democracy in Latin America throughout the 1980s and 1990s has thus been perversely efficient: people "have learned to live without their governments."[46] Governments, in turn, have learned to operate without a citizenship that matters in fundamental ways – apart from elections and the exigencies of their ritualized stagings.[47]

The new cosmopolitism: Its transformative effects on the meaning of the polity within the Latin American milieux

Some profound transformations stemming from the surge of international and domestic phenomena are affecting concrete realms of experience today, with far-reaching consequences not only for the actors directly involved but for the very notion of political society.

Neither emigrants nor inmigrants: The redefinition of migrant experiences

The lack of correspondence of the nation-state with the social spaces that people inhabit, and the implications of this for politics and culture, are things that we learned from the extensive research of the 1970s and 1980s on the urban popular sectors. Today such lack of correspondence is being problematized by a vast and increasing literature on "multiple communities," and the fluidity and hybridization of identities this would engender within the context of circular migration experiences. The implications of the emergence of such types of communities for the meaning of the polity are significant. These kinds of circuits involve "the creation of imaginary communities that transcend territorial frontiers [operating] outside the discourse of the nation state."[48]

Some authors are looking at the configurations of divided loyalties that these new migratory experiences entail.[49] Transnational communities have implications for the interplay between politics and culture on the basis of the simultaneous participation in two or more political systems "that define the citizenship [of migrants] in different and possibly contradictory ways."[50] Other writers focus upon the reconfiguring of loyalties that such communities may entail. For example, Roger Bartra emphasizes the new allegiance to localities in the case of the Mexico of the 1990s:

This regionalism is not a reanimated version of old centripetal caciquist tendencies; it is rather the consequence of the modernizing experience of the hundreds of thousands of Mexicans who have traveled and worked in the United States.... It is a postmodern conservatism that has lost faith in progress and dreams of tranquility.... It is a conservatism that is much closer to its counterpart in myriad small cities, towns and suburban neighborhoods in the midwestern and southwestern US than to the state conservatism espoused by military men such as Almazan or movements such as sinarquismo.... The PAN, especially in Northern Mexico, attracts much of this regionalist, conservative element ..."[51]

It should be noted that far from being limited to the experience of Mexico, Puerto Rico, and other countries of the region with populations whose "transnational communities" link them mostly to the United States, the question of circular migration and its implications for the transformation of politics and culture is of major importance at the turn of the century in cases such as Argentina (Bolivian migrants in Buenos Aires), Chile (Peruvian migrants in Santiago), or Ecuador's experience with Spain and Italy since 1999, when the collapse of the Ecuadorean economy propelled the growth of long-standing migratory flows of unprecedented size and speed.[52]

The circuits and networks that redefine the sites of identity and meaning at the local or transnational level are not limited to these factors. Apart from a burgeoning body of literature on transnational communities, the new cosmopolitanism and its impact have other aspects less explored but nonetheless quite significant, in connection with the reconfiguration of political society in Latin America.

Living there, but not quite: Buying my way out of public space
Parts of Latin America are firmly anchored in the new cosmopolitanism, which, though thus far thematized mostly in reference to "advanced societies," constitutes a major transformation for the region's milieux. In those societies, social hyperdifferentiation translates itself into new forms of competition, new symbologies of status, and changes in consumption habits following the patterns of an increasingly globalized aestheticism.[53] For the cosmopolitan elites of Latin America the same applies.[54] I will simply outline two elements of relevance here.

Firstly, the new cosmopolitanism introduces the possibility of "secession," with implications that go far beyond the well-identified differences and segregations among areas of residence of the upper, middle, and lower classes, which inhibit the development of basic "senses of larger community"[55] and experiences. Perhaps even more than the walled residential areas that dominate the most exclusive areas of Latin American cities (with their private access roads, means of transportation, and guards), the private suites at football stadiums – football being traditionally the most popular of Latin American sports – in cities such as Guayaquil, inhabited by an overwhelming majority of people in the most precarious socioeconomic conditions, stand today as a dramatic metaphor of secession in the region. Secession is linked to a dramatic increase in inequality; it corresponds to social hyperdifferentiation and operates on the basis of financial capital making it possible to buy one's way out of public space.[56]

The second relevant element of the new comopolitanism is the unprecedented surge of possibilities for carving new definitions of territory connected to electronic networks, removing the need to resort to traditional practices of conviviality. There is no need for an additional litany on the topic. What is relevant here is that within Latin America such access is linked to minority sectors that can connect directly, regularly, and in sustained fashion to circuits of communication and patterns of transnational consumption, and it is part and parcel of ongoing shifts linked to processes of differentiating integration.[57]

But the new cosmopolitanism does not only involve the hyperdifferentiation of patterns of consumption of goods and services and the consequent shifting of previous sites for the construction of identities and meanings. It also entails the emergence of transnational modes of collective action.

The politics and culture of transnational networking
The emergence of transnational modes of collective action was a major transformation in the Latin American landscape throughout the 1980s on into the 1990s, with far-reaching implications for the construction of identities and meanings. As early as the 1970s the international-domestic articulation of networks of collective action has been surging as part of the new cosmopolitanism. The scope of these networks is ample. It includes nongovernmental organizations, women's networks, environmentalists, indigenous organizations – in general, the social movements included under the rubric of "cultural citizenship"[58] – as well as urban municipalities and transnational professionals.

Transnational networks have been regarded as sites of empowerment and processes of alternative citizenship construction, of multiple impact at the local national and global spheres simultaneously. As Brysk has pointed out, the region's ethnic movement was "born transnational."[59] Visibility and influence were obtained through the 1980s and 1990s in national and international arenas previously unavailable to excluded collectivities – the indigenous movements prominent among them. Taking this as an indicator, transnationalism has become a formidable site of empowerment. The indigenous organizations of Guatemala, Ecuador or Brazil – not to mention the EZLN (Zapatista National Liberation Army) of Mexico – and the international visibility acquired by their leaders and plight are quite remarkable in this respect.[60]

But how do these sites of empowerment connect with the polity? In general, they have been portrayed as having an impact upon the traditional institutional sites – advancing their "democratization" – through the empowerment conferred by the transnationalization of collective action to nongovernmental organizations, for instance. Nonetheless, there are aspects of the relationship that require further scrutiny, for instance, the gap between the empowerment of indigenous movements and NGOs firmly anchored in transnational circuits of action and the increasing problems of socio-economic exclusion that confront the majority in the region – including peasants and women. For instance, what does the incorporation of leaders of the ethnic movement into the hierarchies of governmental power in Ecuador in recent years mean? What kinds of systemic incorporation do they configure? What kinds of exclusion are still remain? What is the role of "old" practices of clientelism and traditional mechanisms of co-optation in the encounters of the new actors with traditional sites of "doing politics"? Furthermore, what sorts of meanings may be read into the installation of the discourse of "cultural citizenship" in the official realm in Latin America? And what continuities and discontinuities may be read into the political culture of these actors as they gain increasing access to the conventional political system? The case of Ecuador's three-hour military-civilian junta of 21 January 2000 provides sufficient grounds for taking these questions seriously, suggesting that new questions emerge as the indigenous movements enter a new phase: that of becoming salient actors within the national political arena at the very same institutional sites from which they once distanced themselves.

The following reflections, made in connection with women's movements, seem quite relevant here as well:

Women's movements did help restore democratic governments to the region, and they continue to broaden traditional patterns of representation, which are class and race as well as gender biased. But much of what women have accomplished for themselves and their families in this recent wave of mobilization has been marginal redistribution or self-help. With the exception of the issue of violence against women, political progress on a woman's agenda – including such crucial issues as reproductive rights and family law – has been less than one might expect given the extent and intensity of women's political engagement.[61]

For the time being, and without underestimating the emancipatory significance of the new sites of empowerment in granting visibility to previously excluded actors and themes, it seems unwarranted to assume that the transnationalization of empowerment advances citizenship. It can also, in principle, introduce new disconnections and new modalities of co-optation.[62]

A major structural (class) and cultural (meaning) transformation: The surge of transnational networks of professionals
In close articulation with such networks for collective action stand the new professional transnational circuits, whose cultural capital (in terms of knowledge, prestige, accreditation, and rank) and labour practices are not contingent upon career structures or institutional settings "contained" in eminently national spaces. This makes them part of the new cosmopolitanism.[63] Cosmopolitan Latin American professionals are understood here as those firmly anchored to transnational networks and circuits not only through international professional associations but, most fundamentally, through intense interpersonal and intragroup networking with their peers throughout the world.[64]

Transnational professional networks matter in Latin America. They have been key for the configuration of women's networks, ethnic empowerment, and environmentalism on the world scale since the early 1970s until the present. The leaderships of the ethnic and environmentalist movements of Brazil, Guatemala, Bolivia, and Ecuador are prominent in these networks.

These topics are part of a new agenda for research. For the time being, it seems plausible to suggest that the great protagonist of empowerment in the Latin America of the 1980s and 1990s has been the transnational intelligentsia. For the past fifteen years an unprecedented process of integration of ever-increasing numbers of Latin American professionals into transnational circuits has been taking place, from whence they derive recognition, prestige, as well as, increasingly, their sources of employment. This is occurring regardless of their linkages to the governmental regimes in their countries – be they advisors to or vocal opponents of the regimes; of the fragility of their home-base institutions and academic centres; of the coexistence of logics of exclusion and secession in their countries of residence; and of the precarious socio-economic situation of the overwhelming majority of the region's inhabitants.

Many questions emerge, all of them relevant for envisioning the (re)-construction of political society from the perspective of culture and its transformation. How do we account for the breach between the significant integration of the intelligentsia in many countries of the region to trans-national professional circles and the pervasive fragility of the institutions that house those very individuals in their respective countries? What happens when and if belonging to transnational professional networks becomes a new and perhaps the main point of reference for the configuration of identities and meanings for a professional elite? And what does this mean, not only for the notion of citizenship entertained by such professionals but also for the struggles for citizenship, the organization of which is highly contingent upon the leadership provided by the owners of cultural capital?

Final remarks

Disturbing transformations and (equally disturbing) stubborn features relating to the question of politics and culture intersect in today's Latin America, making the politics of disjointedness a major feature. The problem goes well beyond democracies of regimes. It is not a question of whether more or less democratic cultures have or have not been in place in the region in the past two decades, or of whether or not "trust" or "distrust" in elected regimes or in general, allegiance to the idea of "democracy" prevails or not at different moments and conjunctures. The problem does not lie in lack of "favorable political capital"[65] to sustain liberal democracy, either. Above and beyond recurrent crises of political parties and general mistrust of politics and politicians, there are people in Latin America who have been able to craft important collective citizenship movements in contexts and circumstances as different as Chile's 1988 plebiscite; Ecuador's February 1997 "civic coup"; the 1991 Constituent Assembly in Colombia; or the attempts to grant new meaning to electoral politics in Mexico's 2000 presidential election. Beyond the diversity of situations confronted by the polities of Latin America, the fundamental questions revolve around the whethers and hows of eliminating those features that signal the dislocation of the polity under overwhelmingly complex scenarios.[66]

Rethinking the polity and envisioning the (re)construction of political society requires us – at least for heuristic purposes – to ponder the disturbing implications of the transformations in the "known" territories of politics suggested in this essay.[67] In such milieux the global axis redefines – expanding and making more resilient – the disturbing features displayed, insofar as it introduces new patterns of differentiation of the quality and texture of the systems of coexistence to which hyperdifferentiated publics can accede. Again, at least for heuristic purposes, we should not discount the fact that the emergence of a new underclass of "denizens,"[68] marked by their restricted access to transnational space, may be in the offing. The Latin American denizens would include vast sectors of the traditional middle classes who are in no position to obtain access to the new sites, circuits, and networks through a financial or cultural capital that these classes do not, and (structurally) cannot, command. Far from being able to accede to "the cultivation of multiple identities"[69] as a strategy of socialization so as to confront increasingly complex milieux, the new denizens would be those legal citizens without the possibility of exercising a citizenship "that matters," as a result of precarious or inexistent social security systems, mediocre systems of public education, and slim chances of upward mobility – as well as limited possibilities of mobilization to voice their discontent and gain "the power of visibility" like their transnational counterparts.

For the time being the transnationalization of empowerment does not seem to imply a shift of the axis of citizenship from the nation-state to the global community, nor does it resolve what is lacking in the traditional sites for providing space for citizenship as a central feature for structuring the polity. The discredit, as well as the perverse routinization of traditional mediations mean that the secession from public space through financial capital and interpersonal and private contacts through the new technologies, as well as ritualized encounters with new socialization agents,[70] acquire an unprecedented role as mechanisms for making it possible to circumvent the traditional spaces for societal encounter –

dissociating from the public sphere or constructing alternative repertoires of territorialities, proximities, and belongingnesses.

This does not result in a double process of "transnationalization and national disintegration," as it is often suggested. It suggests, rather, the disjointed polity as a feature of the Latin American milieux in the foreseeable future. The tormenting issue here is that for an overwhelming majority of Latin Americans, "the place where I live" – neighborhood, city, province, country, and what happens there – remains the basic site for experiencing politics, the system, government, and the quality and texture of public life. Peoples' circuits of action and meaning remain basically anchored to traditional sites; the selective presence of the state continues to have consequences; the nation-states of Latin America may exhibit "quasi-imperial" styles of government; and, furthermore, the institutions of the state – above and beyond their weakening and discredit – still constitute, as Roberts puts it, "a significant repository of power."[71] Such features may bring no major repercussions within the larger context of international affairs and the global political economy, but they impact significantly, if not decisively, on those most vulnerable to the existing nation-states' decisions. For the time being it seems analytically uncalled-for to assume that the emergence of empowerment logics linked to the transnationalization of identities and meanings preludes the emergence of a new offensive against dramas that – as far as an overwhelming majority of the excluded publics are concerned – are staged, lived, and experienced within their immediate milieux.[72] But without such an offensive it seems unlikely that one may envision the (re)construction of a political society that matters.

Notes

The ideas presented in this essay partially draw from my ongoing research on political learning and citizenship, undertaken under the auspices of FONDECYT-Chile (199-0606). The essay also draws, in part, from a study I am conducting within the overall framework of a collaborative project with Alfredo Joignant, "Political Socialization: The Learning of Citizenship in France and Chile" (C97H01), supported by the ECOS-CONICYT-France Programme. In Santiago, I benefited from the able research assistanship of Ana Maria Mujica, one of my graduate students at the Universidad de Chile. At Macalester College, my student assistant Erica Kaster provided invaluable research support. Both deserve a special note of thanks. I would also like to thank Manuel Antonio Garretón and Edward Newman for their comments and suggestions. The essay also benefited from the comments provided by the participants in the 2000 Mexico meeting as well as by the anonymous reviewers of earlier drafts.

1. Catherine M. Conaghan and James M. Malloy, *Unsettling Statecraft: Democracy and Neoliberalism in the Central Andes* (Pittsburgh: University of Pittsburgh Press, 1994), p. 3. The emphasis is the authors'.

2. In William C. Smith and Roberto Patricio Korzeniewicz, "Latin America and the Second Great Transformation," in *Politics, Social Change and Economic Restructuring in Latin America* (Boulder, Colo.: Lynne Rienner, 1997), p. 1. The emphasis is mine.

3. Note, incidentally, that in his excellent *Duda/Certeza/Crisis: La Evolución de las ciencias sociales de América Latina* (Caracas: Unesco–Nueva Sociedad, 1988), Heinz R. Sonntag introduces a third kind of emphasis, namely, decoupling the notion of "crisis" from its exclusively nefarious connotations to conceive it, instead, precisely as a moment of fundamental transformations – regardless of the "direction" of change.

4. Uruguay's José Enrique Rodo's *Ariel* (first published circa 1900) comes to mind, as well as several works of Nicaragua's Rubén Darío and José Martí of Cuba among other noted intellectuals of the time.

5. This point is made by Ann L. Craig and Wayne A. Cornelius, "Political Culture in Mexico: Continuities and Revisionist Interpretations," in Gabriel A. Almond and Sidney Verba (eds.), *The Civic Culture Revisited* (Boston: Little, Brown, 1980); and restated in Frederick C. Turner, "Reassessing Political Culture," in Peter H. Smith (ed.), *Latin America in Comparative Perspective: New Approaches to Methods and Analysis* (Boulder, Colo.: Westview Press, 1995).

6. See Gabriel A. Almond and Sidney Verba, *The Civic Culture: Political Attitudes and Democracy in Five Nations* (Princeton, N.J.: Princeton University Press, 1963).

7. See Levine's "Constructing Culture and Power in Latin America," in Daniel H. Levine, (ed.), *Constructing Culture and Power in Latin America* (Ann Arbor: University of Michigan Press, 1993).

8. See, for instance Lawrence E. Harrison, *Underdevelopment Is a State of Mind: The Latin American Case* (Lanham, Md.: University Press of America, 1985). By the same author see *Who Prospers? How Cultural Values Shape Economic and Political Success* (New York: Basic Books, 1992); and *The Pan-American Dream: Do Latin America's Cultural Values Discourage True Partnership with the United States and Canada?* (Boulder, Colo.: Westview Press, 1997) – a publication that has been referred to by two distinguished scholars, both Latin American specialists, as "a disconcertingly arrogant view of Latin America's alleged failings"; Thomas E. Skidmore and Peter H. Smith, *Modern Latin America*, 5th ed. (New York: Oxford University Press, 2001), p. 449.

9. In the 1960s an inventory of sorts with the presumed features of "the culture of poverty" was developed in several writings by Oscar Lewis. Even though Lewis conceived his work as social denunciation, the "culture of poverty" notion soon became a widely acclaimed interpretation of "marginality" that, the well-meaning intentions of the author notwithstanding, placed the responsibility for the social order on the poor themselves – portrayed as alienated, lacking in aspirations, overwhelmingly concerned with immediate gratification, inclined to antisocial behaviours, trapped by material and moral disintegration, and thus incapable of overcoming the "culture of poverty." See, for instance, Lewis's *The Children of Sanchez* (New York: Random House, 1961) or "The Culture Of Poverty," *Scientific American* October 1966; p. 215. Such visions of the urban poor would be seriously challenged through extensive empirical research, pioneered by studies such as Janice Perlman's *The Myth of Marginality: Urban Politics and Poverty in Rio De Janeiro* (Berkeley: University of California Press, 1976). A restatement of the central argument of that demythologizing literature may be found in Alejandro Portes and Jose Itzigsohn, "The Party or the Grassroots: A Comparative Analysis of Urban Political Participation in the Caribbean Basin", in Smith and Korzeniewicz, *Politics, Social Change and Economic Restructuring in Latin America*, esp. p. 205.

10. A topic that I have dealt with extensively in *La conquista del voto: De Velasco a Roldos* (Quito: FLACSO-CEN, 1986) esp. pts. 3 and 4, pp. 269–456.

11. This, of course, took place within the context of the significant epistemological shifts that

were becoming increasingly apparent in the social sciences at the time. I have discussed these shifts in "Pero dónde y para qué hay cabida? Comentando la cuestión de la ciudadania hacia el cierre del Milenio: Una mirada desde America Latina" (mimeo, 1999). Also see Sonntag, *Duda/Certeza/Crisis.*

12. Paul Lawrence Haber, "Identity and Political Process: Recent Trends in the Study of Latin American Social Movements," *Latin American Research Review* 1996; 31 (1): p. 172. A study that bridges the literature on the urban poor and on the new social movements, albeit implicitly, is Willem Assies, Gerrit Burgwal, and Ton Salman, *Structures of Power, Movements of Ressistance: An Introduction to the Theories of Urban Movements in Latin America* (Amsterdam: Center for Latin American Research and Documentation, 1990). For an excellent analysis of popular organizations and the political system, see Joe Foweraker, *Theorizing Social Movements* (London: Pluto, 1993). On popular organizations, civic movements, and social movements from an empowerment perspective the main compilations are Susan Eckstein (ed.), *Power and Popular Protest: Latin American Social Movements* (Berkeley: University of California Press, 1988); Joe Foweraker and Ann L. Craig (eds.), *Popular Movements and Political Change in Mexico* (Boulder, Colo.: Lynne Rienner, 1990); Arturo Escobar and Sonia Alvarez (eds.), *The Making of Social Movements in Latin America: Identity, Strategy and Democracy* (Boulder, Colo.: Westview Press, 1992); Sonia E. Alvarez, Evelina Dagnino, and Arturo Escobar (eds.), *Culture of Politics/Politics of Cultures* (Boulder, Colo.: Westview Press, 1998).

13. See Levine, "Constructing Culture and Power in Latin America."

14. Claudio Lomnitz-Adler, *Exits from the Labyrinth: Culture and Ideology in Mexican National Space* (Berkeley: University of California Press, 1992).

15. See the section entitled "Mexican Identity: Many Mexicos?" in Joseph Klesner's review essay "Political Change in Mexico: Institutions and Identity," in *Latin American Research Review* 1997; 32 (2): p. 198.

16. In other writings, such as Rubin's splendid essay "Decentering the Regime: Culture and Regional Politics in Mexico," *Latin American Research Review* 1996; 31 (3): pp. 95–126, culture as content is approached to show how "political and cultural processes at local and regional levels accommodate or resist national projects and in so doing create new political forms." Note that in Rubin's treatment such "new configurations of power in turn become the terrain on which the center acts, as well as a primary source of knowledge for envisioning and implementing such action" (p. 119).

17. See, for instance, Susan C. Stokes, *Cultures in Conflict: Social Movements and the State in Peru* (Berkeley: University of California Press, 1995); and Jorge Duany, *Quisqueya on the Hudson: The Transnational Identity of Dominicans in Washington Heights* (New York: Dominican Studies Institute, CUNY, 1994).

18. On the "rescue" of culture for the study of politics and society since the mid-1980s see, for instance, Richard Munch and Neil J. Smelser (eds.), *Theory of Culture* (Berkeley: University of California Press, 1992). On the "power of culture" and its strategic deployment today see Peter Brown 's review essay "Cultural Resistance and Rebellion in Southern Mexico," *Latin American Research Review* 1998; 33 (3): pp. 217–29.

19. Among both North American and Latin American analysts. For an example of the "Iberian heritage" school, see Howard J. Wiarda, "Introduction: Social Change, Political Development and the Latin American Tradition," in Howard Wiarda (ed.), *Politics and Social Change in Latin America: Still a Distinct Tradition?* (Boulder, Colo.: Westview Press, 1992). For a "national character" interpretation, see, for instance, David Hojman, "Economic Policy and Latin American Culture: Is a Virtuous Circle Possible?" *Journal of Latin American Studies* 1999; 32: pp. 167–90.

20. It was not that long ago that in debates among comparative specialists concern was

voiced that little attention was being granted to the role of new social movements and NGOs in the definition of the political and its boundaries. This acknowledgement would later on become a widely shared premise. See Judith Adler Hellman, "The Riddle of New Social Movements: Who They Are and What They Do," in Sander Halebsky and Richard L. Harris (eds.), *Capital, Power and Inequality in Latin America* (Boulder, Colo.: Westview Press, 1995).

21. In his excellent critique of the neoconservative thesis on citizenship represented by Gertrude Himmelfarb's *The De-Moralization of Society*, Keith Tester discusses "culture" and "civilization." Here I am paraphrasing his formulation of the notion of culture. See Keith Tester, "Making Moral Citizens: On Himmelfarb's Demoralization Thesis," *Citizenship Studies* February 1997; 1 (1): p. 65.

22. See Leigh A. Payne, *Uncivil Movements: The Armed Right Wing and Democracy in Latin America* (Baltimore: Johns Hopkins University Press, 2000), which contains extensive analysis of the contras of Nicaragua, the *carapintada* in Argentina, and the Rural Democratic Union of Brazil as case studies.

23. Arguably, the establishment of "reasonable" horizons of durability for the electoral mode of government throughout the 1990s in Latin America bore stronger direct association with contextual factors – among the most salient, the foreign policy of the United States; the dynamics of intraregional relations; the state of financial markets; the relative proximity, distance, conflict or rapprochement between and among national elites (politicians, entrepreneurs, and so forth) at specific conjunctures; the ability to manage critical episodes of the conjunctures by those in office; as well as various combinations of these factors.

24. I borrow this expression from Levine, "Constructing Culture and Power in Latin America," but apply it differently.

25. See this idea applied to the European Union by Alastair Davidson in "Regional Politics: The European Union and Citizenship," *Citizenship Studies* February 1997; 1 (1): pp. 33–56.

26. Fernando Bustamante and I discussed the question of transnational networks and the implications of their increasing salience at some length elsewhere. See Amparo Menéndez-Carrión and Fernando Bustamante, "Purposes and Methods of Intraregional Comparison," in Smith, *Latin America in Comparative Perspective: New Approaches to Methods and Analysis*.

27. See, for instance, M. Horsman and A. Marshall, *After the Nation-State: Citizens, Tribalism and the New World Disorder* (London: HarperCollins, 1994).

28. Globalization is, of course, a contested notion. Sources particularly relevant for understanding the political economy of globalization are Robert W. Cox and Timothy J. Sinclair, *Approaches to World Order* (Cambridge: Cambridge University Press, 1996); Stephen Gill and David Law, *The Global Political Economy: Perspectives, Problems and Policies* (Baltimore: Johns Hopkins University Press, 1988). See also Jorge Nef, *Human Security and Mutual Vulnerability: An Exploration into the Global Political Economy of Development and Underdevelopment* (Ottawa: International Development Research Centre, 1999). A solid contribution to understanding recent debates is provided in David Held and Anthony McGrew (eds.), *The Global Transformations Reader: An Introduction to the Globalization Debate* (Cambridge: Polity Press, 2000).

29. Michael Mann's comment is illustrative: "It may seem an odd position for a sociologist to adopt but if I could I would abolish the concept of society altogether ..." See Michael Mann, *The Sources of Social Power*, vol. 1 (Cambridge: Cambridge University Press, 1986), p. 2.

30. The expression is borrowed from the title of a paper by C. Conaghan, *Democracy That Matters: The Search for Authenticity, Legitimacy and Civic Competence in the Andes,*

Project Latin America 2000 Series, Working Paper 1 (Notre Dame, Ind.: University of Notre Dame, Kellogg Institute, 1994).

31. George Reid Andrews and Herrick Chapman, *The Social Construction of Democracy, 1879–1990* (New York: New York University Press, 1995), p. 6.

32. This point is made, among other authors, by Eric Hershberg in "Democracy and its Discontents: Constraints on Political Citizenship in Latin America," in Howard Handelman and Mark Tessler (eds.), *Democracy and Its Limits: Lessons from Asia, Latin America and the Middle East* (Notre Dame, Ind.: Notre Dame University Press, 1999). Also, see my "Pero dónde y para qué hay cabida?"

33. Roberto Alejandro, *Hermeneutics, Citizenship, and the Public Sphere* (New York: State University of New York Press, 1993), p. 9.

34. Toby Miller, *The Well-Tempered Self: Citizenship, Culture, and the Postmodern Subject* (Baltimore: Johns Hopkins University Press, 1993), p. 12.

35. Alejandro, *Hermeneutics, Citizenship, and the Postmodern Subject*, p. 8.

36. On the different conceptions of the public/private axes in the American, English, French, and German traditions, and the different "types" of citizenship associated with these distinct traditions see Bryan S. Turner, "Citizenship Studies: A General Theory," *Citizenship Studies* February 1997; 1 (1): pp. 5–18.

37. Within the context of present debates a predominant stream in political science defines and "measures" democracy in terms of the notion of polyarchy. See Robert Dahl, *Polyarchy: Participation and Opposition* (New Haven, Conn: Yale University Press, 1971).

38. Julio Cotler, "Crisis política, outsiders y democraduras: El 'Fujimorismo,'" in Carina Perelli, Sonia Picado S., and Daniel Zovatto (comps.), *Partidos y clase política en América Latina en los 90* (San José, Costa Rica: Instituto Interamericano de Derechos Humanos, 1995), p. 121. The translation is mine.

39. The standard reference on the market is Nestor García Canclini, *Consumidores y ciudadanos: Conflictos multiculturales de la globalización* (Mexico City: Grijalbo, 1996). In the past five years technopolitics, "virtual" territories of politics, global politics, and "the Net," etc., have become the themes of an exploding literature. Perhaps the most ambitious attempt to comment on these topics is provided by Manuel Castell's recent three volumes on themes that had been present in the burgeoning scholarly literature on things global since the late 1980s – from the impact of globalization in the organization of capital and labour to the media and its culture; to the modifications of concepts of time and space; to the problem of the state, the crisis of democracy, and the problem of identities; the centrality of networks; and the gender movement as well as environmentalism, ethnicity, new insurgency movements, and so forth. See Manuel Castells, *The Information Age: Economy, Society and Culture*, vol. 1: *The Rise of the Network Society*; vol. 2: *The Power of Identity*; vol. 3: *End of Millenium* (Cambridge, Mass.: Blackwell, 1996–98). Also see the (demolishing) review by Peter Waterman, "El mundo feliz de Manuel Castells," *Nueva Sociedad* September–October 1998; (157).

40. The notion comes from Eric Hershberg's typology of Latin American polyarchies, in his "Democracy's Discontent." The literature on polyarchy in general is extensive. Some sources that I find especially useful are the following. On disenchantment with politics, Hoskins's review article "Democratization in Latin America" is of great interest. On "democracy's discontents" see Hershberg's article with that title and references therein. Several works by Manuel Antonio Garretón also come to mind, among them: *Los partidos y la transformación política de America Latina* (Santiago: FLACSO, 1992); *Hacia una nueva era política: Estudio sobre las democratizaciones* Santiago: Fondo de Cultura Economica, 1995). The "crisis of representation" and the weakness of political parties and political institutions in South America is ably dealt with in Juan Rial, "Los partidos políticos en América del Sur en la primera mitad de los años Noventa," in Perelli et al.,

Partidos y clase política en América Latina. On the crisis and collapse of the party system in Colombia a recent and useful analysis is Eduardo Pizarro Leongomez, "La crisis de los partidos y los partidos en la crisis," in Raul Urzua and Augusto Varas (eds.), *Fracturas en la gobernabilidad democratica* (Santiago de Chile: Centro de Analisis de Políticas Publicas, Universidad de Chile, 1998). On the Central Andes (Bolivia, Ecuador, and Peru) see Conaghan and Malloy's comparative analysis in *Unsettling Statecraft.* On Central America, Edelberto Torres Rivas's *Repression and Resistance: The Struggle for Democracy in Latin America* (Boulder, Colo.: Westview Press, 1989), remains a "must read" source in order to understand more recent issues and dilemmas.

41. For excellent analyses of these topics, see Elizabeth Leeds, "Cocaine and Parallel Polities in the Brazilian Urban Periphery: Constraints in Local-Level Democratization," *Latin American Research Review* 1996; 31 (3): pp. 47–84; and Jonathan Fox, "The Difficult Transition from Clientelism to Citizenship: Lessons from Mexico," *World Politics* January 1994; 46 (2): pp. 151–84.

42. Michael J. Sandel, *Democracy's Discontent: America in Search of a Public Philosophy* (Cambridge, Mass.: Belknap Press, 1997).

43. A recent publication of seminar proceedings on the topic of "political parties and strategic management" by ECLA's ILPES (Instituto Latinoamericano y del Caribe de Planificación Económica y Social) states that "Criticisms of the way political parties are financed and the behaviour of party leaderships are generalized in the region." The book is presented as part of ILPES efforts to "undertake a serious diagnosis of the causes of the discredit of the present political systems; to identify and evaluate proposals oriented towards rescuing the prestige of (political) institutions and actors ..." These statements indicate that towards the end of the 1990s the discredit of political parties was taken for granted in Latin America even in official circles. ILPES, *Partidos políticos y gestión estratégica* (Santiago: DOLMEN, 1997), p. 7.

44. An excellent recent collection on the topic of "political learning" in Latin America, though its concerns differ from those that frame this essay's treatment of learning processes, is Jennifer L. McCoy (ed.), *Political Learning and Redemocratization in Latin America: Do Politicians Learn from Political Crisis?* (Boulder, Colo.: Lynne Rienner, 2000). It seems worth emphasizing at this point is that at the dawn of a new century democracies in Latin America do not seem to require that "things public" in general are well thought of; and by further noting the perverse socialization process introduced by the equivalence of the idea of "public" in people's thinking with poor or run-down (physical) spaces – schools, recreation centres, hospitals; or with inefficient public policies; or with the abandoned, rejected, or feared – the meeting of others in societally shared spaces. The exception, perhaps, is Uruguay, where the "quality" of "things public" is part and parcel of its citizenship ethos as of today.

45. The expression is Eric Hershberg's, in his "Democracy and Its Discontents."

46. Here I am quoting Colombian political scientist José Gabriel Murillo – who used the phrase in reference to a specific conjuncture in Colombia (personal communication, Bogotá, 17 August 1996). I borrow his expression and apply it more broadly because it describes well the political learning resulting from the perverse institutionalization of the disconnection between governmental regimes and would-be citizens, given governments regarded as "alien" rather than as part and parcel of a "citizenship order" within the framework of which it would be taken as a matter of course that government policies should be aimed at nothing more or less than administering citizens' *entitlements.*

47. To be sure, passive forms of citizenship are features of plebiscitary democracy for which there is indeed room in Latin America. What should be underscored at this point about the linkages between citizenship and elections in Latin America – a topic sufficiently treated in the literature emphasizing the limitations of elections as a significant dimen-

sion of participation – is that even the electoral requirements placed on civilian regimes are "soft" inasmuch as electoral participation, where not compulsory, is dismally low – except in Uruguay and Costa Rica. High abstention rates are a recurrent theme throughout the region. The banalization of participation introduced by public opinion polls as ever-present actors in official discourse; the idea of "participation" as entertainment introduced through television evening news, with "What do you think?" applied to every conceivable topic, from the scent of a new soap to whether a specific presidential candidate dresses better or worse than his opponents, to whether the death penalty should be established as a "remedy for increasing crime in the streets"; and the promotion of the hyperindividuation of the social symbolized by the new populism of consumerism, offer ever-present "models" of what "to participate" means. At the same time, these technologies operate as forms of "resolution" of the problem of participation, freeing the established order from systemic overloads that otherwise it would not be in a position to absorb. On the role of public opinion polls in the production of passive citizens see Benjamin Ginsberg, *The Captive Mind: How Mass Opinion Promotes State Power* (New York: Basic Books, 1986).

48. Jorge Duany, "Imagining the Puerto Rican Nation: Recent Works on Cultural Identity," *Latin American Research Review* 1996; 31 (3): p. 252.

49. For instance, see Arjun Appadurai, "Disjuncture and Difference in the Global Cultural Economy," in Mike Featherstone (ed.), *Global Culture, Nationalism, Globalization, and Modernity* (Newbury Park, Calif.: Sage, 1990); and "Global Ethnoscapes: Notes and Queries for a Transnational Anthropology," in Richard G. Fox (ed.), *Recapturing Anthropology: Working in the Present* (Santa Fe, N. Mex.: School of American Research Press, 1991); Leo Chavez, "The Power of the Imagined Community: The Settlement of Undocumented Mexicans and Central Americans in the United States," *American Anthropologist* March 1994; 96 (1): pp. 52–73; and Duany, "Imagining the Puerto Rican Nation."

50. Duany, "Imagining the Puerto Rican Nation," p. 252. On transnational communities see Alejandro Portes, Luis E. Guarnizo, and Patricia Landlot, "The Study of Transnationalism: Pitfalls and Promise of an Emergent Research Field," *Ethnic and Racial Studies* March 1999; 22 (2): pp. 217–37. Also see essays in Liliana R. Goldin (ed.), *Identities on the Move: Transnational Processes in North America and the Caribbean Basin* (Austin: University of Texas Press, 2000).

51. Roger Bartra, as quoted in Klesner, "Political Change in Mexico," p. 198.

52. An excellent study in this emerging field is David Kyle, *Transnational Peasants, Migrations, Networks, and Ethnicity in Andean Ecuador* (Baltimore: Johns Hopkins University Press, 2000).

53. See John O'Neill, "The Civic Recovery of Nationhood," *Citizenship Studies* February 1997; 1 (1): pp. 19–31.

54. Though many other cases may be found throughout the Latin American landscape, the highly refined elites of Lima's Barranco and their sophisticated habitats provide a striking case in point, inasmuch as their cosmopolitanism stands in astonishing contrast to the squalid urban environment that surrounds them.

55. See David J. Meyers, "Latin American Cities: Internationally Embedded but Nationally Influential," in *Latin American Research Review* 1997; 32 (1): p. 122.

56. Sandel, *Democracy's Discontent*; and O'Neill, "The Civic Recovery of Nationhood."

57. On differentiating integration, see Menéndez-Carrión and Bustamante, "Purposes and Methods of Intraregional Comparison."

58. See Jan Pakulski, "Cultural Citizenship," *Citizenship Studies* February 1997; 1 (1): pp. 73–86.

59. Allyson Brysk, "Acting Globally: Indian Rights and International Politics in Latin

America," in Donna Lee Van Cott (ed.), *Indigenous Peoples and Democracy in Latin America* (New York: Saint Martin's Press, 1994), p. 30.

60. See the essays in Van Cott, *Indigenous Peoples*. See also Bice Maiguashca's thoughtful essay, *The Role of Ideas in a Changing World Order: The International Indigenous Movemnt*, Occasional Papers in Latin American and Caribbean Studies no. 4 (Toronto: CERLAC/York University, 1993); Scott H. Beck and Kenneth J. Mijeski, "Indigena Self-Identity in Ecuador and the Rejection of Mestizaje," *Latin American Research Review* 2000; 35 (1): pp. 119–37; and Rodolfo Stavenhagen's essay in this volume.

61. Jane S. Jaquette, "Rewriting the Scripts: Gender in the Comparative Study of Latin American Politics," in Smith, *Latin America in Comparative Perspective*, p. 126.

62. To be sure, the problematization of transnational networks might benefit from greater articulation with the vast and rich research on *sectores populares urbanos* and new social movements acting in the national sphere, as portrayed in the literature of the 1980s. See Alberto Adrianzén and Eduardo Ballón (eds.), *Lo popular en América Latina: Una visión en crisis?* (Lima: DESCO, 1992); Fernando Calderón, *Movimientos sociales y política: La década ochenta en Latinoamérica* (Mexico City: Siglo XXI, 1995); Allyson Brysk (ed.), *The Politics of Human Rights in Argentina: Protest, Change and Democratization* (Stanford, Calif.: Stanford University Press, 1994); Marguerite Guzmán Boward, *Revolutionizing Motherhood: The Mothers of the Plaza de Mayo* (Willmington, Del.: Scholarly Resources, 1994); Luis Pásara et al., *La otra cara de la luna: Nuevos actores sociales en el Perú* (Lima: Centro de Estudios de Democracia y Sociedad, 1991); Ponna Wignaraja, *New Social Movements in the South: Empowering the People* (London: Zed, 1993), among others. Two excellent treatments of the analytical implications of the literature on social movements are Haber, "Identity and Political Process"; and Kenneth M. Roberts, "Beyond Romanticism: Social Movements and the Study of Political Change in Latin America," *Latin American Research Review* 1997; 32 (2). The scope of the emancipatory and democratizing impulse of social movements and the complexities surrounding their impact on the redefinition of the linkages between micro- and macropolitical spaces are emphasized in both. Haber warns against romanticizing social movements; Roberts places the literature reviewed expressly "beyond romanticism," but at the same time, and apropos one of the volumes reviewed, warns of the problems with disempowering views.

63. On the shift in the axis of class struggles in postmodern society see Alvin W. Gouldner, *The Future of Intellectuals and the Rise of the New Class* (New York: Oxford University Press, 1976); and Ivan Szelenyi and B. Martin, "The Three Waves of New Classs Theories and a Postcript," in C. C. Lemert (ed.), *Intellectuals and Politics* (Newbury Park, Calif.: Sage, 1990). Also see Engin F. Isin, "Who Is the New Citizen? Towards a Genealogy," *Citizenship Studies* February 1997; 1 (1): pp. 115–31. I discuss this point more at length in "Pero dónde y para qué hay cabida?"

64. This is a striking feature of the social sciences. On the role of professional associations and foundations in supporting the establishment and consolidation of professional networks, see, for instance, Peter H. Smith," The Changing Agenda for Social Science Research on Latin America," in Smith, *Latin America in Comparative Perspective*. In his excellent analysis of the role of intellectuals in the 1988 Chilean plebiscite, Jeffrey Puryear offers rich empirical material to demonstrate the impact of transnational networking in the configuration of a major political event that is usually situated within the confines of the "national" and/or the "international." Jeffrey Puryear, *Thinking Politics: Intellectuals and Democracy in Chile, 1973–1988* (Baltimore: Johns Hopkins University Press). See also the comments in Menéndez-Carrión and Alfredo Joignant (eds.), *La caja de Pandora: El retorno de la transición chilena* (Santiago: Planeta-Ariel, 1999) chap. 1.

65. This is Juan Rial's expression. See Rial, "Los partidos politicos."

66. At century's end Uruguay and Costa Rica seemed to remain the exceptional cases – less so Chile, after the profound transformations of the past two decades. On the republican ethos in Chile see Arturo Valenzuela, "Chile: Origins, Consolidation and Breakdown of a Democratic Regime," in Larry Diamond, Juan Linz, and Seymour Martin Lipset (eds.), *Democracy in Developing Countries*, vol. 4: *Latin America* (Boulder, Colo.: Lynne Rienner, 1989); for specific reference to the erosion of features of citizenship in Chile, see Menéndez-Carrión and Joignant, *La caja de Pandora*, chap. 1.

67. The question of transformations as hybridization comes to mind here. I discuss this topic and the relevant debates in "Pero dónde y para qué hay cabida?"

68. Authors such as Thomas Hammer, *Democracy and the Nation State: Aliens, Denizens and Citizens in a World of International Migration* (Aldershot, Hants.: Avebury, 1990), have resorted to the term "denizen" to refer to foreign residents of a state who do not pursue naturalization. Here I use the term to refer to vast numbers of legal citizens whose access to legal citizenship coexists with the denial of meaningful citizenship.

69. Sandel, *Democracy's Discontent*.

70. For a useful review article on the topic, see Elizabeth Mahan, "Media, Politics and Society in Latin America," *Latin American Research Review* 1995; 30 (3): pp. 138–62.

71. Roberts, "Beyond Romanticism," p. 145. On the consequences of the selective presence of the state and the generation of fragmentations within the context of parallel structures of power – with far-reaching implications for the polity – the splendid longitudinal analysis of Leeds on the connections between microspaces and macropolitics in the operations of the drug-trafficking networks in Rio de Janeiro is must reading; Leeds, "Cocaine and Parallel Polities." On "quasi-imperial" styles of government, see Catherine Conaghan, "Polls, Political Discourse and the Public Sphere: The Spin on Perú's Fuji-golpe," in Smith, *Latin America in Comparative Perspective*, p. 230.

72. Again, remarkable feats have been accomplished by transnational social movements. The Pinochet affair is a clear illustration of empowerment at the transnational level that impacts significantly on the traditional site of the nation-state. Alfredo Joignant and I have discussed the impact of this case on the Chilean polity; Menéndez-Carrión and Joignant, *La caja de Pandora*, chap. 1. This, however, does not detract from the validity of the main argument set out in this essay.

11

The international dimension of democratization and human rights in Latin America

Ellen L. Lutz and Kathryn Sikkink

The arrest of General Augusto Pinochet in London in October 1998, and the British court's decision to let him be extradited to Spain for trial for human rights abuses in Chile, signalled again the significance of the international dimension of human rights and democracy promotion in Latin America. Although British authorities concluded that Pinochet was too ill to stand trial, the international events had important domestic political repercussions that did not end when Pinochet returned to Chile. An unprecedented number of human rights cases thereafter moved ahead in Chilean courts, and the Chilean Supreme Court removed Pinochet's immunity from prosecution. The involvement of international actors in the democratic crises in Paraguay, Ecuador, and Peru in 1999–2000 similarly highlighted the continuing importance of the international dimension of democratization. But the inability of international pressures to affect the increasingly authoritarian rule of President Alberto Fujimori in Peru from 1993 to 2000 prior to his flight from the country, or contribute to a peaceful settlement and improved human rights protection in Colombia, reminds us of the limits on the ability of such pressures to bring about political change.

The study of international dimension of democratization and human rights is far from a new avenue of inquiry.[1] Many observers initially suggested that as democratization proceeded in the hemisphere, the international or regional dimension would become less influential.[2] The Pinochet case (and similar judicial processes underway in Spain in relation to Argentina and Guatemala) show that international and regional factors still play an important role even decades after the formal transition to democracy. We argue that international and regional actors, buttressed by changing norms that justify and legitimate their involvement, are playing a more active role in domestic processes of democracy and human rights than ever before.

The arrest of Pinochet was more than an international attempt to provide a measure of justice for victims of human rights abuses in Chile – something the Chilean government previously was unwilling or unable to do. It was part of a complex process of change of international human rights norms and laws. This essay looks not only at the impact international norms have had on human rights and democratic practices in Latin America, but also on the impact that Latin American struggles for human rights and democracy have had on international norms. The Pinochet case is a key turning point in international human rights law, and thus the genesis of the case is important to understanding not only change in Chile, but change in the international system. Chilean activists and Chile solidarity groups around the world made Pinochet an international symbol of flagrant human rights abuse. Chileans, and their allies, sought and secured extensive international involvement as a means of pressuring for domestic human rights change. Because Pinochet was such a powerful symbol – and because Chilean activists helped make him so – the case attracted widespread attention and altered the contours of international human rights law. In a similar vein, the inter-American system, through recent innovations in regional norms and practices with respect to democracy, has been pioneering more effective ways of exerting external pressure to sustain democracy in the region.

The puzzle is to understand how international forces interact with domestic political factors to produce particular political outcomes. The impact of international and regional pressure for democracy or human rights is variable and depends on how it complements domestic political processes. The four democracy scenarios discussed in the introduction to this volume – foundation, transition, reform, and regression and crisis – help explain different domestic political processes of democratization, and provide a starting point for exploring how each democracy "path" interacts with international and regional factors. This essay analyzes cases from each scenario and explores what role international and regional actors played. In addition, it looks at how international and regional laws, norms, institutions, and policies on human rights and democracy have changed over time. This change is particularly dramatic when external responses to human rights and democracy events in the early 1970s are compared to external responses in the late 1990s.

Changing international and regional context for democracy and human rights

Human rights and democratic principles have long resonated in Latin America. Latin American policy-makers, legal scholars, and activists have historically been vocal supporters of the development of international law, in part because they perceived such law as a means of protecting weaker states and their peoples from unlawful interventions by more powerful states, particularly the United States. Many early pan-American leaders stressed the importance of international law in promoting the doctrines of sovereignty and non-intervention, but they argued that the doctrine of non-intervention needed to be harmonized with other principles of international law, including human rights.[3] This legal tradition led Latin American governments to support human rights language in the United Nations Charter, to adopt in 1948 the American Declaration of the Rights and Duties of Man, and to unanimously support, later that same year, UN General Assembly adoption of the Universal Declaration of Human Rights.

Actual practice in adhering to international human rights law in the region often fell far short of this commitment, especially in the period from 1950 through the mid-1970s. Few institutional mechanisms existed to enforce human rights and democracy standards. At the height of the Cold War, concern for the promotion of human rights and democracy was subordinated to anti-communism.[4] The U.S. Alliance for Progress was in principle committed to the promotion of democracy, but in practice led to a dramatic increase in counter-insurgency training and funding for Latin American militaries, thus reinforcing antidemocratic forces throughout the region. In the 1960s and 1970s, a wave of military coups swept the region. National security ideology, with its assumption that authoritarian rule and human rights violations were acceptable in the struggle against insurgencies and communism, reigned. Thus the international and regional environment between 1950 and the mid-1970s was at worst hostile and at best indifferent to democracy. No policies or programmes existed to promote democracy, while the intense anti-communism and the predominance of national security doctrine in U.S. policy strengthened antidemocratic forces. European countries, caught up in their own processes of reconstruction and decolonization, played relatively little attention to the situation in Latin America. The UN was not a significant player in the region, while the OAS was dominated by the United States and by the region's military governments.

This international and regional environment provided cover and impetus for the wave of repression in Latin America in the 1970s and 1980s.

Many countries had levels of state repression not previously witnessed since the colonial or independence periods. Argentina, Brazil, El Salvador, Guatemala, Honduras, Nicaragua, Bolivia, Paraguay, Uruguay, Peru, and Mexico experienced unprecedented repression and human rights abuses in the 1970s and 1980s. When we look closer at four cases for which more precise data are available – Argentina, Chile, El Salvador, and Guatemala – another striking pattern stands out. Despite differences in political histories, economies, and cultures, these four countries had intense peaks of deaths and disappearances in a relatively short two-to three-year period, preceded and followed by serious, systematic, but lower-level violations. Not only did repression take similar forms in each country, but all the peaks of repression occurred during a single decade – between 1973 and 1982.[5] This pattern suggests the value of studying this period – or wave – of intense repression as an interconnected phenomena, not as a series of separate country events.

In part as a response to this wave of repression, since the mid-1970s Latin American countries increasingly have accepted democracy as the norm. In the mid-1970s, a series of international human rights treaties began to enter into force. In addition to the Universal Declaration of Human Rights and the American Declaration of Human Rights, both of which establish human rights norms but have little binding effect on individual countries, international human rights norms relevant to Latin American states are articulated in the International Covenant on Civil and Political Rights, the International Covenant on Economic, Social, and Cultural Rights, and the American Convention on Human Rights. These treaties were adopted by the United Nations and the Organization of American States in the late 1960s and entered into force between 1976 and 1978. Some Latin American countries, especially the handful of long-established democracies, immediately accepted the human rights regimes established by these treaties. For example, Costa Rica, Uruguay, and Colombia all ratified the International Covenant on Civil and Political Rights and its Optional Protocol between 1968 and 1970, well before the covenant entered into force in 1976; Costa Rica and Columbia also ratified the American Convention. But in 1977 and 1978, ten Latin American countries ratified the American Convention. This willingness of states to ratify relevant treaties signalled greater regional attention to the value of human rights and democracy.

Once the American Convention entered into force (July 1978), the Inter-American Court was installed and countries began to accept its compulsory jurisdiction. More highly elaborated norms were subsequently expressed in treaties such as the Convention against Torture and Other Cruel, Inhuman, or Degrading Treatment or Punishment; the Inter-

American Convention to Prevent and Punish Torture; and the Inter-American Convention on Forced Disappearance of Persons, which were drafted and entered into force in the late 1980s and early 1990s.

Between 1978 and 1991, most authoritarian countries in the region returned to electoral democracy. This revival of democracy in turn contributed to the adoption of specific norms in laws for the promotion of democracy. In 1991, the OAS General Assembly adopted the Santiago Commitment to Democracy and the Renewal of the Inter-American System.[6] The following day the OAS General Assembly established a process for convening an ad hoc meeting of the region's Foreign Affairs Ministers in the event of any sudden or irregular interruption of democratic governance in a member state.[7] Members of the OAS later strengthened the regional commitment to democracy by amending the OAS Charter with the Protocol of Washington. That protocol, which entered into force in 1997, provides that two-thirds of the OAS General Assembly may vote to suspend a member state whose democratically elected government has been overthrown by force.[8] This significantly enhanced the level of obligation to enforce the norm of democracy in the Americas, particularly for ratifying states. The Santiago Declaration and the Protocol of Washington have provided the procedural basis for many regional actions in favour of democracy in the region in the last decade.

In addition to these institutional mechanisms to implement the commitment to democracy, the OAS also set up an internal unit for the promotion of democracy. Beginning in the 1980s, the United Nations also began to play a more significant role in the region by helping to broker peace agreements, establishing truth commissions, and running UN peace operations – such as those in El Salvador and Guatemala – that helped facilitate transitions to democracy. Even the World Bank became increasingly concerned with issues of "good governance," and began funding democracy-reinforcing programmes such as judicial training.

Finally, the bilateral policies of other states changed significantly. In the mid-1970s, the U.S. Congress and the Carter Administration adopted human rights policies. The Reagan administration initially tried to dismantle those policies, but was unable to mobilize the political support to do so, and eventually supported adding a more explicit democracy promotion policy to the human rights policies pioneered under Carter.[9] The foreign policies of diverse European countries also came to stress human rights and democracy to a greater degree in the 1970s and 1980s, and European countries expanded their development assistance programmes in the region. Thus, while no country explicitly incorporated democracy promotion into its foreign policy prior to the 1980s, it is now an important part of the foreign policy of the United States and European countries, as well as of a number of key Latin American countries.

In addition, in the 1970s and 1980s, an international human rights advocacy network emerged committed to documenting and spotlighting violations, drafting and implementing international standards, and pressuring governments to implement bilateral and multilateral policies.[10] Domestic human rights organizations throughout the region demanded that their governments respect human rights and ally with international networks to publicize violations and demand change.

These international changes contributed to, and in turn were fed by, regime changes throughout the region as every Latin American country except Cuba either retained or returned to electoral democracy between 1978 and 1991.[11] These electoral regimes are far from perfect democracies, but as a result of these changes, most Latin American countries today face a new set of issues – not the problem of military coups, but rather the dilemmas of moulding existing electoral regimes into fuller democracies.

The return to democracy was generally accompanied by improved human rights practices, although there were important exceptions, like Colombia, where electoral democracy coexisted with increasingly high levels of repression. By the late 1990s, torture was less widespread throughout the region than it was in the 1970s.[12] By 1996, the UN Working Group on Disappearances concluded that political disappearances had almost ended in the Western Hemisphere, although several countries still had backlogs of unexplained cases. By 1998, the UN Working Group and Amnesty International reported disappearances in only two countries in Latin America: Colombia and Mexico.[13]

Because of the wave-like nature of the trends in repression in the 1970s and 1980s, and of the return to democracy and improvement in human rights in the late 1980s and 1990s, it seems unlikely that domestic factors in each country fully account for the regional trend in democracy and human rights. Reflecting on this wave-like quality, Laurence Whitehead has pointed to the importance of international influences on democratization.[14] Whitehead and other commentators suggest that democratization involves interactive processes in which domestic political actors operate simultaneously in an international and a domestic political context, and must be aware of both the domestic and the international repercussions of their actions. We argue that this international context has changed dramatically in the last two decades to become more supportive of human rights and democracy.

International law is one part of this broader regional and international trend that has influenced human rights practices in the region. But international law is less important in and of itself, and more important as one manifestation of a broader norm shift that has led to increased regional and international consensus with respect to an interconnected bundle of human rights norms. The popular, political, and legal support and legitimacy these norms now possess is reinforced by diverse legal and non-legal practices developed to implement and ensure compliance with them.

In the 1980s, Latin America experienced a regional human rights "norms cascade" – a rapid shift towards recognizing the legitimacy of human rights norms, and international and regional action on behalf of those norms.[15] The Pinochet case is an example of this, but the precedents and roots of the norms cascade go back far deeper into Latin American history.

The norms cascade is a source, and an indicator, of political learning at the domestic and the international level. High-profile cases like the Pinochet case are major vehicles through which changes in international law and norms are communicated to a wide audience, thus permitting them to become a source of political learning about the costs and benefits of certain kinds of behaviour.[16]

Active enforcement of new human rights and democratic norms occurs in a variety of ways. Latin American human rights advocates help focus international attention on domestic human rights abuses. Transnational advocacy networks then promote adverse international publicity about a state's violations of human rights so that non-compliance leads to embarrassment or a blow to reputation. Once a state's misconduct has been exposed, more damaging bilateral or multilateral enforcement measures may follow. Bilateral foreign policy sanctions may be imposed on states that violate human rights. Courts in other countries, relying on their own domestic civil and criminal law, may hold individuals who fall within their jurisdiction responsible for violations of international human rights that occurred in other countries. In recent years there has been increased multilateral willingness on the part of regional or international organizations to apply sanctions to rights-violating states. While bilateral and multilateral enforcement continues to be selective, such measures frequently impose high costs on recalcitrant states.

To illustrate these arguments, we show how they operated in cases from each democracy scenario in which international and regional pressures were brought to bear on governments in different ways. These include the impact of international and regional pressures on preventing coups in the region, in both the foundation and regression cases of Guatemala, Peru, and Paraguay; the role of the United Nations in contributing to the peacemaking and the foundation of democracy in El Salvador and Guatemala; the genesis and effects of the Spanish trials for past human rights abuses in Argentina and Chile on the transition cases; and the impact of international pressures on the democracy reform project in Mexico, and on human rights and conflict resolution in Colombia. After surveying the role of international actors in the four scenarios, however, we conclude that the major difference in the influence of international actors has been over time, rather than among the different scenarios.

The role of international actors in the promotion of democracy

The manner in which states and other regional actors respond to an interruption of democracy in the hemisphere has changed significantly from 1973 to the present. Comparing the international responses to the coup in Uruguay in 1973, and to similar coups in Guatemala and Peru in the early 1990s, illuminates the development and implementation of norms in favor of democracy in the region. In many ways the three coups were similar: all were *auto-golpes* or "self-coups," in which the elected president, with the support of the military, undermined the constitutional order, closed Congress, censored the press, and arrested members of the political opposition. All three countries faced an armed guerrilla movement.

Yet the coups in Uruguay (and in Chile) in 1973 illustrate international actors' indifference and hostility to democracy in the region. Although Uruguay was one of the best-established democracies in the region at the time, the initial international response to the coup was extremely muted: it took over five years for international actors to develop the same sort of pressure that is today commonplace when a coup in the region occurs.[17] In Chile, the hostility of the U.S. government and key transnational corporations to the Allende government was one factor contributing to the breakdown of democracy. Even when international pressures on Uruguay and Chile increased after 1976, almost all criticisms were directed against the human rights practices of the military regimes, not against the interruption of democracy per se. Military coups were considered part of the standard political repertoire in the region.

International opposition to coup attempts in Guatemala and Peru twenty years later was rapid, clear, and forceful. Nevertheless, the differences in the way those two self-coups played out suggests how the impact of international factors today varies in the "foundation" scenario of Guatemala and the "regression" scenario of Peru. A significant "critical juncture" for democracy in Guatemala came in May 1993, when elected President Jorge Serrano carried out a self-coup by closing Congress and the judiciary, and censoring the press. Two large groups in civil society – the Multisectoral Forum, led by CACIF, the business association; and the Social Multisectoral Forum, led by unions and social movements – formed and took the lead in opposing the coup and pressing for a return to democracy.[18] The judges of the recently formed Guatemalan Constitutional Court declared that the coup decree was unconstitutional, and, before the military shut the court down, faxed their decision all over the world.[19] Journalists ignored the censorship orders, and people poured into the streets to demonstrate in favor of democracy.

International pressure operated in synergy with domestic legal processes and the domestic opposition, and it was this interaction of domestic and international opposition that was essential for undermining the coup attempt. Domestic groups informed international public opinion about what was occurring. Networks of NGOs then coordinated a lobbying effort to pressure their governments to strongly oppose the Guatemalan coup. Germany, the Netherlands, and the United States suspended economic and military aid.

Bilateral policies towards Guatemala were made more effective because they were co-ordinated with and channelled through the OAS. Just four days after the coup, an OAS fact-finding mission, headed by Secretary General of the OAS João Baena Soares, arrived in Guatemala. The mission's discussions with diverse civil society groups helped to send a clear message in their meetings with Serrano and members of the military high command, that the self-coup had violated the Constitution, and that unless a legal resolution was found to the crisis, the OAS would probably adopt economic sanctions against Guatemala.[20] Eventually the Guatemalan military responded by ousting Serrano and his vice-president. Once Serrano was out, Congress elected Ramiro de León Carpio, the former Attorney General for Human Rights, as the new president of Guatemala.

The Guatemalan case suggests that although internal forces must be the promoters and protectors of democracy, external groups can offer crucial support and assistance. In order for such pressures to be effective, however, they need to be prompt and concerted, and to include a willingness to apply international political and economic pressure (as opposed to political pressure by itself). In the early moments after a coup, the new regime is still unstable. Forceful and rapid action can disarticulate the coup coalition before it has a chance to consolidate, opening up the possibility of reversal. The reversal of Serrano's self-coup did not immediately improve the human rights situation in Guatemala, but it did permit the process of democratic foundation to continue. A less successful international response occurred after the 1992 coup in Peru, when elected President Fujimori closed Congress and the judiciary and assumed dictatorial powers. Within days the OAS foreign ministers met, condemned the coup, and sent a fact-finding mission to Lima. The United States, Spain, Germany, and Japan suspended economic aid, and international financial institutions froze debt relief and development grants. Non-governmental human rights organizations issued reports and sent missions to Peru. Although the international response was rapid, clear, and forceful, and pushed Fujimori to reinstate some elements of democracy, it was insufficient to fully restore democracy. The biggest difference between the situation in Peru and that in Guatemala was that civil society in Peru was not unified and mobilized against the self-coup. On the contrary, large segments of the public vocally supported Fujimori's actions. In particular, the military, local businessmen, exporters, and the urban middle and lower classes supported the coup.[21] Various opinion polls taken in the months following the coup showed that 60 to 90 per cent of the public supported Fujimori's policies.[22] Fujimori's popularity was in part due to the public perception of his success in the fight against the Shining Path guerrilla movement. His popularity was enhanced when, five months after the coup, his security forces captured Abimael Guzmán, the Shining Path's leader, and seven other of its top leaders.

In response mainly to international economic pressures, Fujimori took measures to move Peru back in the direction of democracy, including holding elections for a new constituent assembly in November 1992, and municipal elections early in 1993. Nonetheless, the post–*auto-golpe* Fujimori regime must be characterized as semi-authoritarian. Levels of basic civil and political liberties were not sufficient to ensure the integrity of democratic competition and participation in elections. The semi-authoritarian nature of the Fujimori regime became more overt in the early summer of 2000 when accusations of vote fraud in the presidential election led international and domestic observers to conclude that the second-round elections had to be delayed in order to put into place the necessary mechanisms to ensure fair elections. When Fujimori refused to delay the elections, the leading opposition candidate withdrew, undermining further the legitimacy of Fujimori's election to a third term in office and contributing to his downfall.

Despite significant efforts over a seven-year period, international pressure appears to have had relatively little impact on semi-authoritarianism in Peru. Despite Fujimori's downfall, this case clarifies the limits of international and regional actions to promote democracy, especially when authoritarian leaders retain high levels of domestic legitimacy and popularity.

This does not mean that international and regional pressure will always be ineffective in regression and crisis scenarios. Indeed, international and regional actors have played very important roles in sustaining democracy in another regression and crisis case – Paraguay. The most important intervention came during a coup attempt by General Lino Oviedo in 1996. Oviedo yielded following an immediate display of diplomatic clout by the OAS, the Clinton administration, and the Argentine, Brazilian, and Uruguayan governments, which joined forces to back the elected president.[23] Cesar Gaviria, secretary-general of the OAS, traveled to Paraguay to support President Wasmosy during the coup attempt. Gaviria apparently persuaded Wasmosy not to resign, and international and domestic pressure also dissuaded him from rewarding Oviedo with an appointment as minister of defense.[24] In Paraguay, as in Guatemala in 1993, international pressure interacted with an activated civil society that poured into the streets and plazas of Asunción in support of democracy.

Over the next four years General Oviedo continued to be an impediment to democracy in Paraguay. Accused of having inspired the assassination of the vice-president in 1999, Oviedo fled to Argentina, where he was granted asylum, to the dismay of the Paraguayan government. Oviedo became a fugitive in December 1999 when he feared that the new government in Argentina would be less sympathetic to his case. Eventually the Brazilian and Argentine governments decided to arrest Oviedo, and in June 2000, the Brazilian police found him disguised and alone, hiding in the bathroom of a luxury apartment near the Paraguayan border.[25] Though the general's future was unresolved at the turn of the century, the image suggests that once powerful military coup-makers can be brought to justice by a combination of international and domestic political efforts.

How can we explain the very different international responses to these comparable coup attempts in Latin America? Between 1990 and 1993, strong normative developments in the region coalesced around the "right to democracy." The Santiago Declaration and Resolution 1080 provided the procedural means for rapid regional response to attacks on democracy in Guatemala, Peru, and Paraguay, and put the OAS in the forefront of efforts by international organizations to promote democracy. Actions under the Santiago Declaration or the Protocol of Washington in response to military coups in the region are examples of political enforcement of regional norms regarding democracy. At the same time, the end of the Cold War diminished anti-communist sentiment that had 'justified' authoritarian regimes in the region.

The involvement of international actors in peacemaking in foundation democracies

The most far-reaching and effective involvement of international actors in Latin America in recent decades was that of the United Nations in helping negotiate, implement, and monitor peace accords in El Salvador and Guatemala in the 1990s. Edelberto Torres Rivas provides historical background and highlights the role of the Contadora Group and the United Nations in these peace processes in his essay in this volume, so we will only discuss these cases briefly so as to contribute to the broader argument made here.

As in the other cases discussed in this essay, international actors were able to play a constructive role in contributing to peace and democracy only after domestic political actors had arrived at a consensus that peace was necessary. In El Salvador the government and guerrillas had fought to a stalemate. With the end of the Cold War, it became unlikely that the United States would continue to supply the extensive military aid that had sustained the Salvadoran government counter-insurgency campaign for over ten years, especially given that government's continuing high levels of human rights violations. The end of the Cold War, and the electoral defeat of the Sandinistas in Nicaragua, also made the future scenario for the guerrillas unclear. Thus both sides had incentives to negotiate a peaceful end to the conflict.[26]

By the time negotiations were underway, the changing international and domestic context had led to real willingness on the part of both sides to bring an end to the conflict. The settlement had broad support from all political sectors of Salvadoran society. Nevertheless, international actions provided crucial impetus to negotiations and to implementation of the agreements. In addition to U.N. involvement, outside countries, especially the "Group of Friends" of the Secretary-General, played a critical role in supporting and moving ahead the negotiation process.[27] Thus, here again, successful promotion of democracy required domestic political will and forceful and coherent international pressure working in concert with civil society.

The subsequent transition to democracy in Guatemala in 1994 benefited from the learning process of the El Salvador experience. Once again, a UN human rights monitoring mission, MINUGUA, provided a confidence-building measure that helped ensure that rights would be protected while more complex negotiations continued. According to Suzanne Jonas, MINUGUA was "the most concrete expression of the international community's interest in Guatemala." Its presence provided a constant reminder "that the world was watching," and thus discouraged further human rights violations. MINUGUA was also involved in institution building to strengthen domestic capacity in the area of human rights protection, including the judicial system, the public prosecutor's office, and the national police.[28]

International donors formed a Consultative Group of Donor Countries and sent a clear message that major funding would be withheld until the peace accord was signed and tax reforms were made. The government of Alvaro Arzu and the private sector realized that increased international funding depended upon reaching a peace agreement.

In the end, while making peace depended on the political will of domestic actors, "extensive UN involvement (and that of the international community as a whole) made a decisive difference."[29] One guerrilla leader acknowledged, "We couldn't have kept it alive among Guatemalans. Without the persistence of the UN, the peace process would have been impossible."[30] Many elements of the peace negotiations still need to be implemented, but by the late 1990s, movement towards improvements in the human rights situation had taken place, especially with regard to torture and disappearances.[31] By 2000, the country had sustained its still fragile democracy, and two truth commissions, one sponsored by the United Nations and one by the Catholic Church, had produced definitive reports on human rights violations in the past.

In both Guatemala and El Salvador, during the negotiations actors on both sides of the political spectrum went through a process of identity transformation as they increasingly committed themselves to international and regional norms of democracy and human rights.[32] Torres-Rivas points out in this volume that what mainly contributed to settlements in Central America was a change in the "subjective perspective of the players."[33] We believe that international factors provided much of the context within which those subjective perspectives began to change.

International actors and transitional justice for past human rights abuses: The involvement of the Spanish court in Chile and Argentina

The most important ways in which international political actors have been involved in the transition cases is through the role that foreign courts have come to play in the search for accountability for past human rights violations. The increased judicial activism of foreign courts on cases of human rights violations in other countries caught many by surprise. As late as mid-1998, few imagined that a European government would arrest Pinochet, or any other Latin American official responsible for human rights abuses. Indeed, in 1982, France and Sweden had an opportunity to seek the extradition of an Argentine national alleged to be responsible for the torture, disappearance, and murder of their nationals, but declined to do so. Argentine Naval Captain Alfredo Astiz, whom NGOS had accused of being involved in notorious human rights violations at the Naval School of Mechanics in Buenos Aires, including the disappearance of two French nuns and the arrest and killing of a Swedish girl, was captured by the British during the Falklands/Malvinas war. France and Sweden asked to have questions put to Astiz concerning these abuses. The British government transported Astiz to the United Kingdom and put the questions to him, but, availing himself of his Geneva Convention prisoner of war protections, he refused to answer. Despite substantial evidence against him, and the fact that he was not protected by the Geneva Convention from criminal prosecution for violations of international human rights law, neither country sought his extradition, nor did Britain entertain the possibility of trying him.[34]

The British government's decision in 1998 to imprison Augusto Pinochet pending the outcome of extradition proceedings brought at the request of a Spanish court signalled that human rights law and norms had moved ahead, and had done so even more quickly than most observers had predicted. The arrest was part of a process begun more that two years earlier in a special court in Spain. The Argentine and Chilean exile communities in Spain first raised the possibility that their nationals could be tried there for human rights abuses committed in Latin America. In the context of the twentieth anniversary of the Argentine coup, exiles in Spain organized an impressive campaign to focus Spanish public opinion on human rights violations during Argentina's military dictatorship.[35] In March 1996, an association of Spanish prosecutors (Union Progresista de Fiscales), acting in their private capacity, filed criminal charges against former military leaders for human rights violations committed during the military regime. In July 1996, similar charges were filed against Augusto Pinochet and other Chilean military leaders. After the prosecutors' actions set the criminal process in motion, lawyers for human rights victims took over the prosecution of the claims. In preparing the cases, these lawyers received extensive assistance from human rights organizations both in Spain, and in Argentina and Chile.

The cases against Argentine and Chilean military officers have had the unanticipated effect of spurring the willingness of Argentina and Chile to try human rights cases. The decision by the Argentine government to imprison, pending trial, both Admiral Massera and General Videla, apparently was in part a pre-emptive measure in response to Judge Garzon's international arrest warrants.[36] In Chile, the arrest of Pinochet appeared to have lifted psychological, political, and juridical barriers to justice by weakening the powerful forces that had blocked trials in Chile since the return to democracy. International pressures bolstered by routine retirement and replacement in the Chilean judiciary and military have yielded a more liberal judiciary and a younger, less implicated officer corps. In July 1999, for example, Chile's Supreme Court upheld a lower court decision that the Amnesty Law was no longer applicable to cases in which people had disappeared. Until the bodies of the victims were located, the crime was not murder but kidnapping, meaning that the crime was a continuing event that went beyond the 1978 amnesty deadline.

When British authorities allowed Pinochet to return to Chile after deciding that his ill health prevented him from standing trial, many feared that these legal advances in Chile would be reversed. But, despite a hero's welcome, and his surprising vigour on the Santiago tarmac, New York Times reporter Clifford Krause's description of Pinochet as "a real nowhere man" most accurately reflected his position.[37] His future was being negotiated without him by military and civilian officials. His return speeded up negotiations between military and civilian officials on a human rights accord that created a mechanism to uncover what happened to approximately 1,200 people who disappeared during Pinochet's dictatorship. On 5 June 2000 a Santiago appeals court ruled by a vote of 13 to 9 that Pinochet could be stripped of his lifetime immunity from prosecution and could be tried for the disappearance of at least 19 people in October 1973. The Supreme Court is reviewing that decision, and even if it overrules the decision, lawyers are waiting in the wings with other disappearance cases that they plan to file in the courts.[38]

The Spanish court cases have raised the hopes of human rights activists throughout Latin America that justice for rights abuses in their countries is possible. Following the lead of Argentine and Chilean human rights activists, Nobel Peace Prize winner Rigoberta Menchu filed a case in the Spanish court against several Guatemalan military leaders, including former president Efraín Ríos Montt, who currently is president of the Chamber of Deputies. The suit is based on three specific cases: the military assault on the Spanish embassy in Guatemala in 1980 in which 37 people were killed; the slaying of four Spanish priests; and the torture and murder of Menchu's family members. Ríos Montt's lawyers have counterattacked by filing a suit against Menchu in Guatemalan courts charging her with treason, sedition, and violation of the Constitution for filing charges in a foreign court. Nonetheless, Ríos Montt is clearly feeling some pressure: in April 2000 he cancelled a holiday trip to France to avoid arrest.[39]

In contrast, Bolivians hoping for a Spanish court indictment against former military dictator and current President Hugo Banzer have been stymied by a lack of cooperation from domestic political forces that enjoy international support. Some 200 Bolivians disappeared during the Banzer regime from 1971 to 1978. Bolivian NGOs sought to gather the evidence needed by the Spanish court to indict Banzer for those abuses and his regime's participation in Operation Condor, a Chilean secret intelligence service operation whose purpose was to track down Chilean political exiles living abroad and eliminate them. Bolivians, more concerned with current economic problems than past human rights abuses, elected Banzer as president in 1997 and his government has received strong support from the Clinton administration and the United Nations for its coca eradication campaign. In November 1998, the Bolivian Chamber of Deputies approved a resolution asking its human rights panel to assemble evidence on Bolivian involvement with Operation Condor and turn it over to the Spanish court. But after the evidence was garnered, senior government officials lobbied hard against any congressional transfer of the documents to Spain. In February 1999 the Chamber of Deputies reversed itself; but it did not bar an opposition political party from transferring the documents.[40] Later that year the Inter-American Commission on Human Rights found Bolivia responsible for the disappearance of a student during the Banzer dictatorship and ordered the country to pay compensation. Banzer then announced that he was willing to open an investigation into the fate of Bolivia's disappeared.[41]

Elsewhere on the continent, hopes have been rising that more trials of high-ranking officials accused of human rights abuses will occur. In June 2000, Congressman Marcos Rolim, who heads the Human Rights Commission in Brazil's Chamber of Deputies, asked President Fernando Henrique Cardoso to strip former Paraguayan dictator Alfredo Stroessner of his political asylum. Once it is lifted he plans to ask Brazilian prosecutors to charge the former dictator with human rights violations during his nearly 35-year rule in neighbouring Paraguay.[42]

Notwithstanding the readiness of NGO activists to submit human rights cases to foreign courts when justice at home is foreclosed, the clear preference is for justice in the courts of the country where the abuses took place. Thus, while Pinochet was still in London, many Chileans from all political standpoints argued that if he were to be prosecuted at all the trial should occur in Chile. In the Stroessner case, Congressman Rolim agreed that it would be preferable to try the ex-dictator in Paraguay, but argued that in light of the failed military coup there, and the continuing ties many current political actors in Paraguay still have to Stroessner, such a trial could generate further political unrest. In his view, "Brazil, by giving asylum and protection to Stroessner, has responsibility for his destiny."[43]

International trials are a second-best scenario as compared to justice in the courts of the country where the abuse took place. But the Pinochet case may reveal how international and domestic factors can interact to yield a better outcome than either working alone. The international arrest of Pinochet helped to open the possibility for domestic justice which had previously been blocked.

International and regional pressures in reform processes: Mexico and Colombia

The political and human rights situation in Mexico was different from that of the transition and foundation scenarios. Mexico had an elected civilian government that had been under the control of the official political party, the Institutionalized Revolutionary Party (PRI), from the party's formation in 1929 until its electoral defeat in 2000. Although murders and disappearances of the kind that occurred in Guatemala did not occur in Mexico, human rights abuses were common in the 1970s and 1980s. The police routinely used torture to extract confessions from both common and political prisoners, prison conditions were often abysmal, and electoral fraud and press censorship were commonplace.[44] In spite of this record, the more serious violations in Central America and the Southern Cone occupied the attention of human rights advocates, and virtually no international attention was directed to the Mexican human rights situation in the 1970s and early 1980s. The existence of an elected civilian government, Mexico's progressive stance on international human rights (it became, for example, a haven for political refugees from Pinochet's Chile, and later a firm critic of human rights violations in El Salvador), and the absence of Mexican human rights organizations kept Mexico off the international agenda.

Elsewhere, we have argued that international pressures together with changing domestic political circumstances came together in the early 1990s to contribute to political reform in Mexico.[45] Reports by domestic and international human rights organizations first began to draw attention to human rights violations in Mexico in the mid-1980s.[46] Although these reports upset the Mexican government because they marred its carefully cultivated image as a human rights defender, government practices did not change.

Change started after 1988 when a different domestic and international political context made human rights a more salient issue. The split in the PRI before the 1988 presidential election, led to a political challenge from the left-leaning Revolutionary Democratic Party (PRD) led by Cuauhtémoc Cárdenas. In 1990, Mexico initiated discussions with the United States and Canada over a free trade agreement. Both of these situations made the Mexican government more sensitive to charges of human rights violations.

The OAS Inter-American Commission on Human Rights (IACHR) considered its first Mexican cases in 1989–1990, when it took on three cases of electoral irregularities brought by members of the National Action Party (PAN). Refuting the Mexican government's claim that the IACHR was barred by OAS Charter from addressing electoral issues, the commission recommended that the Mexican government reform its internal electoral law.[47]

In 1990, under pressure from the IACHR, domestic political parties, and human rights organizations, and in response to widespread allegations of fraud in the 1988 elections, the Mexican government entered into negotiations with political parties and began to modify electoral laws and procedures. In June 1990, in anticipation of the impact that an Americas Watch report on human rights conditions in Mexico would have in Washington, where the initial negotiations for the North American Free Trade Agreement were under way, President Carlos Salinas de Gortari took preemptive measures to project a positive human rights image and created the National Commission on Human Rights.[48] Electoral reform and the creation of the National Commission on Human Rights were steps meant to defuse U.S. scrutiny by making it appear that the Mexican government had its democracy and human rights problems under control.[49]

Governmental, intergovernmental, and non-governmental election observers helped guarantee that the 1994 elections were relatively free of fraud, paradoxically legitimizing the PRI victory. The elections in July 2000 turned out to be the most free and fair in Mexican history, and led to an unprecedented victory by the opposition candidate of the PAN party for the presidency.

In the period 1988–98, international and regional pressures began to focus on Mexico, in concert with domestic political parties and human rights groups. This provoked a relatively rapid and forceful response from the Mexican government, contributing to a decline in human rights violations, and a strengthening of democratic institutions.

International and regional pressures have had much less impact in bringing about change in the second "reform" scenario, Colombia. Indeed, the differences between the current path of Colombia and that of Mexico are so striking that they call into question the very categorization of a single reform path. The human rights situation in Colombia is currently one of the most alarming in the hemisphere. Human rights violations have been at high levels for the last ten years, but the situation has recently become worse. The Colombian Commission of Jurists estimated that in 1998 an average of nine persons per day were victims of violence, but that number increased to twelve in 1999 (of these, six died from extrajudicial executions, and one disappeared). These violations are taking place in the context of escalating armed conflict between the government, three major guerrilla organizations, and paramilitary organizations that often have links to state security forces. The paramilitary groups are responsible for approximately 73 per cent of the violations, the police and armed forces for 5 per cent, and the guerrilla forces for 22 per cent.[50] The Office of the People's Advocate documented a 50 per cent increase in massacres, with a 36 per cent increase in the total number of victims of massacres in 1999 over 1998.[51]

International and regional actors have actively focused on human rights issues in Colombia for many years. In 1996, the UN High Commissioner for Human Rights set up an office in Colombia to monitor the human rights situation and advise the Colombian authorities on how to improve human rights in the context of armed internal conflict. Both the reports of the UN High Commissioner and those of the IACHR concluded that the most serious current problem is the high level of violence carried out by paramilitary organizations, often with links to government security forces. Other high-ranking UN officials, including the Special Representative to the Secretary-General on Internally Displaced Persons and on Children and Armed Conflict, have visited Colombia to call attention to these issues.

International organizations and NGOs have called on the government to take effective action to disband these paramilitary groups, to bring their members to justice, and to remove any public official for whom there is evidence of involvement in human rights violations or support for paramilitary groups. They also recommended changes in the penal code, the adoption of a law that would criminalize forced disappearances, and a series of other legal changes that would help overcome impunity for human rights violations. The Colombian government has ignored these recommendations and the human rights situation continues to worsen.[52]

One problem with international efforts is that the United States, as part of its efforts in the "War against Drugs," has continued to supply very high levels of military and economic assistance to Colombia. By 1999, Colombia was the third highest recipient in the world of U.S. assistance, after Israel and Egypt. During the second half of the 1990s, the U.S. Congress sent the bulk of aid to the Colombian police, who were seen as less implicated in human rights violations. But in 2000 the U.S. Congress approved a very large aid package that will significantly increase aid to the Colombian military. This puts U.S. policy at cross-purposes with that of international organizations involved in Colombia. The U.S. Congress inserted numerous human rights conditions, but the aid package will still strengthen the capacity of the military vis-à-vis other actors.

In Columbia, the drug trade increased the number of both international and internal actors who had the necessary resources for and a vested interest in the continuation of violent politics.[53] At the turn of the century, neither the guerrillas nor the paramilitaries have reached the point where they are committed to a negotiated resolution to the conflict. Until there is greater domestic political will for a resolution to the conflict, international actors are unlikely to have much of a positive effect on human rights and democracy. At a minimum, international actors such as the United States should avoid policies that exacerbate the potential for conflict.

Conclusions

These cases reveal the range of international and regional pressures that have been at work in Latin American democracy scenarios over the last two decades. In all of these cases, international pressure was at work, but the outcomes depended on how these pressures interacted with domestic political processes. International pressures were effective in helping contribute to some change in at least one case from each of the four scenarios. Thus, the particular democracy scenario does not determine whether or not international pressures will have an impact. The clearest variation in the amount of international pressure was not between countries or scenarios, but over time. The most important explanatory factors for the changes in human rights practices that we document in this essay appear to be the existence and strength of the norms cascade, the intensity of international and regional human rights pressures, and the level of domestic political will and pressure to conform to the norms. Where domestic pressures are strong, as in Chile or Guatemala, international pressures can provide critical leverage; where domestic opposition is weak or divided, international pressures have less influence.

These social processes may have been especially effective in Latin America because they resonated with a tradition of commitment to international law and human rights norms. These norms were embedded in the belief system of influential individuals and sectors of civil society, and were articulated in positive domestic law. In this situation, international pressures reverberated domestically as external pressures reinforced domestic movements. As international human rights norms were increasingly articulated and clarified, individuals in Latin America both demanded that their governments live up to them and sometimes welcomed external pressure upon their governments to do so.

After redemocratization in the region, the effectiveness of past international human rights pressures reinforced the confidence of newly democratic governments in the efficacy of international legal institutions. Some became enthusiastic supporters of efforts to further develop international and regional human rights law and institutions. Serious international human rights problems continue to plague Latin America, and the quality of democracy throughout the region needs to be strengthened and deepened. But diverse Latin American states have sustained democracies and human rights violations have diminished over the last two decades. International norms and international law, implemented through a wide range of channels and institutions, are important parts of the explanation for these changes. Ultimately, however, consolidating democracy and protecting human rights require a well-organized and coherent domestic civil society, and the willingness of all actors to work to these ends. In these circumstances, international pressures play the crucial but subsidiary role of supporting and reinforcing strong internal movements for democracy and human rights.

Notes

1. See, for example, the excellent study *The International Dimensions of Democratization: Europe and Latin America*, edited by Laurence Whitehead (Oxford: Oxford University Press, 1996) from which we partially borrow our title.
2. See, for example, Kathryn Sikkink, "The Emergence, Evolution, and Effectiveness of the Latin American Human Rights Network," in Elizabeth Jelin and Eric Hershberg (eds.), *Constructing Democracy: Human Rights, Citizenship, and Society in Latin America* (Boulder, Colo.: Westview Press, 1996), p. 75.
3. See, for example, Alejandro Alvarez, *La reconstrucción del derecho de Gentes* (Santiago, Chile: Editorial Nascimento, 1943); for a survey of this historical tradition, see

Kathryn Sikkink, "Reconceptualizing Sovereignty in the Americas: Historical Precursors and Current Practices," *Houston Journal of International Law* Spring 1997; 19(3): pp. 705–29.

4. David Forsythe, *Human Rights and World Politics*, 2d ed. (Lincoln: University of Nebraska Press, 1989), p. 104.

5. Based on a comparison of data from: Comisión Nacional sobre la Desaparición de Personas, *Nunca más: Informe de la Comisión Nacional sobre la Desaparición de Personas* (Buenos Aires: Editorial Universitaria de Buenos Aires, 1984); Comisión de Verdad y Reconciliación, *Informe Rettig: Informe de la Comisión de Verdad y Reconciliación* (Santiago: Talleres de La Nación, 1991); United Nations, *From Madness to Hope: The 12 Year War in El Salvador*, Report of the Commission on the Truth for El Salvador, in United Nations, *The United Nations and El Salvador, 1990–1995*, United Nations Blue Book Series, vol. 4 (New York: Department of Public Information, 1995), pp. 301–4; Commission for Historical Clarification, *Guatemala: Memory of Silence: Report of the Commission for Historical Clarification*, http://hrdata.aaas.org/ceh/report/english/toc.html; and Patrick Bell, Paul Kobrak, and Herbert F. Spirer, *State Violence in Guatemala, 1960–1996: A Quantitative Reflection* (Washington, D.C.: American Association for the Advancement of Science, 1999).

6. Reproduced in Viron Vaky and Heraldo Muñoz, *The Future of the Organization of American States* (New York: Twentieth Century Fund, 1997).

7. AG/RES. 1080-(XXI-0/91), Representative Democracy, Resolution Adopted at the Fifth Plenary Session, June 5, 1991, reproduced in Vaky and Muñoz, *The Future of the OAS*.

8. 1-E Rev. OEA Documentos Officiales OEA/Ser.A/2 Add 3 (SEPF). Signed 14 December 1992, entered into force 25 September 1997.

9. Thomas Carothers, *In the Name of Democracy: U.S. Policy toward Latin America in the Reagan Years* (Berkeley: University of California Press, 1991).

10. See Margaret Keck and Kathryn Sikkink, *Activists beyond Borders: Advocacy Networks in International Politics* (Ithaca, N.Y.: Cornell University Press, 1998); and Sikkink, "The Emergence, Evolution, and Effectiveness of the Latin American Human Rights Network."

11. Scott Palmer, "Peru: Collectively Defending Democracy in the Western Hemisphere," in Tom Farer (ed.), *Beyond Sovereignty: Collectively Defending Democracy in the Americas* (Baltimore: Johns Hopkins University Press, 1996), pp. 257–58.

12. Nevertheless, in 1999, Amnesty International reported that torture was frequent or widespread in four countries in Latin America (Brazil, Colombia, Mexico, and Venezuela), and that "some" or "several cases" of torture had been reported in nine additional countries. Amnesty International, *Annual Report 1999* (London). The United Nations Special Rapporteur on Torture in his 1999 report discussed numerous cases of torture in Brazil, Colombia, Mexico, and Venezuela, and added Peru as a country where torture was frequently used. The Special Rapporteur discussed six additional Latin American countries from which he had received cases alleging torture. Sir Nigel Rodley, *Report of the Special Rapporteur on Torture* (U.N. Commission on Human Rights, 1999).

13. Amnesty International, *Annual Report 1999*; Rodley, *Special Report*. The Working Group also reported it had received one newly transmitted case from Ecuador.

14. Whitehead, "Three Dimensions of Democratization," in *The International Dimensions of Democratization*.

15. On "norms cascades," see Cass Sunstein, *Free Markets and Social Justice* (New York: Oxford University Press, 1997); and Martha Finnemore and Kathryn Sikkink, "International Norm Dynamics and Political Change," *International Organization* Autumn 1998; 52(4): pp. 887–917.

16. This is consistent with the basic argument in Jennifer McCoy (ed.), *Political Learning and Redemocratization in Latin America: Do Politicians Learn from Political Crises?* (Miami: North South Center Press, 2000), but it places emphasis on the international sources for political learning, especially the role of international law and norms, which are not discussed in the McCoy volume. It is also consistent with a point that Edelberto Torres Rivas makes in his contribution in this volume, when he says that UN mediation of conflict in Central America contributed to changing attitudes.

17. Amnesty International initiated a country campaign of publicity about human rights abuses in Uruguay in early 1976. The OAS waited until 1978 (five years after the coup) to condemn human rights violations in Uruguay. The U.S. Congress did not hold hearings on the human rights situation in Uruguay until three years after the coup. Congress suspended military aid one year later, against the will of the president. In 1981, the European Parliament passed a strong resolution, urging European states to suspend arms sales to Uruguay.

18. Rachel McCleary, *Dictating Democracy: Guatemala and the End of Violent Revolution* (Gainsville: University Press of Florida, 1999), p. 135.

19. Interview with Judge Jorge Mario García Laguardia, Mexico City, 6 June 1996.

20. McCleary, *Dictating Democracy*, p. 135.

21. *Latin American Monitor: Andean Group*, May 1992.

22. Ibid., June 1992, September 1992.

23. Thomas Lippman, "Joint Effort Helps Head Off Coup Threat in Paraguay: U.S., South Americans Pressure General Aside," *Washington Post*, 26 April 1996, p. A30.

24. "Paraguay: Threat of Coup by Defiant General Averted," *NotiSur – Latin American Political Affairs*, 3 May 1996.

25. Sebastian Rotella, "Paraguayan General's Arrest Ends Odyssey in Lawless Zone," *Los Angeles Times*, 18 June 2000, p. A9.

26. William Stanley, *The Protection Racket State: Elite Politics, Military Extortion, and Civil War in El Salvador* (Philadephia: Temple University Press). Also see United Nations, *The United Nations and El Salvador 1990–1995*; Ricardo Cordova Macias, "El Salvador: Transition from Civil War," in Jorge Dominguez and Abraham Lowenthal (eds.), *Constructing Democratic Governance: Mexico, Central America, and the Caribbean in the 1990s* (Baltimore: Johns Hopkins University Press, 1996), pp. 26–49; Mike Kaye, "The Role of Truth Commissions in the Search for Justice, Reconciliation, and Democratization: The Salvadoran and Honduran Cases," *Journal of Latin American Studies* October 1997; 29(3): pp. 693–716; Charles B. Rockett, "El Salvador: The Long Journey from Violence to Reconciliation," *Latin American Research Review* 1994; 29(3): pp. 174–87.

27. This paragraph draws on Tommie Sue Montgomery, "The United Nations and Peace-making in El Salvador," *North-South Issues* 1995; 4(3): p. 6.

28. Suzanne Jonas, *Of Centaurs and Doves: Guatemala's Peace Process* (Boulder, Colo.: Westview Press, 2000), pp. 47–48.

29. Ibid., p. 58.

30. *New York Times*, 27 March 1996, cited in Jonas, *Of Centaurs and Doves*, p. 58.

31. United Nations, General Assembly, "The Situation in Central America: Procedures for the Establishment of a Firm and Lasting Peace and Progress in Fashioning a Region of Peace, Freedom, Democracy and Development," Annex: "Seventh Report on Human Rights of the United Nations Verification Mission in Guatemala," A/52/330, 10 September 1997, pp. 16–17.

32. Mark Peceny and William Stanley, "Liberal Social Reconstruction and the Resolution of Civil Wars in Central America," *International Organization* Winter 2001; 55(1): pp. 149–82.

33. See above, p. 106.

34. Nigel Rodley, *The Treatment of Prisoners under International Law* (Oxford: Clarendon Press, 1987), pp. 102–4.
35. See, for example, the symposium organized in Barcelona in October 1997. Plataforma Argentina Contra la Impunidad (ed.), *Contra la impunidad en defensa de los derechos humanos* (Barcelona: Editorial Icaria, 1998).
36. Interview with Dr. Martin Abregu, Director of the Centro de Estudios Legales y Sociales (CELS), Buenos Aires, July 1999.
37. Clifford Krause, "Pinochet at Home in Chile: A Real Nowhere Man," *New York Times*, 5 March 2000.
38. Steve Anderson, "Pinochet Trial," *UPI*, 19 July 2000.
39. Mike Lanchin, "Guatemala's Indians Take Their Former Army Tormentors to Court," *San Francisco Chronicle*, 13 July 2000.
40. Clifford Krause, "Bolivian's Dark Past Starts to Catch Up with Him," *New York Times*, 14 March 1999.
41. "Disappearances," *Latin America Weekly Report*, 15 February 2000.
42. Kevin G. Hall, "Ex-Paraguayan Dictator Stroessner May Be Second S. American Strongman to Face Trial for Human Rights Abuses," Knight Ridder/Tribune News Service, 10 June 2000.
43. Ibid.
44. Americas Watch, *Human Rights in Mexico* (New York: Human Rights Watch, June 1990), p. 1.
45. See Kathryn Sikkink, "Human Rights, Principled Interest Networks, and Sovereignty in Latin America," *International Organization* Summer 1993; 47(3): pp. 411–42. Ellen L. Lutz, "Human Rights in Mexico: Cause for Continuing Concern," *Current History* February 1993; 92: p. 79.
46. Americas Watch, *Guatemalan Refugees in Mexico: 1980–1984* (New York: Human Rights Watch, September 1984); Amnesty International, *Mexico: Human Rights in Rural Areas* (London: Amnesty International, 1986).
47. *Annual Report of the Inter-American Commission on Human Rights 1989–1990*, pp. 106–23.
48. See Denise Dresser, "Treading Lightly and without a Big Stick: International Actors and the Promotion of Democracy in Mexico," in Tom Farer (ed.), *Beyond Sovereignty: Collectively Defending Democracy in the Americas* (Baltimore: Johns Hopkins University Press, 1996); and Jorge Luis Sierra Guzmán et al., *La Comisión Nacional de Derechos Humanos: Una visión no gubernamental* (Mexico City: Comisión Mexicana de Defensa y Promoción de los Derechos Humanos, 1992), p. 1.
49. Denise Dresser, "Mr. Salinas Goes to Washington: Mexican Lobbying in the United States," Conference Paper no. 62, presented at the Research Conference "Crossing National Borders: Invasion or Involvement," Columbia University, 6 December 1991, p. 5.
50. "Written statement submitted by the Colombian Commission of Jurists" to the Commission on Human Rights, 10 February 2000, E/CN.4/2000/NGO/26.
51. As cited in the "Report of the United Nations High Commissioner for Human Rights on the Office in Colombia," Commission of Human Rights, 9 March 2000 (E/CN.4/2000/11), p. 9.
52. Carlos Rodríguez Mejía, "The International Community and the Colombian Human Rights Crisis," presented at "Democracy, Human Rights, and Peace in Colombia" Roundtable, University of Notre Dame, 6 October 1999; "Effective Functioning of Human Rights Mechanisms," written statement submitted by Human Rights Watch to the Commission on Human Rights, 1 February 2000 (E/CN.4/2000/NGO/24), p. 2.
53. George Lopez, "An Anomaly Plagued by Analogies: Colombian Realities Confront U.S. Policy," "Democracy, Human Rights and Peace in Colombia" Roundtable, p. 6.

Contributors

MARCELO CAVAROZZI studied at the University of Buenos Aires and the University of California, Berkeley, where he received a Ph.D. in 1975. He has been Professor of Public Policy and Chair of the Department of Politics and Government, University of San Martín, since 1998, and has served in visiting positions at Georgetown University (where he remains Faculty Associate), Massachusetts Institute of Technology, the University of Buenos Aires, and Yale University. Professor Cavarozzi was the Director of CEDES (Center for the Study of the State and Society), Buenos Aires, between 1984 and 1988, and a Fellow of the Woodrow Wilson Center for International Scholars in 1982. He has published extensively on democracy, political learning, and political participation in Latin America.

MANUEL ANTONIO GARRETÓN M is Professor of Sociology at the University of Chile. He studied Sociology at Universidad Católica de Chile and was awarded a Ph.D. in sociology at the Ecole des Hautes Etudes en Sciences Sociales, University of Paris. During the years of dictatorship in Chile he was involved in human rights work around the world, whilst also serving in visiting positions at Oxford University, the Wilson Center in Washington, D.C., the University of Notre Dame, the Catholic University of Peru, the University of Chicago, and the University of California at San Diego. Dr. Garretón has been Professor and Senior Researcher at FLACSO-Chile since 1976, and was Chief Adviser at the Ministry of Education from 1990 to 1994. His many publications cover political theory and sociology.

MARIA D'ALVA KINZO is Professor of Political Science at the University of São Paulo. She was a Research Fellow (1991–92) at the Institute of Latin American Studies, University of London, where she also worked as part-time Senior Lecturer in 1997–98. She is the author of *Legal Opposition Politics under Authoritarian Rule in Brazil* (1988); *Brazil: Challenges of the 1990s* (1993) and, with Victor Bulmer-Thomas, *Growth and Development in Brazil: Cardoso's "Real" Challenge* (1995). Her articles on political parties, elections, and democratization have appeared in various edited volumes and journals. Professor Kinzo studied at the University of Oxford and the Pontifícia Universidade Católica de São Paulo.

ELLEN L. LUTZ is the Executive Director of the Center for Human Rights and Conflict Resolution at Tufts University's Fletcher School of Law and Diplomacy. She is an attorney with over two decades of experience as a non-governmental human rights advocate, as well as a trained mediator and arbitrator. Her research and consulting focus on Latin America, the prevention of human rights abuses, and the relationship between accountability responses and the long-term prevention of future abuses or conflict. She is an Adjunct Professor of Law at Fletcher where she has taught international human rights law and international organizations, and currently teaches international criminal law.

AMPARO MENÉNDEZ-CARRIÓN studied International Relations and Comparative Politics at the University of Minnesota and at The Johns Hopkins University School of Advanced International Studies, where she received her Ph.D. She has held senior positions in teaching, research, and policy throughout Latin America and North America, most recently in Chile, where she taught in the doctoral program on Latin American Studies at ARCIS University and at the University of Chile's *Instituto de Ciencia Política*. In Peru, she was Visiting Researcher at the *Instituto de Estudios Peruanos* in Lima (1982–85). In Ecuador, she was Director General of FLACSO-Ecuador for two consecutive terms (1987–91 and 1991–95). In Chile, she was the Vice-President of the Chilean Association of Political Science (1998–2000). Her current academic affiliation in Latin America is with the University of Chile where she is Senior Adviser to the Graduate School of International Studies and, since 1997, Professor of Comparative Politics at the *Instituto de Estudios Internacionales*. In the United States she is at present the Hubert H. Humphrey Distinguished Visiting Professor of International Studies and Comparative Politics at Macalester College.

EDWARD NEWMAN is an Academic Programme Associate of the Peace and Governance Programme at the United Nations University. He was educated at the University of Keele (UK), and the University of Kent (UK), where he received a Ph.D. in international relations. He has taught as a lecturer at Shumei University and Aoyama Gakuin University, both in Japan. He is also a founding editorial board member

(Executive Editor) of the journal *International Relations of the Asia Pacific*. Recent publications include *The UN Secretary-General from the Cold War to the New Era: A Global Peace and Security Mandate?* (1998), *The Changing Nature of Democracy* (co-edited, 1998), and *New Millennium, New Perspectives: The United Nations, Security, and Governance* (co-edited, 2000). His co-edited volume, *The United Nations and Human Security*, will be published in 2001.

KATHRYN SIKKINK is the Arlene Carlson Professor of Political Science at the University of Minnesota. She has an M.A. and Ph.D. in political science from Columbia University. Her publications include *Ideas and Institutions: Developmentalism in Brazil and Argentina* (1991); *Activists beyond Borders: Advocacy Networks in International Politics*, (co-authored with Margaret Keck, 1998), which was awarded the Grawemeyer Award for Ideas Improving World Order (1999) and the International Studies Association's Chadwick Alger Award for best work in the area of international organization (1999); and *The Power of Human Rights: International Norms and Domestic Change* (co-edited with Thomas Risse and Stephen Ropp, 1999). Her current research interests focus on transnational social movements and networks, the role of ideas and norms in international relations and foreign policy, and the influence of international law on domestic politics, especially in the area of human rights. She is a member of the Editorial Board of the journal

International Organization, the International Advisory Board of the *International Studies Review*, and the Council of the American Political Science Association, and is program co-chair for the APSA 2002 Annual Meeting.

HEINZ R. SONNTAG is a sociologist, who obtained his Ph.D. in West Germany and has worked since 1968 in Latin America, mainly Venezuela. He has been a Professor of Sociology at the Central University of Venezuela since December 1974. He is also a Senior Research Fellow of its Center for Development Studies (CENDES), and has been three times elected its director. A former President of the Latin American Sociological Association, he has received, among other awards, a Guggenheim Fellowship 1999–2000. He has been a Visiting Research Professor at Brown University, and Visiting Professor at the University of Massachusetts at Amherst and at Yale University (2000–2001). He is author or co-author of more than 20 books and more than 60 articles and essays in different languages.

RODOLFO STAVENHAGEN is Research Professor of Sociology at El Colegio de México. A former Assistant Director for Social Sciences at UNESCO, he has worked extensively on issues of social development, agrarian problems, ethnic conflicts, indigenous peoples, and human rights in comparative perspective, and particularly in Latin America. He is the author of *The Ethnic Question: Conflict, Development and Human Rights* (1990), *Ethnic Conflicts and the Nation State* (1996), *Social Classes in*

Agrarian Societies (1970), *Derecho indígena y derechos humanos en América Latina* (1988), *Los derechos humanos de los pueblos indígenas* (2000), and other books. As member of the International Commission on Education in the Twenty First Century, he is co-author of the UNESCO report *Learning: The Treasure Within* (1996). In Mexico he was a member of the National Human Rights Commission for ten years, and is currently Vice-President of the Inter-American Institute of Human Rights and Member of the Board of the United Nations University for Peace.

LAURENCE WHITEHEAD is an Official Fellow in Politics at Nuffield College, Oxford University, and Senior Fellow of the College. He is co-editor (with Guillermo O'Donnell and Philippe Schmitter) of *Transitions from Authoritarian Rule* (1986). Since 1989 he has been co-editor of *The Journal of Latin American Studies*. He is also general editor of an Oxford University Press book series, Studies in Democratization, and edited the first book in the series, *International Dimensions of Democratization: Europe and the Americas* (1996).

EDELBERTO TORRES-RIVAS is a sociologist, former Secretary-General of FLACSO, and professor and researcher at various universities in Latin American countries and Spain. He is the author of many books and articles on democracy and politics in general. His most recent publications are: "Why Guatemalans Do Not Vote" (2001) and "Guatemala: From Authoritarianism to Peace" (2000). He is presently Director of the Postgraduate Programme in International Relations, Universidad Rafael Landivar, and Co-Director of the Project for the Human Development Report (UNDP) for Guatemala and Central America.

Index

Catalogue Request

Name: _____

Address: _____

_____

Tel: _____

Fax: _____

E-mail: _____

To receive a catalogue of UNU Press publications kindly photocopy this form and send or fax it back to us with your details. You can also e-mail us this information. Please put "Mailing List" in the subject line.

 **United Nations University Press**

53-70, Jingumae 5-chome
Shibuya-ku, Tokyo 150-8925, Japan
Tel: +81-3-3499-2811 Fax: +81-3-3406-7345
E-mail: sales@hq.unu.edu http://www.unu.edu